Let's talk it over

interpersonal communication in relationships

5th edition

gerald L. Wilson
University of South Alabama

Pearson
Custom
Publishing

Please visit our website at www.pearsoncustom.com

ISBN 0–536–60264–6

BA 990646

PEARSON CUSTOM PUBLISHING
160 Gould Street/Needham Heights, MA 02494
A Pearson Education Company

COPYRIGHT ACKNOWLEDGMENTS

PHOTO CREDITS

This book is fondly dedicated to Rita G. Schlecht who lovingly keeps my life together. Her dedication to the students and faculty of the Communication Department at the University of South Alabama is greatly appreciated. Rita, you are loved by so many. Thank you.

PREFACE

I celebrate the effort of students who have studied this text over the past fifteen years. Much has changed in the academic field of interpersonal communication, but the goal of this book has not. It continues to emphasize the themes of relationship management and growth.

Interpersonal communication is for many reasons one of the most rewarding courses we teach. Students are eager learners because they come to the course expecting to take away knowledge and skills that will allow them to be more effective in their relationships. They want to know what they can do to make their interpersonal experiences more rewarding. They want answers to why things go wrong in relationships that they very much wanted to go right. Students are hungry for what this course has to offer.

It is with this need in mind that I wrote this book. It has been a popular text because it focuses on relationships and their growth through communication.

This fifth edition of *Let's Talk It Over* builds on the strengths of the fourth edition, while thoroughly updating research, theory, and application. I continue to emphasize the themes of relationship management and growth—themes I find central to the reasons students enroll in our course.

The aim of the book is to integrate theory and practice, both carefully grounded in research and carefully focused on the variables that influence maintenance and growth in interpersonal relationships. I also specify, throughout, the communication behaviors that are implied by and based on the supporting research presented in each chapter.

THE FORMAT

The coverage and sequencing of the materials are designed for introductory interpersonal communication courses as they are generally taught. My understanding of these courses is based on much feedback from my colleagues across the country, some of whom used the previous editions and some of whom did not. In addition, over the years my publishers have conducted both quantitative and qualitative market research in this area. Thus I am confident that my general organization and the particular sequence of the chapters will be compatible with most introductory courses. However, because some professors like to teach materials in varying sequences, my chapters are self-contained and cross-referenced to permit alternative presentations.

CONTENT FEATURES

I believe that learning to manage interpersonal relationships is as important to a person's health as diet. But *the skills involved in managing relationships are not always consistent with the common wisdom of our society.* For example, our society teaches competition and a "win-lose" orientation as the underlying assumption of play. However, such an approach is generally inappropriate in managing a relationship. In this text. I have directly addressed this and similar problems.

Part 1, The Basics, focuses on the primary issues and concerns in interpersonal communication. It recognizes that messages serve two functions, communicating meaning and defining relationships. Chapter 1 unites the ideas of interpersonal communication and relationship management. It presents the basis for our suggestions in the remainder of the text for managing various parts of relational communication.

Part 2, Foundations, treats particular aspects of an individual's communication behavior: the individual's intrapersonal communication system. Chapter 2 traces how a person's self-concept emerges and develops. An examination of interpersonal needs and how these impact self-concept follow this. Chapter 3 addresses how perception occurs and how to avoid perceptual errors. Then, perception is examined as it impacts relationships.

Part 3, Creating Messages, focuses on message production. Chapter 4 is devoted to the study of language, including the nature of language, language use in relationships, the pitfalls in language use, and what can be done about them. Chapter 5 addresses understanding and communicating feelings, wants, and expectations. This is followed by an investigation of nonverbal communication in chapter 6. Here how general and particular body cues, sound, space, and time form messages is addressed. Next, the topic of listening is presented. Chapter 7 lays out the components of the listening process and provides help, within the relational context, for understanding ineffective and effective listening.

Part 4, Relational Concerns, carries the study of interpersonal communication to specific relational issues. Chapter 8 talks about the relational engagement process and the basics for establishing a relationship. Self-disclosure is thoroughly investigated as a relational building block. The chapter closes with a discussion of how a relationship moves through stages, as well as how to enhance this process. Chapter 9 addresses issues related to climate. It explains why defensiveness occurs. what to do about it, and how to build a positive climate. Chapter 10 explores the use and abuse of power in relationships and management of power games. It also discusses interpersonal conflict; what it is, how we tend to respond to it, and how to intervene in conflicts more intelligently than common wisdom teaches. Finally, Chapter 11 discusses interpersonal ethics and diversity. It develops a set of guidelines that can be applied to situations where ethics is an issue and provides help in communicating with those people who are different.

NEW FEATURES OF THE FIFTH EDITION

I have made a number of changes and additions that will make the fifth edition more exciting and useful to students and professors. Of course, I have made considerable effort to update my references and readings for every chapter. In addition, these changes are especially significant:

- The book is now organized using a chapter format.
- The idea that a qualitative characteristic dimension distinguishes interpersonal communication from impersonal communication is added to Chapter 1.
- Chapters 1 and 6 place a greater emphasis on the reciprocal nature of interpersonal communication.
- The idea that communication competence is culturally based is added to this discussion in Chapter 1.
- I've broadened the discussion of self-concept in Chapter 2 to include the collective image that groups and communities of people have of themselves.

- I've expanded the discussion of "Guidelines for Self-Concept Development" in Chapter 2.
- More information about use of "I messages" is added in Chapter 5.
- I've broadened my discussion of the significance of touch in communication in Chapter 6.
- I've added more on empathy and taking on the perspective of the other as listening behaviors in chapter 7.
- I've expanded the discussion of similarity in attraction and engagement in relationships in Chapter 8.
- I've suggested empathy has three dimensions: perspective taking, experiencing feelings, and caring in Chapter 9.
- The section on functional and dysfunctional conflict in Chapter 10 is expanded.
- New sections on warning signs of relational deterioration and gender and terminating relationships have been added to chapter 10.
- A significant part of Chapter 11 is devoted to the issue of diversity.

LEARNING AIDS

Opening Pedagogy

Each chapter in our text opens with a Preview, a brief list of Key Terms, and a statement of Objectives. These are designed to give the student the clearest possible insight into the nature and content of the chapter.

End of Unit Pedagogy

At the end of each chapter is a Summary of the most important ideas in the chapter. The Discussion Questions may be used by the student privately to study the chapter or by the teacher to lead the class in practicing the analytical and performance skills described. The Endnotes following each chapter include carefully selected references to the literature. I have tried to cite a manageable number of both classic and current works. The Read More section is an annotated reading list indicating excellent sources for further information.

Glossary

The Glossary presents important terms used in interpersonal communication courses and in this book.

Experiences

A set of experiences, arranged according to chapter sequence, that offer the teacher a broad range of interesting, directly applicable, and easily used in-class activities is found at the end of the text. These pedagogical devices are directed toward the chapters they support and show how each relates to some aspect of relationship management and growth.

ACKNOWLEDGMENT

I wish to thank my many colleagues who have so generously given their time to improve this book. Their insights have proved to be especially helpful in refining the presentation of concepts and adapting the work to a variety of viewpoints.

Authors write manuscripts, which are turned into books by extraordinarily able and dedicated people. Terry Gets deserves thanks for his encouragement to begin this project. I am also especially thankful to my editors, Terry Brennan and Jennifer Carlson, who contributed their exceptional expertise and knowledge to this project.

I also thank Nancy Merrill who helped me in the preparation of this manuscript.

Gerald L. Wilson

Brief Contents

Preface   ix

Part 1: The Basics

    Chapter 1: Interpersonal Process   3

Part 2: Foundations

    Chapter 2: Self-Concept   29

    Chapter 3: Perception   61

Part 3: Creating Messages

    Chapter 4: Language   101

    Chapter 5: Feelings and Emotions   141

    Chapter 6: Nonverbal Communication   173

    Chapter 7: Listening   219

Part 4: Relational Concerns

    Chapter 8: Relationships   239

    Chapter 9: Climate   281

    Chapter 10: Conflict   317

    Chapter 11: Ethics and Diversity   361

Experiences   385

Glossary   435

Index   449

CONTENTS

PART 1: THE BASICS

Chapter 1: Interpersonal Process   **3**

What Is Interpersonal Communication?   6

    Interpersonal   6

    Communication   7

    Transactional   7

    Process   8

    Messages   9

    Information   9

    Relationship   12

Communication Competence   12

    Competence Defined   12

    Characteristics of Competence   13

A Process Model of Communication   16

An Interpersonal Exchange Model   *19*

    Sensitivity   21

    Self-Disclosure   21

    Trust   22

    Risk   22

Summary   *23*

Discussion Questions   *23*

Endnotes   *24*

Readings   *26*

PART 2: FOUNDATIONS

Chapter 2: Self-Concept   **29**

Definition of the Self-Concept   *31*

Ideas about Who We Are   *31*

Components of the Self-Concept   *32*

    Beliefs   33

    Values   36

    Attitudes   38

The Development of the Self-Concept   *40*

Guidelines for Self-Concept Development   *44*

Interpersonal Needs and the Self-Concept   *45*

Maslow's Hierarchy of Needs   *48*

Schutz's Interpersonal Needs   *50*

    Need for Inclusion   50

    Need for Control   51

    Need for Affection   53

Self-Concept Maintenance   *54*

Interpersonal Needs and Communication in Relationships *55*

Summary   *56*

Discussion Questions   *57*

Endnotes   *57*

Readings   *58*

Chapter 3: Perception   61

The Nature of Perception   63

Characteristics of the Perceptual Process   65

Perception Involves Selection   65

    Selective Exposure   65

    Selective Attention   66

Perception Involves Organization and Interpretation   67

    Organizing and Interpreting through Closure 69

Influences on Perception   70

    Assimilation and Accommodation   70

    Other Factors that Affect Our Perception   74

Building Perceptual Skills   76

Perceiving People   77

Mutual Perception Affects Interpersonal Relationships   78

    Interpersonal Attraction   78

    Attribution   79

    Role Assignment   82

Expectations Influence Interpersonal Relationships   83

    Expectations and Rules   84

    Expectations and Relationship Positions   85

    Change and Perception in Relationships   91

Building Interpretive Skills   92

Summary   93

Discussion Questions   94

Endnotes   96

Readings   97

PART 3: CREATING MESSAGES

Chapter 4: Language   101

The Nature of Language: What is Language?   103

Language and Experience   104

The Triangle of Meaning   105

The Abstraction Process   107

Abstraction in Relationships   111

Language and Relationships   114
     Using Language in Relationships   114

Denotative and Connotative Meanings   115
     Influences on Connotation   117

Language and Our View of Relationships   121
     Language Expresses and Reveals the Self   121
     Naming in Relationships   123
     Symmetry and Complementarity in Relationships   123

Indiscrimination with Language   125
     Stereotyping   126
     Self-Fulfilling Prophecy   127

Problems with Inflexible Language   129
     Rigidity in Naming   130
     Static Evaluation   130
     Reification   131
     Polarization, Two-Valued Orientation, and Disconfirmation   133

Summary   135

Discussion Questions   136

Endnotes   138

Readings   139

Chapter 5: Feelings and Emotions   **141**

Expressing Feelings, Wants, and Expectations   143

Feelings, Wants, and Expectations Must be Shared   143

Learning to Separate Feelings from Emotions   145

Emotions Are under Cognitive Control   147

How We Limit Our Expressions of Feelings   149

Learning to Talk about Feelings   151

Learning More Emotion and Feeling Words   155

Learning to State What You Want   156

Ask for Clarifications   157

Appropriate Expression of Wants and Needs   158

*Characteristics of Nonassertive, Aggressive,
and Assertive Language and Behavior*   158

When and Why We Fail to Communicate Assertively   162
    Response to the Situation   163
    Response to Personalities   163
    Response to the Topic   164
    Response to Behavior   164

Improving Assertive Communication Skills   165

Summary   168

Discussion Questions   168

Endnotes   169

Readings   170

Chapter 6: Nonverbal Communication   **173**

Body Communication   175

Body Movement and Gestures   176

Posture   177

Face and Eye Behavior   181
    Controlling Face and Eye Behavior   183

Touching Behavior   184

Clothing   187

Using Nonverbal Skills Effectively   191

Silence   193

Vocalics   194
   Vocal Quality and Vocalizations   194

Space   196
   Territoriality   196
   Angle of Interaction   198

Personal Distancing   200

Time   204

Applying Nonverbal Concepts to Relationships   207

Summary   208

Discussion Questions   209

Endnotes   210

Readings   217

Chapter 7: Listening   **219**

Listening: What's Involved   220
   Sensing   222
   Attending   222
   Understanding   222
   Remembering   222

Ineffective Listening Patterns   223
   Fake Listening   224
   Self-Centered Listening   224
   Assumptive Listening   224
   Closed-Minded Listening   225
   Defensive Listening   225
   Neutral Listening   225
   Hostile Listening   225

Effective Listening Within a Relationship   226
   Relational Listening Requires Effort   226
   Relational Listening Requires
   Withholding Advice and Judgements   227
   Relational Listening Requires Empathy   228

Active Listening 230

   Benefits of Active Listening 231

   Active Listening Techniques 232

Summary 234

Discussion Questions 234

Endnotes 235

Readings 235

PART 4: RELATIONAL CONCERNS

Chapter 8: Relationships **239**

Engagement 241

Why We Engage 241

   Physical, Social, and Task Attractiveness 241

   Proximity 243

   Similarity 243

   Basic Interpersonal Needs 244

   Expectations of Relational Benefits 244

Engaging Another Person 246

Relational Definition and Rules 248

   Relational Definition 248

   Relational Rules 249

Self-Disclosure and Relational Growth 251

The Johari Window 252

Benefits of Self-Disclosure 255

   Better Self-Understanding 255

   Sharing of Concerns 256

   Self-Revelation 256

   Relationship Nurturance 257

Risks of Self-Disclosure 257

   Vulnerability 257

   Overexposure 258

   Dislike 258

   Computer-Mediated Communication and Self-Concept 258

Guidelines for Self-Disclosing 259

Friendship and Commitment   260

Initiating   260
  Situation   260
  Attraction   262
  Inviting   262

Experimenting   263
  Collecting Information   263
  Promoting Relational Growth   264

Intensifying   265
  Signs of Intensifying   265
  Promoting Relational Growth   266

Integrating   266
  Signs of Integrating   267
  Promoting Relational Growth   268

Renegotiating   269
  Examining the Relationship   270
  The Renegotiation Process   270

Summary   272

Discussion Questions   274

Endnotes   275

Readings   278

Chapter 9: Climate   **281**

Defensive Communication   283

Why We Defend Ourselves   284

When and How We Defend Ourselves   285

Defensive Behavior   285
  Evaluation   285
  Superiority   286
  Certainty   286
  Control   287
  Neutrality   287
  Strategy   287

Consequences of Defensive Behavior   *288*

   Regret   290

   Hostility   290

   Damage to the Relationship   290

Reflexive Behavior   *290*

Supportive Communication   *291*

Characteristics of Supportive Climates   *292*

Supportive Communication Behavior   *293*

   Description   293

   Equality   294

   Provisionalism   294

   Problem Orientation   295

   Empathy   296

   Spontaneity   297

Benefits of Supportive Communication   *299*

   Supportive Behavior Provides Encouragement   299

   Supportive Behavior Enhances the Possibility of Acceptance   299

   Supportive Behavior Encourages Dialogue
and Understanding   299

   Supportive Behavior Encourages Relational Growth   300

Remaining Supportive   *301*

   You Can Disagree and Remain Supportive   301

   Understanding the Need for Interdependency   301

   Look for the Best Time to Talk   302

   Practice the Supportive Skills,
Especially Empathy and Equality   302

Engaging in Appropriate Self-Disclosure   *303*

Achieving Role and Rule Agreement   *303*

Giving Support   *304*

Demonstrating Affection   *304*

Managing Relational Problems Constructively   *305*

   Assessing and Understanding Relational Problems   305

   Developing a Course of Action   305

Guarding Against Stagnation   309
    Set a Time for Sharing   309
    Agree to Do Something New Together   309
    Express Caring Frequently   310
    Understand That it is OK to Disagree   310
    Give Your Relationship a Periodic Checkup   311

Summary   311

Discussion Questions   312

Endnotes   313

Readings   314

Chapter 10: Conflict   **317**

Power   319

Power Defined   319

Power Is Relational   319
    Endorsement Factors   319
    Commitment to the Relationship   320

Power Bases   321
    Referent Power   321
    Expert Power   322
    Legitimate Power   322
    Reward Power   323
    Coercive Power   323
    Information/Persuasive Power   324

Costs and Benefits of Power Use   324

Managing Power Games   325
    Ignoring the Partner   325
    Creating an Obligation   326
    Name Calling   326
    Expressing Utter Disbelief   327
    Interrupting   327

Conflict   328

Interpersonal Conflict Defined   329

Functional and Dysfunctional Conflict   329

Intervention Techniques   330

Outcomes of Intervention Techniques   *331*

    Win-Lose Techniques   331

    Lose-Lose Techniques   332

    Win-Win Technique   333

Using Forcing Strategies   *333*

Using a Confrontation/Problem-Solving Strategy   *336*

Typical Use of Interpersonal Conflict Strategies   *336*

Managing Interpersonal Conflict   *338*

    A Plan for Managing Conflict   338

    When Agreement Is Not Possible   342

Relational Conflict   *343*

Why Relationships Deteriorate   *343*

    Loss of Attractiveness   343

    Unfulfilled Needs   344

    Inability to Manage Differences   346

The Stages of Relational Deterioration   *348*

    Differentiating   348

    Circumscribing   349

    Stagnating   349

    Avoiding   350

    Terminating   350

Warning Signs of Relational Deterioration   *350*

Gender and Terminating Relationships   *351*

Managing the Loss of a Relationship   *351*

    Understanding and Coping with the Loss   351

    Utillzing Your Support System   352

    Avoiding Reminders of the Relationship   353

    Engaging in Healthy Self-Talk   353

    Learning from the Experience   353

Summary   *354*

Discussion Questions   *356*

Endnotes   *357*

Readings   *359*

Chapter 11: Ethics and Diversity   **361**

Ethical Communication in Interpersonal Relationships   362

Ethics Defined   363

General Principles of Ethical Behavior   364

Interpersonal Ethics   365

White Lies, Equivocation, and the Ethics of Evasion   366
   White Lie   367
   Equivocation   370
   The Ethics of Evasion   370

Diversity   371
   Diversity Defined   372
   The Difficult Side of Diversity   372
   Differences Do Make a Difference   373
   Biology Makes a Difference   373
   Culture Makes a Difference   373

Communication and Diversity   375
   Some Approaches Are Inappropriate   375
     Prejudging   375
     Stereotyping   375
     Name Calling   376
     Inappropriate Humor   376

Communicating with People Who Are Different   377
   Using Language Appropriately   379
   Working in a Culturally Diverse Group   379
   What to Do When the Dominant
   Culture is Different from Your Own   381

Summary   381

Discussion Questions   382

Endnotes   383

Readings   384

Experiences   **385**

Glossary   **435**

Index   **449**

PART 1

THE BASICS

1

INTERPERSONAL PROCESS

PREVIEW

The study of interpersonal communication can be an exciting effort because a great part of life's meaning comes from our relationships. A deeper understanding of interpersonal communication gives you new insights that allow you to make your relationships even better. We hope this is your goal in the study of interpersonal communication.

The aim of this chapter is to provide the foundation for your study of the remainder of the text. Growth and interpersonal competence are the central themes of *Interpersonal Growth Through Communication*. Here, you will learn a useful definition of interpersonal communication and explore what it means to be a competent interpersonal communicator.

In this chapter you will study two models of the communication process to discover how the various components of the process work and how they interact with each other. This information will help you communicate effectively because you will be much more sensitive to the enormous complexity of the process and more aware of where communication difficulties can occur.

KEY TERMS

channel	communication
communication competence	context
decoder	encoder
feedback	frame of reference
messages	noise
persuasive	process
receiver	risk
self-disclosure	self-expression
transactional	

OBJECTIVES

1. Explain why variability is a characteristic of relational life, using examples from a particular relationship.

2. Define and explain *interpersonal communication*.

3. Define and explain each main idea in the definition of interpersonal communication, including:

information	relationship
messages	transactional
process	

4. Suggest what it means to be a competent communicator. Identify the characteristics of a competent interpersonal communicator.

5. First, draw from memory and label the components of a process model of communication. Then define and explain the components.

6. Define and give an example of each of the following parts in the communication process:

channels	receiver
context	risk
decoder	self-disclosure
encoder	sensitivity
feedback	source
messages	trust
noise	

7. Explain each step in the interpersonal exchange model.

If you have brothers and sisters, your relationships with them will undoubtedly differ from those with your friends.

Many of life's greatest joys flow from our relationships with those who are close to us. It is in these relationships that we find encouragement when we are feeling down and comfort when we are hurting. These relationships also provide nurture for our self-concept and sense of well-being. Unfortunately, the opposite is also true. Our most unhappy moments can come from relationships that are not going well. Clearly, all relationships have the potential for both joy and heartache. It is the aim of this book to help you discover how you can increase the joy in your relationships and minimize the potential for unhappy moments. We believe that the knowledge you gain through the study of interpersonal communication will be very helpful in your effort to grow in your relationships.

Relationships of all kinds are an important part of your life. You have a relationship with each of your parents, if they are living, and with each of your friends. The relationships with your friends differ in the degree of intensity or quality. If you have brothers and sisters, your relationships with them will undoubtedly differ from those with your friends. If you have a job, your relationships there will include elements of subordination and power that distinguish them from relationships with your friends. Our many important relationships differ dramatically.

You will certainly agree that your relationships are characterized by *variability*. For example, you may limit your interactions with your boss to formal, task-related talk, preferring to keep her at a distance because of the power component in your relationship. At the same time, you may engage in a broad range of interactions with your best friend: at one moment you may take out your frustrations on your friend, at another you may turn to your friend for support and comfort or extend support and comfort, and at still another moment you may seek information from your friend to reduce your uncertainty[1] or strengthen your concept of yourself. This enormous variability in interpersonal communication has led scholars to try to define and illustrate the term precisely.

WHAT IS INTERPERSONAL COMMUNICATION?

Interpersonal communication is a transactional process of exchanging messages and negotiating meaning to convey information and to establish and maintain relationships. This definition makes clear that our focus is not only on the exchange of messages but also on their joint interpretation and negotiation. The definition includes some key ideas that bear further explanation.

Interpersonal

The term *interpersonal* means between people. Interpersonal communication usually, but not always, occurs face to face. When the face-to-face communication involves only two persons, we refer to it as *dyadic communication.*

Interpersonal also suggests something about what is going on between the people involved. Contrast interpersonal and impersonal to see what we mean. Interpersonal implies that a relationship is established, whereas impersonal suggests no such thing. In establishing a relationship, there is an attempt to take the other person and that person's needs into account. This is what people do when they establish a relationship in the sense that we use the word. There is a qualitative dimension to interpersonal communication. Some scholars believe this is what distinguishes interpersonal communication from impersonal interaction.[2]

Communication

There are generally two basic understandings of the term *communication*. Perhaps the most common is that it is a process of transmitting messages. With this definition in mind, scholars have developed important models of message transmission, which have been very helpful as highly technical communications systems such as radio, television, and computer-assisted, voice-activated interactive teaching machines have evolved.

A second common yet more complex (and more interesting) understanding is that communication involves the meaning of messages—their interpretation as well as transmission. Meaning is thus a function of the interaction of the communicators. It is this second focus that is more interesting to us as we study interpersonal communication.

Transactional

The term *transactional* suggests that the messages from persons involved in the act of communicating are being sent and received simultaneously. This happens because most people monitor and process the other person's reactions while they are talking. So when a person is sending a message, that person is also receiving, decoding, and responding.[3] Suppose, for example, that you ask a person for a date. The other person's warm smile and pleasant expression suggest this person is receptive. As you continue, you notice an ever-so-slight frown as you suggest a movie you'd like to see. This leads you to ask, "Would you rather do something else?" What is going on here is a back-and-forth exchange—a transaction—even though the other person didn't utter a word.

Transaction also suggests a mutual negotiation of the meaning. Each interpersonal communication is a mutual event whose meaning is negotiated by participants. In fluent conversation, we use signs and symbols as we talk with each other. A *sign* is something that indicates something else. It "announces" a natural relationship, as dark clouds announce rain. A *symbol* is something that stands for something else, as the word *chair* symbolizes the actual object. Our

use of signs and symbols depends on our unique, individual understanding of them. The concept of transaction suggests that the individuals arrive at some mutual agreement about the meanings for communication to be effective.

The fact that what one person communicates effects and even shapes the other's communication is an important outcome of transactional combination. So, as a study with parents and children suggests, the quality of interaction between those involved is a two-way affair—the interactants effect each other by their communication. Thus, the children influence parents just as much as the reverse.[4]

Process

The word *process* is used to suggest that interpersonal communication is a continuing and continually changing phenomenon. When you talk with someone, the act of talking changes both you and the other person. As you grow, as you learn, as your self-concept evolves, and as your image of the relationship develops, you change your basic assumptions, as does the other person.

One teacher, trying to explain the notion of process, asked a student to try to tell another how she felt and then to report on how she attempted to communicate her feelings. The result was that the student's report was obsolete by the time it was finished because the act of telling how she felt changed the way she felt.

Messages

A *message*, another key idea in our definition, is any symbol or combination of signs or symbols that functions as a stimulus for a receiver. These messages may be auditory, such as language and vocal cues, or visual, such as body, face, and eye movements. They may also be tactile if we communicate by touch. We may generate messages by using the environment (for example, how we place objects or arrange furnishings) or the clothing we wear. When we arrive for an appointment or date at a particular time, we express our view of the situation.

Messages are intentional means of achieving *a goal*. Sometimes we are not as aware of our purposes as we might be, as in when we say or do something and later regret it. But, even when this happens, others assume that we are acting with intention. We expect people to mean what they say and do, and say and do what they mean. The more intentional we can be in our communication, the more likely we will be able to select messages appropriate to our purposes. Competence in interpersonal communication implies just that. It implies that we are aware of our goals and how to communicate so that we are most likely to achieve them.

The messages we create provide information to those around us. Let's examine what we mean by information.

Information

The term *information* has spurred much interest in communication studies. Some scholars believe information deals with the amount of uncertainty and unpredictability that exists in a situation.[5] When a situation is completely predictable, no new information is present. This view of information is often a little confusing, however, for it has nothing to do with message, facts, or meaning. It suggests instead the number of messages required to eliminate all uncertainty in a situation. Others have argued that information must be more human. They focus on the notion that anything conveyed in a communication that reduces uncertainty and increases predictability is information.[6]

This second understanding of information is closer to our definition of the term as anything in a communication event that helps or causes us to attach meaning. Thus, talk and the nonverbal messages that surround it and allow you to know how to interpret the talk are information.

Information serves two broad purposes: creating understanding and persuading. If its aim is *creating understanding*, then it suggests how we are thinking, how or why we are acting, or even our emotional state. Telling your boss about your impressions regarding your work is an example of communication to express how you are thinking. Or, instead, you might explain to your boss why you were unable to turn a report in on time. This would be communication about your actions.

Sometimes we communicate our emotional state. Certain verbal and nonverbal messages, known as *self-expressive messages*, point to our emotional state. If you walk near a playground, you will be able to see and hear examples of such messages. The child who jumps up and down just because he is excited is sending a powerful nonverbal message about his excitement. The child who shouts for joy is using her voice for the same purpose.

Similar observations can be made when you watch your friends on the dance floor. Some will be sending messages for a persuasive reason, but many more will be moving their bodies and occasionally vocalizing just for the joy of self-expression.

Some people use language to express their emotional states, not pausing to think about the denotative implications of their word choice. These people may choose strong language without intending anyone to take them literally. For example, a teenage girl was recently overheard saying to her best friend, "I'm going to kill you if you do that again." The statement was made in the kitchen, while the two girls were doing the dishes. The friend had just used the rubber spray hose at the sink to soak the first girl in a surprise attack. Such excessive use of language is probably common in your experience, too.

Sometimes extravagant uses of language can create grave problems in a relationship. How you talk with someone says a lot not only about yourself but also about your concept of the other person. Excessive language may well be giving messages that create relationship problems. For example, you may know an unhappy person who habitually uses strong, negative language to describe experiences of the world and appears to believe that you see the world in the same way. "It's awful at this school. The teacher is a jerk. The quarter system is dumb. The student newspaper is stupid. The dormitory is a pigsty. The campus is a dump." Clearly this language says that the speaker does not like the school. If you were to ask this person about the literal meaning of each of these strong words, the person might be surprised, for he or she is thinking metaphorically. Even so, you would undoubtedly grow weary of such a person.

A second use of information is *persuasive* messages. If you set out to change the thoughts, feelings, or behavior of someone, you have sent persuasive messages. Change is thus an important component of persuasive communication. As you will see, learning to set appropriate, well-defined, positive goals is a valuable persuasive skill.

Not all persuasive messages are consciously structured for the particular communication event. For instance, we believe that individuals carefully nurture the images and impressions they project, although they may not deliberately select the message at the moment they send it.[7] For example, a woman may carefully choose the clothing she buys to conform to certain standards she holds. The

Self-expressive
messages point
to our
emotional state..

clothes thus become part of the image she projects. On some occasions, her selection of items from her closet may be very deliberate; at other times—as when she is late for work—her choice may be relatively unconscious. Even at such moments, however, the woman's impression management is intentional.

Persuasive messages operate in at least two ways. When you manage your relationships, that management can take a positive, nurturing, and maintaining direction, or it can move in the direction of conflict. In either case, effective goal setting seems a critical interpersonal communication skill.

Relationship

We will define *relationship* as a series of encounters that create a connection between two people, regardless of its source. Relationships can be permanent, such as by blood, or transitory. Most of your relationships are transitory and therefore also tentative. Whether by blood or by any other connection, the quality of your relationships is a matter of choice, for to sustain them in a mutually satisfying way, you have to nurture and reinforce them.[8]

COMMUNICATION COMPETENCE

What does it take to be a competent communicator? This is an important question for you to consider as you begin reading this book. Most of us are fairly confident that we can identify a competent communicator. Yet, communication competence turns out to be such a complex issue that researchers are still struggling to define it. There is, however, a great deal that we know about communication competence.[9]

Competence Defined

Most communication scholars agree that communication competence should be defined in terms of two basic ideas: achievement of a goal and maintenance of the relationship. Although scholars are struggling with a definition, *communication competence* is communication that achieves what you want from the other person while maintaining the relationship in a way that is acceptable to both persons.[10]

Goals are only meaningful when taken within a particular situation. This implies that competence is best viewed with a situation and person in mind. Communication that is competent in one situation might not be in another. You might be successful in achieving a goal with a friend if you use humor, while the same approach might fail with your professor. Your experience bears this out. We conclude that there is no ideal way to communicate. *Different styles of communication will be effective in particular settings and will vary in their effectiveness from setting to setting.*

Communication competence also includes a relational component. Our definition indicated that the relationship should also be maintained in a way that is satisfactory to both persons. *We must judge competence by asking how well the relational needs of those involved were met.* You might get along fine in relationships with your peers but have difficulty with your parents. Your competence at meeting relational needs may vary from relationship to relationship. So, meeting relational needs is part of being competent; none of us would label a communicator competent who achieved his or her aim but failed to meet relational needs or who, in attempting to meet those needs, damaged the relationship.

Keep in mind that competence is culturally based. What is seen as competent in one culture might not be in another.[11] For example, self-disclosure and speaking clearly are valued in the United States, but are likely to be viewed as overly aggressive and insensitive in some Asian cultures. These cultures value subtlety and in directness, instead. But even within a society different ethnic groups may have different ideas of competence. For example, one study revealed that how good friends should communicate varied from one ethnic group to another. As a group, Latinos valued relational support most highly, while African Americans looked for respect and acceptance. Asian Americans emphasized caring and positive exchange of ideas, while Anglo Americans valued friends who noticed their needs as an individual.[12]

Characteristics of Competence

Communication scholars have discovered several characteristics of communication competence.

1. *A competent communicator has a range of communication behaviors from which to select for any particular communication event.* The importance of this characteristic can easily be seen by considering a common experience most of us have had. Suppose you would like a close friend to help you with a project. Here are some options you might consider in attempting to achieve this goal:

   - You might decide to say nothing, figuring that you will be turned down anyway.

   - You might invite the friend over and plan to be working on the project when he or she arrives. You hope that your friend will notice your struggle and volunteer to help.

   - You might hint about how difficult the project is, hoping the friend will volunteer to help.

   - You might joke about your discomfort in having such a difficult project, hoping for your friend's help.

- You might straightforwardly express your need and ask for help.
- You might demand that the friend help. (You have helped your friend in the past, so this person ought to help you now.)

We could go on with other choices for communicating in this situation. Our point is not to exhaust the possibilities but rather to show that there are many options. If you are confined to only one or two options, then you may not be able to select one that will provide you the best chance of success.

2. *A competent communicator possesses rhetorical sensitivity. Rhetorical sensitivity* is the ability to analyze a situation and pick the right communication approach to it.[13] Having a range of behaviors from which to select is not enough; you must be able to select an appropriate behavior for the particular situation. You must be able to tell that an approach that worked yesterday may not work today because the situation has changed. You will notice the change and select a different way to communicate because you are rhetorically sensitive.

   The need to be rhetorically sensitive if you want to be effective is supported by research. Researchers found that no type of behavior was effective or ineffective in every relationship. They concluded that what works with some people can be harmful to others. Thus, a need for rhetorical sensitivity arises as the individual communicator analyzes the situation and decides what ways of communication will work for him or herself and the other persons involved.[14]

3. *A competent communicator will have the ability to enact the appropriate communication behavior.* Skill must be developed in using various communication behaviors. Developing skill in communication is very much like developing skill in anything you decide to do. If you were to decide to develop your skill as a tennis player, you would seek instruction and then practice what you learned. You will find that this is the approach of this book—we provide information about a particular concept and then instruction in how to develop skill in applving it.

   Developing communication skill also requires self-monitoring. *Self-monitoring* means paying close attention to behavior and using that information to shape future behavior. This suggests that you need to be both a participant in and observer of the communication event. You need to be constantly asking "How am I doing? Could I do this differently next time and be more successful?" People who are aware of their behaviors and the impression they make are more skillful communicators than those who are low self-monitors.[15] *It is only through this kind of analysis, making mental notes of what you have learned and using that information, that you will be able to make intelligent choices in future communication encounters.*

We have suggested that the best way to get your desired results from your interaction with others is to develop communication competence. Research supports this notion. Rebecca Rubin and Elizabeth Graham identified a positive relationship between interpersonal competence and college success.[16] Of course, this may not be surprising to you because of the central place communication takes in relationships with roommates, other students, faculty, and administration. In addition, other researchers have found a relationship between interpersonal competence and reduced feelings of anxiety, depression, and loneliness.[17] The link might be that those who have interpersonal competence are able to develop stronger interpersonal relationships that counter feelings of anxiety, depression, and loneliness.

For the rest of your life, you will want to polish your analytical and performance communication skills. You will continually ask such seemingly simple but crucial questions as: How can I start a conversation with this person? How can I get other people to open up? How can I let another person know who I truly am? How can I issue an invitation that is likely to be accepted? Is there something I

The best way to achieve interpersonal effectiveness is to develop communication competence.

Developing skill in communication is very much like developing skill in anything you decide to do.

can do to handle criticism more constructively? How can I reduce my anxiety in social situations? Is there a way to know where I stand with someone? Can I change a relationship for the better? Can I change a relationship without damaging it? These questions and countless others about relational effectiveness will be the focus of your study in interpersonal communication.

A PROCESS MODEL OF COMMUNICATION

We have defined interpersonal communication as the transactional process of exchanging messages to convey information and to establish and maintain relationships. This definition is the result of a good deal of thinking about communication by scholars from many different backgrounds and ages.

We can make our definition more concrete and useful to you by constructing a graphic representation of the communication process through the creation of a model. A model is a visual representation; when the subject is somewhat abstract, like the notion of communication, a model can make it more concrete. We will present two models: one model of the communication process and a second of the interpersonal exchange process. This second model introduces several key components of building and sustaining relationships.

The process model of communication is labeled to indicate that two individuals are working together in one setting (see figure 1.1). The *source* is the location of an idea. Obviously, in interpersonal contexts, the source of the idea is an individual. The next term, *encoder*, is used in the same box to show that individuals must translate ideas into codes. The most common, but by no means the only, code is language. You can also encode into many different nonverbal message systems. For example, you can communicate with muscle changes, with peculiar use of space, with the clothes you wear, or with your gestures and tone of voice.

Notice that, at the other side of the model, another individual must *decode* the messages sent. Since these messages do *not* have meaning in and of themselves (meaning is in the minds of those who use the codes), messages must be decoded to be meaningful. Skill in decoding is just as important as skill in encoding.

Figure 1.1
A process
model of
communication.

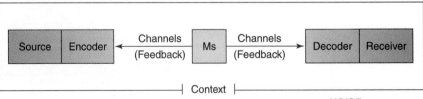

The source/encoder transmits messages—plural. Since more than one code is used every time you communicate, you send more than one message. The *Ms* in the middle of the box suggest these multiple messages.

These messages have to be transmitted through *channels*. A person talking with you is using vibrations in the molecular structure of the air as a channel. If this person is visible as well as audible, you will pick up additional nonverbal messages, too. In that case, light waves are being used as channels. If a phone is used, electrical impulses over a wire are being used to send messages. Even in a phone call, more than one message is sent. Words, phrases, tone, stress, and emphasis are all communicated.

Notice the arrowheads at either end of the middle line labeled *channels*. These arrowheads suggest that messages travel in both directions at the same time. This special feature of the model is feedback. *Feedback*, the receiver's response to the message, can take a verbal or nonverbal form or both. The decoder feeds back a reaction to what is sensed, which enables the encoder to control and correct the message if needed. Feedback can occur instantaneously or sometime after the message has been received. It most often comes in the form of instantaneous vocal and nonverbal cues. For example, it may be a smile, a vocalized hum, or a nod to signal agreement.

Reexamine figure 1.1. Notice that all components of the model are enclosed in the context of the communication event. Everything available to the communicators in that event—including all that the participants brought with them—affects the message exchange. Health, attitudes and opinions, emotional condition, and inhibitions all come into play at the moment.

An important feature of this model is *noise*. But we do not want to limit your understanding of this term to physical, channel noise, for it refers to any sensory or perceptual interference that disrupts or distorts communication. Noise can be both physical (disturbances in the channels) and emotional. Sometimes called *semantic*, emotional noise is anything going on inside the participants that upsets the accuracy of message reception or transmission.

> Noise is any sensory or perceptual interference that disrupts or distorts communication.

A potential for noise is in the source/encoder. If the encoder has a biased perception or uses strong language, for example, noise is introduced. Or there can be noise in the channels. Is the air conditioner or furnace working? Is anything happening in the next room? If so, you are aware of it because of the noise.

There is also the potential for noise in messages, especially when people of different cultures try to talk with each other. Offensive language is also sometimes used by people speaking the same tongue. Noisy nonverbal signs and signals are likewise transmitted. These problems are compounded when the expectations of other cultures are introduced. Often very noisy results are produced.

To illustrate, Tim was working in a restaurant that also employed an Iranian student on the same shift. One day, Tim gestured a friendly OK sign to mean "Everything is good. You did well." The Iranian was working a double shift and had been up most of the night before writing a paper. Thus, he was experiencing a good deal of noise. In his exhausted state, he mistook the sign for an obscene message and knocked Tim down. Noise played an important part in distorting this message.

Let us add noise to the model, then, in all the places where it can occur, namely in the source, the encoder, the channels, the messages, the decoder, the receiver, and the context (see figure 1.2). In sum, the communication process can be a very noisy business.

The critical components of interpersonal communication, then, are *source, encoder, messages, channels, decoder, receiver, feedback, context*, and *noise*.

Now we want to examine a slightly more complicated model of communication—the interpersonal exchange model.

AN INTERPERSONAL EXCHANGE MODEL

The *interpersonal exchange model* shows how we make decisions about sharing ourselves in an interpersonal communication encounter. This sharing process is important to us because it is the basis for relational growth—a central concern of this book and undoubtedly an important issue for you.

This process of sharing ourselves generally begins with an encounter with another person who provides a stimulus for a communication event. Suppose, for the purposes of our discussion, that you see a person you recognize, Frank. Frank becomes a part of your stimulus field. His appearance and behaviors have no intrinsic meaning. So, at this point, since meaning lies within you, we need to examine events going on inside of you to discover what is happening in the exchange process.

Let's follow this process with Frank as our example. First, your *basic sensitivity* comes into play. This suggests the level of ability you utilize in discovering stimuli in your environment and sorting

Figure 1.2
The
communication
process with
noise.

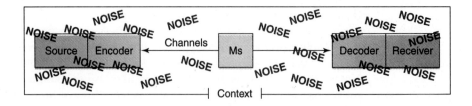

through them. Here, too, your *perceptual process* comes into play as you bring stimuli inside your body and become aware of them. Perhaps you notice that Frank is tall, quick to smile, and said "Hello" with certain vocal emphasis.

Next, you go through a process of *interpreting and understanding* what these stimuli might mean. Part of that analysis is *risk assessment*, a process in which you make decisions about what these stimuli tell you about an appropriate response. There is obviously a range of possible responses you might make, from a cold "Hello" to a warm "It's good to see you!" Your decision about what response to make rests, in part, on your assessment of the probability that Frank's communication will be positive toward you. This decision is the final step in this internal processing of the stimuli. A *prediction* is made about Frank's response and a message formulated based on that prediction. This prediction rests on the *trust level* you have regarding Frank's communication in response to yours. The internal process we described here is represented in the part of the model illustrated in figure 1.3.

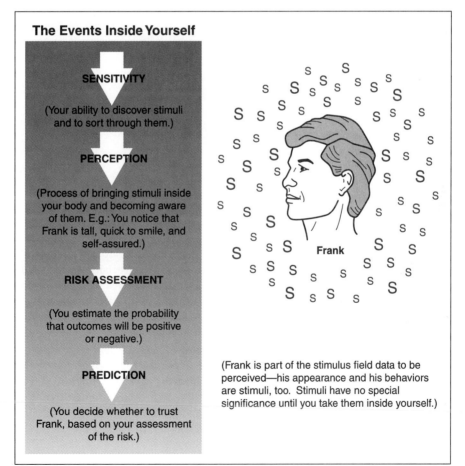

The Events Inside Yourself

SENSITIVITY

(Your ability to discover stimuli and to sort through them.)

PERCEPTION

(Process of bringing stimuli inside your body and becoming aware of them. E.g.: You notice that Frank is tall, quick to smile, and self-assured.)

RISK ASSESSMENT

(You estimate the probability that outcomes will be positive or negative.)

PREDICTION

(You decide whether to trust Frank, based on your assessment of the risk.)

Frank

(Frank is part of the stimulus field data to be perceived—his appearance and his behaviors are stimuli, too. Stimuli have no special significance until you take them inside yourself.)

Figure 1.3
First part of a model of interpersonal exchange.

Figure 1.4
Model of
interpersonal
exchange:
prediction, trust,
self-disclosure,
and message
production.

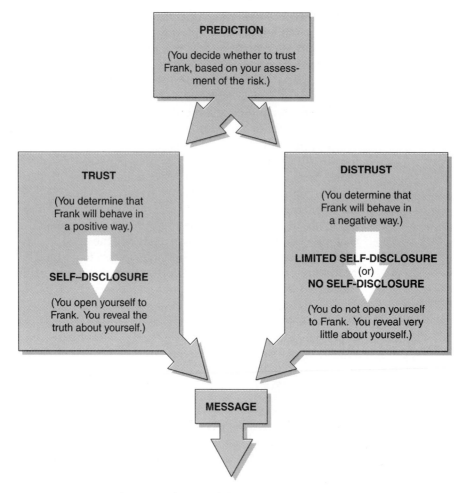

The second part of the interpersonal exchange model, illustrated in figure 1.4, presents the transition of this process from internal to external processes in the formulation and transmission of a message. Suppose the decision is to *trust* that Frank will respond positively through his communication. Perhaps you think he will warmly say, "It's good to see you!" This decision to trust might lead you to open yourself to him through self-disclosure. *Self-disclosure* is revealing something about yourself that Frank might not normally discover unless you told him. In doing so, you allow yourself to be somewhat vulnerable to Frank and thereby demonstrate your trust in him.

On the other hand, your decision might be either that you *distrust* Frank or that you don't know if you can trust him. Perhaps you decide you don't know how he will receive your greeting. Under this circumstance, you may decide to play it safe. So, you either open yourself slightly, *limited self-disclosure*, or do not open yourself at all, *no self-disclosure*.

At this point in the exchange, whatever your message, it becomes a stimulus to Frank—much as his initial communication was to you. He, too, will go through the process, as you did, of sensing the stimuli in his environment, perceiving from the environment the parts that are your message, processing them by making decisions about what they mean, and analyzing the risks of responding to you in each of a variety of ways. He, too, will make a prediction about your behavior, settling on some level of trust. Finally, he will produce a message that will contain some level of self-disclosure or perhaps none at all.

If Frank recognizes self-disclosure on your part, he will probably behave in an accepting and self-disclosing way. If Frank understands your self-disclosure as an invitation to greater intimacy, he will almost certainly provide you with feedback. It is your turn again. If that happens, your relationship has a good chance of growing. But if he understands that your message does not disclose yourself and so behaves in a rejecting way, or if he understands your self-disclosure but rejects you anyway, the relationship will probably not grow. You will probably make the decision to disengage.

We have already identified the critical components of the communication process to be *source, encoder, messages, channels, decoder, receiver, feedback, context,* and *noise.* The exchange model identifies additional terms—*sensitivity, self-disclosure, trust,* and *risk*—that are central to the process of developing relationships.

Sensitivity

Sensitivity is a person's skill and ability to take in information that another person provides and to interpret that information with empathy. *Empathy* suggests identification with another's experiences, feelings, ideas, and/or problems. You are sensitive to the extent that you skillfully observe and accurately interpret what another is saying and are able to empathize. No two people can experience an event identically, but you can experience the moment in essentially similar ways. The key to sensitivity is the awareness that you are guessing and that the guess needs to be checked. Sensitive people empathize because they are willing and able to take others into account frequently. Sensitivity thus deals with the perceptual mechanisms and the interpretations that are made of those perceptions.

Self-Disclosure

Self-disclosure is the process of revealing information about oneself, including thoughts, desires, needs, and goals, that would not normally be known by the other person. You self-disclose when you report your honest attitudes about another or another's ideas or about yourself or your ideas. You self-disclose when you respond candidly, daring to display your ideas.

There are degrees of self-disclosure. Sometimes self-disclosure reveals more about you than at other times. All self-disclosure can be described by some degree of breadth and some level of depth. Irwin Altman and Dalmas Taylor have defined *breadth* as the range of subjects revealed and *depth* as the intimacy of subjects revealed.[18] Relationships are built through willingness to disclose. How can we develop attraction to and liking for a person we do not know? Casual relationships are generally characterized by breadth without much depth. Intimate relationships are likely to have great breadth and depth.

If a meaningful relationship is to be maintained, it is clear that self-disclosure is important. Tracy Schmidt and Randolph Cornelius found, for example, that self-disclosure helps to achieve a closer relationship with another person.[19] Beyond this Susan Sprecher found that couples who engaged in significant self-disclosure remained together longer than couples who did not. She also discovered that we develop increased affection for our partner when we disclose. Yet, the recipient of the self-disclosure may or may not develop more affection for the partner, depending on gender. Men develop increased affection, while women do not.[20]

Trust

Interpersonal trust is confidence in another person's behavior. But what is the behavior we have confidence about in interpersonal communication? We trust that the other person will receive the information we share in a relatively accepting, confirming, and positive way.

Our concern in interpersonal relationships often lies with how our self-disclosure will be received. We are relying on the other person to be accepting, confirming, and positive as we share a part of who we are. Because we rely on the other person not to use the information to be hurtful, trust is the foundation of self-disclosure. You trust that your self-disclosure will be received and accepted. Indeed, the bases of trust include another's character, competence, and judgment as you perceive them.

If a person is open, honest, and discreet and behaves consistently, and if you perceive the person's motives and intentions to be confirming, you trust the other's character. If this person has a record of successes, you trust the person's competence. And if you think this individual makes the right decisions, you trust the person's judgment. If all of these are combined in your image of this person, you trust and will be able to risk disclosing yourself.

Risk

Risk is the process of deciding to accept the chance that adverse outcomes may result from trusting another. The greater the risk, the more you must trust. "Taking the risk" usually expresses a decision to gamble that you will receive positive, not negative, consequences

To trust is to rely on another person's behavior.

from your actions. In its simplest form, to risk is to weigh payoffs and costs and to determine that the payoff for certain behavior is likely to be greater than its cost. When the decision is about self-disclosure, you risk being damaged by trusting another enough to disclose yourself. Self-disclosure is risky because, as John Powell (1969) said in *Why Am I Afraid to Tell You Who I Am?*, "I am afraid to tell you who I am, because, if I tell you who I am, you may not like who I am, and that is all I have."[21]

Summary

Your relationships are enormously varied, but all rest upon interpersonal communication—the transactional process of exchanging verbal and nonverbal messages to convey information and to establish and maintain relationships. Each term in this definition has been defined and explained. We want you to understand that the study of interpersonal communication is complex but worthwhile. Your goal is to manage your relationships with increasing effectiveness. The best way to do this is to increase your communication competence.

Congratulations! Your choice to study interpersonal communication is an important step in that lifelong journey.

Models help scholars and students study the components of the communication process and the relationships among them. We described two such models.

A process model of communication, emphasizes the two-way flow of messages. It also incorporates such central concepts as context and feedback, making it clear that people always send more than one message and that noise can be both physical and semantic. One important implication of such a model is that communication occurs both inside and between individuals.

We also described an exchange model of the interpersonal communication process, which establishes that what goes on within an individual is profoundly important not only to communication in the content dimension but also, more importantly, to communication about our relationships.

Discussion Questions

1. Working with a small group of your classmates, try to construct a *taxonomy*, or classification system, of as many different kinds of relationships as possible (for example, a father-daughter relationship). Base the taxonomy on one of these criteria: degree of intimacy, amount of time spent, degree of importance, or activities engaged in. List your group's taxonomy on the chalkboard and compare it to the lists generated by other groups in your class. What similarities and differences do you find in the *approach* and the *results* of the various group efforts?

Can you draw a lesson about relationship effectiveness out of this exercise?

2. Apply each term in our definition of interpersonal communication to an important relationship in your life.

3. With one or two classmates, act out what you think might happen in the first few minutes of a blind date. Afterward, try to identify examples of auditory, visual, tactile, and environmental messages. Then classify them as self-expressive or persuasive messages.

4. Working with a small group of classmates, develop an original model of the interpersonal communication process, labeling each part. Try to present as complete a picture of the variables that influence communication as you can. Does your model focus attention on certain aspects of communication while minimizing others? Present your finished product to the class for consideration and comments.

5. Using your group's model or the process model presented in this unit, decide whether the model is complete. If not, what changes or additions are needed?

6. Together with one or two classmates, discuss whether you believe the interpersonal exchange model is accurate. If not, what changes would you make? Why?

ENDNOTES

1. For a thoughtful and thorough development of this idea of uncertainty reduction, see C. R. Berger and J. J. Bradac, *Language and Social Knowledge: Uncertainty in Interpersonal Relations* (London: Edward Arnold Publishers, 1982).

2. See, for example, J. Stewart and C. Logan, *Together: Communicating Interpersonally*, 5th ed. (New York: McGraw-Hill, 1998).

3. See, for example, R. K. Shelly, "Sequences and Cycles in Social Interaction," *Small Group Research* 28 (1997): 333–356.

4. M. Dainton and L. Stafford, *The Dark Side of Interpersonal Communication*, B. H. Spitzberg and W. R. Cupach, eds. (Hillsdale, NJ: Erlbaum, 1993).

5. This difficult concept has been very influential. For further discussion, see three classic works: N. Wiener, *Cybernetics, or Control and Communication in the Animal and Machine* (Cambridge: MIT Press, 1948); W. Weaver, "The Mathematics of Communication," *Scientific American* 181 (1949): 11–15; and C. Shannon and W. Weaver, *The Mathematical Theory of Communication* (Urbana: University of Illinois Press, 1949).

6. Y. Bar-Hillel and R. Carnap, "Semantic Information," *British Journal of the Philosophy of Science* 4 (1953): 147–157.

7. See E. Goffman, *The Presentation of Self in Everyday Life* (Garden City, NY: Doubleday & Co., 1959).

8. S. Duck and G. Pittman, "Social and Personal Relationships," in *Handbook of Interpersonal Communication*, 2d ed., M. L. Knapp and G. R. Phillips, eds. (Newbury Park, CA: Sage, 1994).

9. For a review of research on communication competence, see J. M. Wiemann and M. O. Wiemann, *Interpersonal Competence* (Newbury Park, CA: Sage, 1991).

10. J. M. Wiemann, J. Takai, H. Ota, and M. Wiemann, "A Relational Model of Communication Competence," in *Emerging Theories of Human Communication*, B. Kovacic, ed. (Albany, NY: SUNY Press, 1997).

11. G. M. Chen and W. J. Sarosta, "Intercultural Communication Competence: A Synthesis," in *Communication Yearbook 19*, B. R. Burleson and A. W. Kunkel, eds. (Thousand Oaks, CA: Sage, 1996).

12. M. J. Collier, "Communication Competence Problematic in Ethnic Relationships," *Communication Reports* 4 (1991): 22–29.

13. A. P. Bochner and C. W. Kelly, "Interpersonal Competence: Rationale, Philosophy, and Implementation of a Conceptual Framework," *Speech Teacher* 23 (1974): 270–301; B. H. Spitzberg and H. T. Hurt, "The Measurement of Interpersonal Skills in Instructional Contexts," *Communication Education* 36 (1987): 28–45.

14. James C. McCroskey and Linda Wheeless, *Introduction to Human Communication* (Boston: Allyn Bacon), 1976, p. 5; D. Stiebel, *When Talking Makes Things Worse! Resolving Problems When Communication Fails* (Andrews and McMeel, 1987).

15. S. M. Daughton, "The Nature and Correlates of Conversational Sensitivity," in *Interpersonal Communication: Readings in Theory and Research*, M. V. Redmond, ed. (Fort Worth, TX: Harcourt Brace, 1995).

16. R. B. Rubin and E. E. Graham, "Communication Correlates of College Success: An Exploratory Investigation," *Communication Education* 37 (1988): 14–27.

17. B. H. Spitzberg and W. R. Cupach, *Handbook of Interpersonal Competence* (New York: Springer-Verlag, 1989).

18. I. Altman and D. Taylor, *Social Penetration: The Development of Interpersonal Relationships* (New York: Holt, Rinehart and Winston, 1973).

19. T. O. Schmidt and R. R. Cornelius, "Self-disclosure in Everday Life," *Journal of Social and Personal Relationships* 4 (1987): 563–575.

20. S. Sprecher, "The Effects of Self-disclosure Given and Received on Affection for an Intimate Partner and Stability of the Relationship." *Journal of Social and Personal Relationships* 4 (1987): 113–127.

21. J. Powell, *Why Am I Afraid to Tell You Who I Am?* (Niles, IL: Argus Communications, 1969), 12.

READ MORE ABOUT INTERPERSONAL EFFECTIVENESS IN THESE SOURCES

Bochner, Arthur P. "The Functions of Human Communicating in Interpersonal Bonding." In *Handbook of Rhetorical and Communication Theory*, ed. Carroll C. Arnold and John Waite Bowers, 544–621. Boston: Allyn and Bacon, 1984. This essay is a scholarly review of the communication research and theory regarding forming and maintaining interpersonal relationships.

Stewart, John. "Interpersonal Communication: Contact between Persons." In *Bridges, Not Walls: A Book about Interpersonal Communication*, 7th ed. New York: McGraw-Hill, 1998. Stewart shares his view of the differences between interpersonal and impersonal communication in this introductory essay.

Wiemann, John M., and Mary O. Wiemann. *Interpersonal Competence*. Newbury Park, CA: Sage, 1991. This is an excellent source for discovering what we know about communication competence.

READ MORE ABOUT THE INTERPERSONAL COMMUNICATION PROCESS IN THESE SOURCES

Altman, Irwin, and Dalmas Taylor. *Social Penetration: The Development of Interpersonal Relationships*. New York: Holt, Rinehart, and Winston, 1973. This book provides an interesting research-based examination of the relational engagement process.

Johnson, David W. *Reaching Out: Interpersonal Effectiveness and Self-Actualization*, 4th ed. Englewood Cliffs. NJ: Prentice-Hall, 1990. Johnson's chapters on self-disclosure and developing and maintaining trust are helpful readings.

Mortenson, C. David. *Miscommunication*. Thousand Oaks, CA: Sage, 1997. This book discusses the many ways people can have difficulty creating shared meanings when they communicate.

PART 2

FOUNDATIONS

2

SELF-CONCEPT

PREVIEW

Your relational interactions and the images you hold of yourself depend upon one another and influence one another. That is, your images both control and are controlled by your communication. It is important to understand how your self-image has evolved and what you can do to change it.

What motivates communication in our relationships? We have already suggested that we communicate to develop our self-concepts and our styles of self-disclosure. Another reason we communicate is to express and fulfill our basic needs. For example, we may feel a need to hear someone acknowledge that we belong, that we are part of a group, that they like us, or that we are in charge of some aspect of our relationship. We also communicate for relatively unconscious reasons. We may seek out or avoid communication to protect the self-concept and the relationship from challenges and changes we may not want. This chapter explores our interpersonal needs. Reading and thinking about them will help explain why we communicate as we do in our relationships. Attention to the needs that motivate our communication can help us adjust our interactions to promote greater relational growth.

KEY TERMS

abdicrat	adaptable-social
attitudes	autocrat
being conscious	beliefs
democrat	derived beliefs
frame of reference	going unconscious
identity aspirations	interpersonal needs
labeling dominate behavior	material me
multiple selves	need for affection
need for control	need for inclusion
openness to change	overpersonal
personal	self-awareness
self-concept	shared beliefs
significant others	social comparison
social me	spiritual me
surface beliefs	survival orientation
synthesis of beliefs	underpersonal
unshared central beliefs	undersocial
values	

OBJECTIVES

1. Define *self-concept.*
2. Describe how beliefs, values, and attitudes shape your frame of reference.
3. Identify particular beliefs, values, and attitudes that are important to your self-concept.
4. Explain the processes that have contributed to the development of your self-concept.
5. Set goals for the further development of your self-concept and define specific steps for the attainment of those goals.
6. Explain how interpersonal needs affect our communication.
7. Identify and give an example of each component of Maslow's hierarchy of needs.
8. Discuss how each of Maslow's needs might be met through an interpersonal relationship.
9. Define the need for inclusion, and give an example of how it motivated your communication.
10. Define the need for control, and cite an example of how it motivated you to communicate.
11. Define the need for affection, and give an example of how it motivated your communication.
12. Cite an instance in which the need to survive prompted your communication in a relationship.
13. Explain and practice the appropriate expression of interpersonal needs.

DEFINITION OF THE SELF-CONCEPT

We present ourselves through our communication. And, naturally, we present ourselves differently from one encounter to another. However, certain aspects are repeated in many relationships. These flow from the *self-concept*—the summary of the perceptions, ideas, and images we each have of ourselves. The very phrase "perceptions, ideas, and images" suggests that we have both a self *and* a concept of that self. The self-concept is a sense of who we are that may or may not be close to the actual self.

The degree to which our self-concept matches the self others see in us represents our *self-awareness*. We want you to think about your self-concept as you read this chapter. Consider the self you believe you present in various situations and notice how people respond to that presentation. Examine your communication and the messages others send you about it. By increasing self-awareness in this way, you will gain greater control over your self-concept and your communication will be more authentic.

A self-concept is not something we can see or touch but rather a useful idea that enables us to study the way we communicate in our relationships. Self-concept is comprised of the characteristics that we present about ourselves. These take the form of attitudes, values, and beliefs. We choose aspects of self that we think are important to the relationship when we present these images.

> The self-concept is the summary of the perceptions, ideas, and images we each have of ourselves.

IDEAS ABOUT WHO WE ARE

Interest in the self-concept is not new. In fact, twenty-three centuries ago, Aristotle argued that there were physical and nonphysical parts of the person. At the turn of this century, psychologist William James refined earlier ideas about the self. He suggested that there is a *material me*—my body, my home, and the physical objects around me; a *social me*—my awareness of how others see me; and a *spiritual me*—my awareness of myself as a thinking and feeling person.[1] Later, George Herbert Mead observed how people achieve self-identity through viewing those around them.[2] He suggested that the self has two dimensions—the *I* and the *Me*—which exist and function side by side, each controlling as well as stimulating the other. The *I* represents our private, unique aspects. It is this dimension of our self that provides our goals, creativity, and imagination. The *Me* represents our social side. It maintains an awareness of what is appropriate in certain situations. The *Me* understands how to get what the *I* wants in a socially acceptable way.

Self-concept is not merely a concept that applies to the individual. Groups as well as entire communities develop a collective image of themselves. Communication Scholar Donal Carbaugh tells how Americans interact in ways that create their identities in a variety of settings.[3]

COMPONENTS OF THE SELF-CONCEPT

The self-concept is a complex structure. This complexity is illustrated by the idea of *multiple selves.* We seem to be a different person in each of many different situations. An example may clarify this concept.

First, picture yourself at an athletic event. Now, contrast this image with one of yourself taking a final exam. Finally, imagine yourself at work on a very busy day. You would probably describe yourself differently in each setting. Which image is really you? Of course, all are. We have multiple selves, each dependent on a context. Together, they form our self-concept. It is the context that makes certain aspects of our self-concept more important at a particular moment.

Self-concept is composed of our *beliefs, values,* and *attitudes.* Our individuality comes from the unique interaction of these elements. They provide a structure through which we develop and build who we are and how we think. We also make assumptions about others on the basis of our own beliefs, values, and attitudes. Let's take a look at these components.

Beliefs, values, and attitudes reflect our assumptions about the world and our places in it. Each of these elements differs, however, in its function. Our beliefs represent the people, places, and things

The self-concept includes many images of the self.

that exist for us. Our values appraise them, and our attitudes guide our behavior toward them.

Together, these components of the self-concept provide a *frame of reference*, a topic we'll develop in later in this chapter. We experience people, places, and things through this frame much as we look out through sunglasses or a window. In other words, a frame of reference is a set of interlocking facts, ideas, rules, and presuppositions that orient a person and give meaning to situations and experiences. Every combination of beliefs, values, and attitudes creates a different frame of reference. The particular frame through which we look at an event colors the way we interpret it. We will experience the event differently if we shift frames of reference; this is like changing the shade of your sunglasses. The differences caused by our frames of reference are central to our perceptions of people and messages, for they determine the self we present to the other person in a relationship. It is important to remember that the source of our frames of reference is the beliefs, values, and attitudes that make up the self-concept. Each frame of reference "represents" some idea about who we are.

> We experience people, places, and things through a frame of reference.

Beliefs

At the core of our self-concept lie our *beliefs* about the existence and characteristics of people, places, and things. Any idea is a belief if it includes any form of the verb "to be." If you see one of your friends is acting in an unfamiliar way, you might say, "Are you okay? You're not normally like this." This is an expression of a belief that you hold about your friend. Other examples of beliefs are

- "I'm a tough but fair supervisor."
- "I'm an educated person."
- "You're attractive."
- "My doctor knows what to do about my problem."
- "My friend knows which tie will look best with this suit."

Some beliefs are more significant than others. In the examples above, if your friend says she does not know which tie will look best with your new suit, the belief is contradicted, but the results are not earth-shattering. On the other hand, if your doctor says she does not know what your problem is, the consequences are much more serious.

Beliefs may concern ourselves, others, or tangible objects. For example, when you are wondering about something you heard your professor say in class, you might conclude, "He's the teacher and so has a great deal of knowledge on the subject." The connecting of "teacher" and "knowledge" illustrates a belief statement.

Many beliefs are derived through *synthesis*, that is, they are developed from information outside our personal experience. Suppose, for example, you hear that your company is hiring a new vice president for operations, a Mr. Schmidt. During the week before his arrival, you listen carefully to all the speculation about this new manager. You hear Tim say that he knows that four of the seven department heads were fired in Mr. Schmidt's last two years at his previous job. Marie says she overheard the president talking in the elevator about his concern for greater efficiency in the company. You know from your own experience that Mr. Schmidt's predecessor was fired. When asked for your opinion, you might say, "Well, I think we're in for some tightening up around here. Mr. Schmidt must be some kind of efficiency expert that they're hiring to whip all the departments into shape." This statement represents a belief that comes from synthesis. You have had no contact with Mr. Schmidt, yet you believe him to be a taskmaster. This belief is based on your confidence in your friends' reports about Mr. Schmidt, information about his experience, and knowledge of the company.

Milton Rokeach suggests that beliefs are organized in a pattern from a central core of most primitive beliefs. He explains this concept of relative centrality in terms of four principles:

1. Beliefs about one's self, existence, and identity are much more central than other beliefs.

Figure 2.1
The structure of
beliefs.

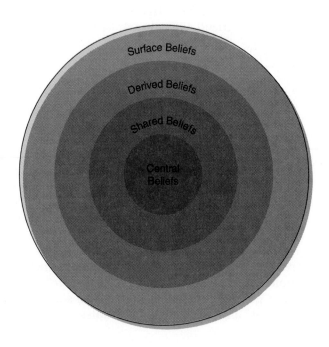

2. Shared beliefs about one's existence and self-identity are much less central than unshared beliefs (ones held by oneself).

3. Beliefs that are derived from other beliefs (rather than from contact with the object of the belief) are less central than shared beliefs.

4. Beliefs concerning matters of taste are less central than others. They are usually seen by the holder as arbitrary in nature and are thus relatively inconsequential in their impact on other beliefs.[4]

These interrelationships are shown in figure 2.1. At the outer ring of the figure are *surface beliefs*, or those that are least central. For example, have you noticed that you tend to sit in or near the same seat every time you come to class? This choice expresses your belief that there is something preferable about that location. This preference is probably flexible and has little impact on other beliefs. Your favorite flavor of ice cream and your favorite color are other examples of surface beliefs.

The next ring inward represents *derived beliefs*, or those we develop from indirect contact with an idea. Your assumption about Mr. Schmidt's character is such a belief. Another such belief might come from your contact with mass media, school, or religious literature.

Shared beliefs are shown in the next ring. These beliefs are held because of experiences that we are willing to discuss with others and often do. These beliefs provide a basis for our communication in interpersonal relationships. For instance, you and your boss may share the belief that you usually speak up for yourself on matters affecting your role in the company. Or you might have developed a belief in the importance of physical fitness from sharing long walks with your parents.

Unshared central beliefs, in the center of the figure, are fundamental beliefs about ourselves that we rarely share with others. Thus, they are not often directly challenged by others. This central core also includes our secret (and perhaps unconscious) hopes and fears, desires and delusions. Although such beliefs are unstated, they do not go unexpressed. Indeed, unshared beliefs serve as an important motivator for much of our communication. When we discuss interpersonal needs, you'll examine some of these.

Beliefs are what we know about the world and our relationship to it. They exist as statements about what is. Beliefs about ourselves are the building blocks of the self-concept. Here, we find the foundations for the images we present.

The nearer a belief is to the outside of the ring, the easier it is to change. Consider these statements, focusing on how difficult they might be to change. Ask yourself what number you would assign to each if 4 represented the hardest to change and 1 the easiest.

• "I think I'll wear my gray suit to this job interview."

• "This company appreciates a neat appearance."

- "I pay attention to detail."
- "I am proud of my careful nature."

The first statement represents a matter of taste—your idea about what looks good. You might have given it a 1 rating. You might easily be persuaded to wear your blue suit and would not feel bad about the change at all.

The second statement may be a derived belief, which you may hold because of what you have heard about the company. Since there is some basis for this belief, it would be more difficult to change than the first statement. You might assign it a 2 rating. It would take some information to cause a change—some other derived belief that would substitute for this one. Remember that what distinguishes a derived belief from other beliefs is that it comes from information and not direct experience.

The third statement might represent a shared belief or one that you intend to share, which suggests that it is more important than the less central beliefs. You might carefully choose your wardrobe for an interview to communicate this characteristic about yourself. You are involved personally with a shared belief, and only a direct experience can change it. You would probably find this belief more difficult to change than the first two and rate it a 3.

The last statement represents a central belief—one that you hold about yourself. These beliefs form the core of the self-concept because they are intensely held and are well protected; hence, you would give this statement a 4 rating. Central beliefs provide stability for the self-concept.

Values represent what is important in our lives.

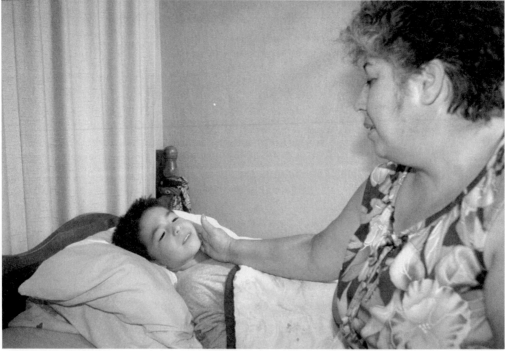

Values

Values provide order and sense to our lives. They include evaluative goals or standards of behavior. Our priorities for wealth, parenthood, inner peace, and a comfortable life are all values. Obviously, values involve beliefs. However, they move a step beyond beliefs. Values sort beliefs into wants, goals, and guidelines that define the desirability and importance of certain beliefs or combinations of beliefs. *While beliefs represent what is, values represent what should be.* For example, you might believe that your professor in this course is difficult but fair. If you think this is the way teachers should be, then you might apply this value as you evaluate other professors. Your statement about how this teacher is represents a belief. Your statement about how a teacher should be represents a value.

Frequently, a value summarizes several beliefs as a statement of goals. For instance, you might believe that sometimes, late in life, people need special help. You might also believe that your parents helped you a great deal at different points in your life. You may observe that as they become older, your parents seem to need and appreciate assistance from you. These beliefs might combine to form a value about the relationship between parents and children as follows:

- *Belief 1* Sometimes, late in life, people need special help.
- *Belief 2* My parents helped me at different points in my life.
- *Belief 3* As they become older, my parents seem to need and appreciate assistance from me.
- *Value:*   Children should lend help to their parents when they grow older. (Figure 2.2, page 38, illustrates this.)

Stewart Oskamp emphasized the significance of the value structure by stating that

> values are the most important element in the individual's system of attitudes and beliefs. They are ends rather than means; they are the goals a person strives for and which help to determine many of his other attitudes and beliefs.[5]

Values contribute much to the image we present to our partners in relationships. They also help us determine an image of others as we assign meaning to their behavior.

Sometimes these value systems come into conflict. Imagine, for example, that you are the sort of supervisor who values a "light touch" on the work of your employees. You don't provide much unsolicited feedback and allow your staff a great deal of freedom. One of your friends, Enrico, holds a different value about how a manager should supervise. He thinks managers should roll up their sleeves and administer with a hands-on approach. What would happen if Enrico came to work for you, or vice versa? The management

Figure 2.2
The structure
of beliefs and
values.

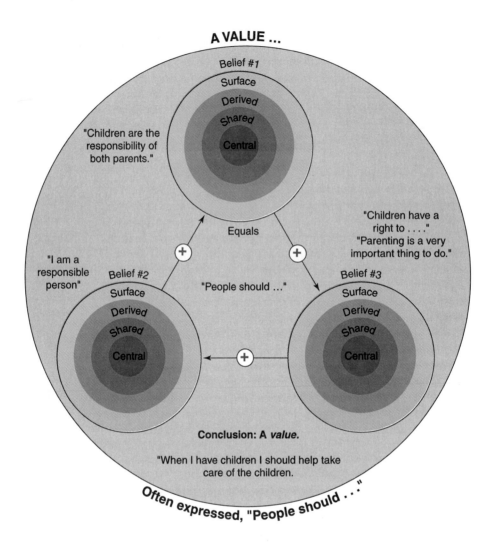

A VALUE ...

Belief #1

Surface

Derived

Shared

Central

"Children are the responsibility of both parents."

"I am a responsible person"

Equals

Belief #2

Surface

Derived

Shared

Central

"People should ..."

"Children have a right to . . . ."
"Parenting is a very important thing to do."

Belief #3

Surface

Derived

Shared

Central

Conclusion: A *value*.

"When I have children I should help take care of the children.

Often expressed, "People should . . ."

approach you value contradicts quite directly the one he values. If you are to work together productively, you will have to work to understand one another clearly.

Attitudes

Gordon Allport defined *attitude* in a way that is useful in a discussion of self-concept.[6] He stated that attitude is a readiness of mind and body, organized through experience, that directs our responses to all objects and situations to which it relates. Our attitudes summarize our belief and value structures. For instance, the person sharing the value that "children should help their parents when they grow older" might possess an attitude of willingness to help her parents. An attitude is the readiness to act on or carry out a value. In simplest terms, an attitude always reflects something that we believe or value.

It is helpful to examine this definition in detail, because it covers all the components of our attitudes. Allport described an attitude as readiness; an attitude is our predisposition to act. Our action might take the form of words, a gesture or movement, or simply an expression, judgment, or thought.

An attitude exists in one's mind *and* body. Have you ever suddenly felt tension in your jaw at the mention of something you really disagree with? This illustrates the mental and physical nature of attitudes.

Our attitudes are organized through experience. This means that we learn these responses through the events and communication in our relationships. These learned responses become our natural responses, or attitudes, toward similar situations and relationships. For example, if we try to look good for a date and our date compliments us on our appearance, we may express gratitude that the person has noticed. We are ready to receive the praise, and in future dates, we will maintain this attitude.

Attitudes are also tied to the organization of beliefs and values. Just as values may summarize a set of related beliefs, attitudes may summarize a collection of values. Attitudes direct our beliefs and values toward action. This attitude structure, as it relates to beliefs and values, is shown in table 2.1.

To illustrate this, suppose you believe that you work well independently. One of the values that helps you to select courses is that professors should encourage students to organize ideas and projects on their own. You find among the course offerings next term a class called "Social Problems" taught by Professor Bettski. You took another course from this professor and found it worthwhile because of her flexible paper assignments. You also found this teacher to be fair and competent. Your beliefs about yourself and your relationship with Professor Bettski, valued positively, result in an attitude that is illustrated by your willingness to sign up for the course.

If you look more closely at this example, you will see the general structure among beliefs, values, and attitudes. You believe you know what is of interest to you. You believe that the professor is competent and fair. You value teachers who act competently and fairly. You value your independence. You value teachers who allow and foster that independence in their classes. You can even predict occasions when you are likely to want to work independently. Therefore, your attitudes are sometimes future oriented; that is, they involve your expectations about what you will think and do.

Table 2.1	The Belief-Value-Attitude System		
	Belief	*Value*	*Attitude*
Essence	"Something is . . ."	"Should" and "good"	Personal intention
Example	"This course is about business ethics." "I am interested in business ethics."	"A good course covers material that interests me."	"I am going to enroll in this course."
Example	"I am an honest person." "Bill did not tell me the truth about his actions last week."	"People should behave honestly. I expect my relationship partners to be honest with me."	"I want to discuss the issue of honesty in our relationship with Bill as soon as possible."

THE DEVELOPMENT OF THE SELF-CONCEPT

Four processes are involved in the complex and ongoing formation of the self-concept: (1) labeling the dominant behavior pattern, (2) reflected appraisal, (3) social comparison, and (4) identity aspirations.[7] Not all of these apply directly to everyone, so ask yourself which apply to you. Keep in mind that these are not stages. Two or more can act at the same time in the development of self-concept.

Some of us observe our day-to-day activities and then *label the dominant behavior pattern.* For example, we may see ourselves constantly taking the initiative in both social relationships and business activities. If others reinforce this behavior by calling attention to it, we may come to think of ourselves as initiators—"take-charge" people. We will have developed an idea of ourselves that is based on a dominant behavior. Although this example accurately describes what happens in some situations, it may also simplify a very complex process.

An example of labeling.

"I'm a pretty fair golfer."

A more thoroughly developed explanation of how the self-concept develops is found in the second process, known as *reflected appraisal,* that evolved from the work of George Herbert Mead[8] and Charles H. Cooley.[9] Mead wrote that our self-concepts are shaped early in life. The self-concept, he said, begins to emerge with the child's observation of the behavior of *significant others* (such as parents and peers).

Then, at play, the child begins to display this behavior. For example, a child may watch and listen to his father as he cooks and talks about cooking dinner. After a while, the child will accompany the father into the kitchen. As the father prepares dinner, the child will get into the cabinets, play with the pots, pans, and utensils, and talk about cooking. Mead calls this "taking the role of the other."[10] The father may support this play by talking with the child about how "they" are cooking dinner. The child learns that fathers cook dinner and adds cooking as an aspect of self-concept. As the child grows, a concept of self is developed by incorporating other appraisals. Thus, the child's self-concept is a reflection of the appraisals of significant others.

An example of *reflected appraisal.*

Significant Other

"You"

The third process, *social comparison,* takes the idea of self-concept beyond the mere reflection of the attitudes of others. Here, our self-concept evolves out of the comparison of self with others. Leon Festinger argued that we possess a basic need to have our beliefs and values confirmed by those around us.[11] We confirm some beliefs by checking facts. Others are confirmed by social comparison. Suppose, for example, you are asked to help hire a new director for a division at your company. Your task is to observe presentations given by each of the finalists and to offer a recommendation based on your preference. You notice that the other observers are comparing notes about the presentations as you leave one of these sessions. You might hear one say, "He really knows what this company is about" or "She understands our mission." While it is true that you are hearing the evaluations of the speakers, you are also hearing these people compare their own views of the company, its mission, and perhaps their part in it by comparing one another's reactions to the speakers' remarks.

An example of
social comparison.

Over time, we develop standards for comparison that we internalize and reinforce through other comparisons. That is, we have an idea about where someone *should* stand on an important issue if we are going to develop a relationship with that person. If he or she does not fit this standard, we may negotiate the standard. The growth of the relationship may be limited if we are not successful at negotiating or if we choose to live with the differences.

For instance, Peg and Sam were in the beginning stages of what both thought would be a lasting and healthy romantic relationship. They had much in common and seemed to get along well. One day, Peg was looking around Sam's house and discovered several guns in the closet. She was disturbed by this because she had very strong negative beliefs and values about keeping guns in one's home. When Sam came into the room, she said, "Sam, what are you doing with these guns? You're not the sort of person to keep guns around the house. You're going to have to get rid of these." Sam was surprised—and a little annoyed—by Peg's inquiry.

Since this is an important issue, growth in their relationship may be limited unless they negotiate some agreement about this issue. We pointed out earlier that values may occur as standards of behavior. In this instance, Peg's beliefs about and values against firearms serve as a standard for evaluating her relationship with Sam. Sometimes, as in this case, different standards or values will produce contradictory results. Several of Peg's values led her to an attitude of willingness to become involved with Sam, yet this one standard repels her. Peg and Sam must now sort through their values and determine which ones are more important than others in defining relationships. Sometimes our standards are so deeply engrained that any change may be ruled out.

Another way people shape their identities is by developing *identity aspirations:* they want to be recognized as a particular kind of person. This goal may cause them to behave in ways that will lead others to identify them as they would like to be identified. For example, a manager may want to be recognized as the best manager in her organization. To be the best of anything implies that someone else must agree that she has those qualities that are accepted as the "best." She may in fact be able to perform so that she feels good about herself as a manager and those with whom she works acknowledge her efforts by calling her the "best." However, she may not be so capable in other areas. Suppose she also wishes to be identified as an athlete but lacks the skill. She might be able to achieve agreement about this view of herself by *scanning the environment* for incidents that will confirm this image. She could call attention to experiences that emphasize her athletic ability on the basis of her ability to selectively perceive. She might also believe that she has to go up and down three flights of stairs in getting to and from her office to show that she is in good shape. The result may be an image of herself as an athlete. She develops an identity aspiration by managing her perception.

"Hummm. If I'm going to be the city tournament champion, I'd better practice."

"I'm going to spend a couple of hours on the driving range."

Your Image of You Holding a Trophy

"You"

An example of an identity aspiration.

Our relationships with others affect the process by which our self-concepts are shaped. We reflect on our communication with others, compare ourselves to others, and use others as models for our own behavior. Our perception of what others think of us and of how they react to our disclosures provides data that support aspects of our self-concepts. Cooley calls this the "looking-glass self," because in effect we use others as a mirror for seeing ourselves.[12] So our self-concept is extremely subjective, being almost totally a product of our interaction with others.[13]

Our relationships with others affect the process by which our self-concepts are shaped.

GUIDELINES FOR SELF-CONCEPT DEVELOPMENT

Here are some suggestions to help you achieve your goals and develop your self-concept.

1. *Begin with a small change.* Recall that many of our beliefs, values, and attitudes were shaped gradually over a long period of time. Also remember that we have surrounded our more important characteristics with a protective layer of supportive information. Some people can change themselves swiftly and easily, but most cannot. For the majority of us, self-change is most successful and long lasting when accomplished in manageable portions. Use your skills to predict how much change you can manage without interfering with your other goals and priorities. Don't hesitate to slow your pace a little if you overestimate.

2. *Let go of the past.* You may be looking at events and experiences that are no longer true of you. Looking back can make our sense of self-worth more difficult to change. These events may even color your *self-talk,* your intrapersonal communication with yourself, so that it effects your behavior and potential for growth. Positive self-talk can have a reassuring impact on your self-worth and in turn your relationships with others.

   Understand that past failures do not have to be an indicator of your future. Consider these examples, Einstein was four years old before he could speak and seven before he could read. Isaac Newton did poorly in grade school, and Beethoven's music teacher once said of him, "As a composer he is hopeless." A newspaper editor fired Walt Disney because he had "no good ideas." Wernher von Braun flunked ninth-grade algebra. Abraham Lincoln entered the Black Hawk War as a captain and came out as a private.[14] All of us have failures in our lives and it is helpful to let them go.

3. *Be specific about the changes you desire.* Wanting to be a "better" person is certainly a desirable goal, but how will you know when you have achieved it? A clearer statement might be, "I'm going to work with the local council the first Saturday morning of each month." The more specific you are, the better able you will be to visualize yourself effecting the changes and the easier it will be to measure your progress.

4. *Make agreements with yourself that will allow you to achieve.* Make agreements with yourself about what to expect. Sometimes it helps to include a reward for successfully carrying out desired changes. Encourage others to expect that of you as well, but take care not to hold them responsible for producing your change.

5. *Seek feedback and support about your self presentation.* The concept of the looking-glass self tells you that the image you think others have of you is important, and it is. Seek the help of those you

trust in monitoring the changes you are working toward. How are they experiencing these changes? Are there ways they can encourage and support you? Enlist their aid where you can. You will find their encouragement and support will help you achieve your goals.

6. *Reward yourself for keeping agreements.* We know that rewards encourage positive behavior in others. Why not use this knowledge to improve yourself? Look at your presentation of self every day, and when you find your image in line with your desires, give yourself a present. Ask friends to notice when you present yourself in a desirable way. Encourage them to reward you by commenting favorably about it.

Changing the self-concept involves overcoming our natural inclination to resist change by using the proper techniques and attention. Although the self-concept does not change dramatically day by day, the complex process by which it is formed and developed is unending. We change gradually over time. As we express messages about who we are, we are guided by information acquired by our interaction with significant others, including family, peers, teachers, and media personalities.

It is valuable to consider certain aspects of ourselves as we see them and as they are seen by others. We must become aware of the characteristics that express who we are if we want to improve our interpersonal communication. To the extent that every message is, at least in part, about us, it is helpful to think and talk about our images.

INTERPERSONAL NEEDS AND THE SELF-CONCEPT

The complex system of beliefs, values, and attitudes that define our self-concept determines the beginning point for our interactions with others. It also serves as the control system for those interactions. In every communication act, there is something that each party *wants.* Each of these desires serves as an expression of who we believe we are and how we wish to be seen. Communication that expresses and meets our needs may preserve and protect the self-concept or enrich and expand it. This relationship is graphically illustrated in this account about a boy named Cliff Evans.

This account provides a clear illustration of the fact that our ability to express our needs, and the ability of others to understand and help fulfill our needs, is significantly related to self-concept and personal happiness.

The aim of this section is to help you understand human needs. We will focus on two useful classifications of needs: first, the hierarchy Abraham H. Maslow[15] has suggested and, second, the three areas of need identified by William C. Schutz.[16] *Interpersonal needs*

Cipher in the Snow

It started with tragedy on a biting cold February morning. I was driving behind the Milford Corners bus as I did most snowy mornings on my way to school. It veered and stopped short at the hotel, which it had no business doing, and I was annoyed as I had to come to an unexpected stop. A boy lurched out of the bus, reeled, stumbled, and collapsed on the snowbank at the curb. The bus driver and I reached him at the same moment. His thin, hollow face was white even against the snow.

"He's dead," the driver whispered.

It didn't register for a minute. I glanced quickly at the scared young faces staring down at us from the school bus. "A doctor! Quick! I'll phone from the hotel. . . ."

"No use, I tell you he's dead." The driver looked down at the boy's still form. "He never even said he felt bad," he muttered. "Just tapped me on the shoulder and said, real quiet, 'I'm sorry. I have to get off at the hotel.' That's all. Polite and apologizing like."

At school, the giggling, shuffling morning noise quieted as the news went down the halls. I passed a huddle of girls. "Who was it? Who dropped dead on the way to school?" I heard one of them half-whisper.

"Don't know his name; some kid from Milford Corners" was the reply.

It was like that in the faculty room and the principal's office. "I'd appreciate your going out to tell the parents," the principal told me. "They haven't a phone and, anyway, somebody from school should go there in person. I'll cover your classes."

"Why me?" I asked. "Wouldn't it be better if you did it?"

"I didn't know the boy," the principal admitted levelly. "And, in last year's sophomore personalities column I note that you were listed as his favorite teacher."

I drove through the snow and cold down the bad canyon road to the Evans place and thought about the boy, Cliff Evans. His favorite teacher! I thought. He hasn't spoken two words to me in two years! I could see him in my mind's eye all right, sitting back there in the last seat in my afternoon literature class. He came in the room by himself and left by himself. "Cliff Evans," I muttered to myself, "a boy who never talked." I thought a minute. "A boy who never smiled. I never saw him smile once."

The big ranch kitchen was clean and warm. I blurted out my news somehow. Mrs. Evans reached blindly toward a chair. "He never said anything about bein' ailing."

His stepfather snorted. "He ain't said nothin about anything since I moved in here."

Mrs. Evans pushed a pan to the back of the stove and began to untie her apron. "Now hold on," her husband snapped. "I got to have breakfast before I go to town. Nothin' we can do now anyway. If Cliff hadn't been so dumb, he'd have told us he didn't feel good."

After school I sat in the office and stared blankly at the records spread out before me. I was to close the file and write the obituary for the school paper. The almost bare sheets mocked the effort. Cliff Evans, white, never legally adopted by stepfather, five young half-brothers and sisters. These meager strands of information and the list of D grades were all the records had to offer.

Cliff Evans had silently come in the school door in the mornings and gone out the school door in the evenings, and that was all. He had never belonged to a club. He had never played on a team. He had never held an office. As far as I could tell he had never done one happy, noisy kid thing. He had never been anybody at all.

How do you go about making a boy into a zero? The grade-school records showed me. The first and second grade teachers' annotations read "sweet, shy child," "timid but eager." Then the third grade note had opened the attack. Some teacher had written in a good, firm hand, "Cliff won't talk. Uncooperative. Slow learner." The other academic sheep had followed with "dull"; "slow-witted"; "low I.Q." They became correct. The boy's I.Q. score in the ninth grade was listed as 83. But his I.Q. in the third grade had been 106. The score didn't go under 100 until the seventh grade. Even shy, timid, sweet children have resilience. It takes time to break them.

I stomped to the typewriter and wrote a savage report pointing out what education had done to Cliff Evans. I slapped a copy on the principal's desk and another in the sad, dog-eared file. I banged the typewriter and slammed the file and crashed the door shut, but I didn't feel much better. A little boy kept walking after me, a little boy with a peaked, pale face; a skinny body in faded jeans; and big eyes that had looked and searched for a long time and then had become veiled.

I could guess how many times he'd been chosen last to play sides in a game, how many whispered child conversations had excluded him, how many times he hadn't been asked. I could see and hear the faces and voices that said over and over, "You're a nothing, Cliff Evans."

A child is a believing creature. Cliff undoubtedly believed them. Suddenly it seemed clear to me: When finally there was nothing left at all for Cliff Evans, he collapsed on a snowbank and went away. The doctor might list "heart failure" as the cause of death, but that wouldn't change my mind.

We couldn't find ten students in the school who had known Cliff well enough to attend the funeral as his friends. So the student body officers and a committee from the junior class went as a group to the church, being politely sad. I attended the services with them, and sat through it with a lump of cold lead in my chest and a big resolve growing through me.

I've never forgotten Cliff Evans nor that resolve. He has been my challenge year after year, class after class. I look for veiled eyes or bodies scrounged into a seat in an alien world. "Look, kids," I say silently, "I may not do anything else for you this year, but not one of you is going to come out of here a nobody. I'll work or fight to the bitter end doing battle with society and the school board, but I won't have one of you coming out of here thinking himself a zero."

Most of the time—not always, but most of the time—I've succeeded.

Jean Mizer, *Today's Education*, November 1964

relate to the development of the self-concept and its projection through self-disclosure. We see ourselves in terms of our needs. For example, if we describe ourselves as well organized, we might be saying that our need to control is important to us. We thus communicate to satisfy our interpersonal needs. It must follow that our self-disclosures are selected by what we think we need.

Suppose we learn that a member of our social group has developed a serious medical problem. We might talk in the group about others we have known who survived similar difficulties. This sort of interaction might satisfy our need to express caring for the friend, and it also establishes something about the group. The friend isn't excluded because of the illness. The friend remains part of the group because through this communication, we let him know we have reason to understand something of his experience.

Most significant interpersonal communication deals with an issue at hand as well as a deeper interpersonal need.

MASLOW'S HIERARCHY OF NEEDS

Maslow's work has had a significant impact on our understanding of needs. The hierarchy of individual needs he suggested is displayed in figure 2.3. He argues that we all have the potential to experience five kinds of needs. We need to have our physiological necessities met. We need to feel secure and safe. In our relationships, we need to feel that we belong and are held in esteem. Finally, we need to feel self-actualized. Maslow contends that these needs generally follow a hierarchical order—that lower-level needs must be met for higher-level needs to become important. For example, if you are starving, it would be somewhat difficult for you to be very concerned about esteem. You might even risk your safety to obtain food.

Physiological needs are our most basic, for they deal with survival. We need food, water, sleep, and shelter to survive. The biological origin of these needs, in that they are important to the life of any organism, gives them their strength. Sometimes we form relationships to help us meet these needs.

Safety needs are the next level of needs in this hierarchy. We need to feel secure and free from fear. We need structure and order to feel that there is some predictability in our lives. Basically, these needs are related to self-preservation—both present and future protection from bodily harm. These needs, too, can be provided by certain relationships, either through financial contributions or physical strength.

Social needs, Maslow's third category, are represented by two distinct sets of needs. The first are those related to the need to accept, associate with, and be accepted by others; the second are those related to belonging to a group. The first is a more intense socialization need. At this level, you want to exchange signs of love, affection, or friendship in appropriate interpersonal relationships. The quest for this kind of relationship finds its outlet in informal groups as well as in marriage and other committed relationships.

The second of these needs, association with and acceptance by others, is primarily an affiliation need. Members of groups want to say and believe that they are part of the group. They do not want to feel alone and set apart.

The fourth level of needs, *esteem need,* is the need to be recognized and rewarded. This need is fulfilled by the respect and recognition of our associates. We may satisfy this need by being a part of a relationship in which our partner gives us status, respect, recognition, and appreciation. We believe that self-esteem may be the most important of all human needs. You can help meet this need through your communication with those you form relationships with.

The top of Maslow's hierarchy, *self-actualization,* is a need for self-fulfillment, for achieving our potential, for self-development, and for creativity. Maslow suggests that this is a "desire to become

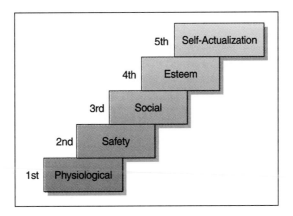

Figure 2.3
Maslow's hierarchy of needs.

more and more what one is, to become everything one is capable of becoming."[17] It is difficult for most people to satisfy this need. We may achieve fulfillment in a relationship with those who give us the freedom to be what we are capable of becoming. We might also receive encouragement to reach our potential from our circle of friends and acquaintances.

There is more connectedness among Maslow's needs than we might imagine. Communication is so important that its presence or absence can affect physical health. So the social needs can be connected to safety and physiological needs. Socially isolated people are two or three times more likely to die than those with strong social ties.[18] So even though we view communication as a means for meeting social and esteem needs, it can affect safety and physiological needs as well.

SCHUTZ'S INTERPERSONAL NEEDS

William Schutz elaborates on the social need identified by Maslow. Schutz's analysis places the needs for inclusion, control, and affection in a framework of interpersonal relationships.

Need for Inclusion

We all have a social need for *inclusion*, which includes our desire to be accepted, to feel wanted, and to be a part of groups, both at work and in our personal lives. It also includes our need to accept others. Yet, clearly, not all of us experience all these needs in the same way. Some of us demand a great amount of inclusion, while others avoid closeness and interpersonal contact. Schutz recognizes these varying degrees of need and labels them accordingly.

People who feel little need for inclusion may behave *undersocially*, isolating themselves from group involvement. *Oversocial* people seek to join and feel a part of many groups. *Adaptable-social* behavior, on the other hand, balances needs for inclusion and privacy. The adaptable-social person often allows the context of the relationship to motivate the degree of involvement.

Consider coworkers Greg, Tom, and Yuka. Each day, Greg comes in and gets right to work. He speaks only when spoken to, takes his breaks and his lunch alone in his office, and never volunteers for any assignment that involves working with other people. Tom, on the other hand, socializes a great deal in the office. He seeks out group assignments, always goes to lunch in the company cafeteria, and frequently initiates conversations with coworkers. During breaks, he goes out of his way to find company. Yuka seems to have a different need for inclusion. She socializes with others and works well with them, but when she is given an assignment to do on her own, she closes her office door and starts to work. She finds working with Greg difficult, because she believes that she has to carry the burden of the conversation. Working with Tom can be rewarding but also frustrating. At times, he wants to talk about everything but the task at hand, which makes work take much longer than it should. Sometimes Yuka finds it difficult to get her point of view across, as Tom tends to monopolize the conversation.

Undersocial individuals like Greg and oversocial people like Tom often experience difficulties in their work. The undersocial person may be seen as aloof, arrogant, or indifferent. The oversocial person may be seen as superficial, dominating, or demanding of time and attention.

Understanding inclusion as one part of everyone's need structure offers insight into their motivation. Greg, for example, does not respond to messages of inclusion because he does not need to feel accepted as part of the team. Tom may need considerable reassurance in this area and Yuka only a moderate amount. In communicating with the undersocial person, it is important to keep the possibility of inclusion open. We must make it clear that if the person wants to develop the relationship, we are willing to do so. We might say to Greg, "I am glad we are working on this project together. We will do a good job if we both contribute to it. So I want to know what you think about it as we go along. OK?"

As we communicate with the oversocial person, we must be clear that the other is included in the relationship. More importantly, we must create language that will communicate our intentions and expectations about the relationship and the task, and the other person must acknowledge that he understands what we want from the relationship. Yuka might have to set some ground rules in working with Tom by saying something like, "Tom, I'm glad we're working on this together because I have some ideas about the way this project ought to go and I know you do, too. I want to be sure that at each stage we both have our say about it. Can we do that?"

The need for inclusion is critical because we may seek new relationships, sometimes abandoning current ones, if it is not satisfied. Communicating clearly about how much contact or inclusion we expect in a relationship can help us fulfill this need and allow the relationship to grow.

Need for Control

Another social need, *control*, is our desire both to exercise power and authority and to be controlled. The need to control is based on two strict principles: we have the need to control our environment and the destiny of our relationships, and our partners in relationships have this same need.

People have differing degrees of this need for control. Schutz describes an *abdicrat* as someone with little need to control. This person abdicates all power and responsibilities to his partner in a relationship. This person's opposite, the *autocrat*, dominates others and

We need to communicate clearly about how much inclusion we expect in a relationship.

feels the need for strong control in relationships. A person who takes the middle ground is called the *democrat*. This person can either take charge or allow others to be in control.

The need to overcontrol can cause serious problems in relationships, as autocrats may try to control everything. Abdicrats, on the other hand, can also create problems. For example, the professional who cannot or will not assume control when needed leaves more work for coworkers. This lack of leadership can often mean failure to a business in which efficiency is critical.

The need *for* control can affect relationships as well. Jim and Maria have been married for several years and have had frequent problems in their relationship. Jim would be characterized as an abdicrat, while Maria might be considered an autocrat. She takes charge of most issues in the relationship and often makes decisions without consulting Jim. One year, she made all the arrangements for them to vacation in the Caribbean. By the time they arrived, she was frantic. By taking on too much, she had ruined the trip for herself. Jim did not understand her problem. He thought she should be enjoying herself. After all, she got exactly what she wanted. The next year, Maria asked Jim to plan their vacation. He missed the dates for booking an economy flight and waited too long to get reservations at a good hotel. As a result, they did not take a vacation that year.

Jim and Maria might work toward more democratic control in their relationship. Having one person take all responsibility does not work for either partner. Understanding this problem may help them avoid it.

Our awareness of this dimension in others will help us focus more closely on how they function in our relationships. In dealing with the autocrat, we must be clear about what aspects of the relationship we want to control and what aspects we would prefer to share in controlling. Again, expressing what we want from the relationship is the key. We might say to an autocrat, "I know that you want to take care of all this, but I'd like to do some of it too—not so much for you as to satisfy my own needs. Can we work out some way to share the responsibilities for this?" Communicating with an abdicrat can be more difficult. We may try to motivate, while remaining clear about how much we are willing to do. For example, "This event can affect both of us, and we can both benefit from it. I am willing to do X, Y, and Z, and I would like you to agree to do A, B, and C. But I don't want you to say you'll do them if you won't. If that is the case, I will take charge of the event alone."

The need to control is powerful in both its presence and its absence. It is important to know when to take on responsibility and when to give it up. We can only learn this through the experiences we have as a relationship develops. We need to watch for it to address this need in ourselves and our partner appropriately.

Need for Affection

A final social need described by Schutz, *affection*, is the desire to like and be liked. Liking, or affinity, is the degree to which people care for or appreciate one another.[19] It is reflected in the development of loving relationships. We often find ourselves identifying more with the person we like when we fulfill this need, for the result of liking is personal closeness and positive feelings. When a person has little need for affection, neutrality is displayed in relationships, and all others are viewed in the same way. Some of us may even respond with hostility to avoid closeness. Schutz refers to people who have a low need for affection as *underpersonal*. Unlike the undersocial person, who avoids contact with others, the underpersonal individual will avoid not contact but self-disclosure. On the other hand, a person with a high need for affection is considered *overpersonal* and will take special pains to avoid being disliked by anyone. An overpersonal individual may become too concerned with the social dimension and thus often spend far too much time talking about his own feelings or inquiring about the feelings of others. A *personal* individual holds the middle ground. She can balance situations in order to be liked when affection is desired but can also maintain distance when affection is not needed. This balance allows people to manage their relationships more productively.

When a person has little need for affection, he or she displays neutrality in personal relationships.

SELF-CONCEPT MAINTENANCE

We are often reminded that the characteristic that most distinguishes humans from other creatures is our sophisticated ability to communicate. Indeed, this enabled us to survive in the most hostile of environments. At first, people developed their communication skills to withstand the threats of the environment and other creatures. In the modern world, we depend on others and our communication with them more than ever. Improving communication in our relationships is thus essential for both our development and our survival.

The most serious problem that may arise from protecting our self-concept is that defensiveness can become a habit.

Although our survival instinct remains, it serves a somewhat different function than it did in the past. Now, the instinct helps us nurture and protect our self-concepts as well as our bodies. At times, the mind works to protect itself from change. This can be beneficial, but it also can inhibit the growth of an individual. We find ourselves behaving without awareness and in a way quite inconsistent with our goals when this instinct takes over. Acting to defend ourselves without much thought is called *going unconscious*. When our self-concept seems threatened, we will often defend it. When we go unconscious, we rely on long-established defense techniques so we can get through the situation without actually thinking about it. Chapter 9 examines defensiveness in relationships in more detail.

Defensiveness affects both our expression and our perception. We are moved to do or say whatever is necessary to emerge from a situation with our self-concept intact.

The self-concept is a relatively stable structure on a day-to-day basis yet is changeable over time. Have you ever had a professor who encouraged students to ask questions but then ridiculed the questions they offered? This same professor may later complain that students never ask questions. We might interpret this criticism as his way of emerging from the situation with his self-concept intact. After all, he could still (unrealistically) view himself as open and competent if he believed that the students would not participate because they had a problem. Because his self-concept is geared to survival, it moves him to resist changing his behavior, even when change might be desirable.

The *survival orientation* usually involves self-concept structures that are centrally and intensely held. The most serious problem that may arise from protecting the self-concept is that defensiveness may become a habit that we are not even aware of.

There is an alternative orientation that is active, conscious, and supportive, which we call *being conscious*. With this orientation, our communication asserts our self-concept and stimulates the growth of our relationships, thereby helping the self-concept to change in a way that facilitates the realization of our goals. The key to being conscious is *openness to change*. We must be willing to listen to and learn from others. The greater the trust in a relationship, the easier it is for us to maintain this attitude. We explore other aspects of being conscious in Chapter 9 on supportive communication.

We must also be honest with ourselves about who we are, who we can be, and who we want to be to present an image that will work in our relationships and will help us to satisfy our interpersonal needs.

An understanding of others' needs for affection will help us determine how to more effectively talk with and listen to the partners in our relationships. We can vary our approach depending on where we believe the other person is on this dimension of personalness.

INTERPERSONAL NEEDS AND COMMUNICATION IN RELATIONSHIPS

A better understanding of how interpersonal needs differ from relationship to relationship can be quite useful. We may know ourselves better if we analyze each of our need areas: Do our basic needs correspond to roles we have chosen? Can we conduct our relationships and have our needs fulfilled? We should not necessarily play amateur psychologist or select roles based solely on our needs, but this analysis might assist us in making choices about relationships.

We are communicating effectively when we understand how all parties operate to satisfy their needs in our relationships. When we do this, we learn how to motivate and reward others, which is critical to the effective development of our relationships. We all possess these needs to some degree that must be met to nourish our relationships and help them grow.

SUMMARY

Interpersonal communication involves the presentation of our images of the people, places, and things in our world. We accompany the presentation of our ideas with images of ourselves. Our images of self and our ideas about what aspects of ourselves to express in a relationship determine the self-concept. The basic components of the self-concept are beliefs, values, and attitudes. These elements work together to provide each of us with a unique manner of presentation. They also form a "window" known as the frame of reference, through which we view our relationships. Four processes operate as the self-concept develops: (1) labeling the dominant behavior pattern, (2) reflected appraisal, (3) social comparison, and (4) identity aspirations. These processes help us to learn new beliefs, organize them into values, and express those values in our attitudes and behaviors. Self-awareness means knowing what messages others receive as you present yourself. Maintaining and changing the self-concept requires self-awareness, attention, and discipline.

Understanding why we express ourselves the way we do can help us more carefully choose the language we use to communicate in our relationships. Our relationships are formed to fulfill needs. Maslow suggests that we have physiological, safety, social, esteem, and self-actualization needs. Schutz focuses on three interpersonal needs: the need for inclusion, the need for control, and the need for affection. We experience these needs in different degrees, and our communication frequently relates to one or more of them. We must be sensitive to the needs that motivate the communication of others, using language that addresses these needs while allowing us to express what we need as well.

The need to survive is internal. We protect our self-concept by using the frame of reference to screen threatening information. This survival need makes changing either our self-concept or our communication style difficult, although we can make adjustments that will allow us to communicate effectively in our relationships through an attitude of openness.

DISCUSSION QUESTIONS

1. Describe the frame of reference you would bring to a job interview. Consider the beliefs, values, and attitudes that would be involved.

2. List your significant others. Think about your communication and theirs, and identify instances of labeling the dominant behavior, reflected appraisal, social comparison, and identity aspirations.

3. Choose an attitude you hold rather strongly. Try to trace the attitude back through your system of values and beliefs. What values came together to shape that attitude? From what beliefs do those values stem?

4. Take a careful look at one of your close relationships. How have you prioritized your values in the relationship? Does the relationship contradict any of your values? How have you reconciled this discrepancy?

5. When and how has the survival need helped you in a relationship? When has it hindered relational growth?

6. Imagine yourself in each of these roles: a religious person, a political person, a student, a partner in a special relationship, a member of a family, and a volunteer in public service. How might each role and your relationships in it affect your self-image?

7. Which of the interpersonal needs discussed in this chapter might you express in each role mentioned above?

8. Try to classify some of the people in your relationships using the Schutz's classification of interpersonal needs: needs for inclusion, control, and affection. Do certain groups of people in your relational world seem to have similar needs? What, besides these need characteristics, do these people have in common?

9. What role do you suppose context plays in the way we choose to communicate about our needs? Can you identify certain needs that are tied to certain situations? What needs do you experience as more general, permeating many of your relationships?

ENDNOTES

1. W. James. *Psychology* (New York: Holt, 1910), 177 and following.

2. G. H. Mead, *Mind, Self and Society* (Chicago: University of Chicago Press, 1934), 16–42.

3. D. Carbaugh, *Situating Selves: The Communication of Social Identities in American Scenes* (Albany, NY: SUNY Press, 1996).

4. M. Rokeach, *Beliefs, Attitudes, and Values: A Theory of Organization and Change* (San Francisco: Jossey-Bass, 1968), 5.

5. S. Oskamp, *Attitudes and Opinions* (Englewood Cliffs, NJ: Prentice-Hall, Inc., 1977), 13.

6. C. W. Allport, "Attitudes," in *Handbook of Social Psychology*, C. Murchison ed. (Worcester, MA: Clark University Press, 1935), 810.

7. K. Gergen, *The Concept of Self* (New York: Holt, Rinehart, and Winston, 1971).

8. Mead, *Mind, Self and Society*, 173.

9. C. H. Cooley, *Human Nature and Social Order* (New York: Scribner's, 1912).

10. Mead, *Mind, Self and Society*, 150–152.

11. L. Festinger, *A Theory of Cognitive Dissonance* (Stanford, CA: Stanford University Press, 1937).

12. Cooley, *Human Nature*, 152.

13. P. Killock and J. O'Brien, eds., *The Production of Reality*, 2nd ed. (Thousand Oaks, CA: Pine Forge Press, 1997).

14. Milton E. Larson, "Humbling Cases for Career Counselors," *Phi Delta Kappan* 54, no. 6 (February 1973): 374.

15. A. H. Maslow, *Motivation and Personality* (New York: Harper & Row, 1970).

16. W. C. Schutz, *The Interpersonal Underworld* (Reading, MA: Addison-Wesley, 1969), 18. Third edition revised by R. Frager, 1987, 35–38.

17. Maslow, *Motivation*, 82.

18. R. Narem, "Try a Little TLC," research reported in *Science 80* (1980): 15.

19. See, for example, R. A. Bell and J. A. Daly, "The Affinity-Seeking Function of Communication," in *Interpersonal Communication: Readings in Theory and Research*, M. V. Richmond, ed. (Fort Worth, TX: Harcourt Brace, 1995).

READ MORE ABOUT
THE SELF-CONCEPT IN THESE SOURCES

Cupach, William R., and Sandra Metts. *Facework.* Thousand Oaks, CA: Sage, 1994. This work is a summary of ways people manage their identity and maintain face in problematic communication situations.

Jourard, Sidney. *The Transparent Self*. New York: D. Van Nostrand Company, 1971. Jourard's writing about the role of the self-concept in everyday interactions is considered essential reading for persons who wish to improve their presencation of self. As you read this work, think about how you can apply Jourard's ideas about "being yourself."

Singer, Peter. *Practical Ethics*. London: Cambridge University Press, 1983. Reading this short volume will help you to think carefully about your values and their sources. Singer outlines a clear theory of utilitarian values in the first three chapters and then examines several controversial issues in the remainder of the book.

READ MORE ABOUT INTERPERSONAL NEEDS IN THESE SOURCES

Goldhaber, G. M. *Organizational Communication*, 6th ed. Dubuque, IA: Wm. C. Brown, 1993. If you are interested in how interpersonal needs operate as a communication variable in the workplace, study chapter 4 of this classic text.

Maslow, Abraham, H. *Motivation and Personality*. New York: Harper & Row, 1970. This classic work explores the hierarchy of human needs as major variables in the communication process. The book is clear and accessible. Its content is still valid for today's interpersonal relationships. Third edition revised by R. Frager, 1987, 35–58.

Miller, Gerald, ed. *Explorations in Interpersonal Communication*. Beverly Hills. CA: Sage, 1976. This collection of research on interpersonal communication includes studies of the process of relationship development. The material in this work is for those interested in reading examples of research studies, and so the content is somewhat advanced.

3

PERCEPTION

PREVIEW

The different points of view you experience as you communicate with others represent an important area of study for students of interpersonal communication. The world that exists outside us is not the same as the world within us. Our communication and relationships depend more on our perceptions of the external world than the world itself. This chapter explores the ways we select, organize, and interpret the information we use as a basis for relational action and communication. First, we explore the frame of reference, the filter through which we view and understand the world. Next, we examine the perception process. We also look at how perceptions are organized and how this organization affects our views of relationships. We will suggest some limitations that may interfere with the perception process. We suggest also ways to improve the accuracy of your perception through heightened awareness and concentration.

Our perceptions influence communication in our relationships from start to finish. They shape the attraction we feel for others, the traits we assign to them, our expectations of them, and the way we understand what they do and say. Our perceptions function together with our expectations for ourselves and others to create communication rules for our relationships and influence our relationship positions. These positions summarize how we view ourselves in relation to the other person. Finally, both the nature of perception and the derivation of expectations can change. In this chapter, you will learn about how to improve your perception in relationships.

KEY TERMS

accommodation
attribution
closure
expectations
frame of reference
inferential statements
interpersonal attraction
mutual perception
perception
perceptual filtering
perceptual organization
relationship position
rules
selective exposure
sociological aspects of roles
transactional analysis

assimilation
change
communication roles
external attributes
gender roles
internal attributes
leveling
observational statements
perceptual distortion
perceptual interpretation
psychological aspects of roles
role
selective attention
sharpening
stereotyping

OBJECTIVES

1. Define *frame of reference* and give an example of how different frames of reference affected your communication in a relationship.
2. Explain how perceptions affect the frame of reference.
3. Cite examples of the active, inductive, and unconscious characteristics of perception.
4. Provide examples of the way selective exposure and selective attention work in the process of perception.
5. Define closure and explain its importance to organizing perception.
6. Describe an experience that shows the impact of assimilation and accommodation on your frame of reference.
7. Define leveling, sharpening, and perceptual distortion.
8. Describe physical, environmental, social, and cultural influences on perception.
9. Discuss the improvement of perceptual ability through concentration and attention.
10. Explain what is meant by the mutual nature of perception.
11. Name two ways in which perception affects our attraction to others.
12. Give examples of sociological and psychological roles.
13. Recall an experience in which the mutual nature of role assignment posed a problem for a relationship.
14. Give examples of how internal and external attributions affect perception.
15. Define expectation as a component of interpersonal communication.

16. Define communication rules. Explain the difference between the two ways communication rules are formed by giving an example of each from experience.

17. Create dialogues representing each of the four relationship positions.

18. Tell of an instance in which your perception in a relationship changed.

19. Distinguish between a statement of observation and a statement of inference.

THE NATURE OF PERCEPTION

Perception is a fundamental aspect of interpersonal communication. Perception gives meaning and stability to the communication in our relationships because it is a process through which we select and organize information about what has happened around us. Understanding perception can help us comprehend our responses to others and the formation of our views of relationships. Perception is not only a process but also a skill. After working with this chapter, you will know how to improve your ability to perceive.

Perception is not only a process but also a skill.

Our senses are the basic tools of perception. They take in information as raw data in constructing experiences. Remember that all five senses operate simultaneously, each providing data. While we look at someone, for example, our other senses do not shut down. This means, as we communicate, we are tasting, smelling, seeing, hearing, and feeling the touch of our relationships as well.

We perceive through a *frame of reference*—a set of interlocking observations, beliefs, values, and attitudes.[1] This frame of reference is the basis for our understanding of people, events, and experiences. It has a structure in that we order our experiences to fit together in a way that is sensible to us. As we take in new information, we use our frame of reference to process it in one of three ways: we may reject it because it doesn't fit with our frame of reference, we may use it to support the frame of reference; or we may use it to change the frame of reference. Figure 3.1 illustrates the way the frame of reference screens and organizes information to provide meaning.

Frame of reference also provides stability for our perception. Rather than seeing our experiences as constantly shifting in response to various senses, perception within our frame of reference gives them a flowing quality. For instance, try this experiment. Hold your hand at arm's length and examine it for a moment. Now move it quickly toward you and then back out. Although the movement of your hand created sensory differences in size and color, you probably experienced it as the same size and color when you were moving it as when you were not. Your frame of reference contains an understanding of the size of your hand, and it will not let your senses fool you.

This same principle of stability applies to our perceptions of people in our relationships. Perhaps you have had the experience of encountering a friend who has changed his appearance somewhat, maybe by getting a haircut or shaving off a mustache. If you did not notice this change at first, it is because your perception was acting to maintain your frame of reference for this person. Once the change is called to your attention, your frame of reference adjusts to accept a new vision.

The events that occur around us may be but are not necessarily connected. However, for us to understand groups of sensory events as whole experiences, they must be interrelated and placed within our frame of reference. Perception allows us to connect separate experiences.

Consider how this applies to the important relationships in your life. Think about what it feels like to be near someone for whom you care deeply. You feel the touch of his skin, smell the fragrance of his clean hair, hear his breathing and heartbeat, and see his calm, relaxed expression as you think about the relationship, recalling its important, warm moments. All of your senses operate together to produce sensations that you understand as the emotion called love.

Figure 3.1
Frame of
reference:
screening and
organizing
information.

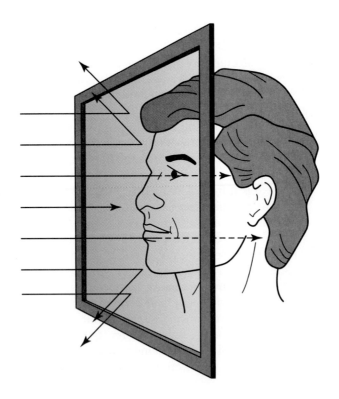

CHARACTERISTICS OF THE PERCEPTUAL PROCESS

Although research on perception continues, scientists have clearly identified several aspects of the process.[2] These shed light on the way we perceive ourselves and others. First, perception is active. Because we cannot take in and accept all of the stimuli available to us, we must sort, screen, and sometimes reach out for information. We must perceive selectively to maintain our sense of structure and stability as we use the perceptual process to fit it together.

Perception is active and works inductively.

Second, the perception process works inductively. Through perception, we generate whole images of things and people built from the observation of their parts. Our perception process takes in clues about the way things are and then puts the clues together to form a conclusion representing the whole thing.

Third, perception generally occurs relatively unconsciously. We usually think no more about perception than we think about our heartbeats or breathing patterns. Unlike the latter, however, we cannot even focus on the act of perceiving because attention is one of our tools of perception. We can, however, focus on *what* we are perceiving, and this focus is very important to accurate perception.

Perception generally occurs relatively unconsciously.

PERCEPTION INVOLVES SELECTION

Selectivity is choosing information. Even with all five senses operating at optimum efficiency, there is just too much going on around us for us to absorb and interpret everything. We must, therefore, select from available stimuli. We select what we will expose ourselves to, and we select what we will pay attention to.

Remember the first day of class? Certain people captured your attention more than others. You were exposed to the messages of those people and paid attention to some of those messages more than the messages of other people in the class. After several classes, you began to notice more people as well as more *about* them. This is because repeated exposures tend to increase our knowledge of the people around us. There are some things about people in the class—habits, manners of speaking, physical attributes—that you may not have noticed until several weeks had gone by. Although the information was there at every meeting, your perception process ignored it if it was not needed to accomplish your goals in the class.

Selective exposure and selective attention are two types of selectivity that are important to our interpersonal communication. These processes occur in order, with exposure first, followed by attention.

Selective Exposure

When we turn on the radio and tune in a frequency, we are engaging in *selective exposure* as we expose ourselves to one station and exclude others. When we participate in any conversation, we similarly become open to some stimuli while disregarding others. Sometimes selective exposure can help us both avoid unwanted communication and receive needed communication. For example, you may find yourself in a meeting with a group of people that includes someone with whom you frequently argue. When he speaks, you may look away or read something to avoid exposure. On the other hand, you may be at a crowded gathering looking for a particular person you expect to see there. Amid the noise and confusion, you see her across the room, and she sees you. As you concentrate your senses on her and struggle to communicate clearly, you try to shut out much that is happening around you. If you are successful, you may not even notice who was standing by you and what they said. You limit your exposure to the verbal and nonverbal messages your friend sent across the room by shutting out everything else.

There are more subtle bases for selective exposure to people and things; many are personal preferences. For example, we may choose to expose ourselves to information coming from someone who uses our name. (Direct mail advertisers assume we make this choice when they have their computers insert our names in the appropriate spaces on their form letters.) In the example above, your exposure to your friend across the room might have been interrupted if the person next to you spoke your name. We thus expose ourselves to ideas and people selectively, although such exposure does not necessarily result in communication. It does, however, provide the opportunity for perceiving. To perceive, we must not only be exposed, we must also attend.

Selective Attention

Selective attention occurs when we choose to attend to one or more of the stimuli to which we are exposed. Even though our senses operate simultaneously, we focus best when we focus on one at a time. At this moment, for example, you may see the page in front of you. You may also taste and smell a cup of freshly brewed coffee, hear the faint hum of the air conditioner, and feel both the hardness of your chair and tightness of your shoes. But you must select one of these sensations for attention at a time. If you decide to see the printed page, for example, and the smell of the coffee is overpowering, you will have difficulty reading. Your concentration will flash rapidly back and forth between the sensations, and you will find it hard to concentrate on either.

Suppose you must chair a meeting that will include Anne, who tends to talk too much and wander away from the point of a discussion. When she speaks, you must choose to expose yourself to her communication but listen selectively. Rather than taking in all the content, you may instead monitor her contribution so that if she wanders, you can find a point to break in and move the meeting along. That way, when you try to summarize and focus the discussion, you can genuinely acknowledge Anne's contribution without supporting her wandering.

In the case of finding your friend in a crowded room, you may have engaged in two levels of selectivity. While you looked around for her, you may have been exposing yourself to communication in your immediate surroundings, picking up on some of what was being said. But when you spotted your friend, you very finely narrowed the focus of both exposure and attention.

Exposure and attention are related in important ways. Through exposure we select information to which we will attend either now or later. Exposure occurs in the present—we are exposed to current people, events, and relationships. We attend to some of these now and store the rest for possible attention later. For example, consider meeting your friend at the crowded gathering. After you are united, she may ask, "Who was that person you were talking with when I found you?" Although at the time you did not pay attention to that person because you were focusing on your search, you will probably recall some details of the conversation you were exposed to but not then attending.

Take some time now to explore your own selective exposure and attention processes in terms of people and relationships. Are there people in your interpersonal communication class with whom you talk often? Are there any whom you seem to avoid?

PERCEPTION INVOLVES ORGANIZATION AND INTERPRETATION

Different people may view the same event differently. One reason for this is that people may attend to different parts of the event. Even if they attend to similar facets of the experience, they may *understand* it differently. Since what we do depends on what we perceive, our perception is actually more important to our communication than what the other person intended or what really happened. For example, we may believe that we see two friends arguing. Another observer may view them as joking. We cannot know which perception is true without investigating. The action we take with regard to our friends will differ according to our perception and can significantly affect our relationship with them.

Our responses to our relationships are based on our perceptions. Sometimes we communicate a distorted view of events because of the way we have organized and interpreted them. We turn to these topics now—organization and interpretation—to show how they contribute to the perceptual process.

The stimuli we receive through the perception process are limited first by exposure and then by attention. When we attend to experiences, however, we do not just take them as they are. Rather, we arrange them to fit our frame of reference: this is known as *perceptual organization*. We next give them meaning in light of that frame of reference in what is called *perceptual interpretation*. Organization and interpretation are both necessary for us to respond to the stimuli. We can see how this works by applying it to a perceptual task.

Look at the four drawings in figure 3.2. Which do you like the most? Why? Compare your perceptions with those of others in the class. People will assign different meanings to what they see in the figure. Those who are attracted to a different drawing than you were will give reasons that reflect differences in the way they organized and interpreted the pictures. Sometimes they will have seen parts of a picture that you did not notice at all, but you may still prefer your original choice even after these hidden features are pointed out.

People may also select one picture over another because of its overall impression, which results from all of the prior experiences, norms, rules, and expectations that formed their individual frames of reference. As you compare your perceptions of figure 3.2 with others, you will notice that your own perception shifts a little to make their meanings valid in your own frame of reference. When you do this, you are accommodating their perceptions into your evaluations.

Figure 3.2
Perceptual
organization
and
interpretation

Organization and interpretation are interrelated. We put data together to give it meaning. One way to view this part of the process is to think about what happens when we sketch a portrait of someone we know. We start with the general shape of the face and rough features—a basic organizational pattern. As we sketch, we organize the drawing to render an image of the subject. We do not create a face and then try to find someone who resembles it; that would put organizing ahead of interpreting. Instead, we organize and interpret together: we give the portrait meaning as we organize it, and we organize it to give it meaning.

In conversations, the stress placed on particular words or phrases may affect our perception of the message. That is, once we have been exposed to and attended to a message, there are characteristics of the message that may influence our understanding of it. To explore this aspect of organizing and interpreting, try this experiment. Repeat each of these phrases, emphasizing a different word in the phrase each time. How does the meaning shift when the emphasis changes?

- I need that report tomorrow.
- I think you're quite attractive.
- Are you going to the game on Saturday?
- I want to talk with you.

The way we organize and interpret information is very important for our relationships. What we hear others say influences our responses to them. For instance, when we asked you to change the emphasis in the statements above, did you think about how you might respond differently depending on where you heard the stress in a sentence? "I *think* you're quite attractive" produces a different response from "I think you're *quite* attractive." Remember, both the emphasis placed by the speaker and the emphasis heard by the listener affect perceptions. If our perception skills are sharp enough, we will hear what was intended. If our skills are not very sharp, we make a mistaken response and thus add confusion to our relationships.

Organizing and Interpreting Through Closure

Very few of our perceptions are based on whole images. Rather, through the process called *closure*, we must create perceptions by putting together bits and pieces of data from our experiences. For example, consider the procedure of forming an impression of someone in an office. The objects you find in this person's space are the information from which you form whole impressions of this individual.

We are using closure when we add finishing touches to our perception of otherwise incomplete events by rearranging and filling in missing parts. We are also using closure when we draw inferences about an event from its bits and pieces, as when you finish another person's sentence or generalize about someone's character or behavior. For instance, Tom and Pete often play doubles tennis together. When Pete serves, Tom always seems to know where to move on the court to get the best shot. If you ask him about it, Tom will tell you that he knows Pete's game so well that he can figure out what sort of serve is coming from the way Pete walks up to the line. Tom observes Pete's actions and, through closure, successfully predicts a complete cycle of behavior.

Look closely at the reproduction of Georges Seurat's painting *Sunday Afternoon on the Island of Le Grand Jatte* (figure 3.3). What would you say is going on in this picture? Describe your perception of this painting. Now look carefully at figure 3.4, which is a small detail of the painting. As you can see, the painting is really just a mass of dots of various shades and densities. You used closure to bring these dots together into the picture you recognized in figure 3.3.

Closure affects perception in relationships also. Our general perception about a friend is really a summary of numerous discrete perceptions, smoothed into a consistent image. Also, in very close relationships, we often find ourselves able to understand the other's intentions with minimal expression. In well-developed relationships, it is not unusual to find whole actions or ideas conveyed in just a word, phrase, or gesture. Because we know the other person well, closure enables us to communicate more efficiently.

Paul says he can always tell the kind of day his spouse, Jill, has had by the way she greets him when she comes through the door. He can then adjust his communication to take into account her thoughts and feelings about the day's events.

INFLUENCES ON PERCEPTION

Perception is not an entirely "clean" process. That is, many things may get in between the events of the world and our perception of them. Some of these influences on perception occur as part of the process, while others represent aspects of the situation in which perception occurs.

Assimilation and Accommodation

Our ability to make sense of what we are observing, such as another person in a relationship, is affected by the way we use the frame of reference to act on it. Two aspects of perceptual organization, assimilation and accommodation, describe this process.[3] With *assimilation*, we *change* what we perceive to fit our frame of reference. We may even use it to defend our beliefs, attitudes, and values. For

Explore your perception using these figures.

• • •   • •   • • • •   • •

Nearness: Do you see four groups of dots?

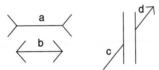

Likeness: The rectangles composed of Xs or circles, exclusively, are easier to perceive than those composed of two circles and two Xs.

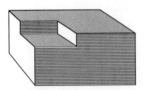

Part-whole relationships: The same set of lines may be seen as forming a block of wood or as outlining a recess in a block of wood.

Shifting perception: The same figure may be organized into different wholes or patterns.

Perceiving parts as a whole: Lines *a* and *b* are the same length. Lines *c* and *d* can be connected to form a continuous line. The illusion results from distorting a part because of the larger whole in which it is found.

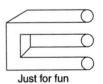

Field-ground relationship

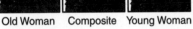

Old Woman   Composite   Young Woman

Past experience: We tend to see objects that are familiar. In the picture at the right, do you see the young woman or the old woman?

Just for fun

example, we might see our partner in a relationship as loving and caring. When we observe the opposite, we may perceive the negative behavior as less intense as we weigh it through our frame of reference. With *accommodation*, on the other hand, we *adjust* the frame of reference to integrate what we have perceived to make room for new information and experiences. It reflects an openness or willingness to be influenced.

Assimilation and accommodation always occur together; that is, a space is made for new information as the information is altered to fit that space. If our frame of reference offers us a generally positive feeling about a coworker, for example, we are likely to use these processes to maintain this attitude. If, for instance, this individual acts sharply toward us, we might assimilate our observations, seeing the attack as less intense than if it had come from someone else. At the same time, we would accommodate the frame of reference about that relationship to include the new information.

The changes that information frequently undergoes during assimilation can contribute to inaccurate perceptions. The assimilation process may level, sharpen, or distort a perception to allow it to better fit our frames of reference. In *leveling*, details of a perception are lost, leaving only those parts that clearly fit the frame of reference. For instance, we may have a friend whose company we enjoy but with whom we've had our ups and downs. As we organize our perceptions about this person, we may retain the general positive feeling we get from several experiences, rather than recall the particular high and low points that might contradict that overall attitude.

Frequently the details omitted are those that contribute to the uniqueness of an experience. That is what the term *leveling* implies—shaving off the peaks and filling in the valleys. An experience is easily assimilated if it looks like many others. If we find ourselves failing to see the uniqueness of people in our relationships, we may be leveling too much, and the relationships may suffer. We need to pay more attention to the individuality that various people bring to our relationships.

Sharpening is the editing of our perception by focusing on details that reinforce our frame of reference while discarding the rest. You can hear examples of sharpening when you listen to the conversation of old friends who are getting together after a long separation. Recalling the highs and lows of their experience serves as a ritualistic way of reminding ourselves of the importance of their relationship. The friends vividly sharpen their perceptions of their shared adventures and forget their more mundane activities to reinforce the feeling they have for one another quickly and strongly.

Perceptual distortion is the outright changing of the content of our experiences to fit our frame of reference. You might alter your memory of the details of an evening if you had a particularly bad time with a friend whose company you normally enjoy. For example, you might come to admit that the service in a restaurant was not very

We sometimes change our experiences to fit our frame of reference.

prompt upon observing your friend's unfair criticism of it. The event can then be assimilated into the existing frame of reference because you distort your perception to believe your friend's behavior was justified.

We also distort our perception of our own behavior. For example, to provide support for the relationship in the example above, you might remember that you too complained about the service. Perhaps when your friend spoke rudely to the waiter, you actually frowned at her. You might, however, distort your memory to recall frowning at the waiter instead. Too much distortion can lead to an unhealthy communication climate in our relationships because our partners may come to question the reliability of our perceptions.

Sometimes two people distort their perceptions of an event so that they can build their agreement into their relationship. In the film *Annie Hall*, Woody Allen narrates a story about two lonely people sitting in a restaurant and talking. "This food is terrible," one says, and the other replies, "Yes, and the portions are so small." The contradiction between their points of view about the food is obvious. But having agreement that something is wrong—whether or not it is the same thing—is perhaps more important than the content of their individual feelings. As a result of this distortion, they build into their frames of reference the same feeling about dinner, but perhaps for different reasons. Distortion can serve the best interests of our relationships when it does not create any harm and builds a sense of unanimity. This sense of common understanding contributes to our notion that we have things in common and, thus, to our attraction to each other.

Other Factors that Affect Our Perception

Outside the perception process, other factors may influence the nature of our perceptions. These include physical things, such as the health of your senses or the distraction of the environment. They also include social things, such as self-concept, our interaction with other individuals and groups, and occupational or gender roles. Finally, cultural differences operate as factors that may also limit our perception.

Physical Health.

We know that our perceptions are influenced by our physical health. When we are feeling ill, our perceptions often become less accurate. We may experience difficulty in keeping our attention fixed on matters at hand or in thinking clearly to process perceptions that are before us. Fatigue and hunger influence perception similarly. It's important to recognize symptoms hunger and fatigue produce in yourself and in your relationships. Pete is particularly susceptible to the influence of hunger on his perception and has difficulty focusing attention when his blood sugar drops. Mimi, his wife, has come to recognize this over the years and often suggests Pete have some orange juice if he seems unfocused.

Environment.

Environment also influences our perception. Our physical surroundings interact with the frame of reference to limit or influence our perception of certain situations. Have you ever wondered why so many people feel comfortable acting more wild than they ordinarily might when at a rock concert or a sporting event? Environments such as these influence our perceptions of the events and of ourselves and thus our behavior.

Our Past.

Sometimes our past images, expectations, or desired outcomes affect our perceptions. For instance, Lauren lives in the mountains but gets away from the stress of work by making several trips to the beach each year. Her perception of events at the beach are always similar. She has been there in the cold of winter, in sunshine and rain, even once in a hurricane. She always returns smiling and refreshed. Her images of the positive value of beach trips, her expectation of a relaxing time, and her desire for more such experiences will let absolutely nothing interfere with that outcome. She thus overlooks many images and events that might ruin such a trip for many other people.

Roles.

The roles present in an interaction also affect our perception. While we'll look more carefully at this issue later in this chapter, it should be noted here that the roles we take in relationships steer us toward certain patterns of perception. These patterns inevitably lead us to pay closer attention to some things while overlooking others. In some aspects of life, roles may limit perception more than in others. Two of the most influential situations involve the interaction of persons through occupational roles and gender roles. For now, just think about how your roles at work shape your perception of the people around you. Think also about how you tend to notice more things related to what you do, even outside the workplace. Think also about the things you've been taught to expect of people because they are male or female and how being male or female has shaped your perspective.

Culture.

We also know that people of different cultures communicate in different ways. These differences occur in terms of language and nonverbal communication. People of cultures and even subcultures other than ours do some things and express some ideas differently than we do. Cross-cultural differences influence perception. Typically, we may expect that a person from another culture will not understand us, so we may make the mistake of speaking louder or more slowly when addressing her. People often incorrectly assume that because another does not speak their language, the other person knows less. The tendency, then, is to talk down to those individuals. We are often surprised at their reactions to this. We examine cultural roles more later in this chapter and cultural influences on communication in the chapters on nonverbal communication and diversity later in this book.

Self-concept.

The difference of feeling confident about yourself versus feeling down on yourself can effect how you see your world. One study provides a good example of this factor. Researchers found the recipient's self-concept was the greatest factor in determining whether people who were being teased saw the teaser as friendly or hostile.[4] This same effect can be seen for other opposing emotions, such as happiness and sadness. Our view of our self has a strong effect on how we interpret others' behavior.

Shared Narratives.

We create a shared perception of the world when we interact with others. This kind of shared perspective is called a narrative. So a group of people make sense of their world by crafting a story that explains the events. The story then gets repeated over and over again, until members accept it as "truth." However, if an outsider were to hear this "truth" and decide to observe the particular situation, he or she may very well discover that it doesn't jibe with the facts.

BUILDING PERCEPTUAL SKILLS

You can improve your perceptual skills by learning how to verify the accuracy of your perceptions and to sharpen your ability to take in and interpret information from your environment. But working on your perceptual abilities can be demanding and time-consuming, so do not expect dramatic improvement overnight. And do not expect to retain any improvements without practice.

The basic tools of perception are your senses and your brain. The keys to developing your perceptual tools are attention, concentration, and time. You must pay attention to what your senses and your body are experiencing in different situations. Remember that improving your sensing ability is an ongoing, long-term process, so persistence is mandatory. Certain meditative techniques might help you concentrate on your senses.

PERCEIVING PEOPLE

Perceiving people involves making judgments about personality and drawing inferences from what we observe.[5] Perceiving people is different from perceiving things. Although the same basic processes are at work, two important distinctions separate these two kinds of perceptions:

First, perceiving people is different from perceiving objects because of the consistency of what is being observed. Objects remain relatively stable and unchanged, so our expectations can remain relatively stable, too. People, however, are less consistent and more complex than objects. This leads to less clear and more numerous expectations in our perception of people than in our perception of objects.

Second, interpersonal perception is *mutual*. As we take in and interpret information about someone, that person is doing the same with respect to us. This important characteristic of person perception has a significant effect. It leads us to be concerned about our self-image. For example, an employment interview with a company's executive officer will involve mutual perception—you are looking each other over. The company executive has an agenda: she wants to decide whether to offer you a job. You also have an agenda: you want to decide whether to accept a job if it is offered. You try to respond in a way that will present yourself at your best. At the same time, you evaluate her based on her questions and interviewing technique. The mutual quality of perception makes it possible for both people in this situation to achieve their agendas. The mutual nature of perception has a significant impact on our expectations in relationships.

In a relationship, both parties have expectations that, although they may differ, influence our perception in that relationship. As we observe the behavior of those in our relationships, we speculate about motives for or causes of their actions. Our guesses about the causes of our partners' behaviors, called *attributions*, contribute to our expectations.

We develop *communication rules* out of our perceptions, attributions, and expectations in a relationship. These are boundaries for the communication in our relationships. If we break the rules, perceptions are confused and expectations become unclear. When we observe the rules or change them through negotiation, expectations are reinforced and relational growth can occur.

The expectations we bring to our communication with others come from a summary evaluation of our feelings about ourselves and our partners in the relationship. These summary evaluations are referred to as relationship positions. For example, if you take the position that both you and the other person are O.K. in the relationship, your communication will be healthy and contribute to the growth of the relationship. However, there are other positions you might take that could harm that growth. We will examine these ideas more closely later in the chapter.

We develop communication rules for our relationships. When we observe the rules or change them through negotiation, relational growth can occur.

MUTUAL PERCEPTION AFFECTS INTERPERSONAL RELATIONSHIPS

Mutual perception affects the development of our relationships in three important ways: it influences interpersonal attraction—our willingness to establish relationships with particular persons; it governs the process of attribution, where we assign motives to the behavior of ourselves and others; and it affects the roles we establish and maintain as relationships develop.

Interpersonal Attraction

Interpersonal attraction describes our willingness to communicate and to develop a relationship with another person. We are attracted to those who are like us, those to whom we are physically close, and those whose physical attributes we admire.[6] Perception is crucial to this attraction because it provides the data we use to decide about whether to engage another person in communication.

We begin to like people and to seek relationships with them in many ways that relate to the process of perception; two ways in particular stand out. First, we usually like people who like us. We perceive their behavior as positive and supporting. Consider, for example, the other students in your interpersonal communication class. There may be several whom you did not know before but have begun to like and talk with. Is there anyone among them who expressed a positive feeling about you before you really thought about a relationship with that person? If so, it was your perception of this event that attracted you to this person. Has this happened to you in other situations? Has it happened at your place of work?

Second, we usually like people who *are* like us. We think they are like us because our perceptions of them correspond to our perceptions of ourselves. These are people we may think we understand and who seem to share a frame of reference similar to our own. Look around you. Perhaps you see people in your classes or at your job who seem to look or act as you do. Focus on those with whom you have begun relationships. Is it true that they are like you?

Occasionally, we are attracted to people because we are in frequent contact. The frequency of interactions may lead to information sharing and eventually to learning to like someone. For instance, since his retirement, Len has become an avid traveler and explorer. His new interest often puts him in the situation of having to live with a group of fellow travelers for extended periods. Often these people are younger and have little in common with Len. However, the close quarters and frequent contact often lead Len to develop positive relationships with his fellow travelers. A more common example of attraction through contact occurs in the workplace. You may not at first especially like those you work with, but frequent contact inevitably results in sharing information and experiences. This sharing leads to some level of attraction that might not have happened if you were able to terminate the relationship based on your first impressions. Our awareness that frequent encounters are inevitable may cause us to perceive positive information selectively. For instance, we might find something to like about a person because we wish to enjoy the time that we know we will be spending with him. The relationship might not grow very much, but it could develop sufficiently for our tasks to be done efficiently.

We also like and seek relationships with others because of physical attraction. Standards for physical beauty are tied very closely to one's individual frame of reference. And, like the frame of reference, these standards will change over time. Perception is very important in this aspect of attraction because we are making judgments about whether to communicate based on physical data that we take in through our senses. Consider the people in figure 3.5. Whom do you consider attractive? Whom do you find unattractive? Compare your preferences and the reasons for them with a friend and a classmate. How are your standards of beauty different? Are the standards of your friend closer to yours than those of your classmates? This kind of comparison will help you appreciate the personal nature of interpersonal attraction.

Attribution

One of the most important ways our perceptions help to shape our expectations of others is through the attribution process. *Attribution* describes the way we figure out why people, including ourselves, behave in particular ways.[7] When we think we understand the motives behind a person's actions, we feel more confident about our expectations of that person. For instance, because Bob believes that Dana sees himself as a good organizer, when Bob finds himself involved with Dana in a project, he expects Dana to take charge and get things arranged.

We divide our attributions into two types, internal and external. When we attribute internal causes to an action, we say that a person did something because it is her nature to do so. We might see that Lawanda has agreed to spend the next four Saturdays registering voters at the local shopping mall. We might say that she does this because she is a civic-minded individual. *Internal attributes* represent a statement about what sort of person we're perceiving. *External attributes,* on the other hand, explain our actions in terms of the situation or environment. We might think that Lawanda volunteered to give up her Saturdays because she was cornered at a social gathering and might have felt embarrassed to say no. Here, we see her response as determined by the situation in which her help was solicited.

Figure 3.5
Whom do you
consider
attractive?

Figure 3.5
Whom do you
consider
attractive?

Both types of attributions influence our expectations of others. When we judge positive behaviors as internally caused, our attraction for another increases, and our expectations of him grow from the personality characteristic we have assigned to him. When we judge negative behaviors as internally caused, our attraction diminishes, but expectations of that person still grow from that characteristic. For instance, if we see Lawanda's actions as self-serving, we would tend to expect her to behave self-servingly in future encounters. When we judge behaviors as externally motivated, a similar process takes place. We assume that the action came from the situation and expect the person may behave differently when the pressure of the environment is gone. So, positive behaviors we see as externally motivated lead us away from our relationships, while negative behaviors we view as caused by the situation bring us closer in our relationships. On the whole, interpersonal researchers have found that we tend to attribute internal causes to others' behaviors more often than we attribute external ones. Doing this enables us to think we understand the person more directly and deeply.

We also explain our own behavior to ourselves and others, but the attribution process is different. First, we more often turn to external motives than to internal ones when describing our own actions. For instance, we recently watched our friend Ted arrive to pick up a date, bringing her flowers. He explained his thoughtfulness, saying, "Well, the flower stand right on the corner wasn't busy, and I know you like flowers, so I figured I might as well stop by."

Second, when we're creating self-attributions, we often engage the self-concept's survival orientation described in Chapter 2. You may remember from the discussion that we possess a powerful force with a mission to preserve and protect the self-concept. Our attributions about ourselves represent the exercise of this force. We use self-attribution to preserve our self-concept and to formulate expectations of ourselves. We tend to attribute internal motives to positive behaviors and external motives to negative behaviors. For instance, if we show up on time for a date, it's because we're punctual individuals. If we are late, it is often because of traffic or some other difficulty that no reasonable person could predict.

Attribution is assigning motives to the actions of ourselves and others in our relationships. Doing this helps us to formulate our expectations of ourselves and others and leads to the creation of communication rules that apply to people and situations in our lives. Monitoring your attributions can reveal a great deal to you about how you perceive others. Are your attributions consistent? Are they reasonable? On what impressions have you based them? Answering questions such as these can help you monitor your attributions, and this will lead to more fair judgment of both your motives and those of others.

Role Assignment

A *role* is a pattern of behavior, a routine that we associate with a particular context. For example, in the classroom, we would expect to find someone taking the role of teacher. This might include meeting and leading a class, stimulating the students' thinking, making assignments, and giving and grading tests. Roles have both sociological and psychological dimensions.[8]

Sociological aspects of roles are those patterns of behavior with social implications. In our various relationships, we may assume many of these roles, such as parent, teacher, student, and friend. The *psychological aspects* of roles are their placement in our frame of reference. This aspect personalizes roles and allows us to "own" them. You have noticed that most college professors have unique ways of fulfilling their role, yet they all fulfill the sociological role of teacher. It is the psychological dimension of the role that provides the individuality of style. When we communicate in a relationship, we begin by assuming roles for ourselves and expecting certain roles of the other person. This establishes guidelines for the communication because roles represent patterns of behavior, many of which are understood socially.

A relationship may involve several roles. For instance, Pamela is a college professor who has had Jolene, an older, part-time accounting student, in her classes for many years. Jolene does Pamela's taxes outside of school, and Pamela goes to her for assistance on tax matters. Look at all the possible role encounters implied by this relationship. Pamela and Jolene sometimes interact as professor and student, sometimes as accountant and client and, since their relationship has some history, as friends. Each must make certain that the expectations formed around one role relationship do not interfere with communication in another.

Cultural and *gender roles* are very important in our development of expectations in relationships. The roles traditionally defined for men and women have changed greatly over the past decade. More women have entered the work force as colleagues and supervisors of men than at any time in history. The increased ease of communication and proximity between cultures has brought cross-cultural contact to the level of the expected, rather than the unusual. Sensitivity to perceptions and expectations based on gender and cultural roles enables us to keep up with these changes.

Our perceptions as well as those of others in a relationship are influenced by the roles we and the others assume. The act of assuming roles is mutual; we jointly work out our role relationships. We must be careful that the two of us are defining our roles appropriately for a given situation. For example, suppose you are accustomed to getting together with your coworkers for refreshments after work on Fridays. This Friday, your boss joins the group. You identify her as your supervisor and assume your psychological version of that role for her. You may be surprised to see her if your understanding of her role did not include socializing with employees as an appropriate pattern of behavior.

Successful role negotiation is important if we are to function effectively in our relationships. Differences in role definitions can be negotiated when we discover them. In fact, successful negotiation is important if we are to function effectively in our relationships. Such differences are frequently encountered when we compare our psychological role definition with that of someone else. When this happens, we assume that the other person will behave in accordance with our definition of the role. Thus, our perception of the person's actual behavior will be filtered through our frame of reference; we do not allow for the other's frame of reference.

Consider how this *perceptual filtering* affects the interpretation of the following situation. Suppose you encounter one of your professors in the hall and he says, "Bring your term paper in and I'll take a look at it." If you see the professor as a disciplinarian, you might hear the statement differently than he intended. You might expect he wants to admonish you about your progress, when he may actually intend to help. In this case, the psychological aspect of your role definition has influenced your perception of his message.

When we generalize role assignments in this way, we sometimes make mistakes that affect the capacity for our relationships to grow. The categories we use and the perceptions that result from them are inaccurate. Such errors are usually reflected in both language and action. For example, we know of patterns in marriage that lock spouses into "woman's work" or "man's work." Detecting these mistakes is a matter of comparing perceptions of the roles with the events we experience. To avoid this problem, remember that interpersonal attraction, attribution, and role assignment are the parts of perception that are *mutual.* We enter relationships based on mutual interpersonal attraction. We develop those relationships through attribution and the mutual assignment and definition of roles. Our relationships continue to grow when we communicate in a way that acknowledges that the other person in the relationship is perceiving us just as we are perceiving that person.

EXPECTATIONS INFLUENCE INTERPERSONAL RELATIONSHIPS

Expectations are an important part of the perception process. When we communicate, we do so at least in part by predicting the other person's responses.[9] We believe that we understand the person when our predictions prove accurate and that we do not understand the person when they prove incorrect. Sometimes, these expectations are based on our rigid impression of the group to which this individual belongs. This is called *stereotyping.* Our expectations are stereotyped when they come from our knowledge of a group, rather than of an individual. This becomes a problem when we fail to go beyond these general group expectations in our actions toward the person and fail to perceive the person as a unique individual. (Chapter 5 examines stereotypes in detail and offers recommendations for dealing with them.)

Expectations relate to our perception of people and relationships in two important ways. First, they govern the establishment of communication rules. Second, our expectations of a given relationship are summarized as a *relationship position*, which guides communication with the other person.

Expectations and Rules

One way expectations influence perception is in the way we use rules to structure our interpersonal communication. *Rules* are patterns of behavior we use to form expectations about certain role relationships and certain situations. Here are some examples of communication rules in relationships:

- "We don't talk about sex in front of the children."
- "When we talk about the people at church, we never use their names."
- "If you touch my elbow, I know you want to take me aside to talk privately."

Communication rules establish which topics are appropriate with various people and in various situations. For example, the rules governing communication in a relationship with a supervisor at work may not allow for the sharing of personal problems. If we break these rules, we might get an unexpected reaction. Similarly, it is probably within your rules to discuss your finances with your spouse but not at a dinner party. Following such rules builds our relationships and encourages others to have confidence in their perceptions of us. Violating the rules makes our partners unsure of their perceptions and thus hinders relational growth. Communication rules are about the appropriateness of messages for relationships and situations. We expect the partners in our relationships to play by the rules. Our expectations and perceptions depend on the use of these relational rules for communication. For example, suppose you and a close friend have agreed not to reveal the depth of your relationship to your coworkers until you both feel more certain about it. You would therefore not expect to find your partner talking about your friendship at an office party. If, however, that person did break this rule, your perception of him would certainly change, and you would have to renegotiate the rule before the relationship could continue to develop.

In their discussion of the formation of family communication rules, Kathleen Galvin and Bernard Brommel identified the basic process by which many communication rules are established.[10]

We expect the partners in our relationships to play by the rules.

These scholars pointed out that one way we create such rules is through direct, conscious negotiation. In the family, for example, certain topics may be forbidden at the dinner table. In the workplace, you may have set a regular time for discussing your performance with your supervisor.

Similar rules emerge through the unspoken repetition of the responses in a relationship. For instance, in family communication, the goodnight kiss may be a long-established ritual. The kiss does not need to be requested; it is an act that we have always performed. When it does not happen, however, we notice and assume that something is wrong. At work, you may know from experience that your supervisor is working and does not wish to be disturbed when you hear music coming from her office. Past experience tells you that she likes music when she is working hard—and only then. And she has learned that whenever she plays music while working, she will find herself undisturbed. Neither of you may have acknowledged this rule, but you both follow it.

The communication rules governing each relationship suggest mutual expectations about the topics we can discuss, the language we can use, and the people with whom we can talk about the relationship. These rules provide us a predictable way of communicating that helps us avoid misunderstanding. When we find that they are not working, we perceive that the relationship must be renegotiated before further growth can occur. In short, our expectations and the communication rules that shape them clarify our perceptions in and of our relationships.

Expectations and Relationship Positions

Eric Berne developed a method of looking at relationships called *transactional analysis*.[11] His ideas are frequently used to explain the way people see themselves and how that vision influences their communication. Some of his concepts relate to our assertion of the importance of mutual perception. Transactional analysis suggests that we go through our lives acting out "scripts" that we write for ourselves or that others have written for us. These scripts have a central theme that establishes our basic attitude about ourselves in relation to others. There are four such central themes, each of which describes first how we see ourselves and then how we see others in relationships. The four positions are: (1) "I'm O.K., you're not O.K."; (2) "I'm not O.K., you're O.K."; (3) "I'm not O.K., you're not O.K."; and (4) "I'm O.K., you're O.K." Berne says that our actions toward one another are guided by these basic "life positions."

Berne's concepts can help explain perception and communication in relationships. Rather than applying these "life positions" to whole personalities, we will look at them as differing from relationship to relationship. We want to suggest that the entire frame of reference for a relationship can generally be summarized in a basic "relationship position." We bring this position to our interactions with relational partners. These summaries guide our perceptions as we communicate in them. These basic relationship positions take a form similar to those originally proposed by Berne:

1. "I'm not O.K. in this relationship, but you are."
2. "I'm O.K. in this relationship, but you're not."
3. "I'm not O.K. in this relationship, and neither are you."
4. "I'm O.K. in this relationship, and so are you."

The difference between our model and Berne's is that, rather than viewing everyone from a single perspective (for example, "I'm O.K., but you're not"), we believe that the relationship influences the perspective. Thus, we approach every person from a different perspective, picking up where we left off with that person and relationship. We may find ourselves feeling that either we or the other person is not O.K. Only one of these themes ("I'm O.K., and so are you") promotes optimum growth in our relationships. The others tend to demean one or both persons and therefore stifle growth. Let's look at these positions and see how they affect expectations and perception.

"I'm not O.K. in this relationship, but you are"

Our expectations are frequently dominated by a desire to give control of the relationship to the other person, whether that person wants it or not. This affects our communication when we find our-

	You're O.K.	You're not O.K.
I'm O.K.	We're equal.	I'm one up on you.
I'm not O.K.	I'm one down on you.	We're both down.

The central themes of transactional analysis.

selves refusing to help make decisions that concern our relationships. This point of view also places all responsibility for making the
relationship work on the other person. This is unfair and may be
resented. Consider the case of Chuck and Kate, a married couple.
Kate has remained friends through the years with Rob, her
boyfriend twenty years ago. Rob calls Kate often to talk over things
happening in their lives. His calling disturbs Chuck, but Chuck can't
put his finger on why it disturbs him. He feels guilty and embarrassed about his jealousy of Kate's friendship with Rob and angry at
himself about being bothered by it. He doesn't communicate about
these feelings with Kate. So, when Rob calls, Chuck's behavior
toward Kate becomes distant, even hostile. He feels not O.K. in their
relationship and also feels that Kate is doing nothing wrong. Sooner
or later, Kate and Chuck will talk or argue about Rob because of
Chuck's relationship position. We can help our relationships when
we recognize that we have taken this position. The best way to do
this is to communicate openly about our feelings about the relationship. We will probably find that the other person is more than willing to work with us to strengthen the relationship and our role in it.

The child: "I'm
not O.K. in this
relationship, but
you are."

"I'm O.K. in this relationship, but you're not"

We find ourselves blaming the other person for problems in our relationships when we approach it from this position. We may view situations with righteous indignation and expect that they will not work out because the other person will make a mistake. We may also be anticipating errors from the other person and be difficult to please. This frame of reference creates a no-win situation for the other person; perhaps nothing that person might do will please us. Often, this results in the deterioration and termination of the relationship by the other person. The basic reason for such an attitude is our failure to acknowledge the other person's contribution to the relationship. Our example about Chuck, Kate, and Rob might have occurred differently. Perhaps Chuck does not feel guilty about his jealousy of the relationship Kate has with Rob. Perhaps he feels that he has acted properly in their relationship but that Kate's friendship with Rob violates some aspect of Chuck's relationship with her. In this instance, Chuck might view himself as O.K. in the relationship and Kate as not O.K. Chuck's behavior might be as hostile but would probably exhibit more aggression than defensiveness. Again, they will eventually have to communicate about the issue in some form, or even greater problems will emerge.

One way to resolve this problem is to review the relationship. Think back to its beginning and recall the other person's contribu-

The woman: "I'm O.K. in this relationship, but you're not."

tions. Then discuss those shared experiences to try to put the relationship in its proper perspective by reevaluating and perhaps redesigning the mutual expectations. Your relationship can grow in a positive direction once successful reevaluation and redesign have been accomplished.

"I'm not O.K. in this relationship, and neither are you"

This orientation suggests that the relationship is in considerable trouble, for we no longer have the motivation to want to control, nor do we believe the other person is capable of handling control. We blame both ourselves and the other person for the problems. We also expect to make mistakes, and we expect the other person to behave badly when we do so.

In the case of Chuck, Kate, and Rob, either of the first two relationship positions on Chuck's part might evolve into this one, in which neither party is seen as functioning well. Chuck might feel insecure in the relationship but also believe that Kate's actions lead him to feel that way. This act of blaming the other person for one's own negative feelings can be extremely destructive to our relationships.

At this point we must seriously consider our goals in the relationship—why we created it and what we want from it—and discuss them with the other person. Whether the relationship can be saved depends very much on the other person's perspective. For

The man: "I'm not O.K. in this relationship, and neither are you."

Being O.K. with
the relationship
and ourselves
helps us
develop a more
positive view of
the relationship.

example, if the other person's perspective is, "I'm O.K. in this relationship, and so are you," then she will be willing to help us develop a more positive view of the relationship. Sometimes an outsider, either a friend or a professional, can help us examine our frame of reference.

"I'm O.K. in this relationship, and so are you"

This is the preferred point of view for healthy, growing relationships. With this attitude, we acknowledge both our and the other's contributions to the success of the relationship. Our expectations tend to match the rules we have established and kept. We are not often confused by surprisingly negative behaviors. However, we do not deny that problems exist but rather set a tone that will enable us to talk to the other person and do something about these problems. If Chuck, to continue our example, holds this view of the relationship, he will know that it is all right to admit feeling the way he does about things. He will expect that Kate is interested in talking about and working out matters that bear on their relationship. This frame of reference anticipates relational growth. We perceive the other in ways that promote effective communication.

The expectations that we bring to our relationships affect the way we perceive the other person and the relationship itself. The communication rules and our relationship position, which summarizes our view of the relationship and provides the basis for our

Both people:
"I'm O.K. in this
relationship,
and so are you."

actions toward the other person, are statements of these expectations. We maintain an appropriate perception of our expectations and those of our partner by clearly understanding the rules as well as our position, which facilitates interpersonal growth through communication.

Change and Perception in Relationships

Appropriate communication about our roles and expectations is critical to the development of our relationships. *Change* is one factor that influences our perception of interpersonal attraction, attribution, role assignment, the development of expectations, and the creation of relationship positions. We must be prepared to deal with change if we are to build long-lasting relationships. Changes in people may be physical, social, psychological, or professional. Of course, changes are not always readily visible—sometimes not even to the person who has changed. Still, changes interact with expectations in person perception.

The expectations we bring to a relationship may not be appropriate in light of changes in the other person. Similarly, the other's expectations may no longer work in light of our own changes. If both people have changed, all expectations may need adjustment, along with the roles in our relationship or our view of their importance.

Think about some of the physical changes you have undergone. How did your way of perceiving shift to accommodate them? Did the changes alter any of your relationships? If so, how? Next, think about an important social change in your life, such as your decision to start college, join a new social group, or find a new job. How did you perceive your new relationships? Did different rules emerge to control them? Did your new associations affect your perceptions of existing relationships? In what ways did your perceptions change? What changes have taken place in your career? If you have not yet begun working, you will find that when you do, your perceptions will shift again. New goals and values will develop around your professional roles, and your perceptions will change as you assimilate information into your new roles. If you already have a career, think about the last important change in your work role or responsibilities on the job. If you changed jobs recently, you may have much to say about the changes in perception that occur when you make a professional change.

Share with your classmates some of the ways change has affected your perceptions of your relationships. You may be surprised to learn that we have all gone through many transformations. Our relationships continue through these changes, and many of them grow along with us.

BUILDING INTERPRETIVE SKILLS

We need to keep in mind two very important aspects of the perception process if we are to understand how to improve our perception of people in our relationships. First, perception occurs inductively. Our interpretations of stimuli represent inferences drawn from what we observe. Sometimes we lose sight of this fact and treat these inferences as though they are facts. This aspect of perception is important to remember because we can improve our ability to give meaning to our perceptions of people and relationships by learning to distinguish more clearly between our observations and inferences.

We must also remember that we perceive relatively unconsciously. We cannot focus on perceiving but only on *what* is perceived. We can improve our powers of perception by learning to recognize inferences when we or others state them.

Herbert J. Hess and Charles O. Tucker have argued that statements of observation differ from statements of inference in three ways.[12] One difference is the extent of description in each. *Observational statements* are faithful descriptions of what was sensed: "I saw you pour the last of the coffee into your cup and then walk away with it." *Inferential statements,* on the other hand, go beyond description: "You poured the last cup of coffee, and I'll bet you're not going to make a new pot."

A second difference is that statements of our observations make no judgments: "I smell something burning." Inferences, however, frequently involve judgments: "It stinks in here." Sometimes a statement of inference goes beyond both observation and judgment: "That inconsiderate oaf must be smoking those disgusting little cigars again." If you assume that this last statement is a fact rather than an inference, you may be surprised when your friend reacts to it defensively.

The third difference lies in the way statements of observation and inference are limited. Observations are limited to a description of what the senses take in. Inferences, on the other hand, are limited only by the imagination of the perceiver. While observations can grow in depth and detail only as long as you concentrate on what you are perceiving, a large number of inferences can be generated from the most limited of observations.

Expectations are important aspects of our communication in relationships, for they represent statements of inference that we must make regularly. But as Hess and Tucker point out, it is useful to recognize guesses as guesses. The unrecognized inference is often the cause of misunderstanding and other relationship problems.

You can practice certain skills to develop your ability to perceive more accurately in your relationships. First, state your observations and then follow them with your inferences. For example,

- "I see that you are shaking. You seem nervous to me."
- "Your eyes are red. Are you tired?"
- "I know you finished your paper. You must be happy."

Practice both alone and with others. When you are alone, remind yourself to clarify the observations that result in your expectations of others. When you are in conversation, actually state the observation and then your inference.

A second skill, and one that we introduced in Chapter 5, is that of checking out your inferences. You can check what is inferred on the basis of one sense against the evidence provided by other senses. For instance, a friend seems less talkative than usual. You may infer that she is tired. You can check this out by looking at her face. Does she look tired? Listen to her voice. Does it sound tired? Compare the data from several senses before drawing your inference. This technique works better at the moment of perception than it does after the fact. After all, remember that perceptual distortion can shape your memory of an event to support your inference about it.

Another way to check your inferences is to repeat your observation; that is, look again. You might repeat yourself or approach the subject from another angle. In the case of your tired friend, you might inquire indirectly by saying, "Have you been working many hours these days?" Then rephrase the question more directly, saying, "You seem tired to me." Find out if there is agreement between your first and second observations. Double-checking your perceptions is sometimes time-consuming, but it can prevent the difficulties that arise from acting on an inaccurate perception. Sometimes it is necessary to ask a person to repeat what was said so that you can observe more carefully. The benefits in taking the time to do this are worth the effort.

The practice of these skills requires a conscious effort, especially at first. But you will soon see an improvement in your ability to express your perceptions of people and events in your relationships more clearly.

SUMMARY

Perception is the process by which we take in and give meaning to information around us. It is on the basis of our perceptions that we understand our relationships. All of our perceptions are filtered through our frame of reference, a collection of our attitudes, values, and beliefs. Perception is able to work as it does because it is active, inductive, and relatively unconscious.

We select information from the wealth of data around us, paying attention to some while discarding most. Our frame of reference helps us to organize and interpret this information using closure, assimilation, and accommodation. Closure helps us feel that our pictures are complete. Assimilation and accommodation bring our perceptions and our frame of reference closer together. Sometimes this coming together of images occurs through leveling or sharpening, and other times through perceptual distortion. Many other physical, situational, social, and cultural variables also influence perception. With practice, you can improve your ability to perceive and thereby improve your ability to communicate appropriately in your relationships.

We have examined the process of perception as it operates directly on our communication in relationships. We began by discussing our perceptions of people. In doing this, we found that the mutual nature of such perceptions and the development of expectations are important.

We next explained how perception functions in the beginning stages of a relationship by looking at its effects on interpersonal attraction and attribution. But perception is also important as it relates to role assignment in the later stages of a relationship. One way to improve communication and perception in relationships is to clarify the communication rules, some of which are stated and some of which are assumed.

Certain expectations in relationships come from the general position we take on the relationship. "I'm O.K. in this relationship, and so are you" represents the most productive position because it enables us to communicate in a way that stimulates relational growth.

As we perceive others, we must also remember to account for relational changes and recognize observations and inferences. Three skills are crucial to the latter: we should first state our observations, then check them out, and finally repeat observations.

DISCUSSION QUESTIONS

1. Try to describe your frame of reference when you entered college. How did it affect your initial perceptions of the people you encountered? Did these perceptions in turn affect your frame of reference? If so, how?

2. Recall the details of your first image of your interpersonal communication professor. How have your impressions of this person changed since the course began? Has this altered your frame of reference? If so, why?

3. Have several class members explain the same important event in your community. How are the explanations different? Is there

any evidence of selective exposure or selective attention? Any leveling? Any sharpening? Any other distortion?

4. It seems that assimilation and accommodation might at times work against each other in ways that at least temporarily confuse your perceptions of a person or event. Describe an experience in which you were simultaneously shaping your perceptions to fit your frame of reference and adjusting your perceptions.

5. What are your perceptual weaknesses in the physical realm? That is, under what conditions do you find your perception skills hampered? What environmental influences on perception have you noticed affecting your communication in the past? Can you relate any cross-cultural perception experiences?

6. Visit the professor teaching a course you have considered taking to learn more about the course. Then answer the following questions.

   a. What tasting, smelling, hearing, seeing, and touching cues did you receive from the professor?

   b. Was the professor in good health? How do you know?

   c. Was the professor tired? How do you know?

   d. How old was the professor?

   e. Did you discover any evidence, either directly related to the person or to the environment, that would enable you to say whether this person is kindly? well read? involved in any extracurricular activity? involved with a family?

   f. Were you tired during this conversation? If so, how did this affect your performance?

   g. How do you think the professor reacted to you? What images did you leave?

   h. What perceptions of you do you believe would still be fresh and vivid in the professor's mind?

   i. Did you and the professor agree completely or even partially about the role expectations for the meeting? What were those role expectations? How do you know?

7. Create a list of expectations you have of a person in one of your relationships. Now, examine the attributions that lead to these expectations. Which expectations connect to internal attributions? Which come from external attributions? Think about other relationships in your experience. Do you follow any particular patterns of attribution?

8. Identify three of your relationships in which the communication rules are very different. List some of the rules to show these differences. How is your perception of people and events guided by the rules in each case? Do you find yourself agreeing to

things in one relationship that you might not in another? Is your communication style different?

9. Describe instances in which you assumed each of Eric Berne's relationship positions. How did the communication in these relationships occur? What was it like? What happened to each of these relationships? Did your position change? If so, how?

10. Go to a movie with several classmates and then discuss what you saw. Note the differences in inferences drawn from the same observed images.

ENDNOTES

1. A. G. Athos and J. J. Gabarro, *Interpersonal Behavior: Communication and Understanding in Relationships* (Englewood Cliffs, NJ: Prentice-Hall, 1978), 137–148.

2. H.C. Triandis, *Interpersonal Behavior* (Monterey, CA: Brooks/Cole, 1977), 94–135.

3. J. Piaget, *The Construction of Reality in the Child* (New York: Basic Books, 1954).

4. J. K. Alberts, U. Kellar-Guenther, and S. R. Corman, "That's Not Funny: Understanding Recipients' Responses to Teasing," *Western Journal of Communication* 60 (1996): 337–357.

5. P. R. Hinton, *The Psychology of Interpersonal Perception* (New York: Poutledge, 1993).

6. M. Ruffner and M. Burgoon, *Interpersonal Communication* (New York: Holt, Rinehart, and Winston, 1981), 179–194.

7. E. E. Jones and K. E. Davis, "From Acts to Dispositions: The Attribution Process in Person Perception," in *Advances in Experimental Social Psychology*, vol. 2, L. Berkowitz, ed. (New York: Academic Press, 1965), 219–266.

8. These ideas were introduced by G. R. Miller and M. Steinberg in *Between People: A New Analysis of Interpersonal Communication* (Chicago: Science Research Associates, 1975), 17–22; also see C. L. Book, ed., *Human Communication: Principles, Contexts and Skills* (New York: St. Martin's Press, 1980), 3–37, 108–138.

9. J. J. Gabarro, "The Development of Trust, Influence and Expectations," in A. G. Athos and J. J. Gabarro, *Interpersonal Behavior: Communication and Understanding in Relationships* (Englewood Cliffs, NJ: Prentice-Hall, 1978), 290–303.

10. K. Galvin and B. Brommel, *Family Communication, Cohesion and Change* (Glenview, IL: Scott, Foresman, 1986), 64–93.

11. E. Berne, *Games People Play* (New York: Grove Press, 1964).

12. H. J. Hess and C. O. Tucker, *Talking About Relationships*, 2d ed. (Prospect Heights, IL: Waveland Press, 1980), 19–31.

READ MORE ABOUT
PERCEPTION IN THESE SOURCES

Athos, Anthony G., and John J. Gabarro. *Interpersonal Behavior: Communication and Understanding in Relationships.* Princeton, NJ: Prentice-Hall, 1978. This work provides both ideas and case study applications of those ideas. The authors emphasize and elaborate on the connection between assumptions, perceptions, and feelings.

Bandler, Richard, and John Grinder. *Reframing: Neuro-Linguistic Programming and the Transformation of Meaning.* Moab, Utah: Real People Press, 1982. Readers will find a detailed examination of what we refer to as the frame of reference. These authors argue that we can alter the meanings we assign to events by "reframing" those events. They offer practical suggestions for implementing their ideas.

Wheeler, Ladd. *Interpersonal Influence.* Boston: Allyn and Bacon, 1970. This short, classic work summarizes seventy years of research on interpersonal influence by describing several landmark research projects in clear detail. In the process, it identifies major findings about the perception process.

READ MORE ABOUT
INTERPERSONAL PERCEPTION IN THESE SOURCES

Cronkhite, Gary. Perception and Meaning. In *Handbook of Rhetorical and Communication Theory,* eds. Carroll C. Arnold and John Waite Bowers. Boston: Allyn and Bacon. 1984. 51–229. This extended essay includes bibliographic materials across the entire subject of perception and communication. The author examines all major variables affecting interpersonal perception in comprehensive fashion.

Ickes, William ed. *Empathic Accuracy.* New York. Guilford, 1997. Ickes presents scholarly works he has collected. These address topics such as the evolutionary and social factors that contribute to empathy, the psychological characteristics and influences that affect empathic ability, and the relationship of empathy to gender.

Triandis, Harry C. *Interpersonal Behavior.* Monterey, CA: Brooks/Cole, 1977. This is an advanced interpersonal communication book based in social psychology. The topic of attribution is treated thoroughly in this work, and the summary of research up to its publication is exhaustive.

PART 3

CREATING MESSAGES

LANGUAGE

We use words to represent our ideas and to talk about the events in our lives. Language, our word system, enables us to establish and maintain connections with others. Understanding the way language works is essential to improving our relational communication. This understanding implies knowing that events and ideas, our thoughts about them, and the words we choose to describe them relate to one another very directly. Growth in relationships is difficult when our use of language is unskilled, inefficient, or inappropriate. As senders and receivers of language, we must keep in mind that words only stand for experiences. Words do not take the place of the events they represent. This chapter explores the nature of language and how it affects relational growth.

The use of language is essential to our relationships because much of the work of relationships gets accomplished through language. Through language, relational communication takes place and relationships grow and change. We must very carefully choose the language we use to talk in and about relationships. Words have meanings that may be common or personalized. We use language to summarize our views of ourselves, other people, and even our relationships in ways that fit our frames of reference. We hold opinions about the relative importance of people in our relationships. These opinions lead to our choices of language to communicate with or about them. This chapter explores how language affects both the sending and receiving of messages and suggests ways of improving the accuracy and meaningfulness of the communication in our relationships.

Quite often the evidence of problems in our relationships comes from the language we use. Sometimes the words we choose to express our ideas do not account for the uniqueness of the other person. At other times, we forget that we are in control of the language we use and instead allow our words to control us. We also create difficulties when the language we use to name ourselves, our partners, or our relationships does not change as our relationships grow. Likewise, masking reality by using words and symbols as substitutes for reality can create problems. Finally, we sometimes use language that expresses extreme points of view rather than our experience. This chapter will help you recognize and deal with these problems by helping you find language that will more effectively promote nourishment and growth in your relationships.

KEY TERMS

abstraction	classification level of abstraction
combining	complementarity
connotative meanings	dating
denotative meanings	focusing
gender	ignoring
indiscrimination	inferential level of abstraction
language	levels of abstraction
multivalued orientation	naming level of abstraction
nonverbal level of abstraction	polarization
possessing the symbol	rearranging
reification	relational depth
relational function	rigidity in naming
self-fulfilling prophecy	self-disclosure
static evaluation	stereotyping
stress	subcultural language
symbol	symmetry
thought	Triangle of Meaning
two-valued orientation	

OBJECTIVES

1. Discuss the interrelationship among events, thoughts, and language using the Triangle of Meaning.
2. Explain abstraction as it applies to language.
3. Recall an example of how abstraction helped or hindered your communication in a relationship.
4. Discuss the significance of the impact of culture on language use.
5. Describe four levels of abstraction we can apply to our relationships.

6. Explain how relationships limit our choice of language.

7. Recall an example in which the nature of the relationship affected the language used in communicating an idea.

8. Define and give examples of denotative meaning.

9. Define and give examples of connotative meaning.

10. Explain how naming affects communication in relationships.

11. Explain how different views of a relationship affect the language used in it.

12. Explain how role, gender, relational depth, and relational function influence connotation.

13. Recall an instance of language stereotyping that resulted in interpersonal problems. Explain how this occurred.

14. Explain "self-fulfilling prophecy." Provide an example from personal experience.

15. Provide a personal example in which rigidity of language posed a problem for a relationship.

16. Recall an experience in which static evaluations influenced the outcome of a situation.

17. Discuss the way reification contributes to problems in relationships.

18. Recall an experience in which polarization, or the two-valued orientation, interfered with communication in a relationship.

THE NATURE OF LANGUAGE

WHAT IS LANGUAGE?

Language is an important part of how we see our relationships and how they develop. As with other parts of the communication process, we must define language before we think about how it affects communication in our relationships.

Many people have studied language and offered definitions of it. We prefer the one offered by Howard Pollio, who said that *language* is a system of symbols governed by rules that describe which symbols are acceptable for use in communication.[1]

Several important ideas about language are suggested in this definition. First, it tells us that language is made up of symbols—that is, words. Second, it implies that the words are abstract, that is, they are not directly related to the objects and experiences they describe. For most of us, there is some relationship between a word and its object, but it may be somewhat different for each person who uses the word. Third, the use of language is governed by rules. We know a great deal about what those around us believe is appropriate language for each particular situation. Part of this knowledge comes from our culture and part from people with whom we communicate.

Language is a system of symbols governed by rules. It is our primary means of expressing ourselves to others.

LANGUAGE AND EXPERIENCE

Language is our primary means of telling others who we are and how we feel about them. We use language both to send and receive this information. We select words that we believe will convey our experience. As we come to understand the other person and his ideas, we attach to those perceptions language that describes what we are sensing. The other person is also using language—perhaps different from ours—to talk and think about his experience.

The language we have acquired is woven into the fabric of our frame of reference. Part of the process of perception entails comparing what we sense to the names we have on file for our experiences. We use the frame of reference and the language that is a part of it to filter, interpret, and shape responses to our experiences. If our frame of reference has limited language to describe feelings and emotions, then our capacity for self-disclosure is similarly limited.

Suppose that a friend comes to you and talks in a tone that you perceive as anger. Perhaps the friend is actually experiencing and attempting to convey frustration. Suppose that "frustration" is not the word you use to label your observations. Instead, you select one that seems to fit your perceptions most closely, in this case, "anger." How do you suppose labeling frustration as anger might affect the relationship? How would this affect your response to your friend? How do you think your frustrated partner would react to being treated as though he were angry?

What one person experiences as frustration may not affect the other person at all.

THE TRIANGLE OF MEANING

Understanding the relationship between the words we use, what they refer to, and our ideas will help us become more aware of what is happening when we communicate our relationships. Charles K. Ogden and I. A. Richards depict this relationship as the *Triangle of Meaning* (figure 4.1).[2]

The *referent* at the lower right corner of the triangle is the subject of our communication. The referent may be a person, object, or event; it also may be a feeling or a want. The referent is the object of our perception and the subject the symbol refers to.

The *thought* at the top of the triangle represents our perception and interpretation of the referent. Our feelings about the referent, past experiences related to it, and other perceptions may also be included. In other words, the thought is a mental image we hold of the referent in our frame of reference.

The lower left corner of the Triangle of Meaning is labeled *symbol.* A symbol stands for something else. In language, words, phrases, and sentences stand for thoughts. We cannot communicate our thoughts directly, so we translate them into language, which is a system of commonly shared symbols.

The arrows in figure 4.1 show the relationships among the elements of the Triangle of Meaning. A solid arrow connects the referent with the thought because the referent acts as a stimulus for the thought. One reason we have a thought is that we perceive a referent. Frequently, our thought is about the referent, but it may also involve something quite apart from what is taking place. For instance, you may be working hard on an assignment when your roommate asks if he or she can get you a cup of tea. Your roommate knows that you enjoy having tea while you work and that it is difficult for you to interrupt your work to make yourself a cup. Your response may be about the cup of tea—the referent in this interaction. But you might

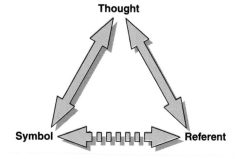

Figure 4.1
The triangle of meaning.
Source: C. K. Ogden and I. A. Richards. The Meaning of Meaning © *1923 Harcourt Brace Jovanovich, New York.*

also respond by saying something like, "You know, I'm really lucky to have a friend like you." This represents a statement of your feelings about your roommate, stimulated by but only remotely connected to the referent.

The reason a relationship exists between the thought and the symbol we use to convey that thought is similar to the reason for the relationship between thought and referent. We use the symbol because we had the thought, and this symbol seems to represent it most conveniently. The symbol, however, does not represent all of the thought, nor does it necessarily represent the thought accurately. We select our symbols to communicate the intended idea as clearly as possible.

The broken arrow connecting the symbol with the referent suggests that these two elements need not correspond at all. There is no direct relationship between the word and the object; the word is not the object, and the symbol is not the referent.

You can understand the relationships illustrated in the triangle by listing your reasons for studying interpersonal communication. They must, inevitably, take the form of symbols. Here are possible answers:

- "To get credits in an interesting subject."
- "Because it's a required course."
- "I heard the teacher was good."
- "I want to improve my relationships."

None of these statements expresses all of your reasons for enrolling in the class. Thus, language only *symbolizes* your reasons and puts them in a form others can understand.

The thought aspect of the Triangle of Meaning includes everything that occurs in our minds when we hear the question or perceive the referent. This includes assumptions, feelings, and reflections making up the frame of reference, as well as physical sensations. These relate to our question about taking this course because the answer is designed to represent some or all of them. Your thoughts also relate to the referent, which in this case is interpersonal communication. You have these thoughts because we gave you the topic to consider.

Remember that there is not necessarily a direct causal relationship between the symbol and the referent. Your reasons for studying interpersonal communication do not stem from interpersonal communication itself. Your words about it are not the same as your experience of it. The thought aspect of the Triangle of Meaning connects the symbol and referent.

Consider another example. If we show you the word "chair," you will think about it and then point to a referent chair. If we show you a chair, you will think about it and then utter the word "chair."

You cannot move from symbol to referent or from referent to symbol without first passing through thought.

All these facts about symbols, thoughts, and referents are especially important in the language we use to describe our relationships. When we describe someone as a "friend," we have chosen this word to summarize thoughts that might have developed over years. Consider the following example of how we use language to symbolize relationships.

George is an important person in Lisa's world. He is her stepfather. Lisa calls him "Dad" when speaking directly to him and "father" when talking about him with others. Their relationship is so close that the term *stepfather* seems inappropriate to Lisa. She describes him by saying, "He cares about me" or "He helps me when I'm down." She recalls their experiences together, elaborating that "he cheered me up when my dog disappeared . . . he really understood what I went through."

If George were your stepfather, you might use labels such as "Dad" or "father," or you might refer to him as George or perhaps a pet name that carries significance only for the two of you. You might find it interesting to recall the experiences that result in our labeling people as "friend," "sister," or "father." Note that the language you use to describe a relationship has a great deal to do with your relational communication.

We have already said that your individual frame of reference influences the way you use and understand language. Another part of that frame that we ought to think about is the cultural dimension. We accumulate language habits and understandings from our experience, and a big part of our experience occurs in a culture or subculture. Some of these represent trivial differences from one region to another in word usage. For instance, in certain regions of the United States, you turn on your VCR by "mashing" the power button, while in other regions, you merely "press" it. However, some *subcultural language* makes a tremendous difference in our relationships. Ethnic subcultures, such as the African-American or Hispanic-American communities, have particular ways of expressing ideas about many aspects of daily life. When we fail to pay attention to these differences, we deny the other person a heritage, something we implicitly acknowledge for ourselves.

THE ABSTRACTION PROCESS

The process of perceiving and making sense of language is called *abstraction*. We use abstraction to translate experience into thought and then into language. John C. Condon explained abstraction as an act of selection.[3] When we attempt to explain our experience of an event or a relationship, many images come to mind. For instance, when we think of "friend," many faces, images, and experiences are evoked. We must select those that will accomplish our purpose. Condon says that we choose by *ignoring* much of what is available to us, by *focusing* on a limited amount of it, and by *combining* or *rearranging* what is left into an expression of our intentions (see figure 4.2).

Figure 4.2
The abstraction
process.

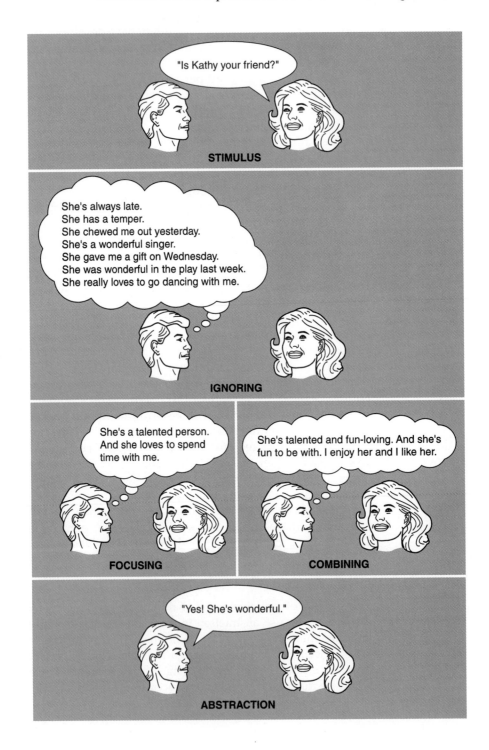

We can describe a relationship on many *levels of abstraction*. Higher levels of abstraction are more general. At these levels, we ignore much of the specific information by focusing less on details. Lower levels of abstraction ignore less by focusing more on specific information.

S. I. Hayakawa offered a useful explanation of how we abstract and how that abstraction relates to language.[4] He said that abstraction is like climbing a ladder. As we climb higher up the ladder, our view of an event changes in several important ways. This affects the language we choose to describe the event. Figure 4.3 illustrates these

Figure 4.3
Content, context, and abstraction.

changes. The higher we climb, the farther we are from the ground, so we can see less detail but more of the surrounding territory. As we climb the abstraction ladder, our ability to relate experience through language is affected similarly. The more abstract our perception of the event, the farther we are from our direct experience of it. Our perception contains much less detail at higher levels. For instance, you might describe getting an A on a tough exam by saying, "That extra study time really paid off—I scored 97 out of 100 and got the highest grade in the class!" At a higher level of abstraction, you might say, "I did better than I usually do on exams." You can see that the lower-level statement is closer to the direct experience of the event and the higher, more general level is much farther.

On the other hand, when we describe an experience from a higher level of abstraction, our perception includes more of the context surrounding the event. That is, it includes information that is not directly related to our experience of the event but helps us understand it.

We can identify four levels of abstraction that we use in our interpersonal communication (see figure 4.4). The *nonverbal level of abstraction* uses no verbal language. It is our direct experience of the other person, and involves our thoughts and perceptions. We communicate at the *naming level of abstraction* when we use language that acknowledges the uniqueness of the other person. Often, calling someone by name brings us to this level. We operate at the *classification level of abstraction* when we think about people in our relationships in terms of the particular group to which they belong. Perhaps the person is a lawyer or a teacher. When we do this, we assign characteristics typical of the group to that individual. At the *inferential level of abstraction,* we use language that suggests broad, often judgmental categories. This level differs from the classification level in that the classification level is descriptive rather than evaluative. Consider how these different levels of abstraction are illustrated in this example.

Kathy is a child psychologist who emphasizes play as a therapeutic aid. Our relationship with Kathy might be described at a number of different levels of abstraction. When we're around her,

Figure 4.4
Abstraction in
relationships .

Inferential Level of Abstraction
Relates a person to broad territory; may be evaluative or judgmental. "Professionals"

Classification Level of Abstraction
Relates a person to a group possessing common characteristics. "Dr. Walker"

Naming Level of Abstraction
Signifies a person as an individual in our world of relationships. "Kathy"

Nonverbal Level of Abstraction
Relates to a person in the immediate experience using sensory data. Our verbal language is inadequate to express this level of abstraction.

our awareness of her presence represents the lowest level of abstractions for relationships. Our perceptions and thoughts about her, our direct experience, cannot be put into words. When we refer to her by name, we move up a level. We recognize her uniqueness and relatedness to us by using her name.

In the presence of others, we might refer to Kathy as Dr. Walker. This represents movement up to the level of classification. While losing some of the uniqueness of our relationship, this language gains information about her "territory." When talking with others outside of her presence, we might refer to her as a professional we know, rather than by her name or title. The word *professional* refers listeners to a few broad characteristics of Kathy and, thus, is at the inferential level. This takes into account the data from our experience of Kathy and is therefore accurate, but it also includes much that is not specific to her. All sorts of people are professionals—lawyers, executives, and college professors. This high level of abstraction tells us less about Kathy than the lower-level abstractions yet serves a communication purpose. Using the appropriate level of abstraction is very important to facilitating communication in relationships because it implies our definition of the relationship as we are seeing it at the moment.

We select levels of abstraction based on how well we know another person—the depth of our experience in the relationship. To use the abstract term *professional* to describe Kathy, we do not have to know her well at all. We have identified four levels we can use to examine our relational communication. These are nonverbal, naming, classification, and inferential. We want you to understand that talking about levels represents our making somewhat arbitrary distinctions. The abstraction ladder is in reality a continuum. The four relationship levels identified here are useful but not rigid. We should exercise care and attention when we talk about relationships. Appropriate abstraction is essential to clear communication.

ABSTRACTION IN RELATIONSHIPS

Levels of abstraction of language are important to relationships in three ways. First, the abstraction level identifies the characteristics of the relationship that we see. This includes not only ways of talking about the relationship but also behaviors that are viewed as appropriate to some degree. For instance, when discussing details of your job with your new supervisor, you may find that your language takes on a very low level of abstraction. However, when talking about personal matters, the level of abstraction may be much higher. Your supervisor might, for example, ask, "How are things at home?" You might reply, "Everything's fine." It is important to use an appropriate level of abstraction in relationships. In the example above, it seems appropriate for the supervisor to inquire about your life at home. A detailed response that was either positive or negative would

Abstraction Ladder

Start reading from the bottom up

Abstraction
ladder. Start
reading from
the bottom up.
*"Abstraction
Ladder" from*
Language in
Thought and
Action, *Fourth
Edition, by S. I.
Hayakawa,
copyright © 1978
by Harcourt
Brace &
Company,
reproduced by
permission of the
publisher.*

8. "wealth"

7. "asset"

6. "farm assets"

5. "livestock"

4. "cow"

3. "Bessie"

2.

8. The word "wealth" is at an extremely high level of abstraction, omitting *almost* all reference to the characteristics of Bessie.

7. When Bessie is referred to as an "asset," still more of her characteristics are left out.

6. When Bessie is included among "farm assets," reference is made only to what she has in common with all other salable items on the farm.

5. When Bessie is referred to as "livestock," only those characteristics she has in common with pigs, chickens, goats, etc., are referred to.

4. The word "cow" stands for the characteristics we have abstracted as common to cow_1, cow_2, $cow_3 \ldots cow_n$. Characteristics peculiar to specific cows are left out.

3. The word "Bessie" (cow_1) is the *name* we give to the object of perception of level 2. The name *is not* the object; it merely *stands for* the object and omits reference to many of the characteristics of the object.

2. The cow we perceive is not the word, but the object of experience, that which our nervous system abstracts (selects) from the totality that consitutes the process-cow. Many of the characteristics of the process-cow are left out.

1. The cow known to science ultimately consists of atoms, electrons, etc., according to present-day scientific inference. Characteristics (represented by circles) are infinite at this level and ever-changing. This is the *process level*.

be inappropriate, given the level of the question. The nature of your relationship with your supervisor suggests a more abstract response.

Second, the abstractness of the language used in a relationship indicates our view of its depth and intensity. We tend to use less abstract terms of endearment, such as *dear* and *honey,* with those to whom we are close. In less intense relationships, we tend to use more abstract, general terms, such as *sir, ma'am,* and *professor.* When Dr. Stevens called the roll for the first time in his class, he asked students to tell him if they had another name that they preferred, such as Fred instead of Frederick. One student, Tom, said that he preferred to be called "Studpuppy." Dr. Stevens and the other students in the class realized that this name was probably not appropriate to their relationship with Tom. After one embarrassing day of being called "Studpuppy" by both the teacher and his fellow students, Tom also realized this and requested that everyone call him "Tom."

Third, the level of language abstraction used by one partner to talk about a relationship is similar to some degree to that used by the other partner. As relationships grow, partners may find themselves using similar language to describe their feelings. For example, when John is upset, he frequently says, "I have a problem, here," and then describes the situation. A little while after John started dating Sue, she was using similar language.

As a relationship grows, partners may find themselves using similar language to describe their feelings.

The more the two descriptions reflect similar levels of abstraction, the more the partners can sensibly talk with one another about their relationship. For example, Sue might say to John, "Are you happy with the way things are going in this relationship?" He might respond, "We go to the symphony together, and we talk about interesting things." Then Sue might say, "Yes, but are you happy with the relationship?" They are not communicating at similar levels of abstraction. Perhaps John should think about the relationship more abstractly, while Sue should lower her level of abstraction somewhat. Then they could both discuss their satisfaction with the same aspects of the relationship.

Language provides a set of symbols that we use to transmit our thoughts to others. Experiences of people, events, and objects are reconstructed in a symbolic form that becomes talk about those experiences. The words we choose to represent the idea we intend to communicate vary in terms of abstraction level. The more abstract our language, the farther we are from direct experience, the more territory our language covers, and the fewer specific details are included in our messages. Now compound the problem—as it is compounded in every relationship. While the complex process of abstracting is going on inside us, it is also going on inside the person with whom we are talking. Thus when we interact, we are truly living in a world of words. Figure 4.5 makes this problem clear. We have turned the abstraction ladders of two people sideways to show their interaction. Notice how far the talk of each individual is from their mutual experience.

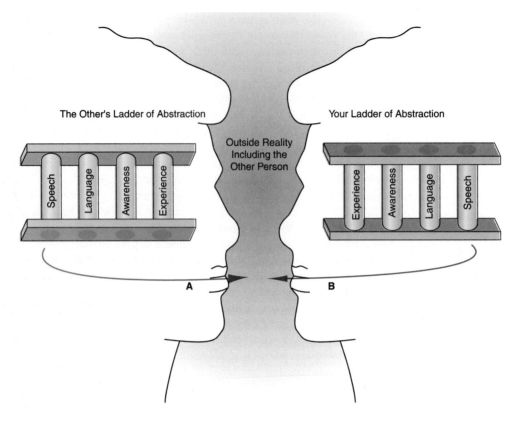

Figure 4.5
Levels of
abstraction in a
relationship.

LANGUAGE AND RELATIONSHIPS

Our relationships are related to our language in three important ways: (1) The relationship limits our choice of symbols. (2) The nature of the relationship affects the meaning of certain symbols. (3) The language we choose reflects our view of the relationship.

Using Language in Relationships

Every time we communicate about a relationship, we find ourselves faced with choices about what language to use. We select the language that seems appropriate to the particular relationship, which varies according to the roles we assign and take, our shared experiences, and the depth of intimacy.

The roles we and others take determine the language available for our use in a particular conversation. Consider the language we might use in describing a strong commitment in a romantic relationship. We might use the words "sharing," "love," "caring," and perhaps even "forever" when talking to another person. As we communicate our intentions to friends or parents, we may feel more comfortable with a different word, such as "serious," "comfortable," or even "compatible." We may be trying to convey similar feelings about our commitment in each case, but we find that the role of lover demands a different menu of words than the role of friend or son or daughter.

What we and the other person have experienced in a relationship also affects our choice of *symbols*. For example, if you wanted to talk with a classmate about interpersonal communication, you would feel comfortable using terms learned in class. You might discuss "abstractions," "improving disclosure," or "the need to control." But in talking about interpersonal communication with someone who has not studied it—that is, a person who has not shared your experience—you would find your symbols more limited and more abstract.

The depth or intimacy of a relationship is a third aspect that affects the language availability for communication. In a more intimate relationship, we have more words for our ideas and are willing to share more fully. Suppose you have been trying to get to know your new boss for some time, but he has remained aloof, detached, and rather formal. Today you experienced a breakthrough and had a long discussion about the goals and expectations that you each hold for one another. You feel really good about this and cannot help smiling to yourself and others for the rest of the day. One of your coworkers notices your apparent satisfaction and inquires about your good mood. You might respond by saying, "I'm having a really good day . . . things are really falling into place for me." When you return home at the end of the day and respond to a similar question from your spouse, you might say instead, "George and I really got down to business today. We had a long talk, and I think we really understand one another better because of it!" In the first instance, the relatively low intensity of your relationship with your coworker does not lead to an extended discussion of your happiness. The language available is thus more limited and more general. In talking with your spouse, however, the greater intimacy of your relationship permits the use of language not only to describe the event but also to comment on its meaning and your feelings about it.

> Three aspects of our relationships influence the language we use in them: the roles we assign and take, our shared experiences, and the depth of intimacy.

DENOTATIVE AND CONNOTATIVE MEANINGS IN RELATIONSHIPS

Denotative meanings, or the common, dictionary meanings of words, are a part of all messages. These meanings usually do not include the context of the communication or information about the relationship between the communicators.

Sometimes we may want to stress the denotative meanings of words, as when we give instructions to someone at work. We want to be as clear and specific as possible to assure that the task is properly done. Denotative meanings are also important when we are reporting an event because they allow the receiver of our message to judge its meaning or significance correctly without the cues that knowing us might provide about meaning. In both these instances, we want to be as clear as possible, so we use specific, unambiguous language. We describe the event at the lowest level of abstraction.

Another sort of meaning takes the listener beyond the denotational level. *Connotative meanings* are our personal meanings for words derived from our experience. They are influenced by the message, the person talking, the subject of the conversation, and even the environment in which it takes place.

Table 4.1 illustrates connotative meanings. The left column displays the conversation. The connotative meanings—what each individual might be thinking—are displayed in the right column. Of course, these are only some of the possible meanings that might have been assigned in this conversation. What judgments do you see implied here? What does each person seem to believe about the subject of the conversation? What are their views of each other? What difference could environment have made in their connotative meanings? For example, what if the conversation had taken place in the teacher's office? In a classroom after class? In the university center, in front of the student's friends?

Table 4.1	Connotative Meanings
Speaker's statement	*Listener's thoughts (connotative meaning)*
Teacher: You know, a course in statistics might be really helpful for you, especially if you're planning to go on to graduate school.	*Student:* He wants to see me take a statistics course. He thinks everyone who goes to graduate school should have it.
Student: Well, I really hadn't thought about it, but now that you mention it, maybe I'll try it next term.	*Teacher:* He's interested. I should encourage him.
Teacher: I've been looking at your work, and it seems to me you'd do well at the graduate level. Do you have any interest in that?	*Student:* I'm surprised that a teacher would show this much interest in a student. It is flattering to hear this. I wonder if I really could handle graduate work.
Student: Do you really think so? I honestly don't know much about graduate school. How would I afford it?	*Teacher:* He is interested but doesn't realize how talented he is.
Teacher: Why don't we go over to my office? I can show you some materials, and we can talk more about it.	*Student:* He wants to get to know me better. He wants to help me along. I like that.

Because people do not always say what they intend in a way that we can understand, it is very important to be aware of the potential for misunderstanding connotative meaning. You can help yourself become better at listening for the intended meaning by practicing the listening skills presented in Chapter 7.

People do not always say what they intend.

Our relationships play an important role in determining the connotations we find in conversations. Just as roles and the nature and intensity of the relationship influence our choice of language, these same factors affect our decisions about meaning.

Influences on Connotation

While it is clear that connotation is a product of the way information is handled by our frame of reference, several factors seem to stand out as influential in assigning meaning. These are roles, gender, relational depth, and relational function (see figure 4.6).

Roles affect connotation quite directly. The same words might mean different things to various people, depending on their roles in a relationship, as the following example shows.

Margaret is a senior communication major taking her last few classes before graduation. The courses she needs are offered only at night, so she is out of the mainstream of activity that normally brings her together with other communication majors. One evening she is sitting in the lobby of a classroom building during a break, as are another student and her teacher, Dr. Garcia. She sees Dr. Adams, one of her favorite professors from past terms, passing through the lobby. Margaret has often sought his advice and support. She

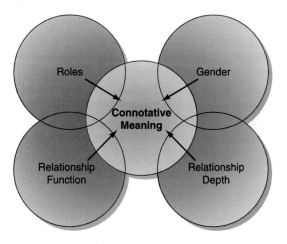

Figure 4.6
Influences on
connotation .

exchanges greetings with him, and then Margaret says, "I have all my classes at night this term, and I never get a chance to see anyone anymore. It's like there's no one to talk with."

Now let's see how the roles of the people involved affect the connotative meaning in this situation. Margaret is in the role of student in a relationship with Dr. Garcia, her new teacher. She also has a relationship with Dr. Adams, but their roles might be better described as friends. Margaret also has a relationship with the other student, which is that of a colleague or perhaps a coworker. Now consider how the connotations might vary for each role. To Dr. Adams, Margaret might sound lonely, saying, "I miss you. Please spend some time with me." Dr. Garcia might think she means, "I don't like night classes." The other student might hear her saying, "I don't feel I can talk with these people." On the other hand, Margaret's words might remind the student of a similar relationship. In this case, she might hear something such as "I like you, Dr. Adams" and then go on to think about how she likes working with her own advisor.

The response that Margaret gets from Dr. Adams will relate to the connotative meaning he associated with her message. Even though the message was intended for someone else, Dr. Garcia's interpretation could influence his future interactions with Margaret. The same is true for the other student.

Roles influence the connotative, or personal, meanings we assign to language. We must consider roles and choose language that will address the range of connotations appropriate to the existing relationships.

Gender also influences the meanings we assign. The impact of gender on many aspects of the communication process is increasingly of interest to communication researchers. Many of the research findings are limited by culture and situation. Another limiting factor in gender communication research is that gender is also a role variable. That is, the physical classification of people as male and female must be accompanied by their classification as actors on a continuum of gender-related communication styles. These range from masculine to feminine, with a style termed *androgynous* marking the center point. People, regardless of physical gender, adopt behavior patterns that fall anywhere along that continuum. That is, you will find men who exhibit feminine styles and women who exhibit masculine styles. The androgynous style, which might be adopted by men or women, represents a blend of masculine and feminine characteristics.

Having listed the limitations of research on gender and communication, we can still note some fairly consistent findings. Men and women do seem to differ in their motivation to communicate, their style of communication, and in the content of their communication.[5] Men often report social reasons for communicating, such as comradery or collegiality. Women report initiating communication in order to seek empathy and understanding, reasons that seem more personal or interpersonal in nature. The style of expression among women has been rated by researchers as more inquiring and aesthetic, compared with the more dynamic, aggressive style observed among men. The subjects addressed by males in same-sex conversations seem more external. Men talk about business, sports, and current events with one another more often than they do with women or than women do among other women. Women, on the other hand, tend to address more internal matters when engaged in same-sex conversations. They talk about relationships and personal experiences. Although few men and women typify all these differences, you can see that communication between genders poses certain difficulties. Motive, preferred subjects, and style all represent variables that might influence connotation. You might understand a message differently based upon the reason you think the message has been sent. Care must be taken when communicating with a person of the opposite sex to understand the differences along these lines. For instance, suppose John characterizes the research findings for men, and Beth does so for the findings about women. John wants to talk about current affairs because he likes talking about them—he finds it socially engaging to argue about politics. Beth, on the other hand, prefers to talk about their relationship and to do so rather deeply. They must both acknowledge these differences as they listen. Otherwise, each will feel, connotatively, that the other is uninterested in the relationship.

The androgynous style represents a blend of masculine and feminine characteristics.

Connotation also depends on the *function of a relationship* for its members. These functions include utility, stimulation, ego support, affirmation, and security. We listen to one another in the context of these relationship functions, and we understand what is said to us in these contexts. Our relationships may grow beyond these initial functions with experience and in different situations. As we do this, we become accustomed to our partner's language and the intended connotations. You might have a friend, for example, who often compliments you, frequently using very affectionate language. The meaning you attribute to this person's language and intentions are connotative and depend somewhat on the breadth of your relationship. You might hear these remarks as romantic overtures if you have had only limited contact with the individual. On the other hand, with wider experience of this person, you might learn that such terms of endearment are only a way of expressing admiration and a desire for friendship. We must be careful about attributing connotative meanings based on limited experience.

Likewise, the *depth of a relationship* greatly affects connotative meaning. The better we get to know our partners, even in a single context, the better we can correctly understand their intentions. Sometimes people in relationships of great depth can talk with each other at a "relational level" about one issue while using language that is connotatively different in meaning to others.

The case of Jim and his big celebration provides an example of this phenomenon. After a number of difficult years in his new advertising business, Jim had a very good year. He decided to give a huge champagne party for all his friends as a way of thanking them for their support. Changes in the location, several caterers, and many other problems plagued the planning of the party. Jim confided in his close friend Martha throughout, and she supported and encouraged him as he organized the event. When the day came and the party was in full swing, Martha arrived. She looked Jim over carefully and said, "Why Jim, you look wonderful . . . very relaxed. How are you?" Jim smiled, saying, "I'm fine, and thank you, Martha. Everything seems to be under control. I'm glad you could come." Martha responded, "I just knew this would turn out to be a lovely party. Do you think you can hold things together here? I want to mingle for a bit." Other partygoers might hear connotations of affection in this exchange, but for Jim and Martha, this conversation was about the trials and tribulations leading up to this event. The connotative affection is there, and beyond that are expressions of caring, gratitude, and even teasing that only Jim and Martha can understand.

It is important to pay attention to the connotations that are unique to relationships, for otherwise much of the meaning in your interactions might be lost. The more involvement you have with another person, the more likely you are to share such relational connotations.

LANGUAGE AND OUR VIEW OF RELATIONSHIPS

The third way language contributes to the growth of our relationships deals with our view of those relationships. This view includes our sense of self in the relationship, the way we see the other person, and our role expectations. In examining our sense of self in relationships, we talk about *self-disclosure*. In thinking about how we see others, we consider *naming*. In studying role expectations in relationships, the concepts of *complementarity* and *symmetricality* are discussed.

Language Expresses and Reveals the Self

Self-disclosure is the use of language to reveal information about ourselves to others. Our language reveals how we see ourselves and how we would like others to see us. Certain language clues are used intentionally. For instance, a child who is lonely may scream as though hurt to get our attention. Consider the following examples of intentional self-expression:

- "I can't do math."
- "I like going out on the town."
- "If I were you, I'd lay it on the line."

These are all direct statements about a person's view of herself. They may have been made to the self or to someone else. What images of this person do you get from these statements?

From Roy Paul Nelson, The Design of Advertising, *Seventh Edition. Copyright © 1994 Wm. C. Brown Communications, Inc., Dubuque, Iowa. All Rights Reserved. Reprinted by permission.*

We use such statements to define what we are and are not willing to do. Sometimes we allow them to become rules that we feel obliged to defend. However, we limit the possible range of our experiences and relationships when we do this. But even when this does happen, such statements still represent intentional messages about how we see ourselves and would like to be seen.

Some language reveals information about our self-concepts in more subtle ways. Listeners may draw conclusions about the way we see ourselves by noticing the frequency with which we talk about certain things or use certain metaphors in describing our experiences. Both of these ways of communicating the self-concept are often conducted unintentionally.

We discuss certain ideas or subjects more frequently than others because they hold some special importance to us. Joseph, for example, tends to respond in conversations using monetary terms. On seeing a new car, he might try to guess its value. Once, after spending a good deal of time waiting to see a customer service representative at a local utility company, he conveyed his irritation by sending the company a bill for his time. If others want to be sure Joseph hears them, all they have to do is listen for a money-oriented response or phrase their message in financial language. Having an idea about what the person believes is important thus helps us select language that conveys our intended meaning.

Anthony Athos and John Gabarro suggest that the language we use in conversation reveals something about all aspects of our self-concept.[6] They encourage the use of active listening techniques as a way of seeking out information about the self-concepts of our partners in relationships. As we listen more to people talking about themselves—either implicitly or explicitly—we find it easier to bring growth to our relationships.

Listening carefully to the language we use to describe our experiences may reveal some consistency among the metaphors chosen and thus suggest what we consider important. If, for example, you place a high value on promptness, you may unconsciously include references to time in your conversations. We frequently use figurative language that is based in things that are important to us but that may be unknown to the people with whom we're talking.

The language we use in everyday conversation also reveals much about us. In fact, we sometimes intentionally choose language to create certain impressions about ourselves. For example, at job interviews, we carefully select language that will clearly convey the contributions we believe we can make to a company.

Our goals, priorities, and assumptions can also be revealed by the style of our nonverbal communication, such as the loudness or softness that we give certain words, the rate at which we speak, and our facial and body expressions. For example, Lavar graduated *magna cum laude* from a distinguished university, and he is very proud of this fact. When he talks with his coworkers or friends and

Our language tells others about our self-concepts, attitudes, beliefs and values, and feelings about our relationships.

the subject of education or credentials comes up, he unknowingly communicates his pride by sitting up straighter and assuming a more authoritative tone. He does this even if his particular credentials are unknown and unmentioned in the group. People talking with Lavar in this situation, though, leave believing he must know something about the subject.

Naming in Relationships

We communicate our view of the partners in our relationships through a process called *naming*, or the assignment of labels to these people. When we characterize a person as a friend, for example, we are naming. Examine the names you use when referring to people in your relationships and when talking directly to them. Thinking about how they are similar and different can help you understand how you see the other person and what you still need to know about him. The names we use at a given moment convey our perception of the other person and also affect that perception.

John C. Condon observed that people tend to notice those things for which they have names.[7] They also tend not to see those things for which they have no names. Our relationships exemplify this principle. The names we have for people are part of our frame of reference, the filter through which we perceive others. We are naming when we assign language to describe our beliefs, values, and attitudes. We tend to notice, recognize, and acknowledge those people whose names we know more than those whose names we do not know. Likewise, we tend to notice those behaviors and characteristics that fit the names we have for people, while sometimes ignoring those actions that are inconsistent with those names.

Symmetry and Complementarity in Relationships

Our expectation of the roles in a relationship is also important to our selection of language. Dennis R. Smith and L. Keith Williamson explained that each of us has a view of every relationship that suggests the perceived status of the other person.[8] The view is *symmetrical* when we see ourselves as equal partners and *complementary* when we see ourselves as in some way unequal to the other person. The complementary view is sometimes characterized as feeling "one up" or "one down" in a relationship.

Our language reflects our view of the relationship, either complementary or symmetrical. When our view is symmetrical, our language might be more "we" oriented, with clear indications that control of the relationship is shared. Our relationships with friends and classmates are typically symmetrical. Classmates usually have the same responsibilities in the course and thus share a common and equal basis for the relationship. A friendship might also be symmetrical when there is an expectation that each partner will contribute equally to its growth.

Relationships between parents and children are frequently viewed as complementary, as are teacher-student relationships. In such relationships, the language used in conversations will indicate that one of the participants has more responsibility than the other for determining their direction, goals, and growth. For instance, consider the language in the following dialogue that took place after class one day:

> *Dr. Penny:* Jim, please stay for a minute. I'd like to talk with you.
>
> *Jim:* Yes, Dr. Penny?
>
> *Dr. Penny:* Jim, you're doing very well in this class. Are you doing equally well in your other classes?
>
> *Jim:* Well, this is my best class, but I'm keeping up in the others also.
>
> *Dr. Penny:* You may have heard that we're starting an honors program. A group of interested students are getting together in the seminar room to discuss it with me and the other participating faculty. You're welcome to join us.

In this conversation, Dr. Penny controls the goals and direction of the conversation and the relationship. She calls Jim by his first name, but Jim refers to her more formally as Dr. Penny. When Dr. Penny asks about his other classes, Jim responds immediately with this private information. (If the relationship were perceived by both as symmetrical, Jim might have said, "Why do you ask?") Dr. Penny asks Jim for what is, in effect, a closer relationship by inviting him to the honors meeting. The invitation carries with it more contact and an introduction to Dr. Penny's colleagues.

Problems can arise when our language reflects different views of a relationship.[9] For example, how would you characterize the following communication between two classmates, one of whom views the relationship as symmetrical while the other views it as complementary?

> *Anitra:* Hey, Joe, are you free tonight? I thought we might work on that project together.
>
> *Joe:* Let me see . . . . No, can't do it tonight, but I can give you Friday. Tell you what, you go ahead and get it roughed out, and then when we meet Friday, we'll have something to work from.

Anitra: I really think we should work on the basics together, Joe. We're going to have to share the outcome. We should each get in our ideas at the beginning.

Joe: OK, fine, Anitra, but you're going to have to type it up . . . . I don't have the time for that kind of work.

In this conversation, Anitra is struggling to maintain the equality that she perceives in the relationship. Joe, on the other hand, sees himself as "one up." He expects Anitra to adjust to his schedule and to do what he considers the less important parts of the task. Their different perspectives of the relationship could bring them into conflict. Before they will get much work done, they are going to have to make some agreement about the nature of their relationship.

How do you think communication between a husband and wife might sound if both viewed the relationship as complementary but each saw the other person as "one down"?

In both these instances, as well as in other combinations of the two views, a third party listening to the conversation might get the impression that the two people talking do not know one another very well or that they do not like one another very much. To avoid this, we need to listen for language that tells us about the other's view of our relationship. We have a responsibility to talk with our partner if what we hear evokes images that are different from our own. We need to clarify our own view, to work at understanding the view of the other person, and to arrive at language that expresses some agreement about who we each are in the relationship.

INDISCRIMINATION WITH LANGUAGE

Language is our principal tool for achieving relational growth. It is so important that the correct use of language has been associated with our basic well-being: we feel better about ourselves and our relationships when we are using language appropriately. Robert Alberti and Michael Emmons are quoted as saying that assertive language and behavior relate directly to our mental health.[10] This is also true for other aspects of language, including the level and flexibility of the words we choose. Alfred Korzybski said that attention to these and other aspects of language can provide a measure of sanity.[11] The noted language scholar S. I. Hayakawa summarized Korzybski's definition of "sanity" as follows:

> The sane individual, he said, does not confuse levels of abstraction; he does not treat the map as if it were the territory; he does not copy animals in their reactions, and therefore is not a dogmatist, or a categorist (the pun is Korzybski's, not mine); he does not treat as identical all things that have the same name; he does not exhibit

a two-valued orientation in which absolute good is pitted against absolute evil. . . .[12]

This definition clearly identifies several language skills that Hayakawa and Korzybski believe are important. Problems with these areas of language use include treating all things with the same name as though they are the same, confusing words and the things they represent, and thinking of and describing our experiences in terms of opposites. When we have difficulty using language, relationship problems inevitably result. And as long as such problems persist, growth is hindered. This section will help you learn to use language effectively by adopting techniques that allow you to avoid these difficulties.

Our language provides categories for the things in our world to help us move through a world in which everything is different. We operate in our relationships and make decisions about our world using these categories. We are *indiscriminate* with our language when we place people or things into categories without carefully examining who or what they are and whether they actually fit into the category. Indiscriminate use of categories is one of the most frequent problems in relational communication. When it affects others, we call the behavior *stereotyping*. When it is applied to ourselves, it takes the form of a *self-fulfilling prophecy*.

Stereotyping

People and relationships are unique. The communication difficulties that result when we ignore their uniqueness affect not only the people involved in an interaction but also the relationship itself. Ignoring the uniqueness of people to the point where we make judgments about them on the basis of some category is called *stereotyping*.

Wendell Johnson is often quoted as saying, "To a mouse, cheese is cheese, that's why mousetraps work."[13] He was saying that because expectations are often not questioned, the uniqueness of a situation is frequently missed. You may have heard this same idea applied to people or relationships:

- "What did you expect? Women are like that."
- "Hey, what can I do? Business is business."
- "You men are all alike. You never pay any attention to the details."
- "I'll have to turn down your offer to introduce the guest of honor. I'd get up and make a fool of myself."

We frequently create traps for ourselves when we choose language carelessly. We react to people as representing a class rather than themselves. We ignore their individuality and miss the opportunity for genuine communication. This is damaging to relationships because we think of our partner as a category of person rather than a unique person. We limit opportunities for new contacts, new experiences, and new or improved relationships when we talk in these ways.

Stereotyping is the act of taking ideas about a group and applying them to a member of that group without seeing whether they actually describe that person. You are probably aware of ethnic or racial stereotyping. You may even have witnessed sexual and age stereotyping. When actions based on stereotyping are widespread, as in these cases, the resulting problems are both interpersonal and societal.

We will consider stereotyping in more personal terms. A relationship is most meaningful when we can really know and deal with someone as an individual. However, it is difficult to appreciate the person fully when your frame of reference is based on a stereotype. Sometimes the stereotype will not be evident in our language but will influence our responses. Consider the following example.

Mark holds certain ideas about older, retired people that affect his expectations of them in conversation. "They're always talking about the 'good old days,'" he says. "They don't really know what it's like in today's world." Imagine the difficulty he experienced when he found his film history class heavily populated with retirees participating in the university's College for Seniors Program.

Stereotyping is common and even beneficial in the early stages of a relationship. It is useful in finding things to talk about with people we would like to know better. We can draw inferences about them, based on stereotypes, that give us topics to explore. We then check out these inferences as we communicate and, based on our findings, build a relationship by comparing and contrasting the person's uniqueness with those stereotypes.

If, for example, we meet a university student, we might guess that the person is interested in the music that students generally enjoy. We test this inference and then expand on it by being more concrete in our talk as we learn about the particular tastes of our partner and share our own. The stereotype thus serves as a basis for engaging the other person.

Self-Fulfilling Prophecy

Stereotyping influences our relationships in another, more indirect way. Sometimes we form an image of a person based on a stereotype and then select language to predict who that person is and what will happen to us. That image may be so real to us that we respond to our predictions rather than to the events themselves. In other words, we act to make our predictions come true. We have created a *self-fulfilling prophecy* by which we ignore our own individuality, as well as the uniqueness of others. Telling ourselves, for example, that we cannot speak before a group of people may lead us to turn down opportunities that might benefit us or, if we do perform, our self-fulfilling prophecy may cause us to perform below

our ability. Research suggests that speakers who feel anxious about giving speeches seem to create a self-fulfilling prophecy about doing poorly that causes them to, in fact, perform less effectively.[14]

Self-fulfilling prophecies also may interfere with the way we act. Telling ourselves, for example, that we are not good at solving problems may lead us to put more energy into rationalizing a poor job instead of carefully analyzing the problem. This self-deception can reinforce the label "not good at solving problems" because we frequently do not notice that we devoted much of our time to creating language that explains our failure. We may believe that we are spending that time trying to solve the problem. Thus, the next time we have to solve a problem, we still have a negative label and, even worse, we have had a recent experience that supports it. As we communicate this to others, we teach them stereotypes of ourselves that contribute to their view of us and may affect their relationships with us. In this instance, when a group problem-solving assignment is given, we may not be sought out by those with whom we would like to work, for they have heard and believed the stereotype that we have promoted through language choices.

Self-fulfilling prophecy can extend to our social rejection. One study found subjects who were sensitive to social rejection had a tendency to expect rejection. They perceived it where it may not have existed and overreacted to their exaggerated perception in ways that jeopardized the quality of their relationship.[15]

The solution to the self-fulfilling prophecy begins with understanding its nature. A self-fulfilling prophecy can only involve something over which we have some control. Remember, we make the prediction and influence events as we communicate about that prediction. If you say, "It will snow Friday," your prediction may or may not come true. There is nothing you can do to influence the outcome. If, on the other hand, you say, "Boy, you're going to be angry with me," you can do a good deal to make this happen or prevent it.

Once we understand that we can control how we describe the state of our relationships, we can choose not to participate in negative fantasies. We then have to create language that presents ourselves and our relationships in new, positive, and realistic ways and work to carry out the behaviors suggested. In the problem-solving example, we must say something such as, "I know I did not do well on my last assignment, but I'm not going to let that get in the way. I know what I did wrong, and I'm going to be careful to avoid making those same mistakes. I'm going to use my last decision-making assignment to improve myself, not as an excuse for another failure. And if I don't do well this time, it will be because of what I did this time, not because of who I am."

The point to keep in mind is that both we and our relationships change. Our language needs to reflect this idea, too. We can use a concept called *indexing* to help us. An index is a mental subscript that reminds us that we and our relationship are changing. We might think of our relationship$_1$ and our relationship$_2$. The index reminds us that we are really talking about a changing relationship.

> A self-fulfilling prophecy can only involve something over which we have some control.

PROBLEMS WITH INFLEXIBLE LANGUAGE

As our relationships grow, our definitions of them must keep pace. Hayakawa pointed out that problems can result when this does not happen.[16] The names that we choose for ourselves and our relationships may "harden" or become fixed. As a result, we come to believe that (1) other definitions must be wrong and (2) we need to protect ourselves and our relationships from experiences that challenge these names. Sometimes this inflexibility takes the form of *rigidity in naming*, when we do not allow our descriptions to change with the people or things they describe. Other times, our judgments and evaluations of people and things become fixed. When this happens, we call the problem *static evaluation*. Hayakawa explained this problem as it relates to the language we use to describe ourselves:

> When the self-concept is thus rigidified, it may remain unchanged for a while. Trouble arises from the fact that the self will not stay put. The self slips away from the self-concept: the individual's ideas about himself

become less and less real as time goes on. In other words, it may originally have been true that the man was the best salesman in the company, but as time goes on and the facts of life change, it will require more and more self-delusion on his part to maintain his self-concept.[17]

Rigidity in Naming

Rigidity also occurs in relationships, as this example of Bart and Tina illustrates. Throughout their twenty-year marriage, Bart's view of their relationship has been dominated by a traditional stereotype about the place of women. About six years ago, Tina decided she wanted to go to college. Bart encouraged her because he viewed "the wife taking classes" as a way for her to get out of the house, a diversion. Tina was very good in school and managed to complete her degree in six years, while juggling housekeeping and child care. She increasingly called on Bart to manage some of the household affairs as she became involved in her studies. Bart helped but grumbled about it, thinking that if his help would allow Tina to finish school and get back into the home sooner, it was worth the effort. He did not alter his view of their relationship, even though its realities were changing. Tina is now talking about graduate school. Bart is flabbergasted: "How can she do this?" He does not recognize what has happened. If they are to be happy, they need to communicate in ways that more accurately convey how they and their relationship are changing and how they can channel these new goals and events into something positive for them both.

Static Evaluation

Static evaluation is very similar to rigidity in naming. This is when we form a judgment about someone or something and fail to change the evaluation in light of other experiences. In fact, we will use the static evaluation we have incorporated into our frame of reference as a part of the interpretation process. This makes changing our attitudes toward others very difficult. For instance, Marcus had a difficult encounter with Latashia several years ago, when she was new on the job. Ever since, each time he has heard someone praising Latashia, he discounts what they tell him about her, saying, "Well, in my experience, she's very difficult to work with." He avoids situations where he may have contact with her and otherwise refuses to allow a relationship to form. His static evaluation has prevented him from seeing that she has become more experienced and capable.

The consequences can be very unpleasant when both parties hold outdated definitions of the relationship. One couple we know remained married for at least five years after the relationship was actually over. Their need to hold an unchanging definition of the relationship led them to pretend that it was working and to communicate as though things were fine. They might have been able to salvage their marriage if they had recognized the problem earlier and, perhaps with professional help, addressed it. The relationship met a tragic end because they recognized only one definition and failed to see that they might have used other, more appropriate definitions.

We must realize that we, our partners, and our relationships all grow and change. We must work to find ways to describe what is really happening, even if we do not like the direction of this growth. Remaining anchored in past views of a relationship will diminish our effectiveness in it. The way to achieve definitions that keep pace with growth is to seek new language to describe our relationship and to communicate frequently about how each partner sees it and its future.

> To keep pace with the constant changes in a relationship, seek new language to describe it and talk about it often.

One way to guard against static evaluations is to try to date your statements and evaluations. *Dating* ideas reminds you that the statement or evaluation is a past-tense event and can prompt you to reevaluate based on current information.

Reification

Reification is treating a symbol as if it were a real thing—an object we can manipulate. Ideas like democracy, friendship, and love have many associations but do not exist in and of themselves. They become reified when we try to find things that correspond to them. We are fooling ourselves when we manipulate the objects associated with these ideas and think that we are changing the ideas. For example, Rekha recently had an idea about the way her company could offer adequate day care for the children of its employees. She expressed her idea as a written proposal, which she showed to her coworkers. At this point, reification took over. As her coworkers made suggestions about how her idea might be improved, Rekha viewed their efforts as denials of her idea and to some extent of herself. She had taken an idea, determined that her plan defined that idea, and decided that any change in her plan was a change in the goal. Her stubbornness resulted in a lack of support for the proposal, even though it was a good idea.

We also do this in relationships. Bart, in the case above, decided that they no longer had a real marriage when Tina began behaving in ways that did not fit his definition. The ideal marriage was reified by Bart. John Condon clarified this problem when he wrote, "The problems of reification are especially common when the terms are preceded by adjectives such as *real* or *pure* or *true* or *essential*. There is no such thing as true love, there is only love. There is no essential man, there are only men, and so on."[18]

When we reify something, we treat the symbol as if it were a real thing—an object we can manipulate.

Another aspect of reification is *possessing the symbol.* We sometimes come to believe that by owning something that symbolizes an idea, we become that idea. Phil, for example, wanted to be recognized as a runner. He believed that the way to do this was to acquire all the things runners have—special shoes and clothing, timing devices, and volumes of information on the subject. But he will not *be* a runner until he starts running. We frequently use things to symbolize relationships. This is all right if the purpose of the things is to remind us of the relationship and how we value it. The problem occurs when we come to believe that the fate of things is the fate of the relationship. We understood Karen's reluctance to part with her dead husband's possessions. However, when we went to dinner at her house and found a place set at the table for him, we began to suspect that the things were serving as more than a reminder: Karen refused to acknowledge her husband's death. She was keeping him by keeping his things. This extreme situation shows just how unhealthy this problem can become. Karen is now fine after much counseling, but her reification of the symbols held her down for quite some time.

Such concepts as power, love, and sensuality do not result from our owning the objects that sometimes represent them. These artifacts do have communicative significance, but we must constantly remind ourselves that symbols *are not the things they represent* and that *possession of the thing is not the same as possessing the quality for which it stands.*

Polarization, Two-Valued Orientation, and Disconfirmation

The term *polarization* describes our tendency to use language that occurs in pairs of opposites. We describe our experiences as good or bad, old or new, black or white, and so on. When we rely too heavily on such language, we encourage a way of thinking in which there are only two options. This *two-valued orientation* limits our ability to see the options that may exist. For example, you may enjoy seeing very friendly relationships among your subordinates but do not know what to think of Emilio. Emilio does his job but *never* socializes with his coworkers. He does not come to company-sponsored social events or parties given by his colleagues. When work is slow, he does not join with coworkers as they relax; he keeps to himself. Some of your employees have begun to complain about Emilio, calling him "stiff" and "difficult to get along with." In the meantime, Emilio has become even more withdrawn. One two-valued orientation might suggest that you fire Emilio. After all, either you get along on the job or not, and Emilio does not. Another two-valued orientation would have you tell your employees to leave him alone and do their jobs. After all, you either do the job or not, and Emilio does.

> Polarization encourages a way of thinking in which there are only two possibilities.

The two-valued orientation surfaces in polarized language. We talk about problems, relationships, and feelings about ourselves in extreme terms. We limit the kinds of relationships we can have when we use this language to define them, since our two-valued orientation dictates that the other person *must* be wrong when we disagree. This orientation can result in rejection—we are unwilling to accept the other's view—or disconfirmation—we dismiss the other's view as unimportant or insignificant. Thus, this orientation can be either rejecting or disconfirming as we present our view in such a way that it denies the other's view or the person. Joseph DeVito provides examples of how we can engage in confirming, instead of disconfirming, talk. We display these ideas in table 4.2.

Table 4.2   Confirming and Disconfirming Communication Behaviors

Confirmation	*Disconfirmation*
1. Acknowledge the presence of the other verbally or nonverbally and acknowledge the contributions of the other by either supporting or taking issue with what the other says.	1. Ignore the presence of the other and ignore what the other says; appear indifferent to the person and to what he or she says.
2. Make nonverbal contact by maintaining direct eye contact, touching, hugging, kissing, and otherwise demonstrating acknowledgement of the other.	2. Make no nonverbal contact; avoid direct eye contact; avoid touching the other person.
3. Engage in dialogue—communication in which both persons are speakers and listeners, both are involved, and both are concerned with and have respect for each other.	3. Engage in monologue—communication in which one person speaks and one person listens, and there is no real interaction, and no real concern or respect for the other.
4. Reflect back the other's feelings to demonstrate your understanding of them.	4. Express one's own feelings; ignore feelings of the other; or give abstract intellectualized responses.
5. Ask questions of the other concerning both thoughts and feelings.	5. Make statements about oneself; ignore any lack of clarity in the other's remarks.
6. Acknowledge the other's requests; answer the other's questions; return phone calls; and answer letters.	6. Ignore the other's requests; fail to answer questions, return phone calls, and answer letters.
7. Encourage the other to express thoughts and feelings.	7. Interrupt or otherwise make it difficult for the other to express himself or herself.
8. Respond directly and exclusively to what the other says.	8. Respond tangentially by acknowledging the other's comment but then shift the focus on the message in another direction.

From *The Interpersonal Communication Book* by Joseph A. DeVito. Copyright © 1992 by Joseph A. DeVito. Reprinted by permission of HarperCollins College Publishers.

The alternative to the two-valued orientation is a *multivalued orientation.* This use of language assumes from the start that it is possible to have relationships in which both parties get what they want. It leads us to look between the extremes for language that will describe our wants, feelings, and experiences.

A multivalued orientation might prove useful in creating a satisfying solution to the problem between Emilio and his coworkers. Many values operate as people communicate in the workplace. In this case, two are productivity and a positive atmosphere. If your goal as a manager is to maintain both values, you cannot take a rigid "either/or" position on the problem. You must take a multivalued approach. Emilio needs to see that getting along with coworkers can help him do an even better job, and his coworkers need to see that while getting along is important, so is doing the job well. Conversations with all the employees about the importance and interrelatedness of both issues would help. In these, it will be important to define the problem clearly as *ours,* as opposed to *yours, mine,* or *Emilio's.* You might state, "We want to get the job done well here, and an important part of that is everyone getting along. That doesn't seem to be happening these days. I want to find out what we can do to make it happen." Perhaps restructuring the work hours or rearranging the space would increase communication between Emilio and the other workers. Can you think of other multivalued approaches to this problem?

Control is also important in the multivalued orientation. We can easily lose control of our relationships when we communicate from a two-valued orientation because this position has built-in ultimatums. We are either "for them or against them," "in or out," or "up or down." Such language launches the relationship toward an inevitable outcome. In the case of Bart and Tina, a multivalued orientation eventually won, although Bart had initially taken the two-valued position. He began to see that there was more to his relationship with Tina than simply her presence in the home. When they looked for other ways to view their relationship, Bart and Tina found much that they still shared and were able to redefine their marriage and take control of it once again.

SUMMARY

This unit focused on the interrelationships among events, thoughts, and language. The Triangle of Meaning shows that thoughts and language are tied to one another but that words are not necessarily related to what they represent. Rather, words are abstractions that exist apart from experiences; they are created to assist in conveying those experiences to others. We describe our relationships using abstractions. We identified four levels of abstraction you can use to examine your communication in relationships. These are the nonverbal, naming, classification, and inferential levels. The language we use indicates how we view the relationship and its intensity. It is important for partners in a relationship to view that relationship and talk about it at similar levels of abstraction. By doing this, they can work together to make the relationship grow.

Language is an important tool for achieving relational growth. Relationship roles, type, and depth limit our choice of language and contribute to the degree that our meanings are either connotative or denotative. Connotations are influenced by role, gender, relationship function, and the depth of our relationships. Thus, we must consider these as we interpret the language of others and as we create messages of our own. Language reflects the way we see ourselves and our relationships. We express our intentions in a relationship by names we give it. We may view a relationship as symmetrical or complementary, and our language will reflect that view. Language can also reveal whether both people in the relationship share the same view, and if not, language can be used to correct the problem and help the relationship grow.

Problems with langauge can damage our important relationships. These problems may take the form of indiscrimination, inflexibility, or polarization. These problems, however, can be managed if we remain aware that we use symbols to express ideas, not to substitute for them. Remember also that usually more than two definitions and options are available as you approach relational problems. Work to adopt and maintain language that expresses and supports a multivalued frame of reference.

DISCUSSION QUESTIONS

1. Interview a friend or close acquaintance about something of personal importance to that individual. If possible, and if it is acceptable to the other person, tape the interview.

   a. What does the language used to talk about the situation tell you about this individual's self-concept?

   b. What does the language tell you about the way this person sees the situation?

   c. Do you find any patterns of language that suggest any consistent image of reality and frame of reference?

2. Secure permission from an elderly person to tape an interview in which the person recounts earlier experiences. Then report your answers to these questions to the class:

   a. Are there any language patterns that suggest an attitude or opinion about technology? progress? politics? religion?

   b. What is this person's image of you? What evidence in the language do you find for your conclusions?

c. Can you identify variations in age, educational level, political affiliation, religious affiliation, or ethnic affiliation in the language people use? How so?

3. Tape an interview with a young child in which you ask the child to talk about some things she likes to do at play. Consider how the child abstracts. Try to identify when the child is operating at higher and lower levels of abstraction and under what circumstances each works for the child.

4. Have you had any experience with cross-cultural language differences? What happened? How did you achieve clarity?

5. Bring an advertisement that includes words to class. How would you characterize the audience for whom it was designed with regard to the following:

age	religious affiliation
sex	socioeconomic class
ethnic identification	geographical orientation
educational level	hobbies or interests
political affiliation	

How did you decide?

6. If connotative meaning is personal, how do we discover the connotative meanings others are using? What difficulties do we encounter in trying to learn them?

7. Are certain views of roles more appropriate for particular relationships? If so, give examples.

8. Although naming places limits on our communication, it also serves important functions in helping relationships grow. At what point does naming cease to be helpful in the development of a relationship?

9. Do you think men and women differ in terms of the ways they determine symmetry and complementarity in relationships? Why?

10. Trace a relationship you've experienced through changes in function and depth. How did these changes affect your connotative process?

11. What stereotypes have people applied to you? In what instances were these helpful to your relationship? In what instances did these hinder the growth of the relationship?

12. Think about the people in your relationships. Is anyone living a destructive self-fulfilling prophecy? What can you do to help this person break this cycle?

13. What topics are you more likely to address through a two-valued orientation? Why do you think this is so?

14. Pick up a newspaper and turn to the "Letters to the Editor" section. Analyze the letters for examples of the language problems described in this chapter. Compare your findings with those of other students.

15. Recall two recent conversations, one that was confirming, the other that was disconfirming. What behaviors contributed to each emotion? Were some behaviors more central to creating these emotions? If so, which ones?

ENDNOTES

1. H. R. Pollio. *The Psychology of Symbolic Activity* (Reading, MA: Addison-Wesley, 1974), 53.

2. C. K. Ogden and I. A. Richards, *The Meaning of Meaning*, 3d ed, rev. (New York: Harcourt Brace Jovanovich, 1959).

3. J. C. Condon, Jr., *Semantics and Communication* (New York: Macmillan, 1985), 25–29.

4. S. I. Hayakawa, *Language in Thought and Action*, 4th ed. (San Diego: Harvest House, 1990), 153.

5. For example, see L. P. Stewart, P. J. Cooper, and S. A. Friedly, *Communication Between the Sexes: Sex Differences and Sex Role Stereotypes* (Scottsdale, AZ: Gorsuch, Scarisbrick, 1986).

6. A. G. Athos and J. J. Gabarro, *Interpersonal Behavior* (Englewood Cliffs, NJ: Prentice-Hall, 1978), 398.

7. J. C. Condon, Jr., *Semantics and Communication* (New York: Macmillan, 1985), 34–35.

8. D. R. Smith and L. K. Williamson, *Interpersonal Communication* (Dubuque, IA: Wm. C. Brown, 1985).

9. C. R. Berger and J. J. Bradac, *Language and Social Knowledge* (London: Edward Arnold, 1982), 78.

10. R. E. Alberti and M. L. Emmons, *Your Perfect Right: A Guide to Assertive Behavior*, 6th ed. (San Luis Obispo, CA: Impact, 1990), 8.

11. A. Korzybski, *Science and Sanity: An Introduction to Non-Aristotelian Systems and General Semantics* (Lakeville, CT: The International Non-Aristotelian Library, 1980).

12. S. I. Hayakawa, *Symbol, Status and Personality* (New York: Harcourt, Brace and World, 1963).

13. P. D. MacIntyre and K. A. Thivierge, "The Effects of Speaker Personality on Anticipated Reactions to Public Speaking," *Communication Research Reports* 12 (1995); 125–133.

14. G. Downey and S. I. Feldman, "Implications of Rejection Sensitivity for Intimate Relationships," *Journal of Personality and Social Psychology* 70 (1996): 1327–1343.

15. W. Johnson, *People in Quandaries* (New York: Harper and Row, 1946).

16. Hayakawa, *Symbol, Status and Personality,* 26.

17. Ibid., 41.

18. J. C. Condon, Jr., *Semantics and Communication,* 3d ed. (New York: Macmillan, 1985), 53.

READ MORE ABOUT
THE NATURE OF LANGUAGE IN THESE SOURCES

Condon, J. C., Jr. *Semantics and Communication.* New York: Macmillan, 1985. Condon's book is brief and to the point. Language, values, culture and relationships are all interrelated. The author demonstrates this main point through numerous interesting anecdotes and examples.

Ferguson, C. A., and S. B. Heath. *Language in the USA.* New York: Cambridge University Press, 1983. This book provides a comprehensive survey of crosscultural differences in the United States. In addition to looking at African-American and Hispanic-American languages, the authors also consider broader, more established ethnic sublanguages. They also examine language differences that result from membership in certain professions, including education, law, and medicine.

Lehman, W. P. *Language: An Introduction.* New York: Random House, 1983. This introduction to the science of language remains the best introduction to the subject available. Students interested in the rules and linguistic aspects of language should read this work.

READ MORE ABOUT
LANGUAGE IN RELATIONSHIPS IN THESE SOURCES

Miller, C., and K. Swift. *The Handbook of Nonsexist Writing.* 2d ed. New York: Harper and Row, 1988. If you plan to do any writing, this manual provides excellent practical advice on all matters of style. It also offers helpful suggestions on what to do about gender problems one may encounter in the writing process. Examples are plentiful and entertaining.

Ng, Sik Hung, and James J. Bradac. *Power in Language: Verbal Communication and Social Influence.* Newbury Park, CA: Sage, 1993. This is a comprehensive examination of how power is communicated to influence others.

Pearson, J. C., and Lynn H. Turner. *Gender and Communication.* Dubuque, IA: Wm. C. Brown, 1991. This work provides a massive summary of the research on male-female communication patterns, along with an excellent bibliography.

READ MORE ABOUT
LANGUAGE PROBLEMS IN THESE SOURCES

Hayakawa, S. I. *Language in Thought and Action.* 4th ed. San Diego: Harvest House, 1990. Of Hayakawa's many works on language, this one offers the most entertaining, readable, and comprehensive view of the impact of language problems in our lives. The book presents many solid examples of the types of language problems that interfere with relational growth.

Johnson, Wendell. *People in Quandaries.* New York: Harper and Row, 1946. Johnson's book makes entertaining and valuable reading for anyone interested in thinking more about language and relationships. He emphasizes the point of view that most relational problems are language-related and offers remedies for them.

5

FEELINGS AND EMOTIONS

PREVIEW

In our society, we are taught, sometimes directly and sometimes subtly, that it is not acceptable to talk about feelings, wants, or expectations. These cultural and social norms work against better interpersonal communication. When our relationships are at risk, there is a good chance that the problem revolves around such issues. The skills involved in talking about them include learning to separate feelings from emotions, learning more feeling words, learning to state what we want in terms of observable behavior, and learning to negotiate interpersonal contracts.

Our language contributes to growth in our relationships when it affirms the self-concepts of both partners, when the style of our communication is authentic in its expression, when we negotiate control of the relationship, and when we work toward the achievement of our goals. Our language must express our wants clearly and place responsibility for them on ourselves. Sometimes we make mistakes in our choices about language. These mistakes may entail giving up too much of the responsibility for an outcome or, at the other end, taking too much of that responsibility. If we look carefully, we can often see a pattern in our communication behavior along these lines. We may respond inappropriately to certain situations, personalities, topics, or behaviors. We can turn these habitual responses into opportunities for relational growth by learning to communicate assertively.

KEY TERMS

action

aggressive language

assertive language

cognitive information

emotions

habits

nonassertive language

response to behavior

response to the situation

value

aggressive behavior

assertive behavior

cognitive control

context

feelings

nonassertive behavior

potency

response to personalities

response to the topic

OBJECTIVES

1. Explain the differences between feelings and emotions and provide examples of each.

2. Describe and explain a three-step system for talking about feelings.

3. List and explain the steps for expressing wants and expectations clearly.

4. Explain how to help another person express feelings and wants clearly.

5. Define nonassertive communication and relate a personal experience of it.

6. Define aggressive communication and relate a personal experience of it.

7. Define assertive communication and relate a personal experience of it.

8. Cite a personal experience that triggered nonassertive or aggressive behavior. Practice an assertive response to this situation.

9. Recall an experience that triggered your nonassertive or aggressive behavior. Practice an assertive response to this situation.

10. Recall a personality who triggered your nonassertive or aggressive behavior. Practice an assertive response to this situation.

11. Recall a behavior that triggered your nonassertive or aggressive behavior. Practice an assertive response to this situation.

EXPRESSING FEELINGS, WANTS, AND EXPECTATIONS

In his wonderfully readable and helpful little book, *The Secret of Staying in Love,* John Powell makes a distinction between dialogue and discussion. Dialogue is communicating or sharing emotions or feelings; discussion is sharing thoughts, values, and decision making. Powell's argument is a pointed one:

> There must be an emotional clearance (dialogue) between two involved partners . . . before they can safely enter into a deliberation (discussion) about plans, choices, values. The assumption behind this distinction and the priority given to dialogue is that the breakdown in human love and communication is *always* due to *emotional problems.*[1]

FEELINGS, WANTS, AND EXPECTATIONS MUST BE SHARED

We agree with Powell: a clear sharing of feelings and emotions must exist before meaningful discussion about plans, choices, and values can take place. You might assume, then, that our society would teach its children how to talk about feelings and emotions. Unhappily, however, this is not easily done, for several reasons.

First, what we say cannot fully express what we experience. No matter how accurately we learn to report our experiences, our words can never *be* the experiences.[2] The words are important tools, of course, in communicating about an experience, but they are only a partial expression of it. What we experience is not at the verbal level but at an "unspeakable level."[3] The unspeakable level is the first of three orders of human experience; the second level is thought, and the third is language.

Although we just cannot express much of what we know, we still must try. If we are going to enjoy and nurture ongoing relationships to which we are emotionally and physically committed, we must share our inner feelings, wants, intentions, and images so that others can know themselves in us. In less committed relationships, we must also disclose ourselves and our feelings.

Second, although sharing our feelings and wants with others affects our relationships with those others, our society discourages clear talk about such personal issues.[4] It does so in at least three ways.

1. *Our society teaches us that some emotions are bad and others are good.* Moreover, when we do share emotions, they are usually positive.[5] To illustrate, most of us are taught from very early in life that it is good to be grateful. "What do you say?" asks the grandmother when she hands her small grandchild a piece of candy. The answer, of course is, "Thank you." On the other hand, it is bad to be angry. "Stop that this minute!" says a mother as she breaks up an angry squabble between her two young sons.

If you listen carefully on the rare occasions when people try to talk about their negative feelings, you will hear at least four different ways they punish each other for expressing such feelings:

The judge: You have no right to feel that way. She didn't mean any harm.

The optimist: Don't worry, everything will be all right.

The analyst: I know why you're feeling that way. You just want . . . .

The rip-off artist: I know exactly how you're feeling. Just the other day, this happened to me.

In each of these cases, the speaker may very well be trying to help. But what the person is communicating instead is, "I do not want you to talk about your negative feelings."

2. *Our society teaches us to suppress "undesirable" emotions.* In almost all families, children learn to be comfortable with the expression and display of certain emotions and uncomfortable with others. For instance, a child who grows up in a large, loud, rough-and-tumble household may learn to be comfortable with expressions and shows of anger and uncomfortable with expressions of tenderness. In contrast, some children learn from their parents that

Our society teaches us to suppress "undesirable" emotions.

displays of anger are simply not acceptable but that displays of affection and warmth are desirable. Research bears this out. In the marriage relationship, for example, we find that husbands and wives rarely share face-threatening emotions ("I'm disappointed in you") or angry emotions ("I'm mad at you").[6] Beyond this, our society even discourages too much sharing of positive feelings.[7]

3. *Our society teaches that some emotions conflict with basic values.* For example, young males are often taught that they should not cry because crying is not manly. If an emotional state conflicts with some deeply held value, that conflict will surely cause people to try to suppress the emotion.

The key words used to teach which emotions conflict with basic values and which do not are "ought," "should," and "right." For example, you might hear a parent saying to a child, "Don't cry. You should behave like a man." These terms harken to rules for behavior that exist only in the minds of the speakers. If you listen to yourself talk, you may be surprised to hear yourself using these words. Each time you do, you are referencing a rule for behavior. The rule is always inside you. Where do you think it came from?

A second problem involved in learning to talk about our feelings, wants, and expectations is that we tend to take our language for granted. We hardly notice the words we use—especially when we use them daily. Instead, we assume that the words we choose are an accurate reflection of our experience of ourselves and the world as well as the experience of others. We are not analytical about our word choices, preferring to use them automatically and without giving much thought to how they can limit and hurt ourselves and our relationships.

Thus, much of what we are taught by our society is contrary to relational effectiveness. We must be willing to examine where we are in relation to what our society is telling us. Then we will be ready to practice more effective ways of talking about our feelings, wants, and expectations.

LEARNING TO SEPARATE FEELINGS FROM EMOTIONS

A definite distinction exists between feelings and emotions. *Feelings* are physical events of the human body experienced in the present tense. They are the body's response to physical stimulation. *Emotions* exist in the language you use to talk to yourself and to others about the feelings you are experiencing.

Of course, there are words that we use to talk about feelings separate from emotions but not as many as you might imagine. Rather, when we try to talk about our feelings we tend to focus on the location of a feeling and then to label it using some combination of

Feelings are
physical.
Emotions exist
in our labeling
of our feelings.

words that, *in that context,* suggest an emotional state. Or else we talk about feeling in metaphorical terms: "It feels like . . .."

What you feel is a physical experience. You feel the condition of parts of your body at some moment in time and space. The feelings exist as tiny firings in nerve endings in the tissues of your body. You feel tense muscles; you feel aching joints; you feel the lining of your stomach signaling to you that you are hungry; you feel the sharp pain "behind the eyes" that sometimes occurs when you have eaten too much ice cream too fast. Feeling is a physical experience.

What you tell yourself about your feelings constitutes your emotions. While your feelings are physical, your emotions exist only in the world of words. Consider this example that illustrates this point.

You might suddenly experience a loud noise while walking in your neighborhood after dark. A barking dog jumps out from an azalea bush. You will have a physical experience—a sudden, electrochemical, very real, physical experience. The blood will rush away from your skin. Your endocrine system will instantly infuse your blood with certain chemicals. Your heartbeat will increase. Your muscles, now strengthened by the dramatically heightened adrenaline levels in your bloodstream, will tense. Your stomach will feel like it is knotting up. And, finally, the hair on the back of your neck will stand up and, chances are, you will begin to tremble. Under these circumstances—in that particular moment in your neighborhood when you are confronted by a barking dog—you are experiencing a set of physical feelings. Notice that the *context* in which the event occurs contributes significantly to your experience. It's dark. You are walking a couple of streets away from your house. All the information in that event becomes part of the context. So does all the information that you carry with you into the event. You are sure you should not be walking alone. You are sure that it is late. You have read of people being attacked, and the thought frightens you.

With all of this context coming to bear on you at that moment, you experience your body responding to the sudden, loud appearance of the dog. Your feelings, again, are the physical events of your body that you experience in the present tense. They are your body's responses to physical stimulation.

What will you call these physical sensations? Will you call them fear? Will you call them something more self-confirming? Will you call them startled? Would it be correct to say that you were surprised? And would it be correct to say that you experienced anger? at what? at the dog? at your own inability to control the fight-or-flight reaction? Will you call that experience cowardice? Will you call it embarrassment? What appropriately describes that physical condition in that moment in time and space? What you choose to call it is most important indeed, since so much depends on it! How you see yourself is at issue in your choice of words.

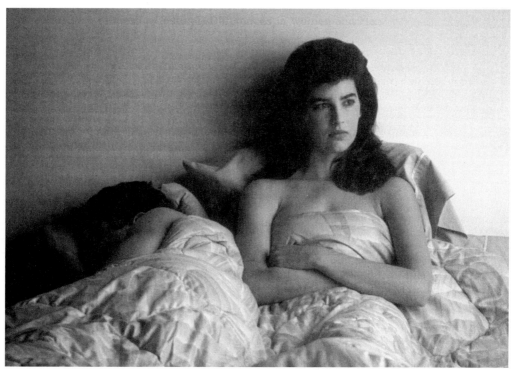

People who do not like themselves or who find it easier to be angry than to feel worthless or inadequate ventilate their pain with a show of temper.

Your emotions exist not in physical feelings but in the words you select to label those feelings *in a particular context*. You *feel* your body, but you experience your emotions in quite a different way, with language.

EMOTIONS ARE UNDER COGNITIVE CONTROL

Because you experience emotions with language, what you experience as emotion contains *cognitive information*. You take the meanings of these physical experience directly from what you say to yourself about them, based upon the context in which you experience them. Even the words you choose to talk about your feelings provide part of that context. The information you derive from that language controls your arousal. Although you may not realize it, and although you may not want to admit it, you make choices about which label to use to think about these physical sensations; your emotions are under *cognitive control*.

We will soon argue that if you will take the trouble to learn a broader vocabulary to talk about your feelings, you will experience a richer emotional range. But we're not quite ready for that idea.

The context in
which an event
occurs
contributes
significantly to
your experience.

When you think about the dog suddenly jumping out at you
from behind a bush you might suppose that the dog made you
afraid. We tend to think of our emotional states as caused by events
outside our bodies. We also tend to think that our emotional states
themselves lead to behavior. So, you may find nothing wrong with
the following logic:

1. A dog barks while jumping out from behind a bush. This makes
   you afraid, so you jump back to get out of the way.

2. Someone you love dies. This makes you sad, so you grieve.

3. The car breaks down. This frustrates you, so you take out your
   frustrations on the car.

In truth, we do not respond directly to an actual event. Rather, we
take information from the event, give it meaning, and then respond
to the cognitive structure of the event that we ourselves have created. Put another way, the event triggers a scanning of our experiences. We sense certain physical responses—our feelings. We draw
an inference about what is going on. That is, we *interpret* the event
and then choose to label what is being experienced with some word
that describes an emotional state.

Because all this happens so fast that we may be unaware of anything more than our experience of emotions, we act on the emotional state, assuming that it was caused directly by the event,

rather than being the result of our thought processes. Look again at the three examples of how emotions occur:

1. A dog barks while jumping out of a bush. You experience certain bodily sensations. You perceive the situation as threatening, immediate, and urgent. You also perceive it as dangerous. *You choose to jump away in fear.*

2. Someone you love dies. You experience certain bodily sensations. You perceive your loss. You understand that you will miss that person greatly. You realize that there were many things that you did not say to the person and regret that you did not work through some of the problems in your relationship. Facing all that, *you choose to label the feelings as distress or sorrow,* emotional states.

3. The car breaks down. You see that you are going to be late. You begin to experience certain bodily sensations. You recall choices you made earlier to put off having the car repaired. You anticipate that dire consequence will result, both from being late and from having to expose your earlier, faulty choices. *You choose to call your emotional state frustration.*

In each example, the response is not to the event per se but to your particular view of the event. You respond to the information you have drawn from the moment and the connections you have made between the information and your prior experience. Your body responds with certain sensations—feelings. These are identified as some particular emotional state. These connections always exist as words. How you talk to yourself about the event, including how you label the emotional state, shapes your response. Could you have chosen other responses if you had chosen to talk about the event differently?

This fact—that people are responsible for choosing their emotional responses—is an important idea. You learn habitual responses to situations that seem to fall into similar categories. You seem to program yourself to respond to certain events in certain ways. Once the program is stabilized, you come to believe (at least, many people do) that you have little choice but to follow through with the programmed behaviors.

But it is possible to rewrite the program. It is possible to make alternative choices of behavior. The key lies deeply embedded in the language you use.

HOW WE LIMIT OUR EXPRESSION OF FEELINGS

We have said that your emotions exist in the words you choose to talk about your body's physical feelings as you experience them in some particular context. We have also said that you choose those words out of habit and from a limited vocabulary. Our argument has been that your emotional range is restricted by these *habits* and limitations.

One way we limit ourselves is by too often confusing our feelings with our thinking. For instance, you might hear someone say, "I feel you spend too much time with the children." The sentence would be far more accurate, we believe, if it started with "I think" rather than "I feel": "I think you spend too much time with the children" makes it clear that the decision-making activity—the conclusion—is in the speaker's mind and that it is not a feeling. How does such a thing actually feel?

Here are a number of examples of how thinking is confused with feeling. We present them because we want you to see how often—and how subtly—we make this fundamental mistake.

1. *"I feel unloved."* How does "unloved" feel? empty? numb? down? Unloved is really the summary of these feelings—an emotional state. Beyond this, who is involved when someone says they feel "unloved"? The speaker, of course—but might there also be another individual involved? We think so. In fact, we think that this speaker may be wrongly taking personal responsibility for someone else's nervous system by accepting "unloved" as his own doing rather than the other person's doing.

2. *"I feel put down."* "Put down" is an assumption (thought) about another person's *intention*. There are feelings associated with "put down." What are they for you?

3. *"I feel you have pulled away from me."* Here, the speaker is making an inference based on some observed behavior. A more accurate statement might be, "I have observed that you have physically pulled away from me. Indeed, you haven't called in several days, and when we have been in the same places together, you have stayed away from me. I feel empty and cut off and am saddened. I miss you very much."

4. *"I feel like a tramp when you look at me that way."* How does a tramp feel? The metaphor, in this case, is entirely a cognitive structure. It is an inference about the other person's *image*, triggered by someone looking "that way." You might ask what the speaker has observed. What does looking "that way" actually look like? In any case, you could change the sentence to make it more accurate by saying, "I see your look. What does it mean? Do you think I am a tramp?"

5. *"I feel used."* This statement is clearly a guess about another's intention or motive. It is not a statement of one's own feeling. Just how does "used" feel?

6. *"I feel tremendously involved."* This statement is also a substitution of thinking for feeling. Does the speaker feel excited? alert? consumed? What does "tremendous" feel like? What does "involved" feel like?

We often confuse our feelings with our thinking.

7. *"I feel as though you're lying to me."* This is obviously a guess about someone's intention, based on an observation. Perhaps the other person's statement seems inconsistent with known fact, or perhaps there is a question of trust inside the speaker. In any case, how does "you're lying to me" feel?

8. *"I feel real bad about that."* Here is a judgment about a feeling state that pushes the feeling into the speaker's head. What does feeling "real bad" feel like—painful? unnerved? tense? shaky?

9. *"I feel wonderful."* Wonder is also cognitive activity. How does "wonder" feel—effervescent? buoyant? energetic? electrified?

These examples show that people habitually confuse feelings with thinking. But this is not necessary, for *you can learn new habits.* You can learn to interrupt the habitual choice of language. One way to do this is to replace "I feel" with "I think." *You can also learn new words* to express and experience a far richer feeling and emotional range. Obviously, learning these techniques will enhance your ability to manage your relationships.

> You can learn new habits. You can learn to say "I think" when you mean "I think."

LEARNING TO TALK ABOUT FEELINGS

A simple, three-step sequence can help you learn to talk about feelings: (1) locate and name the feeling in your body, (2) name the emotional state, and (3) describe the feeling and emotion with a metaphor.

1. *Locate and name the feeling in your body.* Remember that you feel your body and that your emotions exist in the words you use to talk about that physical feeling. To talk about the feeling more effectively, then, you need to identify where you are experiencing the feeling and what it is like. Do a quick inventory of your major muscle groups. It may be convenient to work from your head downward.

   Is the feeling in the muscles of your face? your forehead? your eyes? your mouth? Are your jaws clenched? Are the muscles of your throat or the back of your neck tense and hurting? Is the feeling in your shoulders? between your shoulder blades? in your lower back? in your abdominal cavity? Are the muscles in your chest constricted? Are you feeling the muscles in your pelvic girdle? Are your upper legs tight and hurting? Are you feeling something unpleasant in your knee joints? in your calves? in your ankles? Do your feet hurt? Name the feeling you are experiencing. Use table 5.1 to help you.

Table 5.1	One Hundred Feeling Words		
achy	edgy	jubilant	soft
agitated	effervescent	jumpy	sour
alert	elated	keyed-up	spiritless
alive	electrified	lethargic	steaming
bitter	empty	light	stiff
boiling	energetic	limp	stifled
breathless	expansive	listless	stimulated
bubbly	fast	loose	straight
buoyant	filled	low	stunned
calm	flat	numb	sweaty
churning	flushed	open	tense
closed	fluttering	out of control	tied-up
charged-up	free	paralyzed	tight
cold	fresh	placid	tingly
connected	frosty	pressed	together
constrained	full	puffed-up	tranquil
consumed	glittering	racing	trembling
dazed	glowing	relaxed	twisted
detached	hard	restless	unnerved
disjointed	heavy	restrained	upside-down
dizzy	hollow	rigid	unsteady
down	hot	rushed	vibrant
drained	hurting	shaky	void
dry	icy	sharp	warm
dull	jittery	slow	wired

2. *Name the emotion you attach to the feeling.* After you have located and described the feeling, try to name the emotion that you associate with it. Use table 5.2 to help you.

3. *Describe the feeling and emotion with a metaphor.* Once you have located the feeling and identified the emotion, try to describe them metaphorically. How does it feel? What is it like? For example, if the feeling is painful, what does the pain feel like?

Table 5.2	One Hundred Emotion Words		
affectionate	downhearted	hyperactive	reverent
afraid	eager	impatient	scared
angry	easygoing	indifferent	seductive
anxious	embittered	irate	self-reliant
appreciated	exasperated	jealous	sexy
apprehensive	excited	joyful	shocked
attractive	exhilarated	lively	silly
beautiful	fearful	lonely	skeptical
brave	flirtatious	lovable	sleepy
caring	friendly	loving	sorrowful
comfortable	frightened	mad	supported
committed	frustrated	mean	surprised
compassionate	furious	melancholy	suspicious
competent	generous	miserable	sympathetic
concerned	genuine	optimistic	tender
confident	gentle	overwhelmed	terrified
contented	giddy	peaceful	troubled
creative	glad	perplexed	understood
dejected	grateful	pessimistic	unhappy
despondent	happy	playful	useless
disgusted	hopeful	pleased	withdrawn
dismayed	hopeless	provoked	worried
dissatisfied	horrified	proud	wishy-washy
distressed	hostile	puzzled	youthful
downcast	humorous	resentful	zealous

fire? burning? Is it sharp? throbbing? Does it sting? feel like nee-
dles? cut like a knife? Is it a dull, heavy experience? Does it feel
like something you may have felt before? like the result of a sudden blow? like someone punched you? Is it loneliness—like sitting in the corner of an empty room? Are you as angry as a
hungry, giant black bear awaking from a deep sleep?

To illustrate how you might use this three-step sequence, consider this student's effort to do it:

1. *Locate:* "I'm feeling something in the small of my back and between my shoulder blades."
2. *Name:* "It's depressing, you know? I'm unhappy, and hurt, and tired."
3. *Describe:* "It's like someone is squeezing me in a vise, like a heavy, tight, knotted-up feeling, as if some great pair of hands were holding on to my back and making a fist tighter and tighter."

You might find it helpful to think in terms of *value, potency* and *action* as you try to describe your feeling states. *Value* descriptions might include words along these continua:

good		bad
right		wrong
O.K.		not O.K.
ugly		beautiful

Potency descriptions might include words along these continua:

rough		smooth
hot		cold
bright		dull
hard		soft
sharp		blunt
high		low
strong		weak

Action descriptions might include words along these continua:

fast		slow
moving		still
running		standing
pushing		pulling
lifting		pressing

Another good way to describe your feelings is to try to give them a color. Is the feeling blue? Is it yellow? Is it red? The color metaphors can be very potent in helping you understand and describe feeling states that may otherwise be difficult. The colors often bring to mind a metaphor that someone else can relate to. For example, one student, using our suggestions to describe a feeling in her arm, said:

> The feeling is . . . red and yellow, like . . . uh . . . like, something like an early summer day at the beach, when the sun is shining on you too hot. It is a deep, too hot feeling that seems to be standing still just about a quarter of an inch under my skin, and . . . uh . . . it's from just below my elbow all the way down the outside of my hand and into my little finger. But it's not sharp or jabbing.

Note that she started with a color combination, which brought to mind a metaphor that allowed her to describe the feeling. Then she gave it action and location and finished with a statement of its potency and action. We think anyone hearing her description will fully understand the feelings.

You may find this three-step sequence more difficult than it appears. You will probably have to practice. We are not accustomed to locating our feelings, we do not have much language to talk about our emotional experiences, and we are not very good at developing metaphors to describe feeling and emotional states. If we were, we would experience a far richer emotional range.

LEARNING MORE EMOTION AND FEELING WORDS

One way to learn more emotion and feeling words is to work with your own experience to generate a greater vocabulary. You can do this by working through this simple experience. Because we are not usually accustomed to describing our feelings, sometimes it is easier to begin with familiar emotion words. Recall that we have said that emotion words are the language you use to talk about feelings in a particular situation. If you were listing a set of emotion statements, you might say, "I'm happy," "I'm sad," "I'm angry," "I'm afraid," and "I'm confused." The five words in each of these statements are emotional states. None of them suggest the feelings—the physical sensations that the body is experiencing—that are associated with the emotions.

You can now generate a list of feeling words by considering what feelings go along with this set of emotional states. For example, think of a situation in which you might be happy. Then, make a statement like the following: "When I receive an 'A' in class, I'm happy. When I'm happy I feel _____, _____, and _____." If you fill in the blanks with words that describe what your body is feeling, you will have feeling words. You might have included the words "bubbly," "buoyant," and "effervescent." Or perhaps you chose "electrified," "glowing," and "stimulated." You can list emotion words and use them to generate feeling words through this process.

We asked our students to help us generate lists of emotions and feelings. They took the emotion words listed in table 5.2 and generated the one hundred feeling words listed in table 5.1. You might want to add to these lists. We think these lists can help you expand your vocabulary of emotion and feeling words. If your instructor asks you to practice writing or speaking about your emotions and feelings, use these lists as a reference to help you in the task.

LEARNING TO STATE WHAT YOU WANT

In a relationship, sometimes we have a fairly clear idea of our feelings and those of the other person, but we may be uncertain about what either we or our partner wants. When this uncertainty takes form in talk, a message something like the following often results:

> *He:* What do you want from me?
>
> *She:* I just want you to love me more.
>
> *He:* I *do* love you.
>
> *She:* But I want you to love me *more.*

You can see that she is not giving him much help. How will she judge that he loves her more? Her only way is to observe his behavior and then interpret it to mean that he loves her more.

Consider a different situation, this time at work. Again, the vagueness comes from being unclear about what is wanted:

> *He:* What do you want from me?
>
> *She:* I want you to work better. I want you to increase your level of performance. I want you to be more professional.
>
> *He:* But . . . .

Again, he isn't getting much help from his boss because she has expressed her wants and expectations in very vague and abstract terms. What does "increase your level of performance" mean? What does "be more professional" mean? And what constitutes "better work"?

In each case, the speaker can communicate more effectively by *expressing a want in terms of observable behaviors or measurable results that can be achieved within a specified time.* Here is how one student used this two-step sequence in an exercise in which he was pretending to be a professor:

> *She:* What do you want from me?
>
> *He:* I want you to write a term paper on the dragon ships of the Vikings and submit it in draft form on the day of the midterm exam. I want it in final form on May 15, not later than 4:00 in the afternoon.

However, if many of our students had heard a professor make this request, they would still be frustrated. Surely they would want to know what standards they had to meet. Let's go further in the conversation—you might recognize yourself in it!

She: Do you want it typed? How many pages must it be?

He: Yes. Type it on high rag-content bond paper, not erasable bond. It probably should be about fifteen pages long.

Distinguishing between the observable and the measurable appears to be the most difficult part of asking for what you want. In short, observable behaviors can be seen or heard, whereas measurable results can be counted. Table 5.3 offers help in this area.

ASK FOR CLARIFICATIONS

Interpersonal communication events place you in both the sender and receiver positions. Thus, you often must help others be clear about what they feel about and what they want from you. Your best recourse is, as always, to ask questions. You cannot correctly assume that you can read the other person's mind! Here is a three-step sequence that will help you get clarifications from someone else:

1. Talk about what you observe.
2. Talk about what you are inferring.
3. Ask what the other person wants.

Table 5.3	Observable Behaviors and Measurable Results	
Attitudes	*Observable behaviors*	*Measurable results*
to love	call me on the phone	at least once a day
to improve	arrive at work on time	every day
to be professional	research and write for publication	two essays in refereed journals each year
to care	say you care and show you care by making written and phone contact	three or four times a month
to help or participate	offer to sit with the children and to do the dishes and other household chores	a few times each week

This process is easy to learn and well worth the effort. Here is a sample of it in use:

1. Talk about your observations: "I can see your hands trembling, and I can hear your voice is strained, but I'm not sure what to make of it . . . ."

2. Talk about your inferences: "Are you angry? . . . Are you angry with me personally?"

3. Ask what is wanted: "What would you like me to do? . . . What does that mean? I have to guess?"

APPROPRIATE EXPRESSION OF WANTS AND NEEDS

Appropriate self-expression must include a consideration of the way language influences others' perceptions of our manner and style. The words we choose along with our way of saying them may result in our being perceived as *assertive, nonassertive,* or *aggressive.* Look carefully at this situation and imagine what you might do if you were Mary Ann or Cheryl:

Cheryl and Mary Ann were sitting in the lounge in their place of employment talking about an assignment their boss had given them. Mary Ann, well underway on the project, was listening to Cheryl relate her difficulties in getting started on the assignment when Tim approached. Tim likes to talk and carry on about things and is fun to have around when people want to socialize. However, he frequently interrupts his and other's work to chat. He was in the middle of doing that when Mary Ann politely interrupted him, saying, "Excuse me, Tim. Cheryl and I are working on ideas for a project that Sam assigned to us. If you want to help us with some ideas, that's fine. If not, will you let us get back to it, please?"

Mary Ann dealt with Tim's interruption quickly and assertively. Notice that her response does not attack him but merely states what she wants in precise terms. She might have responded aggressively, saying, "Get lost, you jerk." Aggressive responses are frequently controlling and can be hurtful. With such a response, Mary Ann may get what she wants but at the probable expense of Tim's anger and a somewhat damaged relationship. She might also have given a nonassertive response, such as "Gee, Tim we're working, but you're not interrupting anything." This response is self-denying and completely gives control to another person. In this example, Mary Ann gives up what she wants but may resent Tim because of it.

CHARACTERISTICS OF NONASSERTIVE, AGGRESSIVE, AND ASSERTIVE LANGUAGE AND BEHAVIOR

Our communication with those in our relationships is affected by the degree of assertiveness in our messages. The impact of nonassertive, aggressive, and assertive behavior is felt in four areas of the relationship. These are (1) the self-concept, (2) style of expression, (3) control of the relationship or situation, and (4) achievement of goals or needs. Figure 5.1 summarizes the way these areas vary depending on whether the communication is nonassertive, aggressive, or assertive.

Robert Alberti and Michael Emmons believe that *nonassertive behavior* is generally anxiety-based.[8] *Nonassertive language* has the following characteristics:

- It generally denies (or ignores) the self.
- It can sound hurt, anxious, or inhibited.
- It allows or encourages others to choose and receive what they want from the situation.
- It usually does not achieve the desired goal.

Examine Anne's nonassertive responses below for evidence of these characteristics:

> *Richard:* Anne, if I were you, I'd tell your boss that you have a right to have your vacation anytime you want it.
>
> *Anne:* Maybe you're right, Richard, but I don't know what to say to him.
>
> *Richard:* You've got to start sticking up for yourself. You let your supervisor push you around all the time.
>
> *Anne:* I suppose so, but he is nice to me much of the time, and I could take my vacation later if he needs me. Maybe next month I'll sit down and have a talk with him.

Note that nonassertive behavior involves giving up something in our relationships. Anne is giving up taking her vacation when she wants it. She is denying herself and relying on Richard to solve her problems. Nonassertive behavior such as this can quickly lead to resentment, which compounds the difficulty of achieving relational growth. If Anne lets her dissatisfaction go unattended, she may eventually have an explosive confrontation with her boss, and he

Nonassertive behavior is generally anxiety-based and involves giving up something.

	Aggressive	Assertive	Nonassertive
Self-concept	Self-promoting	Self-enhancing	Self-deprecating
Style	Hurtfully expressive	Authentically expressive	Inhibited
Control	Assumes control	Negotiates control	Gives up control
Goals	Usually achieves but at a great cost	May well achieve	Usually does not achieve

Figure 5.1
Impact of nonassertive, aggressive, and assertive behavior.

may not even understand why it is happening. Repairing a relationship after we have behaved nonassertively requires two steps. First, the built-up resentment must be overcome. Second, the issue that caused us to behave nonassertively must be resolved. Only then can the relationship resume its normal course. Anne is behaving nonassertively toward both her supervisor and Richard. She might respond assertively to Richard as follows:

Richard: Anne, if I were you, I'd tell your boss that you have a right to have your vacation anytime you want it.

Anne: But I'm not you, Richard. I have to approach my boss with respect if I want him to give me what I want.

Richard: You've got to start sticking up for yourself. You let your supervisor push you around all the time.

Anne: Excuse me, but I do stick up for myself when I think I need to. In fact, I'm going to meet with my supervisor tomorrow morning to discuss my vacation. He may or may not agree to let me have it when I want it, but at least he will know what I want.

Aggressive behavior exists at the other end of the spectrum. *Aggressive language* exhibits these characteristics:

- It is self-enhancing but at the expense of another.
- It is expressive but belittles others.
- It assumes control over the choices of others.
- It usually achieves its desired goals but does so by hurting others and damaging the relationship.

See if you can identify these characteristics in Marcus's conversation with Natasha:

> *Natasha:* Marcus, I'm going to the movies Saturday. Would you like to go with me?
>
> *Marcus:* Are you going to one of those stupid, sappy relationship movies again? If you are, I don't want to go.
>
> *Natasha:* Well, I haven't picked one out yet. Which one would you like to see?

Aggressive behavior stifles growth in our relationships because it tends to cut off communication. Our partners will probably lower their esteem for us if we act this way too often. Eventually, they may withdraw from the relationship. Marcus's response to Natasha's invitation above puts her down and removes control of her evening from her. It implies that he knows what "good" movies are and she does not. Natasha will soon tire of this treatment and stop asking Marcus out. Wouldn't you? However, Marcus could have responded to Natasha's invitation assertively like this:

> *Natasha:* Marcus, I'm going to the movies Saturday. Would you like to go with me?
>
> *Marcus:* I'd like to go out with you, Natasha. What are you planning to see?
>
> *Natasha:* I thought I'd like to see that new relationship movie. How about you?
>
> *Marcus:* Thanks, but I really don't think I'd enjoy it. Why don't you go and then we can meet somewhere afterwards?

Assertive behavior lies between the extremes of nonassertive and aggressive expression. It is usually the most appropriate and effective language for a given situation. *Assertive language* is characterized as follows:

- It is self-enhancing.
- It is expressive.
- It indicates choices made by the self, for the self.
- It may achieve the desired goals.
- It does not achieve these goals by putting down the other person.

Aggressive behavior can stifle growth in our relationships.

Assertive behavior and language help us express our ideas while preserving our own dignity and our partner's. Did you notice that in the assertive version of Marcus and Natasha's conversation, he did not criticize her taste but was still able to disagree with her choice. This type of language permits openness in our relationships and provides the opportunity for them to grow through learning, agreeing, and disagreeing in a fair-minded fashion.

WHEN AND WHY WE FAIL TO COMMUNICATE ASSERTIVELY

The major issue in communicating nonassertively or aggressively is one of control. We all have a need to be in charge of ourselves and our relationships, and when we are communicating in ways that satisfy this need, we find ourselves in control. Being in control enables us to appropriately achieve the expression and satisfaction of our interpersonal needs for belonging and affection. We can lose this sense of control in a number of ways. Certain situations, personalities, topics, or behaviors may trigger a nonassertive or aggressive response in us. We need to learn to recognize those that affect us this way so we can learn new assertive language to use in response.

Response to the Situation

Sometimes our choice to communicate nonassertively or aggressively is a *response to the situation.* In some situations, we may act rather timid. For instance, we may feel shy and uncomfortable at large gatherings where we do not know anyone. Our language might reflect this discomfort in a number of ways. We might speak more politely than we usually do, we might choose language that reveals very little about ourselves, or we might remain very quiet, speaking only when spoken to. If our response to such situations is aggressive, we might talk loudly, intrude into the conversations of others, and dominate the conversations into which we are invited.

The assertive response to a gathering where we do not know anybody requires that we first give some thought to what we want out of the situation. Do we want to meet people or participate in some particular aspect of the event? When we are comfortable with our reason for being there, we may be able to act in such a way that we present ourselves and our wants clearly. We might, for example, begin by identifying someone we think is attractive or interesting. Then we would approach this person and introduce ourself. We should keep in mind that we are at the beginning stages of a relationship and must take care to disclose in appropriate amounts and depths.

> The assertive response requires that we give some thought to what we want from a situation.

Response to Personalities

Some of us are assertive or nonassertive only in *response to certain personalities.* We might have difficulty, for instance, choosing language that accurately conveys our wants to an authoritarian, difficult supervisor at work. In this circumstance, we might choose nonassertive expressions that seem to indicate that everything is fine, whether or not it really is. Or we might decide to hint about what we want. On the other hand, if we choose to respond aggressively, we might complain about every task we are assigned.

The assertive response in this situation is one of honesty. If we have concerns that a supervisor might be able to remedy, we must give that person the opportunity to do so. Such assertive communication is free of blame, and the time and place are appropriate to the subject we want to discuss. For instance, when our supervisor asks how things are going, we might say, "Most everything is fine, but I do have two concerns that you may be able to help me with. I'll be finished with this project at 3:00. Can we meet then to talk about them?"

Response to the Topic

We might also find ourselves behaving nonassertively or aggressively in *response to the topic*. For instance, we may have such strong feelings about the way our government should treat its veterans that when the topic comes up, we find ourselves tongue-tied and either withdraw from the conversation or try to change the subject to avoid a confrontation. On the other hand, we might express our strong feelings aggressively by raising our voices to threaten those with differing opinions. This would likely end the conversation, so the goal would be achieved through intimidation.

The key to communicating about sensitive topics is mutual positive regard. We can express our views clearly if we remember that they represent a perspective that others may not have heard before or that they may disagree with. When dealing with sensitive topics, we can strive for an exchange of views. This means that we must use appropriate listening and feedback skills in addition to assertive language.

Response to Behavior

Sometimes we have to choose a way of communicating in *response to behavior* that we think is inappropriate. For example, suppose we are in a group working on a project. Susan, one of the group members, has missed several meetings. She arrives late for the current meeting and without the materials she had agreed to bring. You might respond nonassertively by saying, "Don't worry, Susan, I'll get the materials on my lunch hour tomorrow." Or you might respond aggressively, saying, "Susan, you have been lazy and irresponsible throughout this project! If you don't go and get the things right now and bring them back in an hour, we're going to exclude you from the project." The third alternative, the assertive response, might be, "Susan, would you go get the materials you were to bring now? We have set aside this time to work on our project and must have them before we can proceed." The assertive response is problem-centered and present-oriented. In responding this way, you do not ask for excuses or explanations, only results.

Sharon and Gordon Bower summarized the importance of assertive behavior:

> Above all, as an assertive person you can learn to negotiate mutually satisfactory solutions to a variety of interpersonal problems—from dealing with your neighbor

whose dog likes to march over your marigolds to adjusting an unsatisfactory relationship with a friend or relative.[9]

At times we may see the nonassertive alternative as most appropriate. For example, when someone who normally is quite pleasant is having a bad day and snaps at you, a nonassertive response may be best. You may want to overlook this action or put off discussion of it until a better time. Alberti and Emmons have said that there may be such times when, after examining the possible consequences of assertive behavior, you decide that another response is desirable.[10] They wrote:

> If you *know how* to act assertively, you are free to *choose* whether or not you will. If you are *unable* to act assertively, you have no choices; you will be governed by others, and your well-being will suffer.[11]

Generally, the assertive expression is the most productive. Using language to assert who we are and what we want can help us know ourselves better, present ourselves in a better light, and contribute to the growth of our relationships.

IMPROVING ASSERTIVE COMMUNICATION SKILLS

There are several keys to improving assertive expression. First, we must understand ourselves—who we are, how others see us, and what we want. Chapter 2 suggested ways to clarify the self-concept. Second, we must observe our own actions in relationships. For example, you might keep a diary for several weeks in which you note instances of nonassertive, aggressive, and assertive behavior. Finally, we can analyze our behavior using the information we have collected. The following questions and suggestions can help us achieve insights:

1. *Analyze your behavior.* Is there any pattern to your nonassertive or aggressive behavior? That is, are there certain situations, people, or topics that cause you to behave in a way that you would like to improve?

   Now, consider your assertive behavior. Are you pleased with any examples of your assertive behavior? Compare these events with those in which you were nonassertive or aggressive. Which factors or people in a situation help you to remain in control of your expression? Which trigger nonassertive or aggressive communication?

2. *Develop a plan.* Examine those situations in which you would like to see some improvement and choose one to work on. Recall how you communicated in that situation and consider alternative responses.

The first step in learning to be assertive is understanding ourselves—who we are, how others see us, and what we want.

Plan for your next encounter with the situation, person, or topic that caused you a problem by rehearsing your response. You might get some feedback from a friend. Sharon and Gordon Bower suggest that you actually write out the sort of message you want to communicate.[12] They provide a convenient way of thinking about what you want to say. Suppose, for example, you lent a book to a friend and need it back in order to study. Here is the sequence the Bowers recommend you use to retrieve your book:

- *Describe the situation or idea.* "I lent you my biology book a couple of days ago, and I need to have it back so I can study tonight."

- *Express how you feel about the situation.* "I'm feeling tense about the fact that I have not read for tomorrow's class." After describing the situation from your perspective, let the other person know how you feel.[13] Disclosing your feelings can help build empathy and create a fuller understanding.

- *Specify exactly what you want.* "I'd like to pick it up right after dinner at 6 o'clock."

- *Consider possible responses or consequences you might use if the person does not respond favorably to the expectation you express.* Suppose the friend says, "I'm still using your book." Plan a response in advance. Perhaps you would say, "I still plan to pick up the book by 6 o'clock. If you can't give it to me then, I won't be willing to lend you a book again."

    Notice the use of "I" language throughout this illustration. This languagae clearly identifies the speaker as the source of the message. That language is not only straight-forward, but also takes ownership for the thoughts and feelings. This use of language helps avoid a defensive reaction from the other person involved.

3. *Carry out your plan.* Face the situation, person, or topic assertively, taking care not to get carried away. Remember your goals for the relationship. When we work to change our behavior, the greatest problem we face is that we sometimes go too far in the opposite direction. For instance, we may move from an aggressive expression to a nonassertive one or vice versa. This overcompensation can be avoided through careful thought before *and* during your encounter.

4. *Try another situation.* Apply the same procedures to another encounter. Remember, each situation may pose a different set of circumstances for you to face. Some of your areas of needed improvement are more stressful than others, while some are more complicated. Treat each encounter individually, giving full consideration to the relationship and your goals in it.

Plan for your next encounter with a situation, person, or topic that caused you to behave in a way you would like to improve.

You will find that assertive behavior is, in many instances, easier to achieve than you thought. One reason for this is that such behavior is self-rewarding, for when you behave assertively, you often accomplish what you set out to do. You may not always get what you want, but you will have the satisfaction of knowing that you communicated your wants in a way that helped you express yourself accurately, that fairly considered the other person, and that contributed to the growth and development of your relationship.

Summary

Talking about feelings, wants, and expectations is difficult because of societal injunctions against doing so. But learning to talk about these things can contribute immensely to your ability to manage your relationships. The skills involved in talking about feelings include separating feelings from emotions and learning more feeling and emotion words. We described a method for achieving this goal. Learning to talk about wants and expectations means learning to specify observable behaviors, measurable results, and an appropriate time frame in which the desired results will be performed. It also means learning to help other people be clear about what they are feeling and what they want from you. We provided examples of talk that illustrate these concepts. We have described assertive, nonassertive, and aggressive behavior and language. Nonassertive language denies the self and results in our giving up what we want. Aggressive language is the opposite: we get what we want at the expense of others, often putting ourselves above them. Assertive language enables us to preserve our own dignity and that of our partner while expressing what we need to say. We fail to communicate assertively when we give up control of our language to automatic responses triggered by situations, topics, personalities, or behaviors. We can improve our assertive communication by developing a firm sense of our self-concept and observing our own behavior as we communicate. If we can learn to identify what triggers nonassertive or aggressive communication, we can work to change those habits. Doing this will open the door to greater relational growth.

Discussion Questions

1. Differentiate between a feeling and an emotion. Have you ever confused them in a way that was damaging—or potentially damaging—to a relationship?

2. Working with two classmates, practice the three-step sequence for talking about feelings (locate, name and describe) using these situations:

   a. You are about to respond to a boss who is wrongly accusing you of an error someone else made.

   b. You are about to end a long-term romantic relationship. You do not want to hurt your partner, but you no longer want to be romantically involved.

    c. You are about to assert your right to adult status in your relationship with a parent who, even though you are over twenty, still treats you in a way that you think is "like a child." You are, in large measure, financially dependent upon your parent.

3. In the three situations above, what would you want from the other person? Work with two or three classmates to clarify those wants, and then role play the situation to practice the skills involved in expressing them.

4. Can you think of any situations in which our suggestions would not be helpful? If so, describe them, being as specific as possible. How might you try to assure clarity about your feelings and wants in those situations?

5. Why should we worry about being assertive or improving our communication styles? Can't people just accept us as we are? What would you tell the generally aggressive person who says, "I am what I am, take me or leave me"?

6. Explain how you might help a relational partner overcome nonassertive behaviors in all four of the areas we discussed—situation, topic, personality, and behavior.

7. Try to identify which of the variables influencing assertiveness works most powerfully for you. Is it behavior, personality, situation, or topic? Why do you think the power rests there?

8. Look again at the chart in figure 5.1. Can you recall an instance in which your aggressive behavior illustrated these features? Can you recall situations in which your nonassertive and assertive behaviors illustrated the features in the chart?

ENDNOTES

1. J. Powell, *The Secret of Staying in Love* (Niles, IL: Argus Communications, 1974), 73.

2. S. I. Hayakawa, ed., *Language, Meaning, and Maturity* (New York: Harper & Row, 1954), 27.

3. A. Krozybski, *Science and Sanity*, 4th ed. (Lakeville, CT: The International Non-Aristotelian Library, 1980), 34.

4. S. B. Shimanoff, "Commonly Named Emotions in Everyday Conversation," *Perceptual and Motor Skills* 58 (1984): 514.

5. S. B. Shimanoff, "Degree of Emotional Expressiveness as a Function of Face-Needs, Gender, and Interpersonal Relationship," *Communication Reports* 1 (1988): 1–8.

6. S. B. Shimanoff, "Rules Governing the Verbal Expression of Emotions between Married Couples," *Western Journal of Speech Communication* 49 (1985): 149–165.

7. S. B. Shimanoff, "Expressing Emotions in the Words: Verbal Patterns of Interaction," *Journal of Communication* 35 (1985): 16–31.

8. R. E. Alberti and M. L. Emmons, *Your Perfect Right: A Guide to Assertive Living*, 6th ed. (San Luis Obispo, CA: Impact Publishers, 1990), 91–92.

9. S. A. Bower and G. A. Bower, *Asserting Yourself: A Practical Guide for Positive Change* (Reading, MA: Addison-Wesley Publishing Company, 1976).

10. Alberti and Emmons, *Your Perfect Right*, 206–208.

11. Ibid., 206.

12. Bower and Bower, *Asserting Yourself*, 87–104.

13. D. Cloven and M. E. Roloff, "The Chilling Effect of Aggressive Potential on the Expression of Complaints in Intimate Relationships," *Communication Monographs* 60 (1993): 199–219.

READ MORE ABOUT TALKING ABOUT FEELINGS, WANTS, AND EXPECTATIONS IN THESE SOURCES

Beck, Aaron T. *Love Is Never Enough.* New York: Harper & Row, 1988. Beck makes the cognitive approach to adjustment accessible. He talks about how rational thinking and clear communication help couples enhance relationships.

Metts, Sandra, and John W. Bowers. "Emotion in Interpersonal Communication." In *Handbook of Interpersonal Communication*, 2nd ed., Mark L. Knapp and Gerald R. Miller. Newbury Park, CA: Sage, 1994. Metts and Bowers provide an overview of theories of emotion from scholars representing several disciplines.

Harré, Rom, and Gerrod Parrott. eds. *Emotions: The Social, Cultural, and Physical Dimensions.* Newbury Park, CA: Sage, 1996. This book looks at biological, historical, social, and cultural dimensions of feelings and emotions and their expression.

READ MORE ABOUT ASSERTIVENESS IN THESE SOURCES

Alberti, R. E., and M. L. Emmons. *Your Perfect Right: A Guide to Assertive Living.* 6th ed. San Luis Obispo, CA: Impact Publishers, 1990. This book is the classic presentation of material on the subject of assertiveness. In its sixth edition, the book provides all the basic information covering assertive communication and also additional material on assertiveness in the contexts of gender and occupation.

McCormack, M. H. *What They Don't Teach You at the Harvard Business School.* New York: Bantam Books, 1984. This book provides a very readable, well-illustrated account of the author's experiences as an agent for public figures. He offers practical advice about managing your communication style for success in the business environment.

Phelps, S., and N. Austin. *The Assertive Woman.* San Luis Obispo, CA: Impact Publishers, 1975. This work focuses on the assertiveness problems of women and provides helpful suggestions for dealing with common difficulties.

6

NONVERBAL COMMUNICATION

PREVIEW

In this chapter, we examine the communication potency of general and particular body cues, such as body movement and gestures and face and eye behavior. These cues influence how others interpret our talk and how we interpret theirs. Touching is also extremely important to our relationships and our personal health. The section on body communication ends with specific suggestions about how to apply the information presented to our relationship communication.

Our use of silence, vocalics, space, and time constitutes an especially important nonverbal message system. We base our interpretations of our partner's feelings, wants, and intentions on it. Similarly, the other person in our relationship is continually comparing what we say against how we say it to infer our meaning.

Some of these nonverbal cues, such as what we mean by silence in our relationships, may be unique to an individual or culture. For example, our culture understands time as a series of clicks, sixty to a minute, sixty to an hour. Others think of time differently. Clearly, the personal or cultural assumptions that we make—and that others make—about these matters can affect our relationships.

KEY TERMS

adaptors	affect displays
angle of interaction	antisocial touching
body movement	body territory
clothing	coactive position
competitive position	cooperative position
cooptive position	emblems
face and eye behavior	formal time
friendship/warmth touching	gestures
home territory	illustrators
immediacy behavior	informal time
interactional space	interactive silence
intimate distance	kinesics
love/intimacy touching	monochronic culture
past orientation	personal-casual distance
personal distance	personal space
polychronic culture	posture
present orientation	psycholinguistic silence
public distance	public territory
regulators	relaxation
sexual/arousal touching	social-consultive distance
sociocultural silence	social/polite touching
space	territoriality
time	time-line orientation
yielding	

OBJECTIVES

1. Identify, explain, and provide examples of how behavior in each of these broad categories can communicate:

   a. body movement and gestures

   b. face and eye behavior

   c. touching

   d. clothing

2. Explain the importance of touching to physical health, and suggest the implications of this explanation for interpersonal relationship growth.

3. Describe Heslin's five categories of touching behavior.

4. Discuss what the literature about body cues suggests about your behavior choices.

5. Identify and analyze your own specific nonverbal body cues.

6. Explain and provide examples of how silence can:
   a. convey the inadequacy of language
   b. link words and people
   c. enhance emotion
   d. persuade

7. Identify and describe Bruneau's three forms of silence.

8. Identify and describe features of the vocalic message system, including some of the subcategories of vocalization and vocal quality.

9. Define *territoriality*, and review the four types of territories described by Lyman and Scott.

10. Review Sommer's and Cook's studies of the angle of interaction and suggest the significance of their research for your own relationship management.

11. Identify and explain Hall's categories of personal distancing and suggest their implications for your own relationship management.

12. Explain how time and the ways people use it can communicate important relational messages.

13. Compare and contrast a monochronic and a polychronic culture.

14. Explain the differences between formal and informal time, and suggest the importance of these differences to relationship management.

BODY COMMUNICATION

Some times our verbal communication fails us when we wish to express our thoughts to another person. For example, we can say, "I love you," but the message might be more fully communicated by adding nonverbal behavior such as touch and tone of voice. Or perhaps you are upset and cannot really express the depth of your anguish. In this case, facial expressions as well as gestures and tone of voice would probably add significantly to your verbal message.

We begin our study of nonverbal communication by defining the term. Then we will move to look at body communication. This includes such things as movement and gesture, eye and face behavior, touching, and clothing. Finally we will explore how sound, space, and time communicate.

Nonverbal communication is the messages expressed by other than linguistic means. This rules out some things that may not seem like they are verbal, such as American Sign Language (used by many hearing impaired people), as well as written words.

People use a large number of *cues* to send signals to one another. Five of these are especially important: clothing choices, artifact choices, body movements (the way of walking, for example), habitual and cultural gestures, and face and eye behavior.

Typically we do not pay as much attention to our nonverbal behaviors as we might. In one study less than a quarter of the subjects who had been told to show increased or decreased liking of a partner could not describe the nonverbal behavior they used.[1] This makes the study and control of nonverbal communication more difficult because we need to bring it up to a conscious level if we are to do these things.

Although we may not always be aware of choosing our nonverbal messages, we *can* send such messages more intentionally if we wish. Moreover, we can become more sensitive to our nonverbal behavior, to how others receive it, and to how they interpret it.

Our point is clear. If messages that we send are not interpreted as we intended, we may be causing communication problems for ourselves and those who matter to us. Similarly, if we interpret another's message wrongly or do not pick it up at all, our faulty receiving skills may be causing problems in our relationships. We thus need to understand the nonverbal message systems we share with other people and to heighten our awareness of their use.

BODY MOVEMENT AND GESTURES

Body movement and *gestures* fall within the broad field of nonverbal study called *kinesics*. Gross body movement and gestures, not the subtleties of facial expression, can have an enormous communicative impact, whether or not this is intended. Of course, common sense makes this statement obvious, since our language is full of references to the communicative potential of gross body movement and gestures, such as the following:

- "You really look down."
- "Mary Ann is really wound up tight today."
- "He's so troubled that he looks like he's carrying the weight of the entire company on his back."
- "Perk up, Phil."

Have you thought about the messages you send just by the way you walk? Suppose for instance, that you are in the city—perhaps Chicago, Los Angeles, New York, or Atlanta. You are walking alone down the street. After about six seconds of observation, a mugger could determine whether you were an easy mark! Could you make the same determination?

In a study based on this question, Rubenstein videotaped sixty people walking alone in the late morning hours, then asked a panel of convicts to rate whether they would be easy to mug.[2] The convicts were asked to rate each subject on a scale of one to ten: one meant "a very easy rip-off," and ten meant "would avoid it, too big a situation, too heavy." Each videotaped sequence lasted from six to eight seconds. The expert judges had no difficulty in agreeing about which of the pedestrians would be easy marks: their movements were awkward; they walked as though in a daze; they seemed oblivious to what was going on around them. On the other hand, pedestrians who were seen as "too heavy" walked in evenly paced, determined steps that rocked from heel to toe. They appeared goal-oriented, determined, and confident about where they were going.

Among the first individuals investigating the body's communication independent of voice was Ray Birdwhistell, whose most important work appeared in 1970.[3] You may also have heard about or read such books as *The Body Language of Sex, Power, and Aggression* by Julius Fast. This book, a popularization of some of the research conducted in the early 1970s, was copyrighted in 1977.[4]

Paul Ekman and Wallace Friesen categorized gross bodily movements into *emblems, illustrators, regulators, affect displays*, and *adaptors*.[5] The definition and an illustration of each term are shown in figure 6.1.

Gestures people in the United States generally use include the thumbs-up gesture to suggest that everything is ready, the V-shaped sign with the first and second fingers pointing upward that stands for victory, and shaking the head from side to side to say no or nodding to say yes. But gestures do not always have universal meanings. The familiar OK sign in our culture, for example, made by joining the thumb and forefinger to form a circle, is an obscene gesture that represents the female genitalia in some cultures. Making such a gesture to a woman is the equivalent of making a sexual proposition and to a man is an accusation of homosexuality. This same gesture has still different meaning in other cultures. In France it means "nothing," and in Japan it means "money."[6]

It is interesting to note the differences in the way men and women use gestures. Table 6.1 summarizes what research has yielded regarding this gender-related behavior.

POSTURE

Perhaps even more subtle than gestures, *posture* communicates an enormous amount of information about you. Even so, except for a few moments when you are conscious of posture, you do not think very carefully about how you stand, sit, slump, or slouch.

Posture offers information about your attitudes, status, and self-image. It communicates your sex and whether you conform to the stereotypical gender cues of the American culture. Along with how you move from one place to another, posture reveals your personal and interpersonal style and image. And finally, posture communicates your emotions. Because these cues are so very important, it is surprising that people appear to be so unconcerned about the posture messages they send.

Figure 6.1
Categories of
gross body
movements and
gestures.

Term	Definition	Examples
Emblem	Deliberate movements that can be directly translated into words: discrete, categorical behaviors that are generally known and accepted. *Familiar emblems* are the "O.K." sign, the "come here" sign, and the hitchhiker's sign.	
Illustrator	Deliberate movements used to reinforce and enrich verbal message. The up-and-down movement of the head while saying "yes" and the reaching out and drawing back of the palm while saying "Lets go" are *illustrators*.	
Regulator	Body movements that help us to interact; a gesture system that controls turn-taking in the flow of communication. *Regulators* include nodding our heads, adjusting the focus of our eyes away from the speaker, and raising our hands.	
Affect display	Any movement or gesture that reflects the intesity of our feelings. *Affect displays* may show fear, anger, tiredness, or even surprise.	
Adaptor	Any movement or gesture that is displayed to alleviate psychological tension. *Adaptors* include biting our nails, wringing our hands, and hiding our face.	

Table 6.1	Kinesic (Gestural) Differences in Women and Men
Female behavior	*Male behavior*
Women use fewer gestures than men. Women discriminate in their use of gestures, as they use fewer gestures with other women and more with men.[7]	Men use more gestures than women. Men do not discriminate between male and female partners in their use of gestures.
Women tend to keep their hands down on the arms of a chair more than men.[8]	Men rarely keep their hands down on the arms of a chair.
Women use fewer one-handed gestures and arm movements.[9]	Men use more one-handed gestures and arm movements.
Women play with their hair or clothing, place their hands in their lap, and tap their hands more frequently than men.[10]	Men use sweeping hand gestures, stretching the hands, cracking the knuckles, pointing, and using arms to lift the body from a chair or table more frequently.
Women tend to cross their legs at the knees or cross their ankles with their knees slightly apart.[11]	Men tend to sit with their legs apart or with their legs stretched out in front of them and their ankles crossed.
Women tap their hands.	Men exhibit greater leg and foot movement, including tapping their feet.[12]

From Judy Cornelia Pearson, Lynn H. Turner, and William Todd-Mancillas, *Gender and Communication*, Second Edition. Copyright © 1991 Wm. C. Brown Publishers, Dubuque, Iowa. All Rights Reserved. Reprinted by permission.

Imagine, if you can, that you are sitting on the beach in late afternoon. It is autumn, so there is a crispness in the air, and not many people on the beach are wearing swimsuits. Instead, the costume of the day is blue jeans and T-shirt, a sweater or light jacket, and bare feet. Some blue jeans are rolled up slightly so the walkers can wade along the shoreline. As these people walk in front of you, they are silhouetted against the sun path on the water. What can you tell about them? Can you tell if they are male or female? Can you determine their approximate ages? Can you tell if they are attached somehow? Are they intimate? Can you tell if they have known each other for quite a while or if their relationship is relatively new? Is one dominant? Is one person "showing off" for another? Can you tell how anyone is feeling? And perhaps more importantly, *how* can you tell? For if it is true that you can draw inferences just from the data available in the silhouettes of people who are paying no attention to you, it is reasonable to suppose that other people can draw such inferences about you from the way you present your body, too.[13]

Imagine again the people on the beach. Suppose that one woman leans forward toward a man. She allows herself to brush against him as she smiles into his face. He turns to face her, about eighteen inches from her, and smiles. He touches her eyebrow with his index finger and traces the line of her nose down to her mouth. She nibbles, then kisses, his finger. They clasp hands and amble down the beach, bumping and brushing into each other as they go. Shortly they stop and face each other again, now holding both hands.

These postural and touching cues suggest that these two individuals are nurturing a relationship. They apparently are attracted to each other. Each welcomes the other's proximity and touching behavior. To each other and to you, they have communicated an enormous amount of information. You and they could interpret the behaviors because each of you understands the norms of such behavior in the American culture. Such behavior is called *immediacy behavior*, one of two categories of behavior by which postural and other gross body cues can communicate attitudes, style, status, and emotions. The other category is *relaxation*,[14] which deals with the degree, or extent, to which you are agitated or excited.

If you lean toward someone, smile, reach out, and open yourself to that person, you are expressing immediacy. If you lean away, pull back, withdraw from touch, and never touch; if you frown, glance away, avoid eye contact, and keep your distance, you are also expressing a dimension of immediacy. Thus, immediacy behavior exists along a continuum in context with degrees of relaxation. Don't be confused; the terms are not opposites. Immediacy exists in degrees. Nonverbal behavior that decreases or increases the closeness between us and another or that inhibits or improves visibility between us and another is an important means of relationship communication.

Table 6.2	Kinesic (Posture and Bearing) Differences in Women and Men
Female behavior	*Male behavior*
Women tend to hold their legs more closely together.	Men tend to have their legs apart at a 10- to 15-degree angle.
Women maintain their arms close to their body.	Men hold their arms about 5 to 10 degrees away from their bodies.
Women rely on more closed body positions.	Men rely on more open body positions.[15]
Women tend to engage in less body lean.	Men tend to engage in more backward lean.[16]
Women walk with their pelvis rolled slightly forward.	Men walk with their entire pelvis rolled slightly back.
Women present their entire body from their neck to their ankles as a moving entity when they walk.[17]	Men move their arms independently and exhibit a slight twist of their rib cage.

From Judy Cornelia Pearson, Lynn H. Turner, and William Todd-Mancillas, *Gender and Communication*, Second Edition. Copyright © 1991 Wm. C. Brown Publishers, Dubuque, Iowa. All Rights Reserved. Reprinted by permission.

We observe these behaviors and base our guesses about the components of our relationships upon them. Unfortunately, we rarely talk about them. Instead, we believe that we "know" what they "mean." So, we tend to fall into the dangerous habit of pretending that we can read others' minds by looking at their behavior.

There are differences in the postures and bearing of men and women. Table 6.2 summarizes what we know from research about these gender-related differences.

FACE AND EYE BEHAVIOR

Just as gross body control and movement can communicate, so can particular body cues, such as *face and eye behavior.* Indeed, the face and eyes are probably the most powerful generators of nonverbal messages. So powerful are they that for centuries, they have been the subject of poetry and song and the cause of very dramatic interpersonal and international episodes.

Research shows that women engage in more eye contact than men[18] and that eye contact has both positive and negative aspects. We demand public speakers to establish and maintain eye contact with the audience. We learn early in life that it is not polite to stare,[19] and we especially dislike being stared at when the other person's eyes can not be seen.[20] Eye contact is important in regulating our conversations, especially turn-taking.[21]

Studies have shown that even pupil size can send an important nonverbal message.[22] Larger pupils are perceived as more attractive, so much so that photographers often attempt to enlarge the pupils of their models.[23] There even appears to be a correlation between pupil size and lying.[24] The act of lying actually causes fluctuations in pupil size. Conjuring up the lie seems to make pupil diameter smaller. Actually telling the lie appears to increase pupil size.[25]

Even eye direction communicates. Gur and Gur[26] wanted to know if there was a relationship between eye direction and defensive mechanisms. They discovered that people who tend to look to the right also tend to project and turn against others as a defense mechanism, whereas those who tend to look to the left also tend to repress and deny things as a defense mechanism.

Clearly, face and eye behavior does communicate. But this behavior tends to be so subtle and habitual that we have a very difficult time controlling it. Even so, it bears directly on your relationships. To make our important point again, if you feel that you are in trouble in a relationship or if you become aware of some facial or eye behavior that seems significant, be willing to talk about it. Ask about it. Check your inferences against the actual experiences of the other person. Otherwise you risk acting on a guess that may very well be wrong.

People sometimes manage facial expressions to *neutralize* or *mask* emotions. You neutralize a facial expression of emotion when you try to eliminate it altogether. Perhaps you have heard of someone displaying a "poker face." This expression refers to the generally accepted wisdom that if you are playing cards, you should maintain rigid control of the facial and eye muscles to avoid telegraphing your hand.

Similarly, in American culture, growing up male means, among other things, that it is not acceptable to express your strongest emotions—especially sentimental ones—with your face and eyes. Because of this, many young men have been embarrassed when they were moved to tears. The embarrassment undoubtedly arises from a conflict between experiencing and displaying an emotion. Men are not supposed to display visual expressions of fear and sadness except under extreme circumstances because these are considered feminine emotions.

Neutralizing emotions can be very risky and dangerous. Your entire nervous system could be damaged if you train yourself not to accept and express such emotions as fear and sadness.

Emotions are masked when you attempt to present a facial expression that is different from your experience. People often try to conceal strong or socially unacceptable feelings. For example, even though you may be feeling enraged at work, you will surely try to mask that emotion in public since it is unacceptable in most companies to "make a scene." And an employee would surely be unwilling to display public disapproval of the boss's decision, although a conference might be held in private.

Eye contact in interpersonal communication differs between sexes and among cultures. Women engage in more eye contact than men regardless of the gender of the person they are talking with. The amount of eye contact also varies greatly among cultures. Michael Argyle reports that eye contact is high in Arabian, Latin, and American cultures. It is lowest among Indians and northern Europeans.[27]

Directness in eye contact differs culturally also. A direct gaze is considered normal for a Latin American speaker, and in Arab and southern European countries. In contrast, Indians, Asians, Pakistanis, and northern Europeans do not gaze directly at the listener, and sometimes do not look at the listener at all.

Men and women behave differently in their eye contact and facial expressions. Tables 6.3 and 6.4 display the differences researchers have found.

Table 6.3   Kinesic (Eye Contact) Differences in Women and Men

Female behavior	*Male behavior*
Women establish more eye contact than men.[28]	Men establish less eye contact than women.
Women engage in a higher percentage of mutual looking than men.[29]	Males engage in more mutual eye gazing as they age.[30]
Women avert their gaze more than men.[31]	Men engage in staring behavior rather than in gaze aversion.
Women appear to value eye contact more than men.[32]	Men do not appear to be disturbed by people who do not watch them.

From Judy Cornelia Pearson, Lynn H. Turner, and William Todd-Mancillas, *Gender and Communication*, Second Eddition. Copyright © 1991 Wm. C. Brown Publishers, Dubuque, Iowa. All Rights Reserved. Reprinted by permission.

Table 6.4   Kinesic (Facial Expression) Differences in Women and Men

Female behavior	*Male behavior*
Women use more facial expression and are more expressive than men.[33]	Men use less facial expression and are less expressive than women.
Women are better at conveying emotions than men.[34]	Men do not convey their emotions through their faces.
Women demonstrate superior recognition memory of their own facial expressions.[35]	Men do not recall their own facial expressions.
Women smile more than men.[36]	Men smile less than women.
Women are more apt to return smiles when someone smiles at them.[37]	Men are less likely to return a smile than women.
Women are more attracted to others who smile.[38]	Men are not more attracted to others who smile.

From Judy Cornelia Pearson, Lynn H. Turner, and William Todd-Mancillas, *Gender and Communication*, Second Edition. Copyright © 1991 Wm. C. Brown Publishers, Dubuque, Iowa. All Rights Reserved. Reprinted by permission.

Controlling Face and Eye Behavior

Interestingly, the range of emotions your eyes and face are capable of expressing is very great, but your ability to control and manage such expressions is limited. When you are being fluent—when you are thinking about your ideas or emotions but not your facial muscles—your facial expressions may not be under conscious control.

When you are trying to manage the impressions you are making, you tend to use one of a very limited number of techniques for controlling facial and eye behavior.[39]

Sometimes we manage facial expressions *to intensify or minimize* the emotion we are experiencing. Can you remember attending a surprise party, perhaps one thrown in your honor? Was the guest of honor truly surprised? Or was the guest of honor intensifying the emotion? How do you know? *Intensifying,* in this sense, is nothing more than doing what is expected for the purpose of pleasing friends and maintaining relationships with them. If a friend tries to surprise us and we like her, we will register surprise with a facial expression (or, at least, will try to do so), whether or not we are truly surprised. If a friend is experiencing sorrow, we will register our empathy in a facial expression because we care about him and about our relationship with him. If we reveal our emotions to someone and it seems appropriate or necessary in that context for this person to reinforce our emotions, this will be done so by intensifying.

But, of course, there are times when a facial expression of emotion is unwarranted and unacceptable. We then try to minimize our facial expression. Everyone does this. For example, we have performed well on an exam. But knowing that our friend did poorly, we make an attempt to control our natural sense of excitement.

Some facial expressions seem to be universal in their meaning. Laughter and smiles are a signal of positive emotions around the world. The opposite is also true. The same sour expressions convey displeasure cross-culturally.[40] However, cultural rules do govern the degree of display that is appropriate. For example, identical internal feelings might be more controlled in the Japanese culture than in an Arab culture.

TOUCHING BEHAVIOR

There is little doubt that everyone needs and wants physical contact with others. If someone is deprived of this contact, the deprivation can be damaging. As you mature, much of what you know about conducting your affairs and managing your relationships is a function of the touching behavior you have experienced. Each of these statements has been developed and supported by research. But what do they mean to you, as a student of interpersonal communication?

Touching behavior is generally completely a matter of choice. We can usually choose to touch or to withhold touch. We can choose to respond positively when touched or to withdraw from the touching. Our choices have a very powerful effect on ourselves and the others in our relationships. As you will see, touching can communicate strong messages about attitudes, developmental needs, body contact needs, status, and images about the relationship with the person touched. Touching even has a direct bearing on our personal health and growth.

How does touch
affect your
relationships?

To illustrate the potency of interpersonal touch—and of touch deprivation—we can turn to a very large literature. For example, in 1972, Ashley Montagu published a study involving 173 breast-fed and nonbreast-fed children. Children who had not been breast-fed had four times the number of respiratory infections, twenty times more diarrhea, eight times as much eczema, more hay fever, more asthma, and more of a variety of other diseases than breast-fed children.[41] Although it is likely that other factors contributed to these problems, Montagu concluded that touch was in part responsible. He strengthened his argument by citing cases in which adults suffering from a variety of psychological problems were successfully treated by therapy that employed extensive physical contact. Tactile deprivation has also been shown to be a causal factor in problems involving speech, symbol recognition, and lack of trust and confidence.[42]

Some very dramatic findings in research with animals have also shown the powerful effects of touch deprivation. A very famous early study was published in 1958 by Harry Harlow and R. R. Zimmermann.[43] Laboratory-raised baby monkeys had become so attached to the cloth pads in their cages that they threw temper tantrums when the researchers attempted to replace the pads. So Harlow built a terry-cloth surrogate mother with a light bulb inside to radiate "body heat." He built a second surrogate mother of wire mesh. These "mothers" were placed in cubicles next to the infant monkey's cage. In half the cases, the wire mother provided milk, but the terry-cloth mother did not; in the other half, the terry-cloth mother provided milk, but the wire mother did not. The baby monkeys were allowed to spend time with the mothers on demand, for as long as they wished. The finding was that the infant monkeys spent dramatically more time with the terry-cloth mother, whether or not the mother provided milk. This conclusion makes a powerful statement about touching. Touch is significant for humans too. Research at the University of Miami School of Medicine shows that premature babies grow faster and gain more weight when massaged.[44]

Touching is the first form of communication that an infant knows and is an important aspect of communication throughout life.[45] Among adults, most touching conveys some greeting or symbolic gesture, which differs from culture to culture.[46] For example, psychologist Sidney Jourard found striking differences in the number of body contacts per hour from society to society. He studied touching behavior in cafés in San Juan, Puerto Rico, in Paris, in Gainesville, Florida, and in London. The Puerto Ricans were the most frequent touchers, with up to 180 contacts in an hour. The French touched each other 110 times per hour. The Americans, in contrast, were not very frequent touchers. Jourard counted only 2 contacts per hour in the Gainesville café. But the British were the most reserved. Jourard did not record a single case of physical touching in the London café.[47]

Richard Heslin and his colleagues have been studying touching behavior for ten years and have developed a category system that conveniently organizes the discussion of such behavior.[48] (The category system is Heslin's; we provided the definitions and examples presented in table 6.5.) Of course, we would add the category of *antisocial touching:* touching that violates a person's sense of propriety. Examples here would be unwelcomed sexual advances or a punch in the nose.

While this system is convenient, it cannot be very comfortably used to identify distinct sets of behaviors because communication events always occur within some context. It is the individual communicator's understanding of the context and the relationship within that context that govern the judgment about the appropriateness or inappropriateness of a touch. Moreover, touching behavior can

Table 6.5   Heslin's Categories for Touching Behavior

Category	Definition	Example
Functional/professional touching	Touching that delivers some professional service	Example relationships: physician-patient; barber-client; swimming instructor-student; makeup artist-actor
Social/polite touching	Ritual touching that acknowledges someone's person-hood or essential humanity and/or acknowledges or neutralizes status differences	Examples: handshake, the kiss on the hand, the kiss on a cardinal's ring; ritual greeting hugs
Friendship/warmth touching	Casual and spontaneous touching that signals mutual acceptance and positive regard, but excluding love or sexual touching	Examples: asexual greeting hugs or kisses among friends or family; congratulatory shoulder or back patting; mock-violent behavior, such as the playful shoulder punch
Love/intimacy touching	Touching behavior that signals a special, or bonded, relationship or that assumes or confirms intimate access to be appropriate to that relationship	Examples: hand holding, whether the couple is stationary or moving; mutual hand-on-hip postures; lap sitting
Sexual/arousal touching	Touching that conveys sexual meaning or produces sexual stimulation	Examples: prolonged kissing; petting; sexual foreplay; sexual intercourse

Source: N. R. Heslin and T. Alper, "Touch: A Bonding Gesture," in J. M. Wieman and R. P. Harrison, eds. *Nonverbal Interaction 2* (1983): 47–75.

rarely be isolated in just one category. Human relationships are more complex than this. Thus, two simple but very powerful conclusions can be drawn:

1. Touching behavior suggests a bond between the people who touch and are touched.
2. People respond to touching behavior according to their estimate of its appropriateness within that relationship and within that context.

Based upon these conclusions, it is reasonable to point out, once again, that a person who is concerned about improving interpersonal communication must become sensitive to human touching behavior and to the cues that people send about their estimates of touching appropriateness. We will undoubtedly feel tense and uncomfortable in response to touching that seems inappropriate in its context. However, we only *infer* what the other person means by the touch unless we are willing and able to talk about the experience when it seems fitting to do so.

Touch only *suggests* a relationship—a bond—between the toucher and the touched. It does not explicitly tell us what only the other person can about her feelings, wants and expectations, intentions, latitude or acceptance, and her images of us, herself, and the context. If we want to know these things and want the other person to know these things about us, we must bring them up to the level of talk.

Touching behavior is an area in which there are considerable cultural differences. For example, one study found that students from the United States reported being touched twice as much as Japanese students.[49] Touch also differs on the basis of same-sex associates. In the Middle East men walk with their arms around each other's shoulders. The Middle East, Latin America, and southern Europe are considered to be high-contact cultures that engage in a great deal of touching behavior while talking. People from these cultures may perceive people from northern Europe and Japan as cold, because they are members of low-contact cultures.

The gender differences regarding touching for men and women are markedly different. Table 6.6 displays the differences researchers have found in this area.

CLOTHING

The *clothing* we wear may be used to say something about us. For example, we do not hesitate to "dress up" when the occasion dictates. We have a clear sense of when this is appropriate. Likewise, we do not hesitate to "dress down" under the correct circumstances. And if we are like most people, at times we have not been sure about what to wear for an occasion. Should we dress up? How much? Should we dress down? How much?

Table 6.6   **Tactile Differences between Women and Men**

Female behavior	*Male behavior*
Women touch others less than men do.	Men touch others more than women do.[50]
Women are touched more by others.[51]	Men are touched less by others.
Women value touching more than men do.[52]	Men do not value touch as much as women do.
Women distinguish between touching behavior that indicates warmth and touching behavior that suggests sexual intent.	Men do not make distinctions between various kinds of touch.[53]
Women view touch as an expressive behavior that demonstrates warmth and affiliation.	Men generally view touch as an instrumental behavior leading to sexual activity or as behavior that is childish, indicative of dependency and a lack of manliness.[54]

From Judy Cornelia Pearson, Lynn H. Turner, and William Todd-Mancillas, *Gender and Communication,* Second Edition. Copyright © 1991 Wm. C. Brown Publishers, Dubuque, Iowa. All Rights Reserved. Reprinted by permission.

Differences in clothing communicate about the people and their relationships.

These questions and concerns suggest that we are frequently aware of the messages that are sent by our clothes. Figure 6.2 says a lot about the people in it. Look at the photo very carefully and consider dress. Do you think the people have selected clothes that say something about how they see themselves? Can you infer anything about their socioeconomic levels? about their educational levels? What specifically tells you this?

If you could not see the faces, would you be able to tell anything about the ages of the people in the picture? Could you infer anything about the sexes of the individuals in the photo? What signals are you picking up on?

Nearly all research on the relationship between what people wear and the people themselves has focused upon personality and such characteristics as age, sex, socioeconomic status, and educational level. These demographic variables constitute stereotypes, and you probably are fairly sensitive to them. Some of this research is over thirty years old. For example, M. L. Rosencranz conducted a fairly intensive study about clothes-conscious people in 1962.[55] He found that there was a relationship between married women who were clothes-conscious and their social status. They were usually in the upper social classes; they were usually joiners—that is, they belonged to many organizations; and they usually were rather well-educated and more comfortable in intellectual conversations than were married women who did not care much about clothes. Clothes-conscious women also tended to have fairly high incomes and to be married to white-collar workers.

None of this is surprising, of course. Common experience tells us that dress is a leading indicator of status. But if we look at the phenomenon from a somewhat different perspective, as Aiken did in 1963, we discover some interesting additional information.[56] Aiken wanted to know what kind of woman had an interest in clothing. He found that clothes-conscious women tended to be a bit insecure, quite conscientious, and stereotypical in their ways of thinking. They were also persistent and conventional, given to compliance in the face of authority, and rather tense and uptight.

Aiken also found that women who are interested in and concerned about economy in relation to clothing were responsible, alert, efficient, precise, intelligent, conscientious, and controlled. They would probably spend time shopping for bargains, purchase quality clothing, and be concerned about the clothing budget. Aiken inferred that such care about clothing, reflected in what a woman wears, speaks about the personality of the woman herself.

Aiken asked a third question: What kind of woman prefers elaborately detailed clothing and lots of jewelry—much more than normal? He found that these women were not intellectual but rather conventional and stereotyped. They were also sympathetic, sociable, and conscientious. Moreover, they tended to be somewhat submissive.

Consider the clothes you are wearing now. What are you saying about yourself?

On the other hand, women who conformed to popular norms of dress were found to be socially conscientious and traditional. They were moral women, quite sociable, and they, too, were submissive. They tended to focus upon economic, social, and religious values, but not so much upon the more aesthetic values of the culture.

Finally, Aiken wanted to know what kind of women dressed primarily for comfort. Not surprisingly, such women were self-possessed and self-controlled, socially cooperative, and very sociable. Somewhat surprisingly, however, they were considered to be thorough and deferential to authority.

In a later study, Rosenfeld and Plax discovered that clothes-conscious men were guarded, deferred to authority, and believed that people were easy to manipulate.[57] On the other hand, men who were not very clothes-conscious were fairly independent and aggressive. They did not think people were easy to manipulate. Interestingly, men who were more interested in clothing for such practical reasons as warmth, rather than for aesthetic reasons, were somewhat inhibited and rebellious. Women in this category were clever and confident. Conversely, men who were interested in the aesthetics of dress were generally more success-oriented. They were seen as mature. Women in this category, however, were self-centered and detached.

Another relationship that has been examined is between self-consciousness and clothing. Solomon and Schopler found for both men and women who were highly conscious about their appearance and behavior a markedly significant relationship between public self-consciousness and clothing interest. Interestingly, these researchers found that this relationship between self-consciousness and clothing was exceedingly stronger for women than men.[58]

Other research[59] leaves no doubt that clothes communicate a lot about the wearer. William Thourlby[60] has suggested that clothing is the basis upon which people judge each other in at least ten categories:

1. economic level
2. educational level
3. trustworthiness
4. social position
5. level of sophistication
6. economic background
7. social background
8. educational background
9. level of success
10. moral character

Employment interviewers know the importance of dressing correctly. There has even evolved a "dress code" for interviewing, and interviewers representing the Fortune 500 companies listed correct clothing choices high on the list of characteristics they were looking for in a candidate.[61] Mark Hickson and Don Stacks[62] concluded from their review of the literature on clothing that interviewers tend to hire their own images. To succeed in the interview situation, you should dress much like the interviewer. The interviewer may be dressed in close conformity to the suggestions that John T. Molloy[63] made as a result of his investigation.

Clearly, then, on the basis of common sense and these examples, our clothing choices communicate a great deal about us. Clothes tell about our place of work (formal and informal dress codes), influence the social impression we make, tell people if we are likable or sexy, and say something about our age and social status, and even how powerful we might be.[64]

In all of this work, researchers have only been able to put together a general taxonomy that will allow accurate understanding of the general and particular body cues as they occur in context with each other. Still, we do know that they are important in our day-to-day conversations and especially in our important relationships. Since our grasp of these nonverbal messages is tenuous, it is important to remember that *we cannot read another individual's mind.* If we observe nonverbal messages and then assume that we know what they mean, we may well be doing just that—pretending to read the other person's mind. It is far better to talk about what we have observed and to tell the other individual what we are guessing, for this allows our partner to confirm or deny our inferences. Our relationship will then be better able to grow.

> Researchers have only been able to put together a general taxonomy of body cues. We thus must learn to talk about the inferences we draw from nonverbal messages.

USING NONVERBAL SKILLS EFFECTIVELY

The ideas presented about our nonverbal body messages strongly argue for some common sense and care in our interactions with other people.

Recall that nonverbal communication is two-way and that both we and the other people in our relationships send and receive messages on purpose and by accident. As receivers, we should try to become more aware of our own biases and receiving behavior habits. Are we responding to some behavior of our partner that has no message value? That is, are we responding to some unintentional behavior that really does not reflect how that person is actually thinking and feeling? Or are we assigning meaning based on our own standards and assumptions? For example, our personal dress code may cause us to believe that a person means one thing by his clothing when he actually does not.

Know, also, that your nonverbal behavior effects that of the other person with whom you communicate. Judee Burgoon and her colleagues conclude that nonverbal cues play a key role in how we adapt to others.[65] We often reciprocate behaviors. So if you lean into a person, that person may lean in also. If you talk with your arms folded the other person may do likewise. So don't be surprised if you notice a person with whom you are talking being affected by your nonverbal behaviors.

Try to become more sensitive to your use and interpretation of others' body movements and gestures. At the first moment that you feel confusion or uncertainty about someone's intention, ask about that intention. Say, for example, "I'm aware that you just pulled away, but I'm not sure why. Will you tell me?" The person may be able to help you understand the behavior. Sometimes, however, she may not know why she pulled away. Even when this is the case, talking about the behavior can make the initiator aware of it. Remember to listen carefully to what the other person says, to inquire about her interpretation without defensiveness, and to accept or explain yourself calmly.

Remember also that the face is an important indicator of emotions and feelings. It is also a method of nonverbal expression that is difficult to control. Try to remember to smile when it is appropriate to do so. Smiling and raising the eyebrows are positive, responsive behaviors that are generally encouraging. Of course, if the subject is a very serious one, smiling too much may be an inappropriate response. Also remember to look—not stare—at your partner during conversation. Try to focus your gaze at the speaker. Lack of eye contact often suggests lack of interest, a message that may be far from the one you wish to send.

Think also in terms of what the image you wish to project may mean about your face and eye behavior. Think, too, about your assumptions as you perceive the other person's face and eye behavior. More careful attention to these subtle cues can contribute to your success in managing your relationship.

Try to dress appropriately and even conservatively when appropriate. In addition, research the dress expectations that people are likely to have. All that is required is a phone call, a visit, or direct observation.

Especially in important and tense moments, slow things down and bring your observations and inferences to the level of talk. If you are responding to another's eye shifts, that person may need to know that—especially if these messages are unintentional. If the other person is responding to some facial mannerisms of yours, you need to be aware of that. Candor and direct talk are the best means of remedying a misunderstanding. Practice the skills of talking about relationships. Practice the skills of active listening. In times of conflict, slow down, calm down, and work hard to get and give feedback often.

We trust that our exploration of body cues has been helpful to your understanding of their impact on relational communication. Now we turn to take a look at sound, space, and time and the role they play in our relational communication.

SILENCE

The process you used to decipher the message is similar to the one you use to understand spoken words. The space between the words tells you a great deal about how to interpret them, for *silence* is the background upon which all spoken language is structured. Silence can exist without language, but language cannot exist without silence.[66] The sounds and the silence that surround language constitute an enormously complex set of nonverbal cues. We use silence to communicate threat or to show respect: to demonstrate the inadequacy of language and to enrich spoken messages;[67] to link words and people; to enhance emotion; to communicate judgments: and to spur people into action.[68]

Silence can have both positive and negative impact on our relationships. For example, especially in early stages of a relationship, silences can be very embarrassing—so much so that the participants in an awkward silence will resort to such behaviors as coughing, throat clearing, singing, whistling, and drumming the fingertips to mask the silence.[69] On the other hand, silence can actually communicate intimacy.[70]

What are you saying when you remain silent?

To illustrate the complexity of this one phenomenon as a part of our communication system, Thomas Bruneau[71] identified three forms of silence that are important to communication. *Psycholinguistic silence* is the silence that is part of the temporal sequence of speech in encoding and decoding. *Interactive silence* is a pause, or interruption, in interpersonal interactions that is used for making decisions, drawing inferences, exercising control and power, and adjusting interpersonal distances between the talkers. *Sociocultural silence* includes cultural assumptions and such formally sanctioned silence as the silence we observe in churches or the silence imposed by some authority. This category also includes the silences that people in our society use for deliberate rhetorical or persuasive effect, such as the "silent treatment" that a teenage girl sometimes applies to her boyfriend.

Rollo May pointed out that even infinitesimally small pauses, as well as vocalized pauses—times when we actually vocalize[72] to fill time and allow ourselves to process information—can have enormous communicative significance. A pause is the "locus of the speaker's freedom," he says. That is, the pause, whether short or long, that we fill with vocalizations allows us to stop to think or to listen to others, to "mold" our conversation this way or that, to tell a joke, or even to capture a new idea that is forming. By giving us the freedom to carry out a number of important communication activities, a pause thus helps us shape the uniqueness of a comment or a response and consider and create the next utterance.

Silence is used by people for a multitude of reasons. Silence can be used to psychologically create distance, as in a crowded elevator. Silence can be also used to decrease interpersonal distance, as the silence of lovers that suggests "I understand." Silence is also used in circumstances where people are experiencing strong emotions, such as fear, anger, surprise, or love. Both positive and negative emotions can evoke silence.

What does all this mean to us as we manage our relationships? It means, clearly, that we will do well to become much more sensitive to silences and that we must remember we cannot read another person's mind. *Silences carry important relational messages. Since we cannot read them, we must learn to bring our interpretations of them up to the level of talk and to ask about them if they are troublesome.*

There are cultural differences in how people regard silence. The difference is especially interesting for the Apache. For example, Apache workers are not concerned about introducing a stranger who may be working with them. Mutual strangers are expected to maintain silence, and may do so for several days, while they decide if the other person is OK. Silence also plays a role in courting behaviors among the Apache. The Apache may remain silent for hours. When they do talk, they may say very little. After several months, they will begin to have more lengthy communications.[73] Other cultures regard talk and silence differently, too. Japanese and Chinese believe that remaining silent is proper when there is nothing to be said. People from the United States may resent the silence and try to fill it with talk.

VOCALICS

So far, we have explored some of the body and environmental cues that can have an important impact upon interpersonal relationships. Even so, those messages-without-words have not received nearly as much study over the years as *vocalics*. Indeed, vocalics may constitute the most important nonverbal message system. Vocalics, or the ways we vocalize, are vitally important, for *what* we say cannot exist independent of *how* we say it. Variations in rate, pitch, and force and in how we articulate the elements of language are included in this category. Also included are our particular ways of phrasing, pausing, and even vocal factors like accents.[74] Figure 6.2 illustrates the complexity of this message system. The figure shows that features of vocalization and voice quality directly affect language interpretation and that these elements all work together to produce our unique vocal styles. Each variable is important to your interpersonal communication, and each is one that you can learn to control.

Vocal Quality and Vocalizations

Think of the range of interpretations possible from vocal quality. We suspect that you could expand figure 6.2 under the heading "interpretation" with a little thought and effort. Even so, we have sug-

How do vocalics affect a message? What does an insult sound like?

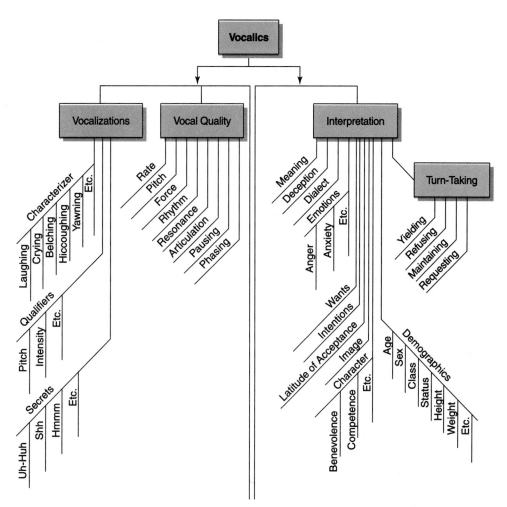

Figure 6.2
The complexity
of vocalics as a
nonverbal
message
system.

gested some of the more obvious possibilities. We determine that someone is lying, for example, partly by the "tone of voice." We make guesses about her emotional state, wants and expectations, intentions, latitude of acceptance, character, and her image of us. We can also tell the age and sex of that individual and something about her social class and status by listening to her vocal quality and vocalizations. We can even try to judge a person's height and weight based upon the sound of her voice. But if we can make these guesses, so can she.

As mentioned before, guessing introduces the risk of error. If we act upon our interpretations as though they were true but they turn out to be wrong, we may very well place our relationships at risk. That is why it is so important to learn to be sensitive to our processing of the nonverbal messages we send and receive and to learn to bring our observations and guesses up to the level of talk when it seems appropriate. Since we cannot read another's mind, we must be told what is happening. Since our culture does not teach us to tell each other these things, we use nonverbal message systems instead. But we can choose and sometimes should discuss them.

Verbal fluency is an aspect of vocalics that has been examined from the perspective of the speaker and listener. Research indicates that less fluent speech—containing more pauses, vocalized pauses, and hesitations—occurs when involvement in the communication is low, when the topic is novel, or when the ideas are being presented by a person who is untrained in message preparation.[75] On the other hand, listeners identify the counterpart—more fluent speech—with authoritativeness, attractiveness, and professionalism.[76]

SPACE

People use *space* in a direct way. For example, there is some evidence that human beings are territorial creatures and that the person-to-space ratio, or *density*, has an important bearing on interpersonal perception and communication. In addition, there appears to be a fairly well-tuned set of cultural norms about the appropriate interpersonal distance that guides individuals in their actions with others. Even the angle of interaction appears to be related to the quality and amount of interaction. Obviously, then, the dimensions of space can operate as communication.

Territoriality

If we "own" space, it gives us a number of behavioral prerogatives that another individual cannot assume with that space. *Territoriality* is this tendency for individuals to claim and "own" space and then use it as an extension of their own personal space. Perhaps you have noticed that at the beginning of a new term, you and other students select the desk or chair in which you will sit and then "claim" that space. We have noticed that our students sometimes will develop such a solid claim on a chair that other students begin to refer to it as "Tim's" or "Elizabeth's chair." We have seen students express, both nonverbally and verbally, their irritation when, after a couple of weeks, someone else sits in a chair that they had claimed.

After a person has staked out, claimed, and begun to own a territory, that claim is very precisely defined—but not only by the individual. It is also defined by the culture. The amount of space that any individual can "own" in this fashion varies from culture to culture.

The territoriality issues that bear directly on relationships evolve out of a complex mix of context and norm. That is, we have learned to occupy the same established spaces according to a powerful, but usually unspoken, set of rules and assumptions. To violate them would be to impose oneself on another and perhaps to risk the relationship.

Lyman and Scott believe that there are four types of territories, which they base on accessibility.[77] *Public territory* is an area that individuals may enter freely. Parks and public playgrounds are both examples of such space, as are certain parts of government buildings, the lobby of a public library, and the common area of a shopping mall. About the only rule for using public territory is that you have a legitimate purpose.

The second category in the Lyman and Scott model is *interactional space.* This territory is mobile. When and where people congregate informally, as well as the consent of the people, mark its boundaries. The boundaries may be larger or smaller and more or less irregular depending upon the people, the context, and the nature of their interrelationships. For example, you and your friends may go to a restaurant to have lunch and to enjoy each other's conversations. The interactional territory will depend in part on the number of people in the group. If the restaurant has only tables and chairs and if the tables all have four chairs, you might very well decide to draw a second table to the first, thus establishing an interactional territory of a different shape and size than the planned seating arrangement in the restaurant. Similarly, your group may decide to stand on a sidewalk waiting for the restaurant to open for lunch. As you stand there, the group's nature, size, loudness, power relationships, and the like will define a space that you will temporarily "own." To experiment with this kind of interactional territory, imagine what would happen if some stranger walked up to your group and stood within its boundaries!

Lyman and Scott's third classification is *home territory.* This is the private space that you occupy with legal sanction, such as your house or apartment. Outsiders must gain permission to enter home territory, or else they are in violation of law. In some cases, the law is so strongly written that the owner of home territory may legally shoot and kill an intruder who is forcibly entering.

The last category in the Lyman and Scott system is *body territory,* or *personal space*—the area immediately surrounding your physical person. It changes size and shape depending upon the nature of your relationships with others and the context. For example, a close relative may actually touch and kiss you, but only within certain unwritten rules and limitations. A close friend may have different prerogatives for entering your body space.

Within each of these categories of territory, we are bound by the rules and assumptions that constantly shift and change according to such variables as the overall size of the space, the number of people,

We are bound by the rules and assumptions that govern the use of space, and we must discover ways to communicate about them.

the nature of their relationships, and the clothing they are wearing. We must navigate through these various territories within the rules that are operating or risk our relationships. And since those rules are entirely in the minds of the people applying them, we often make mistakes. Clearly, a concept such as territoriality can have an important bearing on the success of a relationship. For relationships to grow, people must find a way to communicate about the rules and assumptions they are applying.

Angle of Interaction

Robert Sommer[78] has attempted to relate people's seating choices, or *angle of interactions*, to their perceptions of each other and of the situation. He was especially interested in whether the two-person subject groups of his study would perceive themselves as cooperating, competing, or coacting. Sommer asked people to report how they would seat themselves under the circumstances he wanted to study. His findings were replicated by Mark Cook in the United Kingdom. Their findings are very useful (see figure 6.3 and tables 6.7 and 6.8).

When Sommer asked his subjects to show how they would locate themselves if they were going to compete with each other, they typically took positions opposite each other. The large majority preferred *competitive* positions across a table, face-to-face.

When he asked the subjects to seat themselves in a *cooperative* situation, he found that they assumed closer positions. One of the most common seating choices for this situation was diagonal seating across the corner of the table. Such an arrangement provides some security (the corner of the table intervenes between the participants) while at the same time allows them to make close visual and tactile

Figure 6.3
The four most popular seating arrangements
Source: Personal Space: Behavioral Basis for Design *by Robert Sommer.* © *1969 by Prentice-Hall, Inc. Englewood Cliffs, NJ.*

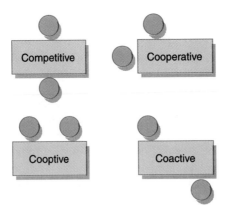

contact. They can work with each other at more intimate distances. This position also permits the individuals to exchange personal and intimate information while maintaining their integrity and dignity and without violating the personal and private space of the other.

Sommer next asked his subjects to show where they would sit if they were in a situation in which they were working on the same task and trying to show mutual support. He called this arrangement *cooptive.* Most agreed that they would sit side by side. This allows the participants to work together, to touch, to maintain personal distances, or choose intimate distances. And at the same time, the position makes it possible for one subject to control—or "coopt"—the other. Interestingly, his subjects also found this position to be fairly satisfying for cooperation.

Finally, Sommer wanted to know where his subjects would sit if they wanted to work privately but on essentially the same task, so they could make contact and exchange views only now and again. In what they called the *coactive* position, the subjects chose to

Table 6.7   Seating Preferences at Rectangular Tables (Cook)

	1	2	3	4	5	6
Conversation						
U.S. sample (151 responses)	42%	46%	11%	0%	1%	0%
U.K. (univ.) sample (102 responses)	51	21	15	0	6	7
U.K. (nonuniv.) sample (42 responses)	42	42	9	2	5	0
Cooperation						
U.S. sample	19	25	51	0	5	0
U.K. (univ.) sample	11	11	23	20	22	13
U.K. (nonuniv.) sample	40	2	50	5	2	0
Coaction						
U.S. sample	3	3	7	13	43	33
U.K. (univ.) sample	9	8	10	31	28	14
U.K. (nonuniv.) sample	12	14	12	19	31	12
Competition						
U.S. sample	7	41	8	18	20	5
U.K. (univ.) sample	7	10	10	50	16	7
U.K. (nonuniv.) sample	4	13	3	53	20	7

Reprinted from M. Cook, "Experimentation on Orientation and Proxemics," *Human Relations* 23 (1970): 63. Used by permission of Plenum Publishing Company.

arrange themselves as far away from each other as they could at the table.

Recall that nonverbal communication can be related to the person's culture. Sommer's study was repeated with British subjects by Mark Cook,[79] who found some differences between the American and British arrangements. Tables 6.7 and 6.8 show Cook's findings.

PERSONAL DISTANCING

The angle of interaction is closely related to the patterns of *personal distance* within a culture. Personal space is used as a communication medium. Special space around you is reserved as private, and you do not let many people invade this private space.

You may have felt uncomfortable when someone came too close to you. At other times, you were very pleased to have people get so close that actual contact was made. Thus, the private bubble of space is very flexible, shrinking and expanding according to your relationships. The prominent anthropologist Edward T. Hall[80] explored

Table 6.8   Seating Preferences at Round Tables (Cook)

	x x	x x	x x
Conversation			
U.S. sample (116 responses)	63%	17%	20%
U.K. (univ.) sample (102 responses)	58	37	5
U.K. (nonuniv.) sample (42 responses)	58	27	15
Cooperation			
U.S. sample	83	7	10
U.K. (univ.) sample	25	31	44
U.K. (nonuniv.) sample	97	0	3
Coaction			
U.S. sample	13	36	51
U.K. (univ.) sample	16	34	50
U.K. (nonuniv.) sample	24	26	50
Competition			
U.S. sample	2	25	63
U.K. (univ.) sample	15	22	63
U.K. (nonuniv.) sample	9	21	70

Reprinted from M. Cook. "Experimentation on Orientation and Proxemics," *Human Relations* vol. 23, 1970, p. 64. Used by permission of Plenum Publishing Company.

this use of private personal space. He discovered that most Americans have what he called *intimate distance*, which extends from their skin to about eighteen inches. People reserve intimate distances for very close relationships or for telling secrets.

For normal, informal conversations, Americans use what Hall called *personal-casual distance,* or from about eighteen inches to about four feet from the skin. However, business transactions and less personal business are conducted at a distance from four feet to about twelve feet, which Hall termed *social-consultive distance.* The closer ranges in this bracket are typically used to present a more personal image in formal or business situations. The more distant space is typically used to keep people of lower power at a distance. If you went to a professor's office, for example, you might find that she has placed her desk between herself and her visitors.

Hall also identified a *public distance,* which extends from about twelve to about twenty-five feet in the near phase, and beyond twenty-five feet in the far phase. This distance characterizes public address and other communication situations outside of buildings. Figure 6.4 illustrates Hall's categories for the use of space.

If you study the figures and apply the research, you will discover that you can use the information to help you attain your goals. Occasions in which seating arrangements and standing distance can be important include:

- a business luncheon
- a dinner date
- a one-to-one conference with a superior on a joint task
- a one-to-one conference with a colleague on the division of tasks on a joint project
- a one-to-one conference with a subordinate in which you are assigning an important task
- an informal social gathering
- an employment interview
- an appraisal interview about your work performance
- an appraisal interview about your employee's work performance

There is evidence that the distance at which we place ourselves and another can say something about the current state of our relationship. Crane found a strong correlation between the emotional closeness of a couple and the distance they chose to separate themselves for conversation. Distressed married couples placed themselves at a distance that was about 25 percent greater than the distance between happily married partners.[81]

Figure 6.4
Hall's categories
for the use of
space in
American
culture. *Source:
E. T. Hall,
"Proxemics," p.
227,* Current
Anthropology:
*93. © 1968 by
Wenner-Grant
Foundation for
Anthropology .*

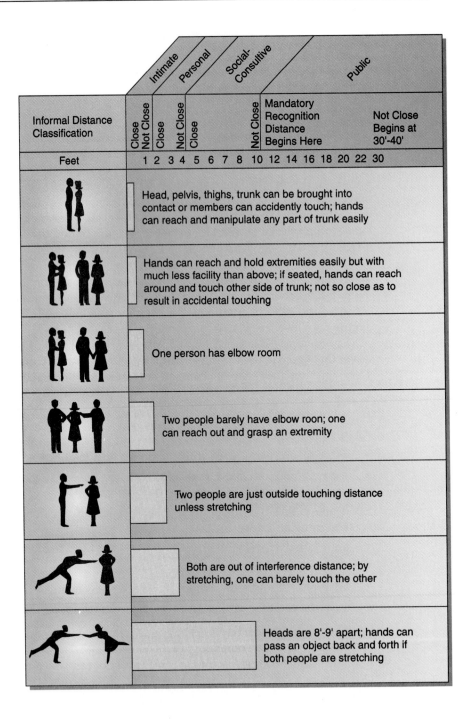

Personal distancing when communicating with another person
is culturally based. We learned from Hall's research that people from
the United States place themselves from 18 inches to 4 feet apart
when participating in an interpersonal communication, unless the

conversation is intimate or secret. Closer spacing is considered intimate and not to be violated. On the other hand, people find this "intimate space" suitable for interpersonal communication if they are from Middle Eastern countries. Thus, when an Arab person talks with a person from the United States, each may feel uncomfortable as they attempt to keep the distance "appropriate."

There also are gender-related differences in the use of space. The research in this area is extensive and is displayed in table 6.9.

Table 6.9   Proxemic Differences between Women and Men

Female behavior	*Male behavior*
Women are approached more closely.[82]	Men are approached less closely.
Women approach others more closely.[83]	Men approach others less closely.
Women discriminate more about whom they approach.[84]	Men discriminate less about whom they approach.
Women's approach creates less anxiety.	Men's approach creates more anxiety.[85]
Women prefer to interact side by side.[86]	Men prefer to interact face to face.
Women are least comfortable with side-by-side invasions.[87]	Men are least comfortable with frontal invasions.[88]
Women are more likely to be placed on the side of a rectangular table.[89]	Men are more likely to be placed at the head of a rectangular table.[90]
High-self-concept women approach others more closely than either low-self-concept women and/or men of high or low self-concept.[91]	High-self-concept men approach others more closely than low-self-concept men but not as closely as high-self-concept women.
Sociability and status of females has no effect on the amount of space they are given.[92]	Unsociable, low-status males are given more room than sociable, high-status males and more room than all women.
Women stand farther away from people who are speaking loudly.[93]	Men maintain the same distance whether the speaker is speaking loudly or softly.
Women respond as easily in close quarters as larger spaces.	Men respond less in crowded conditions than in larger spaces.[94]
Women flee more quickly when invasion is accompanied by talk.[95]	Men flee more quickly when invasion is not accompanied by talk.
Women have less territory.[96]	Men have more territory.

From Judy Cornelia Pearson, Lynn H. Turner, and William Todd-Mancillas, *Gender and Communication,* Second Edition. Copyright © 1991 Wm. C. Brown Publishers, Dubuque, Iowa. All Rights Reserved. Reprinted by permission.

TIME

Edward T. Hall was concerned about more than space-related messages. He also was very interested in *time* as a communication system, noting a number of cultural differences in the way people use time.[97] For instance, Hall described the Navajo Indians' belief that the time to start a ceremony is when all the necessary preparations are made. Such an understanding would defy the expectations of certain North American industrialists for whom time is money. Time is spent; time is made; time is bought and sold as a commodity in advertising; time is saved and managed. Time is never approached casually unless special rules of some subculture allow it. For example, a group of people who clock their workday activities with great precision may go on a weekend canoe trip with the understanding that all watches and clocks must be left at home. "There's no time on the river," says one. This statement verbalizes the subcultural rule that gives the group permission not to manage time.

We *can* make choices about how we will use time. Our guess is that you will make wiser choices if you stop to think about the implications. Does the way you treat time say something about you? Are you comfortable with what it says? Are you imposing an understanding of time upon other people? Is that imposition appropriate? Are you wise enough to examine your own tempo and to set your expectations aside if they are getting in the way?

Hall concluded that cultures fall into two separate categories according to their use of time. A *monochronic culture* uses time in an arbitrary way. American society is monochronic. We are controlled by the clock. Our schools, our television, our businesses, and even our dinner hour (whether or not we are hungry) are set by a monochronic orientation to time. A *polychronic culture,* in contrast, emphasizes interactions and people rather than an arbitrary understanding of time.

To make matters more complicated, within each culture are varying time systems. In our society, *informal time* is experienced uniquely by individuals in terms of punctuality, urgency, activity, variety, and monochronic or polychronic orientation. *Formal time* is experienced in terms of order, cycle, value, duration, and tangibility.[98] Thus, formal time takes its significance from and lends itself to the society's normal expectations. For example, we share our understanding of formal time when we hear someone say, "Bake this cake for 30 minutes at 350 degrees." Informal time is a private matter. Your own notions of "a long time," for example, will surely differ from someone else's. Even your own reaction to time—informal time—differs from one situation to another. Suppose, to illustrate, that you are in a hurry. You are caught at a "long" stoplight. The wait seems interminable because you are rushing. At another nonhurried time, you might not notice the passage of the same number of seconds at that traffic signal.

Does the way you treat time say something about you? Are you comfortable with what it says?

To illustrate the problems sometimes produced by informal time assumptions, what does it mean when a person tells you she will be there "in a second?" What does it mean when someone pledges to love you "forever" (duration)? What does the request to "please be on time" mean (punctuality)? Failure to understand formal time assumptions can also create problems. For example, although we do not have much difficulty understanding that Wednesday comes before Thursday (order) or the age allusion in the sentence, "She was in the autumn of her life" (cycle), we do get into trouble with such concepts as "a long time" (duration). To a twenty-year-old person, two years may be a long time. The fact that her father has had the same car for ten years is incomprehensible. "You have had that jalopy forever," she asserts. "No, I haven't," Dad defends himself. "You've had it for ten years," she says. "That's half a lifetime."

We buy time and spend time, and we determine the monetary value of a person's labor on the basis of how much time that service required of him (tangibility). We sometimes argue about how much our time is worth.

We also find that time and status are intimately linked. Being on time for an appointment varies directly with the status of the individuals involved. If the person we are to meet is of high status, we will likely arrive early so that we do not keep the person waiting. As an employee, for example, we would show up on time or ahead of time for a meeting with our boss. On the other hand, we have all had the experience of a boss keeping us waiting beyond the appointed time. Status and time are even linked to how people manage social engagements. Among lower-status groups, dinner is served relatively soon after the guests arrive. Among higher-status groups, dinner is often delayed for an hour or more.

Finally, Joost Meerloo[99] and Thomas Cottle[100] believe that we live and work in the context of certain time orientations that we assume. For Meerloo, the orientations include a *past orientation* in which we tend to view time as a cycle from which we must learn. A *time-line orientation* is a more analytical approach in which we see time as a systematic progression from past to present to future, and examine the past for its impact on the future. In the *present orientation*, we live in the now. We tend to be unconcerned about future consequences and to set the past aside. In the *future orientation*, we tend to worry about what will happen, often at the expense of our present experience. For example, you may have known the feeling that you are always "in training," always working toward some goal, and postponing your immediate gratifications and sometimes your happiness until you attain it.

Some people seriously jeopardize their relationships because they do not approach time in the same way. In one case, a husband experienced time as a rigid series of clicks sounding sixty times each minute, sixty minutes each hour. He felt it was important always to be on time. By this he meant "at least five minutes before the appointed moment." He felt so strongly about this orientation that he would, for example, leave home at least an hour before an appointment just in case his car had a flat tire.

In contrast, his wife experienced time as process. For her, time was a series of activities connected by transitions. She might decide to bake a pie, for example, and then do it. While she was in the process of baking that pie, time did not click by. Rather, it stopped. It had no significance. When the pie was done, she could make a transition to the next activity.

These conflicting views of time created problems for the couple. He found it easy to criticize her because she was "always late" and "dawdled." She often criticized her husband because he was "so compulsive and uptight" and because he "never gives me time to do anything."

A young couple also reported having problems over time orientations. She was concerned about the future, and he was oriented to the present. She wanted to make plans for a family, careers, and the purchase of a house and a car. He preferred to stay in the present, to concentrate on his studies. "I'll get a job when it's time," he would say. "Right now, I want to get an A on that exam tomorrow." "What good is the A if you don't know what you will do with your education?" she would ask. "Don't you have any ambitions or hopes or dreams? And don't they include me?" These differences in focus—present versus future—made communication and coordination difficult.

You have much to gain and little to lose by adopting a more open, interactive style.

In sum, time talks.[101] We use time to manipulate others, to exercise power, to invest special meaning in our utterances, and to serve as a frame of reference through which we interpret other people's behaviors.

APPLYING NONVERBAL CONCEPTS TO RELATIONSHIPS

Silence, a complex set of vocal cues, space, and time, work together to provide the texture and color of spoken language. It is on these bases, primarily, that we know how to interpret the meaning of a sentence and from which we get relationship cues. What are the implications of these ideas for you in managing your relationships?

For a sender of messages, these ideas strongly argue for clarity in language choice, for directness in expressing feelings and wants, and for candor in responding to others. The solution to vagueness and uncertainty is clarity. But beyond this, you must become much more aware of the messages we send. Remember that you may be sending more messages unintentionally than you are sending on purpose. Take time to ensure that your nonverbal messages are consistent with your intention and to ask for and to understand feedback from others.

For a receiver of messages, these ideas strongly argue for oral feedback. Become aware of the nonverbal messages you are picking up. Remember that you are not consciously aware of many of the nonverbal cues you are interpreting. Again, the solution to vagueness and uncertainty is specificity and clarity. Ask many questions about the other person's intentions and inferences. Verify your own guesses about what the other person means. If you find yourself uncomfortable, bring that discomfort to light. Say, for example, "I'm uncomfortable, confused. And I'm frustrated by the apparent contradiction between what you are saying and how you are saying it. Am I right to understand that you mean . . . ?"

Talk about your habitual uses of time and your wants and intentions regarding your own and the other person's habitual uses of time. Set some ground rules for your relationship by working through your assumptions with your partner. You both need to know how to predict the other's thinking in this matter so that you can identify a true deviation from expected behavior.

Encourage other people to give you feedback often about how they are experiencing your talk. Set your natural defensiveness aside, even if the others are not skillful in giving feedback. Listen carefully to what they say, and reward them for being clear with you. You have much to gain and little to lose by adopting a more open, interactive style.

Especially when you are in conflict, try to slow and calm things down. Both you and the other party will tend to exaggerate nonverbal and vocalic messages. You will talk louder and faster. You will undoubtedly change the pitch and pause patterns of your normal speech. However, you can choose to avoid this behavior.

First, express your intention to calm the situation. Do not hesitate to ask for help in this matter from the other person and to try to work out an agreement about how you will accomplish this important goal. One obvious way is to agree to practice the skills of active listening—to paraphrase what the other is saying and to talk about the inferences you are drawing from each other's nonverbal and vocalic messages. Finally, keep in mind that there is always time to go back and try again. You cannot reverse what happened yesterday, but you certainly can talk about it and make new contracts for the future. These interpersonal contracts, after all, are the foundation of every healthy relationship.

SUMMARY

Messages that we send with our body are directly related to our effectiveness in relationships. Our body movement, gestures, and clothing all convey information about us. Especially significant in relationships, facial and eye behavior and touch communicate our feelings. People even use pupil size as a measure of interpersonal attractiveness.

Since we cannot read another person's mind, the inferences we draw from someone's body messages may be in error. Further, our own body messages may be inconsistent with our words. These facts argue strongly for learning to talk about our observations and the inferences based on them so that errors can be corrected. Similarly, it is important to learn to solicit feedback about how other people are interpreting our body communication.

How we use silence bears directly on our relationships. Bruneau identified three kinds of silence: psycholinguistic, interactive, and sociocultural. Silence forms one of the most important bases on which people draw inferences about their relationships.

In addition to silence, other features of the vocalic message system include vocal quality and such vocalizations as laughing and the vocalized pause. From these data, we infer meaning, emotions, and sincerity. We also use these tiny elements of vocalics to judge such things as competence, sex, and age.

The use and treatment of space can have an important effect on our perceptions of other people and of ourselves and on how others perceive and interact with us. These matters are thus directly related to interpersonal effectiveness.

Our personal health, our sense of interpersonal attractiveness, our "ownership" of territory, and our understanding of appropriate distances are all a part of the nonverbal message system that we use to interpret another person's spoken language and interpretation of our own. These messages do not have to be left to chance, and our effectiveness in our relationships may depend upon a more conscious and intelligent selection of such communication.

Silence is closely related to time and how we use time. Monochronic cultures use time in an arbitrary way, understanding it as a regulating phenomenon over which they have no control. A clock provides a good example of our own culture's monochronic use of time. Polychronic cultures, on the other hand, are more tolerant of individual differences in the use of time because they place more importance on interactions and on people. There are also differences between formal and informal time that may bear importantly on relationships. How we orient toward time may be the most important factor in our perceptions of the behaviors of others and our interpretations of what those perceptions mean.

Clearly, this complex nonverbal message system is somewhat beyond our control. We must learn to bring our inferences about it up to the level of talk if we are going to manage our relationships skillfully.

DISCUSSION QUESTIONS

1. What are some of the general body cues that you and others in your classroom are using right now? Working with one or two classmates, try to identify what messages are being sent, either intentionally or unintentionally. List them under the headings: "clothing," "body movement and gestures," and "face and eye behavior."

2. To what extent do you believe your images of others are based on nonverbal messages you are not aware of receiving? Describe instances in which your nonverbal behavior unintentionally influenced others. Compare and contrast these with those of your class members. What are the similarities and differences?

3. Is it possible to learn to control general and particular body cues as we interact with others? What would be the effect if the other person realized that you were trying to control your nonverbal messages?

4. Is it possible to learn to give and get feedback during a conversation? How might you help yourself and the other persons in a relationship (someone who has not had this course) increase both the quality and quantity of the feedback given and received?

5. Working with a few classmates, list ways that silence can communicate language inadequacy.

6. In what ways do you use language to link yourself to your friends? Do you also use silence as part of this linking process? If so, how?

7. Using figure 6.2 as a guide, try to explore as many ways as possible to change the meaning of this sentence: "Did John say that again?" How do you think the variety of its potential meanings could influence your ability to manage your relationships? Explain.

8. Can you find any evidence of "territoriality" in the room you now occupy? On what basis do you draw your conclusions? Is there any evidence that the "territoriality" assumptions of the people in the room are affecting their interactions?

9. To what extent, if any, does Hall's system of interpersonal distance categories hold true in your own life or in the lives of one or two of your classmates? What are the implications, if any, of this informal research on your conscious use of distance in managing your relationships? In particular, discover any implications from your informal discussion on how you will use distance in relationship to your:

a. parent

b. sibling

c. employer

d. professor

e. favorite aunt or uncle

10. Do you use time differently from people you know? If so, in what ways? Have the differences influenced your relationships with these people? If so, how?

11. How are formal time and informal time different? Give three examples of each. How might these differences affect your ability to develop a new relationship?

ENDNOTES

1. M. T. Palmer and K. B. Simmons, "Communicating Intentions Through Nonverbal Behaviors: Conscious and Nonconscious Encoding of Liking," *Human Communication Research* 22 (1995): 128–160.

2. C. Rubenstein, "Body Language that Speaks to Muggers," *Psychology Today* (August 1980): 20.

3. R. L. Birdwhistell, *Kinesics and Context: Essays on Body Motion Communication* (Philadelphia: University of Pennsylvania Press, 1970).

4. J. Fast, *The Body Language of Sex, Power, and Aggression* (New York: M. Evans and Company, 1977).

5. P. Ekman and W. Friesen, "The Repertoire of Nonverbal Behavior: Categories, Origins, Usage, and Coding," *Semiotica* 1 (1969): 49–98.

6. R. Harrison, "Nonverbal Communication: An Approach to Human Communication," in R. Budd and B. Ruben, *Approaches to Human Communication* (New York: Spartan, 1972).

7. P. Peterson, "An Investigation of Sex Differences in Regard to Nonverbal Body Gestures," *Proceedings of the Speech Communication Association Summer Conference* (Austin, Texas, 1975).

8. Ibid.

9. R. Shuter, "A Study of Nonverbal Communication Among Jews and Protestants," *The Journal of Social Psychology* 109 (1979): 31–41.

10. Peterson, "An Investigation of Sex Differences."

11. Ibid.

12. Ibid.

13. We are assuming that the individuals in our examples and discussions are from the same culture. There is some evidence that both the culture and general body configuration of an individual influence how the body is used and posed and under what circumstances. For example, the ancient Romans are lying down. This position must have seemed as comfortable to them as sitting at a table seems to us. Both are culture-bound examples of posture control.

14. See A. Mehrabian, "Inference of Attitudes from Posture, Orientation, and Distance of a Communicator," *Journal of Consulting and Clinical Psychology* 32 (1968): 296–308.

15. E. Aries, "Verbal and Nonverbal Behavior in Single-Sex and Mixed-Sex Groups," *Psychological Reports* 51 (1982): 127–134.

16. Ibid.

17. R. L. Birdwhistell, "Masculinity and Femininity as Display," in Birdwhistell, *Kinesics and Context*.

18. R. Exline, "Exploration in the Process of Person Perception: Visual Interaction in Relation to Competition, Sex, and the Need for Affiliation," *Journal of Personality* 31 (1963): 1–20.

19. N. M. Henley, *Body Politics: Power, Sex and Nonverbal Communication* (Englewood Cliffs, NJ: Prentice-Hall, Inc., 1972), 151.

20. Ibid., 152.

21. S. Duncan, "Some Signals and Rules for Taking Speaking Turns in Conversations," *Journal of Personality and Social Psychology* 23 (1972): 283–292.

22. For an excellent overview of this literature, see Hickson and Stacks, *NVC*, 140–144.

23. A. S. King, "The Eye in Advertising," *Journal of Applied Communication Research* 1 (1973): 1–12.

24. B. Ambler, "Information Reduction, Internal Transformation, and Task Difficulty," *Bulletin of Psychonomic Science* 10 (1977): 43–46.

25. I. Heilville, "Deception and Pupil Size," *Journal of Clinical Psychology* 32 (1976): 675–676.

26. R. Gur and R. Gur, "Defense Mechanisms, Psychosomatic Symptomatology and Conjugate Lateral Eye Movements," *Journal of Consulting and Clinical Psychology* 43 (1945): 416–420.

27. Michael Argyle, "Intercultural Communication," in Larry Samovar and Richard E. Porter, *Intercultural Communication: A Reader*, 6th ed. (Belmont, CA: Wadsworth, 1991): 36.

28. S. Thayer and W. Schiff, "Eye-Contact, Facial Expression, and the Experience of Time," *The Journal of Social Psychology* (1975): 117–124; Z. Rubin, "Measurement of Romantic Love," *Journal of Personality and Social Psychology* 16 (1970): 265–273: P. C. Ellsworth, J. M. Carlsmith, and A. Henson, "The Stare as a Stimulus to Flight in Human Subjects: A Series of Field Experiments, "*Journal of Personality and Social Psychology* 21 (1972): 302–311; R. D. Muirhead and M. Goldman, "Mutual Eye Contact as Affected by Seating Position, Sex, and Age," *The Journal of Social Psychology* 109 (1979): 201–206; P. C. Ellsworth and L. M. Ludwig, "Visual Behavior in Social Interaction," *Journal of Communication* 22 (1972): 375–403.

29. R. Exline, D. Gray, and D. Shuette, "Visual Behavior in Dyad as Affected by Interview Content and Sex of Respondent," *Journal of Personality and Social Psychology* 1 (1965): 201–209.

30. R. Muirhead and M. Goldman, "Mutual Eye Contact."

31. K. Dierks-Stewart, "Sex Differences in Nonverbal Communication: An Alternative Perspective," in *Communication, Language and Sex: Proceedings of the First Conference*, eds. C. L. Berryman and V. A. Eman (Rowley, MA: Newbury House, 1979), 112–121.

32. C. Kleinke, A. A. Bustos, F. F. Meeker, and R. Staneski, "Effects of Self-Attributed and Other Attributed Gaze on Interpersonal Evaluations Between Males and Females," *Journal of Experimental Social Psychology* 9 (1973): 154–163; M. Argyle, J. Lalljee, and M. Cook, "The Effects of Visibility on Interaction in a Dyad," *Human Relations* 21 (1968): 3–17.

33. A. Mehrabian, *Nonverbal Communication* (Chicago: Aldine-Atherton, 1972); R. Buck, R. E. Miller, and W. F. Caul, "Sex, Personality, and Physiological Variables in the Communication of Affect Via Facial Expression, *Journal of Personality and Social Psychology* 17 (1971): 314–318.

34. A. Schiffenbauer and A. Babineau, "Sex Role Stereotypes and the Spontaneous Attribution of Emotion," *Journal of Research in Personality* 10 (1976): 137–145.

35. D. A. Yarmey, "Through the Looking Glass: Sex Differences in Memory for Self-Facial Poses," *Journal of Research in Personality* 13 (1979): 450–459.

36. M. Argyle, *Bodily Communication* (New York: International Universities Press, 1975); K. Dierks-Stewart, "The Effects of Protracted Invasion on an Individual's Action Territory." Unpublished master's thesis, Bowling Green State University, 1976; S. J. Frances, "Sex Differences in Nonverbal Behavior," *Sex Roles* 5 (1979): 519–535; M. B. Parlee, "Women Smile Less for Success," *Psychology Today* 12 (1979): 16.

37. N. Henley and B. Thorne, "Womanspeak and Manspeak: Sex Differences and Sexism in Communication, Verbal and Nonverbal," in *Beyond Sex Roles*, ed. A. Sargent (St. Paul: West. 1977).

38. S. Lau, "The Effect of Smiling on Person Perception," *The Journal of Social Psychology* 117 (1982): 63–67.

39. P. Eckman and W. V. Friesen, *Unmasking the Face* (Englewood Cliffs, NJ: Prentice-Hall, 1975).

40. S. Weitz, ed., *Nonverbal Communication: Readings with Commentary* (New York: Oxford University Press, 1974).

41. A. Montagu, *Touching: The Human Significance of the Skin* (New York: Perennial Library, 1971), 82.

42. J. L. Despert, "Emotional Aspects of Speech and Language Development," *International Journal of Psychiatry and Neurology* 105 (1941): 193–222. See also J. Bowlby, *Maternal Care and Mental Health* (Geneva: W.H.O., 1961).

43. H. H. Harlow and R. R. Zimmermann, "The Development of Affectional Responses in Infant Monkeys," *Proceedings, American Philosophical Society* 102 (1958): 501–509.

44. T. Adler, "Congressional Staffers Witness Miracle of Touch," *APA Monitor* (February 1993): 12–15.

45. D. Morris, *Intimate Behavior* (New York: Random House, 1971), 31.

46. M. H. Krout, *Introduction to Social Psychology* (New York: Harper and Brothers, 1942).

47. S. M. Jourard, "An Exploratory Study of Body-Accessibility," *British Journal of Social and Clinical Psychology* 5 (1966): 221–231.

48. N. R. Heslin and T. Alper, "Touch: A Bonding Gesture," in *Nonverbal Interaction 2*, J. M. Wiemann and R. P. Harrison, eds. (Beverly Hills, CA: Sage, 1983), 47–75.

49. Dean C. Barnlund, "Communication Styles in Two Cultures: Japan and the United States" in *Organization of Behavior in Face-to-Face Interaction*, A. Kendon, R. M. Harris, and M. R. Key, eds. (The Hague: Mouton, 1975).

50. N. M. Henley, *Body Politics: Power, Sex and Nonverbal Communication* (Englewood Cliffs, NJ: Prentice-Hall, 1977); N. M. Henley, "The Politics of Touch," in *Radical Psychology*, Phillip Brown, ed. (New York: Harper & Row, 1973), 421–433.

51. D. W. Austin, "Nonverbal Cues Influencing Client and Non-client Perception of Counselors." Unpublished doctoral dissertation, University of Wyoming, 1973; Henley, *Body Politics*; Henley, "The Politics of Touch."

52. J. D. Fisher, M. Rytting, and R. Heslin. "Hands Touching Hands: Affective and Evaluative Affects in Interpersonal Touch," *Sociometry* 39 (1976): 416–421.

53. D. Druley, D. Cassriel, and M. H. Hollendar. "A Cuddler's Guide to Love," *Self Magazine* (May 1980): 96–100.

54. Ibid.

55. M. L. Rosencranz, "Clothing Symbolism," *Journal of Home Economics* 54 (1962): 18–22.

56. L. Aiken, "Relationship of Dress to Selected Measures of Personality in Undergraduate Women," *Journal of Social Psychology* 59 (1963): 121.

57. Reported in L. B. Rosenfeld and T. G. Plax, "Clothing as Communication," *Journal of Communication* 27 (1977): 23–31.

58. M. R. Solomon and J. Scholper, "Self-Consciousness and Clothing," *Personality and Social Psychology Bulletin* 8 (1982): 508–514.

59. J. Kelly, "Dress as Nonverbal Communication," paper presented to the annual conference of the American Association for Public Opinion Research, May 1969, and cited in M. L. Hickson III and Don W. Stacks, *NVC: Nonverbal Communication Studies and Applications*, 2d ed. (Dubuque, IA: Wm. C. Brown, 1989), 108.

60. W. Thourlby, *You Are What You Wear* (New York: New American Library, 1978), 1.

61. K. W. Watson and L. R. Smeltzer, "Perceptions of Nonverbal Communication During the Selection Interview," *The ABCA Bulletin* (June 1982): 30–34.

62. Hickson and Stacks, *NVC*, 111.

63. See J. T. Molloy, *The New Dress for Success* (New York: Warner Books, 1988); and Molloy, *The Woman's Dress for Success Book* (New York: Warner Books, 1978).

64. L. E. Temple and K. R. Loewen, "Perceptions of Power: First Impressions of a Woman Wearing a Jacket," *Perceptual and Motor Skills* 76 (1993): 339–348.

65. J. K. Burgoon, L. A. Stern, and L. Dillman, *Interpersonal Adaptation: Dyadic Interaction Patterns* (Cambridge, England: Cambridge University Press, 1995).

66. M. Pickard, *The World of Silence* (Chicago: Regnery, 1952), 1–15. See also S. N. Ganguly, "Culture, Communication, and Silence," *Philosophy and Phenomenological Research* 29 (December 1968): 200.

67. R. L. Scott, "Rhetoric and Silence," *Western Speech* 36 (Summer 1972): 146–158.

68. V. Jenson, "Communicative Functions of Silence," *ETC: A Review of General Semantics* 30 (September 1973): 259–263.

69. M. L. McLaughlin and M. J. Cody, "Awkward Silences: Behavioral Antecedents and Consequences of the Conversational Lapse," *Human Communication Research* 8 (Summer 1982): 299–316.

70. E. G. Beier, "Nonverbal Communication: How We Send Emotional Messages," *Psychology Today* 8 (1974): 53–56.

71. T. J. Bruneau, "Communicative Silences: Forms and Functions," *Journal of Communication* 23 (March 1973): 17–46.

72. R. May, "The Significance of the Pause," in *Freedom and Destiny*, 1981, and excerpted in J. Stewart, *Bridges Not Walls: A Book About Interpersonal Communication*, 4th ed. (New York: Random House, 1986), 86–91.

73. K. H. Basso, "To Give Up on Words: Silence in Apache Culture," in *Language and Social Context*, Pier Paolo Giglioli, ed. (New York: Penguin, 1972).

74. S. H. Ng and J. J. Bradac, *Power in Language: Verbal Communication and Social Influence* (Newbury Park, CA: Sage, 1993).

75. D. A. Coker and J. K. Burgoon, "The Nature of Conversational Involvement and Nonverbal Encoding Patterns," *Human Communication Research* 14 (1987): 61–84.

76. L. A. Hosman and J. W. Wright II, "The Effects of Hedges and Hesitations on Impression Formation in a Simulated Courtroom Context," *Western Journal of Speech Communication* 51 (1987): 173–188; E. J. Clemmer and N. M. Carrocci, "Effects of Experience on Radio Language Performance," *Communication Monographs* 51 (1984): 116–139.

77. S. M. Lyman and M. B. Scott, "Territoriality: A Neglected Sociological Dimension," *Social Problems* 15 (1967): 237–241.

78. R. Sommer, *Personal Space: The Behavioral Basis of Design* (Englewood Cliffs, NJ: Prentice-Hall, 1969).

79. M. Cook. "Experimentation on Orientation and Proxemics," *Human Relations* 23 (1970): 61–76.

80. E. T. Hall, *The Silent Language* (Garden City, NY: Doubleday, 1959).

81. D. R. Crane, "Diagnosing Relationships with Spatial Distance: An Empirical Test of a Clinical Principle," *Journal of Marital and Family Therapy* 13 (1987): 307–310.

82. G. Leventhal and M. Matturo, "Differential Effects of Spatial Crowding and Sex on Behavior, *Perceptual Motor Skills* 51 (1980): 111–119: B. A. Barios, C. L. Corbitt, J. Philip, and J. S. Topping, "Effects of Social Stigma on Interpersonal Distance," *The Psychological Record* 26 (1976): 343–348.

83. B. A. Fisher, "Differential Effects of Sexual Composition and Interactional Context on Interaction Patterns in Dyads," *Human Communication Research* 9 (1983): 225–238; R. Sommer, "Studies in Personal Space," *Sociometry* 22 (1959): 247–260; M. Giesen and H. A. McClaren, "Discussion, Distance and Sex: Changes in Impressions and Attraction During Small Group Interaction," *Sociometry* 39 (1976): 60–70; M. Argyle and J. Dean, "Eye Contact, Distance and Affiliation," *Sociometry* 28 (1965): 289–304.

84. M. A. Dosey and M. Meisels, "Personal Space and Self-Protection, "*Journal of Personality and Social Psychology* 11 (1969): 93–97.

85. P. R. Bleda and S. Estee Bleda, "Effects of Sex and Smoking on Reactions to Spatial Invasions at a Shopping Mall, *The Journal of Social Psychology* 104 (1978): 311–312.

86. G. Leventhal, M. Lipshultz, and A. Chiodo, "Sex and Setting Effects on Seating Arrangement," *The Journal of Psychology* 100 (1978): 21–26.

87. M. Patterson, S. Mullens, and J. Romano, "Compensatory Reactions to Spatial Intrusion," *Sociometry* 34 (1971): 114–121.

88. J. D. Fisher and D. Byrne, "Too Close for Comfort: Sex Differences in Response to Invasions of Personal Space," *Journal of Personality and Social Psychology* 31 (1975): 15–21.

89. D. B. Roger and R. L. Reid, "Small Group Ecology Revisited—Personal Space and Role Differentiation," *British Journal of Social and Clinical Psychology* 17 (1978): 43–46.

90. D. F. Lott and R. Sommer, "Seating Arrangements and Status," *Journal of Personality and Social Psychology* 7 (1967): 90–95.

91. L. O. Stratton, D. J. Tekippe, and G. L. Flick, "Personal Space and Self-Concept," *Sociometry* 36 (1973): 424–429.

92. M. A. Witting and P. Skolnick, "Sex Differences in Personal Space," *Sex Roles* 4 (1978): 493–503.

93. J. G. Ford, R. E. Cramer, and G. Owens, "A Paralinguistic Consideration of Proxemic Behavior," *Perceptual and Motor Skills* 45 (1977): 487–493.

94. F. Prerost, "The Effects of High Spatial Density on Humor Appreciation: Age and Sex Differences," *Social Behavior and Personality* 8 (1980): 239–244.

95. E. Sundstrom and M. G. Sundstrom, "Personal Space Invasions: What Happens When the Invader Asks Permission?" *Environmental Psychology and Nonverbal Behavior* (Winter 1977): 76–82; D. Polit and M. LaFrance, "Sex Differences in Reaction to Spatial Invasion," *The Journal of Social Psychology* 102 (1977): 59–60.

96. I. H. Frieze, "Nonverbal Aspects of Femininity and Masculinity Which Perpetuate Sex-Role Stereotypes." Paper presented at the Eastern Psychological Association, 1974.

97. E. T. Hall, *Beyond Culture* (Garden City, NY: Doubleday, 1976).

98. ———, *The Silent Language* (Garden City, NY: Doubleday, 1959). See also J. K. Burgoon and T. J. Saine, *The Unspoken Dialogue: An Introduction to Nonverbal Communication* (Boston: Houghton Mifflin, 1978): 101–104.

99. J. Meerloo, "The Time Sense in Psychiatry," in *The Voice of Time,* J. T. Fraser, ed. (New York: Braziller, 1966).

100. T. J. Cottle, *Perceiving Time: A Psychological Investigation with Men and Women* (New York: John Wiley and Sons, 1976).

101. Bruneau, "Communicative Silences," 32–39.

READ MORE ABOUT
BODY COMMUNICATION AND
RELATIONAL EFFECTIVENESS IN THESE SOURCES

Burgoon, Judee K. "Nonverbal Signals." In *Handbook of Interpersonal Communication*. Mark L. Knapp and Gerald R. Miller, Newbury Park, CA: Sage, 1994. This essay suggests ways people produce and process nonverbal messages. Included is the infinence of culture and gender on message production.

Hickson, Mark A. and Don W. Stacks. "Physical Appearance Studies. *NVC: Nonverbal Communication Studies and Applications,* 3d ed. Dubuque, IA: Wm. C. Brown, 1993, 89–118. This chapter provides an excellent readable review of the research literature in this area of nonverbal communication.

Montagu, Ashley. *Touching: The Human Significance of the Skin.* 3d ed. New York: Harper & Row, 1986. This interesting book focuses on the importance of touch in human development. You will especially want to read this book if you have or plan on having children.

READ MORE ABOUT
SILENCE, SPACE, TIME,
AND VOCALICS IN THESE SOURCES

Hall, Edward T. *The Hidden Dimension.* Garden City, NY: Doubleday, 1969. This classic book was written by a person who has done more research on use of space than anyone else. It includes animal research that has given us insights into how people use space. One chapter discusses how various cultures use space.

Hickson, Mark L. and Don W. Stacks, "Paralanguage Studies," in *NVC: Nonverbal Communication Studies and Applications.* 3d ed. Dubuque, IA: Wm. C. Brown, 1993, 149–177. This chapter presents a comprehensive discussion and review of vocalic research literature.

Newman, Helen M. "The Sounds of Silence in Communicative Encounters." *Communication Quarterly* 30 (1982): 142–149. This research report provides interesting insights into how moments of silence produce differing evaluations in various relational contexts.

7

LISTENING

PREVIEW

Most of what we know about other people is based on what they say. The rest results from guesses we make based on how they act and what we observe. Listening to people—taking in their messages plus making inferences about the intent of those messages—is very difficult. We can be effective listeners if we understand how to do so. The aim of this chapter is to help you understand listening and how to listen effectively in your relationships.

KEY TERMS

active listening
critical listening
evaluative listening
listening
paraphrasing
remembering
understanding

attending
empathy
forgetting curve
message
passive listening
sensing

OBJECTIVES

1. Construct a model of the listening process and explain each component.
2. Explain the relational significance of saying "you aren't listening" when you mean "we aren't agreeing."
3. Name and describe seven patterns of ineffective listening.
4. Explain why relational listening requires effort, withholding judgments, and empathy.
5. Demonstrate the skill of active listening.
6. Tell how active listening benefits an interpersonal relationship.

A report two students gave of a simple listening assignment illustrates the difficulty and frustration that can be experienced in the listening process. Joycelyn and Tim were to interview Ms. Phillips, a counselor at the University Psychology Clinic, about her view of what it takes to keep a relationship healthy. After the interview, Joycelyn and Tim sat down to compare notes. They agreed in general about what Ms. Phillips had said, but they also differed considerably on some points. Tim believed that he was right, and Joycelyn was just as certain that she was right.

"Tim, you always seem to think you're right. How can you say that you're right?" Joycelyn was a little upset and did not select her words carefully.

Tim's reply was not carefully worded either: "Come on, Joycelyn. If you would listen, we wouldn't have this fight."

"Wrong!" Joycelyn responded. "You aren't the greatest either! You're the one who should listen. I can't wait until we study listening. You'll learn a thing or two, I'm sure!"

This was all Tim could take. He stormed off, muttering that he would show just who was listening. Later, he talked again to Ms. Phillips and found that he was wrong. He apologized to Joycelyn. She had cooled off a bit and was willing to forgive and forget. But surely some damage was done to their relationship, much of which could have been avoided had their listening been better.

LISTENING: WHAT'S INVOLVED

"You're not hearing me" usually does not mean what it seems. Instead, this statement usually means, "You're not listening to me *and* understanding me." *Listening* is much more complex than merely hearing. In fact, it has four components, each of which is critical to effective listening. We have placed these—sensing, attending, understanding, and remembering—in a model to help you visualize the process (figure 7.1).

You may hear and see when a friend comes to you with a problem, but did you really attend to what was said? Did you understand? Did you remember? To understand this point more clearly, focus on the sounds around you. Perhaps you can hear the air conditioner or heater functioning. Perhaps you can hear people talking nearby. If you are indoors, perhaps you can hear sounds from outside, such as cars or birds. Locate one of these sounds. Why didn't you sense this stimulus before? If it was there, you could have sensed it. However, you did not complete the listening process until we urged you to do so. Listening is thus more than sensing. It also involves attending, understanding, and remembering.

We are often not aware of the components of the process of listening because they blend into a nearly instantaneous act of listening. Our hope is that considering each component individually will help you increase your awareness of them.

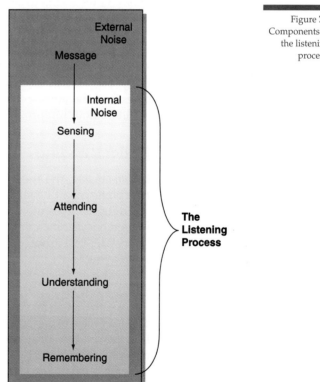

Figure 7.1
Components of the listening process.

Sensing

Sensing is receiving stimuli through the five senses. Generally, though, you concentrate on visual and auditory stimuli. You can hear a clock ticking and see its movement if there *is* a clock and if you have normal sensing capabilities. How is it, then, that you were not sensing it before it was pointed out to you? There was an intentional filter that kept you from listening.

Attending

If you were not aware of the clock, it may have been because you did not *attend* to it—you did not select its particular sound from the many of which you were conscious. Recall that thousands of stimuli are available for your attention. You select only those that seem relevant to the particular situation and ignore the others. This may be why you were able to sense but did not listen. You may have determined that the stimulus from the clock was not relevant, so you ignored it.

Selective attention helps you to concentrate on the message. It also allows you to block out what you choose to ignore. This selectivity contributes to poor listening when you ignore important aspects of the message. Just consider the mistakes Tim made when he filtered out important parts of Ms. Phillips' message.

Understanding

Understanding, the third component of the listening process, is the interpretation and evaluation of what you are able to sense. Understanding involves more than is close to what the speaker intended. Remember that meaning is related to more than the sensing. You get important data from your experience that helps you interpret the words you hear.

Remembering

Tim may have experienced a memory problem when he and Joycelyn interviewed the college counselor. *Remembering* is a difficult task for many people. Would you dare not to take notes if you wanted to remember what was said in a lecture? You might be reluctant to skip note taking for good reason; the *forgetting curve*, a graphic depiction of the retention rate, falls off rapidly. You lose a lot of what is said almost as soon as it has been said.

Just as you perceive and attend selectively, you remember selectively. You remember some ideas more easily than others because you have found them useful. Sometimes you remember because you are particularly intrigued by the thought or see a potential payoff. You encounter problems when you choose not to remember something that later turns out to be important.

You remember some ideas more easily than others because you have found them useful.

INEFFECTIVE LISTENING PATTERNS

We sometimes develop ineffective listening patterns that become habit. The first step in changing unproductive listening patterns is to identify them. Once you have discovered the pattern, you can substitute effective listening habits. This section identifies several ineffective listening patterns. It is followed by a section that will help you learn some effective behaviors to substitute.

Fake Listening

We have all learned to pretend we are listening so that we are not seen as impolite. Undoubtedly, you have caught yourself watching a lecturer—maintaining eye contact, nodding and smiling at the appropriate times, and even following that person with your eyes as he or she moves about the room—but not listening. Perhaps you had something more important on your mind or were just bored. We do this, too, in interpersonal communication situations.

The result of fake listening can be embarrassing and even damaging to the relationship. When we tell someone something that is important to us, we expect that they are treating us and what we say with respect. We also expect that they understand and will respond to what we say with appropriate feedback or actions, especially if they are giving us cues that they are listening. When this doesn't happen, we feel betrayed.

Self-Centered Listening

A self-centered listener focuses on his ideas rather than those of the speaker. Some self-centered listeners spend their time thinking of what they will say next, rather than listening to what you are saying. Other self-centered speakers are so interested in their ideas that they will hold the floor most of the time. When you do get to talk, they will probably be listening for a place to jump in and say more, rather than listening to what you are saying.

This self-centered behavior creates a definition of the relationship that most of us find difficult to take. The self-centered listener is implying that our view is not as important as theirs, even though he does not say this directly. The relational definition that this behavior seems to suggest is one up-one down, superior-inferior. Under many circumstances, this is not acceptable and can result in fake listening or disengagement at the first reasonable opportunity.

Assumptive Listening

An assumptive listener listens to just enough of your message to figure out what you are saying, comes to a conclusion about what your point is going to be, and then tunes out. Recall Tim's fight with Joycelyn in the introduction to this chapter. Remember that they had a dispute over what the counselor, Ms. Phillips, had said about healthy interpersonal relationships. Perhaps the listening problem was that Tim made assumptions about what Ms. Phillips was going to say and tuned out.

Assumptive listening can create relational problems, too. The problem comes when the person acts on what he or she thinks you said. If you were counting on the person doing something or being somewhere, you may be disappointed. The person's intentions might be good, but their actions might be contrary to your conversation because that person decided he or she knew what you were saying and tuned out.

Closed-Minded Listening

The closed-minded listener resists listening to ideas that she does not want to hear. This may be a message about some shortcoming or an opinion contrary to the person's belief system. The person may even nod, but not listen.

The closed-minded listener can create a sense of betrayal. Because this person resists listening and often fakes attention, you may believe he or she is agreeing with you. You think you both are on the same track, that you agree, but you don't. If you later discover this, you may feel bewildered, or worse, betrayed.

Defensive Listening

A defensive listener takes information that has no negative intent as a personal attack. Often some basic distrust in the relationship triggers the listener's negative interpretation and response. Perhaps you have had the experience of asking your parent an innocent question that was met by an explosive response. It is likely that your parent was engaging in defensive listening. You will learn more about defensiveness in communication in chapter 9.

The defensive listener creates the feeling that you are being attacked or ambushed. This puts a strain on the communication that follows. You may retreat to safe, vague language. You may decide the struggle is not worth the effort and change the subject or disengage altogether. If the relationship is ongoing, a regular, underlying tension may frequently present itself in your communication.

Neutral Listening

Neutral listeners are unable to go beyond your words and behaviors to understand the underlying meaning from your point of view. They take your communication at face value, not making any attempt to understand and empathize.

The neutral listener makes communication very frustrating. Neutrality of this kind is difficult to hide, so you often will notice the flat emotional expression in the other person's face. You may feel frustration because you know that the person is not fully understanding you. This kind of listening makes it impossible for the other person to develop empathy for you and your position.

Hostile Listening

The hostile listener provides our final example of ineffective listening. This person listens for the express purpose of disagreement.

This person looks for information that can be used to attack you. What you experience is not necessarily an angry person but one whose intent is finding fault. This person is listening with the intent to be critical.

The hostile listener creates a most unpleasant communication situation. The fault finding this person often engages in tends to produce a defensive reaction. You may occasionally enjoy it when a person picks an argument, but a steady dose of this behavior probably will cause you to have second thoughts about sustaining the relationship. This kind of listening has serious relational consequences.

EFFECTIVE LISTENING WITHIN A RELATIONSHIP

Effective listening in a relationship has specific characteristics. Our goal is to help you develop a basic understanding of effectiveness.

Relational Listening Requires Effort

Effective relational listening is usually active, rather than passive. To listen passively is to avoid displaying behaviors that let the speaker know you are listening.[1] Listening demands that we be alert, with our attention focused on the speaker. This is a mutual process in which we try to tune into the other person's verbal and nonverbal messages to understand both the content of the message and the speaker's feelings about the content. Listening actively suggests that the listener is thinking about—or is involved in understanding—what is received. One way of achieving this kind of involvement is to ask yourself questions while listening, such as:

1. What observations is the speaker reporting?
2. What inferences is the speaker making?
3. What feelings is the speaker expressing?
4. What wants and expectations does this speaker seem to have?
5. What meanings does this speaker intend to share in the message?
6. What degree of acceptance does this speaker expect you to have—for him or her personally and for his or her ideas?

Passive listening, in contrast, suggests that the listener is not as involved with the speaker. Instead, the listener is attending to what is being said without providing much feedback. This may occur when we attend a lecture or watch television. We do not interrupt the speaker or ask questions when we use this kind of listening, although we may provide subtle feedback in the form of nods, smiles, and eye contact.

Sometimes passive listening is appropriate in a relationship. Suppose a friend comes to you with a problem and merely wants you to hear what is on her mind. She does not want any input but

> Effective relational listening is usually active rather than passive.

wants only to tell someone about her frustration. The best way to help this person is to listen without interruption. Of course, you will find it difficult to convey understanding by using such limited feedback, but you will be able to show that you have listened by providing nonverbal cues, such as eye contact and facial expressions, or by giving an appropriate verbal response after your friend has finished talking.

Relational Listening Requires Withholding Advice and Judgments

We all want to be helpful when we encounter a friend who is experiencing a problem if we can. It is clear, though, that advice giving, judgments, and analysis, even when correct, are responses that often fail to help.[2] A study of people who were mourning the death of a loved one reported that 80 percent of the statements made to them were unhelpful.[3] Interestingly, nearly half of the statements were advice, such as "You've got to get out more." The study concluded that a far more helpful response was acknowledgment of the mourner's feelings.

We must make a special effort to keep an open mind if we really want to hear what another person is saying. This is easy advice to give but often difficult to follow! We all have biases. It is often hard to spot them because we think of our biases as the correct view of a situation. Tim had this problem during the Phillips interview incident. He was unwilling to consider that Joycelyn's understanding of what had been said was correct. He was willing, however, to risk an argument with Joycelyn. He was also determined to spend the time to prove that Joycelyn was wrong, but in fact *he* was wrong. Perhaps if Tim had been less rigid, he could have heard Joycelyn's side of the situation. Perhaps hearing her may have prompted a difference in her response to him. Perhaps they could have gone together to talk to Ms. Phillips. Listening while withholding judgment can allow more effective and satisfying communication.

Judgment and closed mindedness cause us to filter what we hear through our attitudes and beliefs. Thus, the only way to set biases aside is to discover a way to identify them and take them into account as we listen. Bringing biases to a conscious level takes some effort, but the payoff is worth it. The question is how this is done. One particularly helpful technique is to ask this series of questions:

Position: What is the speaker's position on the topic?

Agreement: Do I agree or disagree with this position?

Strength: How strongly do I agree or disagree?

Importance: Do I consider this an important issue?

Such questions can help reveal not only our position but also the extent to which we may be closed minded. For example, if there is strong disagreement over an important issue, bias may be interfering with the listening.

There is also a place for *critical listening*—listening and then asking ourselves questions about what we have heard—in relational communication. It is often the second step in a listening task. First, we must listen with an open mind to be sure we get the whole message. Then, we can turn to critical listening as we discuss the message.

Relational Listening Requires Empathy

Empathy allows us to move from our perspective to the perspective of the other. There is a difference between understanding what has been said and understanding what a person has said *from the speaker's perspective;* the latter is a deeper and more reliable level of understanding that has a positive effect on relationships.

This type of listening is especially important in making relationships work or not work. A survey of marital counselors pointed to failure "to take the other's perspective when listening" as one of the most frequent communication problems they saw in couples who were having difficulties.[4]

We can better understand the concept of empathic listening by contrasting it with the listening that Charles Kelley called *evaluative listening.*[5] Kelley said that empathic listening does not impose the listener's frame of reference on the situation, whereas evaluative listening does. Kelley expressed this distinction clearly:

> The difference between empathic listening and deliberative [evaluative] listening is primarily motivational. Both listeners seek the same objective: accurate understanding of communication from another . . . . The empathic listener lets his understanding of the speaker determine his modes of evaluation, which are automatic; the deliberative listener's understanding of the speaker is filtered through his predetermined modes of selective listening, and he actually spends less time as a communication receiver. The empathic listener is more apt to be a consistent listener and is less prone to his own or other distractions.[6]

In other words, empathic listening requires us to withhold our evaluations—our personal views, not just our judgments—to hear the communication more clearly, understand it more fully, and respond more appropriately.

Consider the example of Joycelyn's and Tim's different understandings of the interview with Ms. Phillips. We might imagine that they each had previously disagreed with someone about what had happened in a certain event. This type of misunderstanding was not entirely new to them, yet neither could identify the problem facing the other. They each chose, instead, to see only their own viewpoint.

Imagine what a difference it would have made if they had understood the power of empathy in promoting understanding and cooperation. Empathic listening might also have helped them manage communication and their relationship more effectively.

Ability to empathize is enhanced when we fully understand the speaker. But sometimes the speaker does not give the kind of information we need. There are several response skills that will encourage a speaker to explain more fully.

1. *Express your interest in knowing more.* You can encourage the person to explain more fully by interjecting phrases and questions such as "What else happened?," "Tell me more," "What else were you feeling?," or "Yes, I see." These probing statements and questions are illustrated in the following conversation.

Lou:	I nearly got fired at work today!
Mary Ann:	What happened?
Lou:	You know I was just hired at the Soft Serve Ice Cream Shoppe. New employees are supposed to practice using the ice cream machine. There is a rule, though, about eating ice cream and not paying for it. I ate an ice cream cone that one of the other new people made. The boss really flew off the handle. I thought I was gone!
Mary Ann:	What a shock! How were you feeling?
Lou:	Sort of scared at first. It was like being a kid caught with his hand in the cookie jar. Then I got really mad. I wasn't really doing anything wrong!
Mary Ann:	Do you believe the boss wasn't being fair?
Lou:	No, he was fair. I was warned. I just think it's petty!

    Notice that the questions Mary Ann asked motivated Lou to say more.

2. *Be sure that your response is nonjudgmental.* Judgmental statements are those that reveal evaluation—good or bad, worthwhile or not. Often they convey disapproval, which sometimes arouses defensive behavior in the other person. Suppose Mary Ann had said to Lou, "That was a really crazy thing to do," instead of "What a shock!" This sort of response might have caused Lou to react defensively, which in turn could have led him to withhold information.

3. *Recognize and affirm the other person's feelings.* Give a supportive response. Responding to aspects of the situation other than the speaker's feelings may not be received as well. For example, telling the other person "Don't worry. Things are not really that

bad" might be seen as an insult that effectively says, "You shouldn't be feeling and thinking what you are." Recognizing the other's feelings and empathizing with them avoids this problem. Here, you must pay attention to the nonverbal cues you receive from the other person, as these often carry the feelings. In Mary Ann's dialogue with Lou, for example, she said, "What a shock! How were you feeling?" Such questions emotionally unite the speaker and the listener. When the listener reveals her interest in the speaker and the message, the speaker is likely to feel supported.

ACTIVE LISTENING

We have suggested that relational listening requires an active listening style. This is where the next technique gets the name *active listening*. Active listening is an important response skill for managing relationships productively.

Active listening requires the listener to paraphrase the content of the speaker's message. Often the active listener will also want to mention his own guesses about the feelings of the speaker.

> When we paraphrase, we give our version of what we heard the speaker say.

The act of translating what another person has said into our own words requires processing the information. What we present to the speaker is our understanding of what was said. *Paraphrasing* is thus far more than mere parroting, which is the rote memory task of repeating what was said using the speaker's words.

> You must know the meaning of words to paraphrase them.

To illustrate, some people can vividly recollect learning the Latin responses in the Roman Catholic Mass years ago, although they may not have any notion of what the words mean. You must know the meaning of words to paraphrase them.

Suppose Cheryl engaged Elizabeth in this conversation as they left their work one day:

Cheryl: I met this really neat guy at Rick's last night. He seemed very interested.

Elizabeth: He's really super. It's great that you're so excited!

Cheryl: Excited doesn't really describe how I feel. I'd say I'm ecstatic. I've been waiting so long to meet someone like this. And I agree, he is really a super guy so far.

Elizabeth: I can really hear that sparkle in your voice. Tell me more.

Elizabeth's use of active listening is clearly leading to her understanding of Cheryl's experience and feelings. This represents a deeper understanding than when we merely attempt to understand the idea being conveyed.

Benefits of Active Listening

Active listening offers four major benefits. First, we must listen carefully if we are to repeat what we have heard. We will thus learn to listen and to remember, two of the most difficult parts of the process, more effectively. Second, we will know that we understand the other person. We usually *believe* we understand the other person, but generally, we have no evidence that we do. Active listening provides that evidence. And when we do not understand, we can discover the problem and correct it. Third, active listening allows us to show the other person that we understand. The other person will be able to verify our understanding of the message and discover that we were sufficiently interested to pay close attention.

This third benefit yields a fourth: a relationship may be nourished by the deeper understanding gained through active listening as we listen to both the speaker's message and feelings. This deeper kind of listening occurs all too infrequently.

Finally, we know from the work of Carl Rogers[7] that reflecting a person's ideas back to them when that person is working through a problem helps the person gain insights. Having a good friend who knows how to use active listening is comforting. One survey placed "comforting ability" among the most important skills a friend can have.[8]

Active listening requires that attention be focused on the speaker.

Active Listening Techniques

Active listening sometimes seems awkward to people who have never used it. The techniques described below are designed to help you understand how to use active listening most effectively.

1. *Give the speaker cues that you are listening.* These cues can be both verbal and nonverbal. Verbal cues can be comments such as "Yes," "What else?," or "Tell me more." Be sure you use a variety of these cues. (Imagine how "Yes," "Yes," and "Yes" might be received by your listener.) Such comments invite the other person to give you the details necessary for better understanding and let the speaker know you are paying attention.

   Nonverbal cues also show that you are listening. For example, maintain eye contact, nod, or lean forward slightly to display your interest. Finally, you may want to assume an open body posture by sitting or standing in a relatively direct position to your partner. Do not angle your body away from the speaker, and avoid crossing your arms or legs. Instead, establish a relaxed but alert posture so that you can directly observe your partner's verbal and nonverbal messages.

2. *Paraphrase both the content and feelings of the message.* The content is the easier part of the message for most people to understand. Thus, you may tend to focus mostly or perhaps entirely on this aspect. If there are clear feelings involved, be sure to feed them back, too. This brief example illustrates this type of listening. Ling is responding to Mary:

   > You have been talking for nearly a half hour about whether or not to continue dating Peter. During that time, the only reason you gave for continuing the relationship is that breaking up is such a hassle. From what you've said, I get the impression that you really don't think that you are that much in love with him. And besides this, you know that he will feel hurt and angry. Are you a little scared about the prospects of telling Peter you're through?

   Here is a second example of an active listening response. This time, Charlie has been talking to John about work. John responds:

   > You keep telling me that everything is fine at work, but every time you bring up the subject of your boss, your tone seems to change. All of the enthusiasm leaves your voice. Is something bothering you?

3. *Clarify the areas of uncertainty.* Ask questions about what you have heard to ensure your understanding and receive additional relevant information. Such questions are not meant to probe deeply but rather to stimulate the speaker to express thoughts more

If clear feelings are communicated as part of the message, feed them back, too.

fully. These questions should be viewed by our partners as stimulating and supporting. You can see now that asking questions can help to clarify a message in this dialogue between Annie and Russ. Russ was attracted to Annie. He had considered asking her to go to a movie but decided against this because he knew she was busy studying. He thought she might be willing to spend some time getting to know him if he asked her for a study date. Annie heard him correctly when he asked her to study with him. Russ assumed that she understood that a study date would include a certain amount of horsing around. He was wrong:

Russ: Annie, I'm going to the library to study tonight. Would you like to go along with me?

Annie (with a note of skepticism): Well, I am really snowed with course work, but I guess I'd be willing to go study. In fact, that'd give us a chance to talk about our biology project. Do you understand that I really have to study?

Russ: What do you mean, 'really have to study'?

Annie: Russ, I'd be glad to study with you. And I'd be glad to spend some time just talking. But tonight, if we go to the library to study, I need to study.

Russ: O.K. It's a deal. I'll pick you up at six.

Russ picked up on Annie's nonverbal cues because he was really listening. This prompted him to ask a question. Annie was then able to avoid a misunderstanding and a potential problem by clarifying her initial statement.

4. *Use active listening when the information is particularly important.* Active listening should be attempted only when appropriate. You will need to decide what "appropriate" means for you. For us, it means situations in which understanding is important. For example, a friend may want to tell of a problem or perhaps an exciting experience, we may be discussing a joint project, a child may need the answer to a critical question, or somebody may be explaining a complicated process.

5. *Learn a variety of ways to lead into paraphrasing.* Many people who use active listening for the first time will adopt a "lead-in" phrase, such as "What I heard you say is . . . ." and use it every time. This repetition can become annoying to that person's partners. Among the many lead-in phrases that you might learn are: "I think you just said . . .," "Do you mean . . . ?," "Are you saying. . . ?," "In other words . . . ." "I'm wondering if you mean . . . ?," "Did you say . . . ?," and "So you think that . . . ?" Write down ten such phrases and learn to use them.

SUMMARY

Listening is a process that involves sensing, attending, understanding, and remembering. Sensing is not listening; it is receiving stimuli through the senses. Listening, on the other hand, is more than receiving stimuli. It also includes attending (selecting one of the many stimuli and allowing it to register in the brain); understanding (interpreting and evaluating what is sensed); and remembering (recalling the understood message).

Because of this complexity, listening is a difficult process, especially in a relational context. Effective listening requires effort, withholding judgments, and empathy. We can learn to be more effective listeners by understanding and meeting these requirements. We can also use the technique of active listening to help us to focus on and remember the content and feelings of our partner's communication.

DISCUSSION QUESTIONS

1. Identify a person you would like to get to know better. Ask that person how his or her day is going. Engage in active listening as a part of this experience. Then report to your class:

   a. How did the person respond?

   b. How did you feel while actively listening?

   c. What nonverbal cues did you get?

   d. What were your images of the person?

   e. What image do you think you projected?

2. Turn on the television and sit with your back to it. Listen for the cues, other than words, that are intended to help you interpret the program. These may include sound effects, a laugh track, or music. Identify as many of these auditory cues as possible, and report your findings in class. How did the inability to see the program influence your ability to understand?

3. It is reasonable to suppose that a person with a hearing impairment will have greater difficulty in listening than someone who is not impaired. How might a person with normal hearing impair her own ability to listen?

4. Suppose that you were to seek the advice of a counselor concerning some personal problem. How would you help yourself listen more effectively to receive the information you need? How would you help the counselor to understand your problem?

5. Suppose you receive a low grade on a midterm project. You believe the grade has been unfairly assigned, so you make an appointment to talk to the instructor about the problem. Identify attitudes and other factors that might make listening difficult for both you and the teacher in this context.

ENDNOTES

1. O. Hargie, C. Sanders, and D. Dickson, *Social Skills in Interpersonal Communication* (London: Rutledge, 1994); O. Hargie., ed., *The Handbook of Communication Skills* (London: Rutledge, 1997).

2. D. J. Goldsmith and K. Fitch, "The Normative Context of Social Support," *Human Communication Research* 23 (1997): 454–476.

3. M. Davidowitz and R. D. Myrick, "Responding to the Bereaved: An Analysis of Helping Statements," *Death Education* 8 (1984): 1–10.

4. A. L. Vangelisti, "Communication Problems: The Counselor's Perspective," *Journal of Applied Communication Research* 22 (1994): 106–126.

5. C. Kelley, "Empathic Listening," in *Small Group Communication,* R. Cathcart and L. Samovar, eds. (Dubuque. IA: Wm. C. Brown, 1984), 297.

6. Ibid.

7. C. R. Rogers. "A Theory of Therapy, Personality, and Interpersonal Relationships as Developed in the Client-Centered-Framework," in *Psychology: A Study of Science,* vol. 3. S. Koch, ed. (New York: McGraw-Hill, 1959), 184–256.

8. B. Burleson and W. Samter, "Cognitive Complexity, Communication Skills, and Friendship." (Paper presented at the Seventh International Congress on Personality Construct Psychology, Memphis, TN, August 1987.)

READ MORE ABOUT LISTENING IN THESE SOURCES

Burleson, Brant. "Comforting Messages; Their Significance and Effects." In *Communicating Strategically: Strategies in Interpersonal Communication.* Hillsdale, NJ: Erlbaum, 1990. This study of comforting in everyday life gives insights into its characteristics, types, effects, and implications.

Purdy, Michael, and Deborah Borisoff. *Listening in Everyday Life: A Personal and Professional Approach,* 2nd ed. Lanham, M. D.: University Press of America, 1997. This book is a collection of readings that offer advice about listening in a number of contexts. Chapters are included on the influences of gender, culture, and group settings.

Wolvin, Andrew W. and Carolyn G. Coakley. *Listening.* 4th ed. Dubuque, IA: Wm. C. Brown. 1992. This textbook is a valuable source of information on the listening process and its functions in a variety of contexts.

PART 4

RELATIONAL CONCERNS

RELATIONSHIPS

PREVIEW

Growing, healthy relationships are a great source of pleasure. This chapter addresses the beginning of such relationships. It introduces ideas about the reasons we engage others in relationships, the engagement process, and the role of definition and rules in relationships.

We need relationships to accomplish two important purposes. First, relational communication validates our self-concept. Through it, we reveal ourselves to others. Second, relational communication increases our self-awareness. The uncovering of the self for ourselves and others may not always be easy, but it benefits both relational and personal growth.

The information we reveal varies from one relationship to another, sometimes significantly. Therefore, we need to learn about appropriate self-disclosure and its risks. We provide guidelines in this chapter to help you make decisions about self-disclosure.

This chapter begins our consideration of the factors that influence the development and growth of relationships. This chapter and those that follow will be especially important to you because they focus directly on building, maintaining, and growing in various kinds of relationships. Here, we discuss how relationships develop into friendships and grow into commitment. We also provide suggestions for promoting growth in each stage of a relationship's development.

KEY TERMS

aquaintanceship	attraction
blind self	bonding
"coming together" process	dyadic effect
engagement process	experimenting
hidden self	initiating
integrating	interpersonal attraction
interpersonal needs	intensifying
inviting	Johari Window
open self	relational definition
relational rules	relational stability
renegotiating	revising communication
self-disclosure	similarity
social attraction	social penetration process
task attraction	trust
underdisclosing	unknown self

OBJECTIVES

1. Describe the initiating stage in relational development, including the factors that promote relational growth.

2. List the characteristics of the experimenting stage in relational development, including suggestions for promoting relational growth.

3. Explain the process of intensifying in relational development, including the signs of intensifying and suggestions for promoting relational growth.

4. Explain how relationships integrate. What are the signs of integration, and how can relational growth be promoted?

5. Discuss the role of renegotiating in relationships. What are some of the possible outcomes of this process?

6. Explain what bonding means in a relationship and why a relationship moves to that stage.

7. Define self-disclosure and recall examples of it in at least two relationships.

8. Identify differences in your openness from one relationship to another.

9. Recall an instance in which bringing something about yourself into the open helped a relationship grow.

10. Describe the major benefits and risks of self-disclosure.

11. Suggest appropriate guidelines for self-disclosure.

12. Discuss why people initiate the acquaintance process.

13. Explain some of the fundamentals of attraction.

14. Suggest how the basic interpersonal needs of inclusion, control, and affection affect the decision to engage in a relationship.

15. Describe the engagement process.

16. Identify the function of definition and rules of relationship development.

ENGAGEMENT

The desire to interact with others and to develop meaningful relationships with others is strong in all of us. In fact, there is probably nothing more important to us. This section begins our focus on the development and management of relationships. It asks the question "Why do we engage?" Then it addresses the engagement process itself and lays the groundwork for relational beginnings.

WHY WE ENGAGE

Physical, Social, and Task Attractiveness

Interpersonal attraction is the most obvious reason for forming acquaintanceships that may lead to more committed relationships. This attraction might be physical, social, or task-related.

Physical attraction is clearly an important factor in initiating communication. We are more likely to start a conversation with a person we find physically attractive. But defining attractiveness is a difficult assignment. Everyone has some ideal image of an attractive person—usually of someone who resembles themselves. We may know that we don't fit an ideal image perfectly, but we usually think of ourselves as *within the range* of what we consider attractive.

Along with considering mere attractiveness, we sometimes consider engaging in conversation because of an attribute we believe is related to attractiveness. Researchers find that certain inferences are drawn regarding attractive people. They are thought to be more sexual, personable, persuasive, popular, happy, kind, interesting, confident, sociable, serious, and outgoing.[1] We might engage an attractive person in conversation because we suppose the person possesses some of these attributes.

In our culture, physical attractiveness is an especially important factor for women, for we have been taught to think of women in terms of attractiveness and men in terms of ability. Table 8.1 summarizes the results of a study that shows which qualities were judged to be important in a potential relational partner and how they differ for men and women.

Social attraction, like physical attraction, is highly dependent upon the individual's frame of reference. Socially attractive people seem to draw others into engagement. You might be attracted to a person with a sense of humor, a storyteller who can carry the conversation. On the other hand, someone else might be attracted to a person who is direct but less forward and who can talk about woodworking. Generally, if we look around our social circle, we will discover something about our definition of "socially attractive." We are drawn to a socially attractive person because her behavior meets our needs for social stimulation, which are particular to the persons involved.

A person is *task attractive* if we enjoy working with him. When we appreciate the way people work on a project, whether in a club, social organization, or on the job, we seek more contact with them. Working with them brings enjoyment as well as productivity. Both of these elements, enjoyment and productivity, are important parts of task attraction. So, if we believe that the person is efficient and productive but also boring, we are not likely to engage in conversation with that individual.

Table 8.1	Physical, Social, and Task Qualities Rated as Important in a Partner by Men and Women
For men	*For women*
1. Achievement	1. Physical attractiveness
2. Leadership	2. Erotic ability
3. Occupational ability	3. Affectional ability
4. Economic ability	4. Social ability
5. Entertaining ability	5. Domestic ability
6. Intellectual ability	6. Sartorial ability
7. Observational ability	7. Interpersonal understanding
8. Common sense	8. Art appreciation
9. Athletic ability	9. Moral and spiritual understanding
10. Theoretical ability	10. Art and creative ability

Source: R. Centers, "The Completion Hypothesis and the Compensatory Dynamic in Intersexual Attraction and Love," *Journal of Psychology* 82 p. 117, 1971. Reprinted with permission of the Helen Dwight Reid Educational Foundation. Published by Heldref Publications, 4000 Albemarble St., NW. Washington, D.C. 20016. Copyright © 1971.

Proximity

We have a tendency to be attracted to and form acquaintanceships with those who are in *proximity* to us, the people who live and work close to us. Leon Festinger, Stanley Schacter, and Kurt Back conducted a famous study of how friendships formed among residents of a student housing development. They found that they were based on the distance people lived from each other and whether the unit faced onto the courtyard.[2] The closer a student's room was to another's, the more likely it was that they would form a friendship. In addition, those who faced the courtyard formed more friendships than those who faced the street. Their physical closeness thus provided the opportunity to talk and form friendships. This same principle holds for residents of apartment buildings. People most often form friendships with those who live near them on their floor.

Physical distance is very important in the initiation of the acquaintanceship. We have the greatest opportunity to talk to those who are near us. Thus, where we sit on the first day of class or when we attend religious services will largely determine whom we will be able to engage. As time passes, we may move beyond those who are physically close to us, but proximity will remain a factor in how our relationships develop.

It is not the mere closeness that creates attraction but also that we have the opportunity to interact with these people. We seem to be able to find things that attract us in a variety of persons. As we get to know someone, we gain information about her. We find that we share some interests and come to know how the person thinks and acts. This allows us to be able to predict her behavior. All of this causes us to feel comfortable around the person and to develop attraction. Of course, on the other hand, if the initial exposure is unpleasant, repeated exposure may decrease attraction.

Similarity

We often like people who are similar to us in physical characteristics, intelligence, attitudes, abilities, race, and nationality. A great deal of research confirms this is often the case in most relationships.[3] We are attracted to such people because they validate us. The similarity between their personal characteristics and beliefs and ours confirms that we find them attractive and believe that we are also.

We often like people who are similar to us.

We find that there is a difference between those to whom we say we would be attracted and those with whom we form friendships. We associate with people who are similar to us in attractiveness.

Attitude similarly is especially important. If we believe in God, we may be uncomfortable with a person who does not. This extends not only to what we like but also to what we dislike. Such similarity is particularly important when the attitude is a significant one.

Core values fall into this category. Matters of taste, such as a preference for a certain color, usually do not. As relationships move beyond initial engagement, the salience of attitudes might change. This explains some divorces. Attitudes toward children and spending money, for example, might be neither similar nor very important prior to marriage. Once they become salient, however, they can drive people apart.

We are attracted to people with similar attitudes for two basic reasons. First, their agreement with us reinforces our self-concept and feeling of being OK. It is rewarding to be reinforced in this way. Second, these people are more likely to act in ways we can predict, which makes us feel more comfortable around them. This predictability extends to our ability to predict how we will be received. We are especially attracted to people we think will like us and treat us well.

There are, of course, cases in which opposites attract. If a person likes to control, then he might be attracted to someone who wants to be controlled. In fact, Theodore Reik argues that we seek mates who have a characteristic we do not have but envy.[4] He would say that when we see a couple in which one partner is an extrovert and the other is shy, we can explain their attraction in part by these complementary traits.

Basic Interpersonal Needs

We experience three basic *interpersonal needs* that affect our decision to become acquainted: inclusion, control, and affection. Each may be present to different degrees. Moreover, we both possess and fill these needs. For example, we have a need to include others and a need to be included; we have a need to control others and a need to be controlled; we have a need to love and a need to be loved. Table 8.2 gives examples of how basic interpersonal needs can affect the likelihood of engagement.

Expectations of Relational Benefits

Murray S. Davis suggests that there are four motivations for interpersonal engagement:

1. The impulse to receive stimulation
2. The impulse to express experiences
3. The impulse to assert oneself—to test ideas
4. The impulse to enhance enjoyment of certain activities[5]

Because of their importance, these require individual discussion.

Table 8.2		Interpersonal Needs and Initiating Relationships
Need	*Intensity*	*Impact on initiating*
To include	High	May give parties and include new acquaintances
	Low	May stick to own circle of friends; may avoid initiating
To be included	High	May seek opportunities to initiate; may "push" self on strangers
	Low	May avoid contact; may enjoy being alone
To control	High	May initiate contact with those who appear to be easily controlled
	Low	May initiate contact with those who appear to be equal or able to hold their own in a relationship
To be controlled	High	May initiate contact with those who appear to dominate others
	Low	May initiate contact with those who do not control others; may avoid contact with those who appear to control
To love	High	May initiate contact with those who need "warmth"; may avoid contact with those who appear to be "cold" and uncaring
	Low	May initiate contact with those who appear to need little affection; may avoid initiating contact
To be loved	High	May initiate contact with those who appear to give "warmth"; may avoid contact with those who appear to be "cold" and uncaring
	Low	May initiate contact with those who appear not to give too much affection; may avoid initiating contact

The Impulse to Receive Stimulation

We often experience this impulse when Saturday evening comes along and we have no plans to share the evening. The impulse is also strongly felt when a dating relationship ends and we feel alone.

Sometimes this impulse for stimulation is generated by a relationship that has become too routine; the people become bored, and this boredom gives them the initiative to begin new relationships.

The Impulse to Express Experiences

To visualize this impulse, suppose you have been looking for a car to buy and have just found the right one at the right price. Your immediate impulse is probably to share the news with someone. Everyone has had a similar experience. You feel frustrated and perhaps even a little cheated if nobody is available to share your news, for the joy of sharing such an experience is important.

The same is true about bad news. If the boss has been grumpy and you received the brunt of it, you will want to share this experience. This sharing is an opportunity for you to receive empathy and encouragement from another. It may even prompt the other person to share a similar experience. This reciprocal sharing provides a basis for comparing your experiences to those of others.

Can you recall a time when you felt that you did not do well on a test? It probably did not take you long to seek out others in the class with whom you could commiserate. "That was some kind of a test," you said. "Yeah," your friend answered. "I think it was the hardest one yet. What did you think of that essay question?" You both shudder at the thought of the question before you add, "I'll study harder next time."

The Impulse to Assert Oneself—To Test Ideas

This impulse is not related, as you might suspect, to assertiveness. Rather, it refers to the expression of an idea that needs testing. People have impulses to express ideas of which they are unsure and for which they need feedback. This expression and its related feedback undoubtedly serve to develop an individual's identity and self-concept. We may not be particularly interested in confirming our ideas, but we want to discover how others react to them. We are acting on an impulse for both social contact and comparison when we seek people out for this purpose.

The Impulse to Enhance Enjoyment of Certain Activities

Finally, we are motivated to engage others because being together enhances our enjoyment of an activity. We join together to play games and to engage in other recreational activities. We also join together to celebrate our important events. Imagine celebrating your birthday by yourself. Or picture yourself trying to celebrate Independence Day, July 4th, by yourself. Being together allows us to share our joy, our excitement, and our thoughts so that we gain more enjoyment from the activity.

ENGAGING ANOTHER PERSON

Mere talk is not necessarily interpersonal communication. Interpersonal communication moves beyond the impersonal application of societal rules. Impersonal talk is important, of course, but it relates only minimally to engagement. William and Judith Pfeiffer suggested that the important last step in the *engagement process* is *contact*.[6] They illustrated the engagement process in four steps, as shown in figure 8.1.

Awareness ----------→ Excitement ----------→ Action ----------→ Contact

Figure 8.1
The engagement
process.

Very simply, this process progresses from becoming aware of the person to being excited by the prospect of the conversation to acting on the excitement and finally to making contact. Real contact is never made if there is an intent to remain impersonal. Only an intent to get to know the person psychologically moves us to make interpersonal contact.

The initial engagement is an important step in establishing an acquaintanceship and therefore deserves special attention. We have said a good deal about interpersonal skills. Here, we want to summarize some of the skills and behaviors for you to use as you meet new people:

1. Try to establish appropriate eye contact. This usually means relatively direct contact to signal that the communication channel is open. Experiment with what seems comfortable to you. It is important that you maintain eye contact without staring. You will usually find that too steady a gaze will make the other person uneasy.

2. Experiment to find an appropriate interpersonal distance. Approach the person to the point that you feel comfortable and close. Check your posture. You may want to avoid closed positions, such as standing with your arms crossed or folded in front of you.

3. See if a direct approach to meeting the person works well for you. You might say something like, "Hi, my name is Jerry," rather than the usual game playing, such as "Didn't I see you at Soloman's last Friday?"

4. Try having the person talk about herself. This gives you a chance to respond positively to what the person says. Also, most people seem to enjoy talking about themselves, so this may help them feel at ease.

5. Remember that the face is an important conveyer of feelings. Consider ways to use your face to tell the other that you are enjoying meeting her. One of the simplest ways to do this is to remember to smile. Head nodding can also be effective if used in moderation.

6. Search for similarities between you and the other. Maybe you share classes, hobbies, or other interests. Have you lived in the same cities? An awareness of your similarity is an important source of attraction.

7. Consider how you react to a positive person versus a negative person. We think maintaining a positive demeanor is very important. Sometimes we slip into negative behavior unknowingly, which should be avoided.

8. Be careful not to engage in too intimate self-disclosure. Sometimes we find ourselves enjoying someone so much that we say more about ourselves than we should. Initial engagements are not nourished by overly intimate or overly negative self-disclosure.

RELATIONAL DEFINITION AND RULES

Underlying our developmental view of communication in interpersonal relationships are two fundamental elements—*definition* and *rules*—which have their beginning in the engagement process. The extent of our agreement on these elements with those with whom we have formed a relationship becomes an important measure of a relationship's stability.

Relational Definition

We have a definition of our relationship at every point in its development. A typical definition is "We enjoy each other, but we are mere acquaintances." Another couple might define their relationship by saying, "We are best friends." An eighteen-year-old said, "You'd have to say we're friends—special friends—but just friends."

An examination of how people define their relationship gives an indication of *relational stability*. A *stable relationship* is one in which there is agreement about its kind and nature, as when both say that they are "best friends."

William W. Wilmot presented three aspects of relational stability:

1. Relationships stabilize because the participants reach some minimal agreement (usually implicitly) of what they want (relationally and otherwise) from the relationship.

2. Relationships stabilize at different levels of intimacy.

3. A stabilized relationship still has areas of change.[7]

Outsiders may not understand why the relationship is stable, as, for example, when parents evaluate the relationships their offspring have with others. Outsiders may believe some aspect of a relationship is crucial, while the participants see it as unimportant. For example, consider the marriage that is stable because the participants value the financial resources they can give each other. For them, this security is important. The fact that they hold few interests

Relational stability depends upon agreement by both partners about the kind and nature of the relationship.

in common may not matter. (Of course, some of us may wonder about how satisfactory such a relationship actually is.)

People will not be satisfied unless they can achieve a minimal positive agreement about what they want from their relationship. For example, mere acquaintances may want to receive a happy greeting when they meet each other. They probably will not have any need for deeply meaningful conversation.

Wilmot's second aspect of stability is that individuals fix the relationship at a particular level of intimacy that they find satisfying. When they agree on this, they stabilize the relationship at that level. Such agreement is important if the relationship is to be satisfying. Suppose you meet a professor who shares your particular academic interests. You think that it would be nice to get to know him as a friend. He, however, thinks that the acquaintance level is enough for a student-teacher relationship. You have a definitional problem that could generate some awkward moments, as you try to be a friend and he brushes you off as an acquaintance.

Finally, Wilmot's third point suggests that stability does not mean stagnation. There is always some change in a relationship that requires negotiation. As time passes, people want different things from a relationship. If these wants are met, a new definition is struck and the relationship takes on new stability. If they are not, the resulting instability might lead to relational deterioration.

Relational Rules

People behave according to their cultural, societal, and psychological experience. For example, our culture helps us define an appropriate distance between those engaged in a conversation. Our social contacts will give us a sense of what it means to be polite. The way we see ourselves in relationships—based on how others react to us—and the way we see others will give us rules for behaving. Our behavior is thus governed by a set of *relational rules* that evolve from these three sources.

But how do we discover these rules? The answer lies in the concept of *prediction*. We predict how the other person might act based on cultural, social, and psychological data we get from the person and her verbal and nonverbal behavior. The relationship can be thought of as primarily *impersonal* when the data are cultural and social[8] and *interpersonal* when the data are psychological.

We gain a set of rules from our culture and society related to turn taking and small talk. We are so accustomed to these rules that it is difficult for most of us to specify what they are. Yet, when we or the other person violates a rule, we know it. Here are some of the turn-taking rules that we typically follow:

Behavior is governed by relational rules that evolve from cultural assumptions, social experience, and psychological need.

1. One person talks at a time.
2. If two people talk at the same time, they will do so only briefly.
3. Speakers change frequently.
4. Speakers follow no particular order in taking turns.
5. If an error is committed in turn taking, the speakers will work to "repair" the error. (If two people talk at the same time, one will stop and may apologize.)[9]

Rules related to small talk specify what topics are appropriate for a particular social context and how we may proceed in talking about them. Here are some rules about behavior when we engage in small talk:

1. Maintain a pleasant demeanor.

2. Do not stand too close to the other person.
3. Do not reveal intimate details about yourself.
4. Change topics frequently.
5. Do not disagree too strongly.

Psychological data become available as partners in an acquaintanceship become better acquainted through self-disclosure. They become aware of each other's personalities. This gives them an additional basis for predicting behavior that may be more reliable since it takes into account the uniqueness of the person. Now the relationship has moved from the impersonal level to the interpersonal level. This allows the partners to set rules based upon their respective preferences.

Relational rules that evolve from knowledge of psychological data revolve around similar issues. It might be permissible to talk over each other, especially in an argument. Among a group of friends, for example, it might be permissible for Tim to tease Cheryl about her weight. And the group might permit Tim to express his temper when he is angry. They may also establish the informal relational rule that allows Mary Ann to dominate all the others during a crisis. Each rule is based upon a knowledge of the members' peculiarities and an agreement on rules that will allow the group to succeed. The more often the group members adopt rules based on their relationships, the more predictable, interpersonal, and intimate they become.

SELF-DISCLOSURE AND RELATIONAL GROWTH

We know a relationship is growing when we see that the other person can make accurate predictions about what we would like, say, or do. For instance, suppose Bonita knows that her husband, Julio, has had a hard day at work and she therefore has something special waiting for him at home—perhaps his favorite dinner or a book that he has wanted. This is her way of showing that there is understanding in their relationship. Perhaps on that same day friends call Bonita to invite her and Julio to a party that night. Knowing that Julio would rather relax after such a hard day, Bonita might decline the invitation without checking with him.

The key to correctly anticipating the wants and needs of others is the frequent communication of our own wants, needs, and expectations. The more our partners understand about how we see ourselves, the better their predictions will become and the more the relationship will grow. We call the process of revealing ourselves to others *self-disclosure*. Improving our ability to self-disclose and learning when and where to do this are important elements of relational development.

> Relational growth is apparent when you correctly predict another person's behavior, needs, or wants.

Imagine that we keep all our personal information in a special box that we carry around with us. We select and present items from the box when we meet others. There is some information that we want most people to see and know, so we select these bits most frequently. There are other things we reserve for only select individuals in special situations. There are still other things that we keep entirely to ourselves. Finally, there may be information tucked in the corners of the box that even we do not know exists. These are things we do not discover until we have spent some time and energy rummaging around in the box. Sometimes one of these unknown bits sticks to another bit that we are taking out of the box, and, without our knowledge, is presented to someone else. This is what Anthony Athos and John Gabarro call "a message sent unawares."[10]

THE JOHARI WINDOW

Two contemporary psychologists, Joseph Luft and Harrington Ingham, developed a model, known as the *Johari Window* (figure 8.2), to help people understand the relationship between the various ideas we present about ourselves.[11] The upper left block presents the information about us that is clear both to ourselves and to others. This information includes behaviors, attitudes, feelings, and desires, and makes up the *open self*. Consider for a moment what people in a particular situation—perhaps a club or organization—know about you. Name some of these things. How did they learn them? The things that you and others in the organization know are in the open area of the window.

The square at the upper right represents the *blind self*. This area contains things others know about us that are not evident to us. We may provide leadership in a club or organization, for example, yet not be aware we are doing so. We learn about things that exist in the blind area through communication. Others bring these behaviors, attitudes, and bits of information into the open by telling us about them—perhaps the leader of the club or organization thanks you for your help.

The hidden self and the unknown self are in the lower half of the window. The *hidden self* is that part of our private image we choose not to present to others. Almost everyone has information about themselves that they keep private. This may include information about ambitions, wants, desires, hopes, and fears. Can you think of anything you have *not* revealed to your supervisor at work or to your partner in a romantic relationship? You can see that the size of the hidden self varies from relationship to relationship. This is true for the other areas of the self as well.

Finally, Luft and Ingham reasoned that there is an *unknown self*. This area includes things about ourselves, perhaps talents or phobias, that even we do not know about and have no reason to believe anybody else does either.

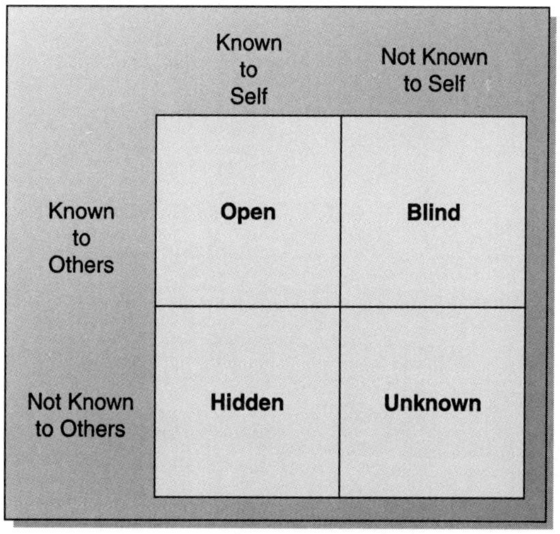

Figure 8.2
The Johari
Window. *Source:*
Group Process:
An Introduction
to Group
Dynamics *by*
Joseph Luft, by
permission of
Mayfield
Publishing
Company.
Copyright ©
1963, 1970, 1984
by Joseph Luft.

How open are you in important relationships? The understanding that comes from shared openness helps each person perceive the other more accurately. Although it is easy to overstate the case for openness, in general, the more we know about someone, the fewer false assumptions we make about that person. It follows that openness is important to relational growth.

On the other hand, if the open self is too large, an opposite effect may result. A person who is too open is said to be imprudent or not completely in control. Revealing information about ourselves that is not yet appropriate in a relationship is called *overdisclosing.* The motives of someone who overdiscloses are often suspect. We have all probably met a person we feel uncomfortable with because he or she overdiscloses, or reveals either overly intimate information or too much information. In such a situation, we would probably withdraw to avoid the overdiscloser. When this is not possible, we may subtly joke or tease about the situation. Generally, people do not come right out and tell the overdiscloser why they are uncomfortable. They hint about it instead.

Openness is important to relational growth, but too much openness may be imprudent.

Complete openness may also harm a relationship. Some things are better left unsaid. Private thoughts in a moment of anger, for example, may be hurtful to the other person and not particularly important to the overall relationship.

We can learn much about ourselves and our style of disclosure by exploring the "blind" area of the Johari Window. Here is information that we are unable to perceive but that is known to others. Suppose, for example, we have a friend, Aroon, who has certain

annoying but unconscious habits. In this case, the unconscious behavior contributes to communication difficulties. Aroon habitually stares off into space during conversations, looking past the person he is talking with and not really hearing what is being said. People frequently avoid Aroon. They report feeling uncomfortable with him because he appears not to listen. Finally, someone calls this habit to Aroon's attention. At first, he does not believe it, but when he pays attention to his communication, he sees that he does have the habits described.

Sometimes we are unwilling to share enough about ourselves to make a relationship work. This is represented by a hidden area that is too large or an open area that is too small. There are many reasons for not wanting to reveal things about ourselves, and sometimes we are right in keeping certain information or feelings hidden. But sometimes we are afraid to take the risk of self-disclosure. Because of this fear, we do not allow the relationship to grow. Has this ever happened to you?

We can use the Johari Window to sort out the information that we impart to others. Select a relationship you would define as close and examine your open area in that relationship. Begin by writing down several of the major things you believe are known both to yourself and to the other person. Next, think about your hidden area in that relationship. Write down several of the major items you have kept private. Is there anything in your hidden area that you might be willing to disclose? Under what circumstances might you be willing to do this?

Learning about your blind and unknown areas in the relationship requires effort from you and cooperation from the other person. Review your lists of open and hidden items. What aspects of yourself were revealed to you as a result of examining the relationship? Finally, ask the other person to talk with you about the way she sees you, herself, and the relationship. Such a conversation may reveal even more about your blind and unknown areas.

By analyzing our self-disclosure, we learn how open we are and how to make more conscious choices about what to disclose. Thus, the Johari Window can be a powerful tool for examining interpersonal communication. It can help clarify the information we share with others and also help us understand ourselves better.

The key objective in self-disclosure is appropriateness: We wish to present an image that is accurate and correct for a relationship and its context. Two general rules will help you gauge appropriateness. First, remember that your window is not the only one present in a relationship. Both partners in the relationship must be willing to self-disclose for the relationship to work. Second, the level of disclosure must be balanced or even, rather than one-sided. If you have a very large open area and the other person has a very small one, you may find yourself overdisclosing or this person *underdisclosing*. Relationships in which disclosure is one-sided will not grow very much. When we disclose, we encourage equal disclosure by our partners. When the other person discloses, we feel encouraged to disclose more ourselves. Relationships grow as disclosures are made by both parties over time.

BENEFITS OF SELF-DISCLOSURE

Self-disclosure is undoubtedly not the most common type of communication for most of us, yet it plays a very important role in establishing and nourishing relationships. Recall from Chapter 1 that the key decision point in the interpersonal exchange model was whether to trust the other person enough to self-disclose. Self-disclosure provides several benefits to the person and the relationship. It enhances your understanding of yourself, enables you to share your concerns, allows the other person to know you, and nutures your relationship.

Better Self-Understanding

Self-disclosure helps you understand yourself better because you can often clarify your ideas by talking them through with another person. When you self-disclose, two things happen. First, the act of expressing an idea forces you to put it into words. Doing so requires mental effort—especially if the idea is important to you—and the process of concentrating and forming a message focuses your thoughts more clearly.

Second, expressing a thought to another provides feedback that helps you understand yourself better. The other person may ask questions that prompt you to think more deeply about the idea. The other individual may also express his or her thoughts about the idea. Often, these thoughts serve to validate or refine your thinking. You might hear, "I think you did the right thing," "That is exactly what I've been thinking about John and Jerry's fight last night," or "I understand your point, but I think you may be misinterpreting his words because you seem to feel hurt."

Sharing of Concerns

Self-disclosure also enables you to share your concerns. You probably know from experience that sharing a concern—that is, talking out a problem—helps you cope with it. Often just being heard and knowing that a friend understands is all you want. At other times, you may want your friend's help in solving a problem.

Research verifies our experience that sharing is related to mental health, but a particular pattern appears when researchers examine the relationship between self-disclosure and mental health. Paul Cozby concluded, after a review of the research literature, that "persons with positive mental health . . . are characterized by high disclosure to a few significant others and medium disclosure to others in the social environment. Individuals who are poorly adjusted . . . are characterized by either high or low self-disclosure to virtually everyone in the social environment."[12] Art Bochner confirms that selective disclosure, or disclosure in moderation, characterizes positive personal adjustment.[13]

Self-Revelation

A third benefit of self-disclosure is that it allows the other person to know who you are. This has two positive effects. First, we believe that communication effectiveness is enhanced when communicators understand each other. Your self-revelation allows the persons you have relationships with to understand you better and thus improves your effectiveness as a communicator. But a second positive effect also occurs. Your self-disclosure usually prompts a phenomenon known as the *dyadic effect*, in which one person's actions become a stimulus for similar actions on the part of the other person. The reciprocal nature of self-disclosure is well documented by research.[14] Thus, as our model of interpersonal exchange suggested, self-disclosure can prompt self-disclosure. Ongoing self-disclosure may be visualized as a spiral: as the reciprocation continues, the disclosure often becomes more and more intimate.[15] The secondary result of your disclosure, then, is that the other person self-disclos-es and you come to know that person better. Better knowledge on both sides can lead to more effective communication.

Relationship Nurturance

Finally, self-disclosure helps you establish and maintain meaningful relationships. Relationships need disclosure to stay healthy and grow. It is through your disclosure that the other person discovers who you are; the person then has something to "hang on to" and value in you. Sidney Jourard spoke to this issue when he said that it is difficult for a person to love another person if he or she does not know that person.[16] You might substitute "like" for "love" to broaden this statement to more than committed relationships. The truth is, though, that to have a relationship you must have something to like in the other person, and what the person reveals to you provides a basis for liking.

Researchers believe that self-disclosure has other relationship benefits as well. Self-disclosure may be linked to trust; your self-disclosure may be seen as a sign of trust. When you are willing to self-disclose, you are saying that you care about the other person and respect that person enough to share some of yourself. Recent research suggests that self-disclosure helps us develop closer relationships. It also indicates that couples who self-disclose tend to remain together longer than couples who do not engage in significant disclosure.[17]

RISKS OF SELF-DISCLOSURE

The power present in self-disclosure for our relationships also presents risks. It is important to weigh both the benefits and risks before you engage in significant self-disclosure. Self-disclosure creates vulnerability, can lead to overexposure, and may even create dislike.

Vulnerability

Self-disclosure makes you vulnerable because you are counting on the other person to treat the shared part of yourself with respect. Is the risk of disclosing yourself reasonable? Is your partner trustworthy and supportive? Take a realistic look at the possibility that self-disclosing may harm you. Realize, too, that appropriate self-disclosure is usually moderate in amount, gradually increasing in intimacy. Understand that even in committed relationships, uncensored candor can be problematic. Self-disclosures about past indiscretions, for example, may ultimately increase or decrease attraction and trust and strengthen or weaken the bonds that hold the relationship together. Unfortunately, making decisions about candid disclosures of this type is difficult because it is not easy to predict the results. The best advice we can supply is to be prudent and to carefully consider the potential benefits and risks.

Overexposure

Self-disclosure can lead not only to vulnerability but to a feeling of overexposure. Significant disclosure does expose you. This, in and of itself, may not be a particular problem if the disclosure has been reciprocal. Disclosure becomes overexposure when you discover that the other person's self-disclosure is less intimate and has less breadth than yours. Disclosure should be appropriate to the stage of your relationship. Generally, the more intimate the disclosure, the closer the relationship should be. Furthermore, you and the other individual should be fairly balanced in your disclosure (unless the relationship is a professional therapist-client relationship).

Dislike

We are generally more attracted toward a person who engages in positive self-disclosure than a person who engages in excessive negative self-disclosure. Negative self-disclosure is negative in content; for example, complaints, discussions of personal failures, and dismal confessions all qualify as negative self-disclosure. This type of disclosure more often takes place within an intimate relationship. If a person engages in excessive negative self-disclosure with a stranger or acquaintance, it can reduce the attraction the other person may feel and stifle the relationship. In fact, people who engage in excessive negative disclosure may be considered "negatively adjusted."[18] In this case, as one communication author put it, "More and more negative communication leads to more and more negative results."[19]

Computer-Mediated Communication and Self-Concept

E-mail communication via the Internet seems to lack the richness of other communication channels. These messages omit much of the nonverbal aspects such as tone of voice, posture, gestures, and facial expression. These omissions can be an advantage to the communicator because the person does not need to worry about managing them.

Communicating via the computer can actually enhance the ability of a person to manage his or her identity.[20] The author of an electronic message can edit what they want to say to create a specific desired impression. E-mail allows the sender to say difficult things without concern about an immediate response from the listener as would be the case in face-to-face interaction. Likewise, the receiver has these advantages in crafting a response or can, if desired, even ignore the e-mail message altogether.

GUIDELINES FOR SELF-DISCLOSING

The fact that there are advantages and disadvantages to self-disclosure suggests that some guidelines for skillfully self-disclosing may be helpful. Recall that our model of interpersonal exchange, presented in Chapter 1, suggests that risk assessment is a step in making a decision whether to share or withhold information about ourselves with other persons. There are no absolute rules about self-disclosure, but we can offer considerations for you to keep in mind.

- *Consider the Stage of Development of the Relationship.* Usually, the intimacy of the disclosure should match the intimacy of the relationship. Research suggests that for most relationships, self-disclosure develops gradually.[21] This means that for a relationship on the acquaintance level, disclosure should be relatively nonintimate, increasing in breadth as the relationship develops. As the relationship develops further and intensifies, integrates, and, perhaps, moves into the bonding stage, greater depth and intimacy also become appropriate.

- *Consider the Reasonableness of the Risk in Self-Disclosing.* It is wise to consider carefully the risk involved in a particular self-disclosure. Is it likely that your disclosure will produce negative results? Do you sense almost certain rejection if you say what is on your mind? Is the relationship strong enough and important enough to allow disclosure of infidelities or dissatisfactions without risking the relationship? Might telling secret information risk that person's relationship with some other person? Certain kinds of disclosure might be too risky for the relationship.

- *Consider Whether the Self-Disclosure Is Reciprocated.* Have you ever found that you seem to carry the conversation, that you say a good deal about yourself, and the other person does not? An imbalance in disclosure will likely lead you to feel uneasy. Such an imbalance may suggest that your disclosure is not welcome at this time. Disclose gradually and monitor the other person's behavior so that you can gain a sense of how your disclosure is being received. Research suggests couples are happiest when their levels of openness are roughly equal.[22]

- *Consider the Effect of the Self-Disclosure.* Complete candor can be harmful to the relationship and to the other person. Confessions such as "I made love to your best friend," may lead the confessor to feel better but harm the relationship. They can also be devastating to the self-esteem of the person who receives the confession. Ask yourself if there is a reasonable expectation that your self-disclosure will have a positive effect for the other person and your relationship as well as for you.

Self-disclosure and trust are two of the "building blocks" of relationships. They are key factors in the growth of friendships and committed relationships. In this next section you will discover how self-disclosure and trust operate to relationships and move folks through stages in them.

FRIENDSHIP AND COMMITMENT

A relationship that fails is a most frustrating experience. In fact, we sometimes insulate ourselves from this disappointment by expecting that relationships might not grow, mature, and prosper. Yet in spite of our emotional preparation, we are surprised and even saddened when we discover that relationships we value are failing.

We believe the ability to care for a relationship is a skill that is central to happiness. But the alarming rate of divorce in the United States attests to the difficulty of maintaining healthy, growing relationships. In fact, roughly one of every two marriages will end in divorce.[23] If we assume that people do not enter marriage expecting failure, why does this happen? There is no simple answer to such a complicated question, but we believe that skill in caring for a relationship contributes significantly to its success or failure. In this chapter, we focus on *relational growth*—making friends and moving to commitment.

The concept of developmental stages in interpersonal relationships has been investigated by a number of scholars.[24] One of the clearest explanations was presented by Mark Knapp,[25] who says that the "coming together" process occurs in five stages: (1) initiating, (2) experimenting, (3) intensifying, (4) integrating, and (5) bonding. Table 8.3 presents these stages and representative conversation for each category.

INITIATING

Initiating occurs when we make decisions about a person's attractiveness. We observe the person from afar and decide whether we will invite the person to interact. This decision is based on at least two factors: the situation and our attraction to the person.

Situation

The situation may encourage or inhibit communication. Social situations, such as parties, for example, give us permission to mingle and involve others in conversation. The odds that we will talk to people we have never met increase because of the situation.

Table 8.3	Stages of the "Coming Together" Process
Stage	*Representative dialogue*
Initiating	"Hi, how you doin?" "Fine, you?"
Experimenting	"Oh, so you like to ski? So do I." "You do? Great! Where do you go?"
Intensifying	"I . . . think I love you." "I love you, too."
Integrating	"I feel so much a part of you." "Yeah, we are like one person. What happens to you happens to me."
Bonding	"I want to be with you always." "Let's get married."

Source: M. L. Knapp, *Interpersonal Communication and Human Relationships* (Boston: Allyn and Bacon, 1984), p. 33.

We are much more likely to meet people when we share an interest.

Likewise, we are more likely to initiate a conversation when the situation gives us something in common with the other person. If you are interested in sailing and attend a boat show, you would be likely to talk about sailing with someone there.

On the other hand, the situation might detract from our willingness to engage another person. As a freshman college student at orientation, it may have been difficult for you just to walk right up to people and talk to them. The newness of the situation and doubts about appropriate behavior may have acted as constraints. But suppose that during orientation, you shared a dormitory room with another entering student. The fact that you were living in such close proximity increased the likelihood that you initiated a relationship.

Attraction

Attraction is the second factor that may invite or keep us from initiating communication. When we consider what we know about people without talking to them, it is easy to understand why attraction is a key ingredient. For example, we can observe physical appearance and compare it to our likes and dislikes. Perhaps we like people who are close to our age, who smile frequently, or who have medium-length hair. It would be a safe guess that many of the characteristics we like are very similar to our images of ourselves.

Sometimes, however, we are intrigued by someone who is very different from us. Although our attention and imagination may be excited by the person, we will usually pass up the opportunity to develop a relationship. The person represents too many unknowns and does not appear to share our background, values, and beliefs.

Usually such a decision is influenced by what we want from the situation. If we are looking for someone we would like to date, we apply one set of standards; if we are looking for advice about sailboats, we are likely to apply quite different standards. Although there is very little concrete data available on which to base a decision at this early stage, we still make decisions about continuing or breaking off the relationship.

Inviting

Once our decision is made, we search for an appropriate way of *inviting* communication. The message we send may be "I'm a nice person, and I'm fun, too. Let's talk." We may then make a friendly inquiry about the situation, such as "I see you are taking interpersonal communication, too," or "What kind of boat do you like to sail?" With such statements, we suggest that the communication channel is open and that we want to discover a topic for conversation.

This inviting process takes only about fifteen seconds, but the outcome is crucial to further relational development. At this point, we decide to: (1) disengage, (2) keep the relationship at a superficial level, or (3) move to the next developmental stage.

The decision to disengage usually results when we discover that our schedules and situations do not coincide and thus would make a continued relationship difficult. Or we may decide that we share so little that even casual acquaintance would not be worth the effort.

The decision to keep the relationship at a superficial level is a common one. Usually one person decides there is not enough in common to warrant a more meaningful relationship. A number of other reasons may lead to such a decision. For example, we might see ourselves as not having time to develop a new relationship. Or perhaps we want to wait to see how the other person responds before we decide to intensify our contact. We expect to continue to see the person and make small talk when we choose to remain at this level.

A decision to move the relationship to the next stage represents a willingness to make an investment. We want more than mere small talk. We want to get to know the other person. We set aside time to be together. We extend our contact with the other, which clearly represents a deeper commitment to the relationship.

Willingness to set aside time for a relationship is a measure of our commitment.

EXPERIMENTING

Exploration of the unknown characterizes the *experimenting* stage in relationship development. The focus in this stage is on exploring the possibilities for a relationship. The data collected here help us decide whether to keep our relationships on a relatively superficial level or to move on to greater commitment. We usually decide to maintain fairly casual relationships. If a relationship is to grow, we must collect more information about the other person.

Collecting Information

Strangers often begin experimenting by collecting standard information—names, hometowns, and places of employment. Students often exchange their major, year in school, and perhaps social organizations to which they belong.

Which of these bits of information do you ask for when you are beginning a relationship?

names	year in school
hometown	social organizations
place of work	religious affiliation

academic major	marital status
kind of work	sexual preference
academic minor	hobbies

Since talking about such standard information quickly becomes superficial, we search for some common interest or experience to which we can shift. This moves us to a new depth of self-disclosure and to more meaningful and slightly more personal topics. As we share values as well as information, we begin to develop relational norms. This even more personal, more revealing conversation becomes the basis for decisions about the future of the relationship.

In this stage of relational development, we begin to risk disclosing our private selves. Initially, of course, we will be cautious and tentative about what we say. We wait to see if the other person also discloses. Most of us will not take on this risk unless we wish the relationship to grow.

The experimenting stage varies in length. Sometimes we discover a significant difference between us and our partner almost immediately. This might cause us to retreat instantly to talk that is more characteristic of the initiating stage. At other times, we are intrigued by a person but wish to pursue a gradual exploration process. Perhaps we have several other significant relationships and assume a "wait and see" attitude. Of course, we may decide very quickly that we have so much in common with our partner that we have no difficulty visualizing a more serious and committed relationship.

Promoting Relational Growth

Relationships are not sustained and do not grow if they are fed only by small talk. We must discover significant areas of common interest as well as cognitive similarity if our relationships are to prosper. Research has shown that common interests and especially similar attitudes, values, and beliefs are most important for maintaining interpersonal attraction.[26]

For example, if you believe that doing well in classes is important, you may want your relational partner to feel the same way. If you place great value on a particular religious belief, you will want the other person to value it as well. We experiment with and explore more and more topics as we work through this experimenting stage. We are disclosing ourselves, demonstrating trust, and making decisions about the other person's compatibility. In terms of what Irwin Altman and Dalmes Taylor call the *social penetration process*,[27] we are experiencing more and more breadth in our self-disclosure but are not yet willing to go deeper.

During all this checking and double checking, the commitment remains at the acquaintance level. And, as is true of the initiating stage, there are several possible relational choices throughout the experimenting stage. We might end the relationship because there is not enough commonality to sustain interest. Or we might decide to remain at the acquaintance level. In fact, this is the fate of most of our relationships; the contact remains occasional and the talk is not particularly intimate. Work relationships are frequently maintained at this level. The third possibility, of course, is for us to intensify a relationship if we find it satisfying and see that there is the basis for building a deeper and more significant relationship. Of course, if we are to do this, the other person in the relationship must make a similar decision.

INTENSIFYING

Intensifying signifies a change in our relationship; we move from acquaintanceship to friendship. Because intimacy and trust increase as we commit more fully, this represents a major step in relational development. This stage gets its name from the fact that communication actually becomes more intense. We are enjoying the relationship, so we talk more often and for longer periods. We may also spend more time together, which also suggests increased commitment.

During this stage, we show more and more of our private selves. We are willing to risk more because of the intimacy of the relationship and the *trust* we are developing in each other. We also may learn about some of our partner's secret fears. This sharing helps us understand each other as unique individuals. We begin to understand our partner's perspective on the world. In terms of the social penetration process, we are not only reaching for more breadth but also for much greater depth in our self-disclosure.

Signs of Intensifying

Knapp identifies numerous verbal cues that indicate that a relationship is intensifying,[28] including:

1. Forms of address become more informal: first name, nickname, or some term of endearment.

2. Use of the first-person plural becomes more common. "*We* should do this" or "*Let's* do this."

3. Private symbols begin to develop, sometimes in the form of a special slang or jargon, sometimes using conventional language forms that have understood, private meanings.

4. Verbal shortcuts built on a backlog of accumulated and shared assumptions, expectations, interests, knowledge, interactions, and experiences appear more often: one partner may request that a newspaper be passed by simply saying, "Paper."

5. More direct expressions of commitment appear: "We really have a good thing going" or "I don't know who I'd talk to if you

weren't around." Sometimes such expressions have an echo: "I really like you a lot" or "I really like you, too."

6. Increasingly, a partner acts as a helper in the daily process of understanding the other person: "In other words, you mean you're . . ." or "But yesterday, you said you were . . . ."

Nonverbal behavior also changes. More touching and closer interpersonal distances occur at the intensifying level. Sometimes attempts are made to coordinate clothing styles and more time is consumed in interactions.

Promoting Relational Growth

Whereas in previous stages, reciprocity was the most common reason for self-disclosure, now the strongest influence on our disclosure is how well we have come to know the person.[29]

Relational growth at this stage is enhanced through increasing the amount of self-disclosure. You begin to share information that is generally withheld from acquaintances. You may talk about your problems in other relationships or reveal your fears and even your personal failures. This willingness to make yourself vulnerable is a sign of trust. Increased trust and self-disclosure allow you to know more about each other, to discover areas of commonality, and to increase liking.

INTEGRATING

We may move beyond viewing ourselves as separate and begin *integrating* when the intensification of self-disclosure in our relationship has been satisfying. It is at this stage that we move closer together. Knapp suggests that "two individual personalities almost seem to fuse or coalesce, certainly more than any other previous stage."[30] Relational partners spend more time talking to each other and may even share a house or apartment, which allows them to increase their contact.

Partners enjoy their relationships so much that they often distort their perceptions of each other. Frequently, the distortions can be heard in their talk about each other. One might say, for example, "This is the most wonderful person I've ever met," "He is so nice; I'm so lucky," or "We never fight because we see everything the same way." Such overly positive statements are gross generalizations and frequently distortions of reality.

Signs of Integrating

The verbal and nonverbal behaviors that characterize the integrating stage can be described as intensifying, sharing, and minimizing differences. You share where possible, and minimize differences between you and the other person in your relationship. Knapp found that this sharing and minimizing process has several forms:[31]

1. Attitudes, opinions, interests, and tastes that clearly distinguish the pair from others are vigorously cultivated: "We have something special; we are unique."

2. Social circles merge, and others begin to treat the two individuals as a common package. They send one present, one letter, and one invitation.

3. Intimacy "trophies," such as pictures, pins, and rings, are exchanged so that each can "wear" the other's identity.

4. Similarities in manner, dress, and verbal behavior develop that accentuate the oneness.

5. Actual physical penetration of various body parts contributes to the perceived unification.

6. Sometimes common property is designated: "our song," a joint bank account, or joint authorship of a book.

7. Empathic processes seem to peak so that explanation and prediction of behavior are much easier.

8. Body rhythms and routines become closely attuned.

9. Sometimes the love of a third person or object will serve as glue for the relationship: "We just built our dream home."

Knapp stated that these behaviors (or at least some) do not characterize only male-female relationships. Any relationship in the integrating stage will exhibit some of them.

Interaction in this stage is characterized by self-disclosure that increases in both scope and intimacy as partners come to know each other in new ways. They are able to share their worlds and even create a new, common world in the process. This leads to deeper trust, which then enables people to risk sharing themselves even more.[32] Frank Dance has illustrated this process as a spiral (figure 8.3).[33] The act of sharing reflects the commitment that has developed during the integrating stage of the relationship.

Language patterns change during the integrating stage, too. You will hear more use of "we," "us," and "our," instead of "I," "me," and "mine."[34] Integrating partners develop their own language to describe recurring events. For example, in a work situation, one partner might say, "Let's go fishing." What he really means is, "Let's quit work early and go play." Nicknames may also be developed for one another.

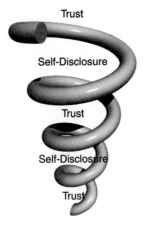

Talk about the relationship also develops. You hear signs of both integration and optimism if you listen carefully. Two sisters might say, "It's so wonderful the way we are able to talk to each other. I can't imagine it being any better for us." Or two lovers might say, "I can't believe the way I feel when I'm away from you. We just seem to fit together. I can't imagine not being together forever." These statements reflect the decision to examine the relationship more closely. This moves the pair to the next stage.

Promoting Relational Growth

Relational growth can be enhanced by being aware that several significant relational behaviors and skills are forming during the integrating stage. Definitions of roles and rules for behavior may develop that either enhance or hinder the relationship. You can influence the adoption of effective roles and rules.

People in this stage develop unique roles, rules, and definitions. For instance, one person may generally have the last word in arguments. These people may have begun to define their relationship as superior-subordinate. On the other hand, they may share in the decision making and hear each other out. Equality defines this relationship.

Characteristic conflict management techniques may also emerge during this stage. If the persons in this relationship start to "manage" conflict by yelling at each other, this style of conflict management may be accepted as appropriate. But if problem solving is adopted instead, they will develop certain rules related to this style. They have an opportunity to promote relational growth if they are able to create a productive conflict management style.

Activities and hobbies are integrated into the relationship during this period as well. If, for example, you like to go fishing and your partner does not, he probably will not define that activity as part of your relationship. But usually friends do not mind giving things up and adopting particular interaction patterns that they would not generally display. People sometimes do this just because they find each other attractive. They feel excited about each other. Sometimes they perceive the relationship and their activities within it selectively, changing, for them, the nature of that activity. A young woman in our department reported that her boyfriend loves to sail but that she is afraid of the water. Nevertheless, she goes sailing with him almost every weekend. We asked her to account for this apparent inconsistency in her behavior. "I just feel so safe when I am with Charlie," she answered.

Julia T. Wood suggests that such distortion presents a special irony. Individuals are less attentive to the communication patterns and rules at a time when many important understandings and rules are developing. For example, they begin to form unsatisfying methods for handling conflict that could lead to deterioration later in the relationship when the incompatibilities in managing conflict are discovered. Wood suggests that "the critical process of generating rules and roles for the relationship thus proceeds almost without partners' awareness."[35]

RENEGOTIATING

Questioning the relationship is a natural part of the development process. The intensity that represents the previous stage, which is characterized by an idealism, cannot go on forever. At some point, we take a more careful look at our relationship as we begin to wonder where it is going. We consider if a more formal, lasting commitment ought to be the next step. We are ready to think seriously about our relationship, its value, its problems, and its future. We feel a need to make a decision to keep the relationship as it is, to scale it down, or to make a deeper, more public commitment to it. Wood has termed this stage *revising communication*.[36]

Although Knapp does not include this stage in his relational development scheme, we think, that it should be considered so that the bonding stage makes sense. Bonding represents public and perhaps legal commitment. Before we take such a step, we frequently will want to examine the relationship more carefully than we did during the integration stage. Furthermore, we may attempt to negotiate changes in things we do not like. If this is not possible, we may begin the disengagement process.

Examining the Relationship

The first step in *renegotiating,* then, involves a private examination of the relationship. Many questions and thoughts are raised: "Can I tolerate this person who wants to take a dominant role?" "I wish she didn't argue so negatively." "Can this relationship really last?" "Do we really have enough in common?" Such examination is vital to the decision to make a public commitment.

We base this examination process on a cost-benefits analysis. Costs might include the pain involved in putting up with some irritating behavior, the time involved in a deeper commitment, and restrictions associated with adhering to the other person's schedule. Beyond these usual costs might be giving up your self-identity. For example, you may have a vision of a person wanting to control you in ways that seem alien to you. On the benefit side, we consider the satisfaction we get from sharing with someone we enjoy. We think of the fun involved in our joint activities. We see a good deal of confirmation of ourselves. These and many other positive aspects of our relationship are weighed against potential costs. This analysis process is not likely to be as straightforward as simply listing all of these costs and benefits. We are usually aware that we have questions about our relationships that we must answer. We are likely to compare our experiences to those we have had with others.

The answers and conclusions from this examination may generate dissatisfaction with some aspect of the relationship. We have listed some options for renegotiating a relationship (see figure 8.4).

The Renegotiation Process

The renegotiation process begins with the discovery of the pain created by dissatisfaction with some aspect of the relationship. Suppose you begin to weigh alternatives: "Should I ask her to try to change her ways? Should I offer to change my ways? Should we both give up a little in order to smooth things out?" We will decide to negotiate if we believe that there is good chance of success and that the effort is worth the potential pain involved: "She's certainly the best woman I've ever known. So what if she doesn't do this the way I'd like? Her compromise makes sense, and my own part of the bargain may be better than what I was doing before." When we think that

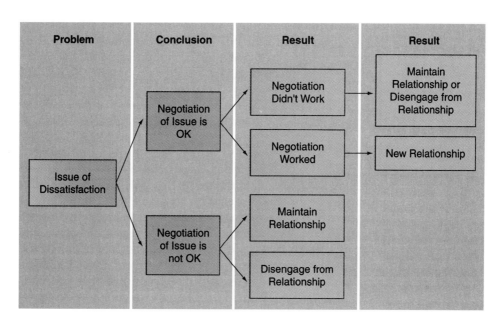

Figure 8.4
The renegotiation process.

there is not much chance of success or that the pain is too great, we may put the relationship on hold or begin the disengagement process: "She'll probably never change. Anyway, she says she won't change, and I believe her. Hmm. That leaves me with no alternative, because I can't stand to be around that behavior."

Irwin Altman and Dalmas Taylor have described this process as a movie shown in reverse.[37] The relationship may move backward through the successive stages. This means less disclosure and less contact. If you and the person in your relationship decide that negotiation is reasonable, you may begin to discuss differences but fail to come to agreement. This might then result in either a "holding pattern" or disengagement. But if you and your partner successfully renegotiate your differences, you are ready for the final developmental stage—bonding.

BONDING

Bonding is different from the stages already discussed because all the others are part of a process rather than an event in themselves. This process is relationship evolution. Bonding, however, is different. It is a special kind of commitment but not necessarily sexual intimacy—although sexual intimacy is part of bonding between lovers. Bonding is a voluntary, ongoing commitment to the renegotiated relationship.

There is some disagreement about the public nature of the commitment represented by bonding. Knapp suggests that it is "a public ritual which announces that commitments have been formally contracted."[38] In contrast, Wood says that "bonding may occur privately between partners or it may be public, as in a ceremony."[39]

Public bonding can create a different kind of relationship than private bonding. Private bonding must rely more on the strength of the relationship to keep it intact. The fact that outsiders have witnessed a public bonding can help to preserve the relationship.

The central features of bonding are its voluntary nature, its indefinite length of commitment, and the special rules attached to it. Its voluntary nature and indefinite length are symbolically important. They signify a powerful force that changes the nature of the relationship.[40] Bonding permits you and your partner to deal with each other with new freedom because you no longer need to be concerned that minor infractions will destroy your relationship. You can be yourself in ways that were previously impossible because of your commitment to the future. Thus, new rules of behavior are generated based on the new definition of the relationship.

SUMMARY

The desire to interact with others and to develop meaningful relationships is strong in all of us. Our decision to engage a person, or to begin an acquaintanceship, rests upon a number of factors. Attractiveness—physical, social, or task-related—may influence the decision. Our willingness to make the contact is also influenced by the proximity of the other person. We are more likely to engage those who are physically close to us. Similarity is another key factor in our decision to form an acquaintanceship. We are attracted to people who share our interests and beliefs. Those we like often possess similar physical characteristics, intelligence, attitudes, abilities, race, and nationality. Of these factors, attitude similarity is especially important. We even want our partner to share our dislikes. Similar attitudes attract because this congruency reinforces our self-concept and increases our ability to predict how our partner will act.

We also engage to fulfill our needs. We need to receive stimulation, to express experiences, to assert ourselves—to test ideas—and to enhance our enjoyment of activities. In addition, we seek fulfillment of our needs to include and be included, to control and be controlled, and to love and be loved.

The initial engagement process involves awareness that leads to excitement. This is followed by action and contact. Several skills can help you to engage others. Be sure to establish eye contact and maintain a comfortably close distance. Introduce yourself and perhaps say something about who you are. Try to be active, positive, and involved. Remember that the face conveys feelings, so smile some of the time. Look for commonalities, as these will help you and your partner see your similarities. Regulate your self-disclosure so that it is appropriately intimate for an initial contact. Relational definitions and rules will begin to form from this first contact as we develop definitions of the relationship and appropriate behavior for us and the other person in the relationship.

Self-disclosure is the act of revealing something about ourselves to another person. We do this to help ourselves and our relationships grow. We can use the Johari Window as a tool to analyze our disclosure in various relationships and then decide whether our levels of disclosure are appropriate for these relationships.

Self-disclosure provides several benefits to the person and the relationship. It can help you understand yourself better, allow you to share concerns, help others better understand you, and nurture your relationships. However, self-disclosure also carries risks. Disclosure makes you vulnerable, may lead to overexposure, and can cause dislike.

Several guidelines can help you make decisions about self-disclosure. Consider the stage your relationship is at, the reasonableness of the risk involved, whether your disclosure is usually reciprocated, and the potential effect of the disclosure. Sometimes relationships do not seem to work very well, but you can increase your chances for successful relationships by knowing how to care for them. This involves understanding how relationships grow and come apart and being able to promote relational growth.

Relationships move through stages of growth. The pattern usually appears as follows:

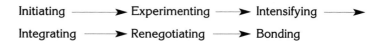

Initiating ⟶ Experimenting ⟶ Intensifying ⟶

Integrating ⟶ Renegotiating ⟶ Bonding

Initiating involves making a decision to engage another person in conversation based on the situation and on your attraction. If the situation seems right and there is sufficient attraction, initiation is likely. Since there is still much that is unknown at this stage, you move to the next level, *experimenting.* Here you exchange information to discover common interests. Generally, this talk moves from superficial to more meaningful disclosure. The disclosure allows comparisons that are useful in deciding about the future of the relationship.

Intensifying signals a change in the relationship from acquaintance to friend. Self-disclosure increases dramatically as you and your partner are willing to make yourselves vulnerable by discussing personal problems and failures. Nonverbal behavior becomes intensified in this stage as more touching and closer interpersonal distances are desired.

Integrating suggests coming together in ways that create increased contact. This could be living together or just more frequent contact. Activities that your partner does not enjoy may be dropped, as the emphasis is on doing things together. There is an infatuation with the other person.

Renegotiating takes place as you try to decide if you want to make this friendship more permanent and committed. At this stage, you and your partner are conducting a private examination of your relationship. When attempts to negotiate the dissatisfactions fail, disengagement may begin. Successful negotiation leads to a new relationship and bonding.

Bonding signals a special kind of commitment to intimacy, a voluntary commitment to your partner for an indefinite period, with new rules. These rules are the result of successful renegotiation of the relationship.

DISCUSSION QUESTIONS

1. As a group, consider why people engage in acquaintanceships. Generate a list of answers and compare them with those offered in this chapter. Are there differences? Do motivations relate to people's age or place in life?

2. It has been suggested that the ideal person we think we would be attracted to and those who actually are our friends are different. In practice. is this true? If so, why?

3. Do similar or different characteristics attract others? Why?

4. Consider someone you would describe as an acquaintance. How would you define this kind of relationship? Would the definition differ if the acquaintanceship is male-female rather than between people of the same sex? Now think about rules that might be shared in such a relationship. List as many as possible.

5. What would your Johari Window look like if you were communicating with a friend? with a college professor? with a brother or sister? with a parent?

6. If you feel comfortable doing so, share a few of the kinds of things you have stored in your hidden self. How are these like the items your classmates have stored in their hidden selves?

7. Explore the conditions under which people self-disclose. When are people most likely to disclose? When is self-disclosure least likely? What factors in a relationship encourage self-disclosure? What factors inhibit it?

8. Considering all the complex factors operating in a relationship, how do you determine whether your partner is open?

9. Can you recall an instance in which you found yourself overdisclosing and seemed unable to stop yourself? How do you account for this?

10. Trace one of your long-term relationships through the stages of development outlined in this chapter. Discuss how closely it mirrored these stages. Did it skip any? Did it backtrack? Were there stages in your relationship that we did not mention? If there were differences, how do you account for them?

11. What happens to a relationship if bonding occurs before renegotiation?

12. Can you make a relationship work? If so, how? Can you renegotiate a relationship more than once? If so, how?

13. More than half of the marriages in the United States end in divorce. Where do these relationships go wrong? What information in this chapter will help you to identify the pitfalls in such relationships?

14. Are working relationships in business any different from working relationships at home? Why or why not?

15. Can a person make you love him or her? Can you make someone love you? Does this have anything to do with attraction? Does attraction have anything to do with loving?

16. Can you disclose yourself too much in a relationship? If so, how much is too much?

ENDNOTES

1. See Keith Gibbins, "Communication Aspects of Women's Clothes and Their Relationship to Fashionability," *British Journal of Social and Clinical Psychology* 8 (1964): 301–312; E. Berscheid and E. Walster, "Physical Attractiveness," in *Advances in Experimental Social Psychology* 7, L. Berkowitz, ed. (New York: Academic Press, 1974); C. L. Kleinke, *First Impressions: The Psychology of Encountering Others* (Englewood Cliffs, NJ: Prentice-Hall, 1975); R. C. Bailey and T. S. Schreiber, "Congruency of Physical Attractiveness Perception and Liking," *Journal of Social Psychology* 115 (1981): 285–286; and E. D. Tanke, "Dimensions of the Physical Attractiyeness Stereotype: A Factor-Analytic Study," *Journal of Psychology* 110 (1982): 63–64.

2. L. Festinger, S. Schacter, and K. Back, *Social Pressures in Informal Groups: A Study of Human Factors in Housing.* (New York: Harper & Row, 1950).

3. B. R. Burleson and W. Samter, "Similarity in the Communication Skills of Young Adults: Foundations of Attraction, Friendship, and Relationship Satisfaction, *Communication Reports* 9 (1996): 127–139.

4. T. Reik, *A Psychologist Looks at Love* (New York: Farrar & Rinehart, 1945).

5. M. S. Davis, *Intimate Relations* (New York: The Free Press, 1973).

6. W. Pfeiffer and J. Pfeiffer, "A Gestalt Primer," in *The 1975 Annual Handbook for Group Facilitators,* J. W. Pfeiffer and J. E. Jones, ed. (La Jolla, CA: University Associates, 1975), 183.

7. W. W. Wilmot, *Dyadic Communication,* 3d ed. (New York: Random House, 1987), 152.

8. G. R. Miller and M. Steinberg, *Between People: A New Analysis of Interpersonal Communication* (Palo Alto, CA: Science Research Associates, 1975): 22–25.

9. H. Sacks, E. A. Schegloff, and G. Jefferson, "A Simplest Systematics for the Organization of Turn Taking for Conversation," in *Studies in the Organization of Conversational Interaction,* J. Schenkein, ed. (New York: Academic Press, 1978), 7–56.

10. A. G. Athos and J. J. Gabarro, *Interpersonal Behavior* (Englewood Cliffs, NJ: Prentice-Hall, 1978), 25.

11. The Johari Window was created by Joseph Luft and Harry Ingham during a summer laboratory in group development at The University of California-Los Angeles in 1955. Their idea was later published by Luft. See J. Luft, *Group Processes: An Introduction to Group Dynamics,* 2d ed. (Palo Alto, CA: Mayfield Publishing Company, 1970), 11–20.

12. P. Cozby, "Self-Disclosure: A Literature Review," *Psychological Bulletin* 79 (1973): 73–91.

13. A. Bochner, "The Functions of Human Communication in Interpersonal Bonding," in *Handbook of Rhetorical and Communication Theory,* Carroll C. Arnold and John Waite Bowers, eds. (Boston: Allyn & Bacon, 1984).

14. V. J. Derlega and A. L. Chaikin, *Sharing Intimacy: What We Reveal to Others and Why* (Englewood Cliffs, NJ: Prentice-Hall, 1975).

15. J. H. Berg and R. L. Archer, "The Disclosure-Liking Relationship," *Human Communication Research* 10 (1983).

16. S. M. Jourard, *The Transparent Self* (New York: Van Nostrand Reinhold, 1971).

17. T. O. Schmidt and R. R. Cornelius, "Self-Disclosure in Everyday Life," *Journal of Social and Personal Relationships* 4 (1987): 365–73; Susan Sprecher, "The Effects of Self-Disclosure Given and Received on Affection for an Intimate Partner and Stability of the Relationship," *Journal of Social and Personal Relationships* 4 (1987): 115–127.

18. C. L. Kleinke, "Effects of Personal Evaluations," in *Self-Disclosure: Origins, Patterns, and Implications of Openness in Interpersonal Relationships,* Gordon J. Chelune, ed. (San Francisco: Jossey-Bass, 1979).

19. D. Stiebel, *When Talking Makes Things Worse! Resolving Problems When Communication Fails* (Andrews and McMeel, 1997).

20. J. B. Walther, "Computer-Mediated Communication: Impersonal, Interpersonal, and Hyperpersonal Interaction," *Communication Research* 23 (1996): 3–43.

21. Kleinke, "Effects of Personal Evaluations."

22. L. B. Rosenfeld and G.I. Bowen, "Marital Disclosure and Marital Satisfaction; Direct Effect versus Interaction Effect Models," *Western Journal of Speech Communication* 55 (1991): 69–84.

23. Source: National Center for Health Statistics, Public Health Service, Washington, D.C.

24. See C. R. Berger and R.J. Calabrese, "Some Explorations in Initial Interaction and Beyond: Toward a Developmental Theory of Interpersonal Communication," *Human Communication Research* 1 (1975): 99–112; S. W. Duck, *Personal Relationships and Personal Constructs: A Study of Friendship Formation* (New York: The Free Press, 1973); T. M. Newcomb, *The Acquaintance Process* (New York: Holt, Rinehart, and Winston, 1961); and J. T. Wood. "Communication and Relational Culture: Bases for the Study of Human Relationships," *Communication Quarterly* 30 (Spring 1982): 75–83.

25. M. L. Knapp, *Interpersonal Communication and Human Relationships* (Boston: Allyn and Bacon, 1984), 29–57.

26. Newcomb, *The Acquaintance Process;* W. Griffitt and R. Veitch, "Preacquaintance Attitude Similarity and Attraction Revisited," *Sociometry* 37 (1974): 163–173.

27. I. Altman and D. A. Taylor, *Social Penetration: The Development of Interpersonal Relationships* (New York: Holt, Rinehart, and Winston, 1973).

28. Knapp, *Interpersonal Communication and Human Relationships,* 37.

29. L. B. Rosenfeld and W. L. Kendrik, "Choosing to Be Open: Subjective Reasons for Self-Disclosing," *Western Journal of Speech Communication* 48 (1984): 326–313.

30. Knapp, *Interpersonal Communication and Human Relationships,* 38.

31. Ibid.

32. G. L. Wilson, "Trusting and Self-Disclosure in Dyads" (Ph.D. dissertation, University of Wisconsin, 1979).

33. F. E. X. Dance, "Toward a Theory of Human Communication" in *Human Communication Theory: Original Essays,* F. E. X. Dance, ed. (New York: Holt, Rinehart, and Winston, 1967): 288–309.

34. M. S. Davis, *Intimate Relations* (New York: The Free Press, 1973), 56–91.

35. J. T. Wood, *Human Communication: A Symbolic Interactionist Perspective* (New York: Holt, Rinehart and Winston, 1982), 177.

36. Ibid., 178–180.

37. Altman and Taylor, *Social Penetration*, 174.

38. Knapp, *Interpersonal Communication and Human Relationships*, 39.

39. Wood, *Human Communication*, 180.

40. Knapp, *Interpersonal Communication and Human Relationships*, 39.

READ MORE ABOUT
BECOMING ACQUAINTED IN THESE SOURCES

Aronson, Elliot. *The Social Animal*, 5th ed. New York: Freeman, 1988. The author provides an understandable survey of factors that influence interpersonal attraction.

Berscheid, Ellen, and Elaine Walster. *Interpersonal Attraction*, 2d ed. Reading, MA: Addison-Wesley, 1978. This book offers a readable discussion of theories of attraction.

Miller, Gerald R., and Mark Steinberg. *Between People: A New Analysis of Interpersonal Communication*. Palo Alto. CA: Science Research Associates, 1975. The authors describe their developmental theory of interpersonal relationships involving levels of data and levels of rules.

READ MORE ABOUT
SELF-DISCLOSURE IN THESE SOURCES

Derlega, Valerian J., Sandra Metts, Sandra Petronio, and Stephen T. Margulis. *Self-Disclosure*. Newbury Park, CA: Sage, 1993. This interesting book looks at the connection between self-disclosure and the needs for intimacy versus privacy. A chapter examines the role of gender in self-disclosure and how men and women reveal themselves differently in same-sex and opposite-sex relationships.

Johnson, David W. "Self-Disclosure," *Reaching Out: Interpersonal Effectiveness and Self-Actualization*, 4th ed. Englewood Cliffs. NJ: Prentice Hall, 1990, pp. 29–78. This excellent chapter further develops our material and provides interesting exercises for you to try.

Luft, Joseph. *Of Human Interaction*. Palo Alto, CA: National Press Books, 1969. This book introduces and develops the idea of the four selves as depicted in the Johari Window. In addition to describing the Johari Window, the author offers valuable, in-depth advice about self-disclosure in interpersonal relationships.

Miller, Gerald R., and Mark Steinberg. *Between People: A New Analysis of Interpersonal Communication*. Chicago: Science Research Associates, 1973. While this book offers a general introduction to interpersonal communication, the part covering both the positive and negative aspects of self-disclosure is especially worthwhile. The points these authors make about the dangers of "apparent" self-disclosure have been strongly upheld in research over the past fifteen years.

READ MORE ABOUT FRIENDSHIP AND COMMITMENT IN THESE SOURCES

Cahn, Dudley D. *Letting Go: A Practical Theory of Relationship Disengagement and Reengagement*. Albany, NY: State University of New York Press, 1987. This book looks at the role of communication in the relational development process in the context of various types of relationships.

Fitzpatarick, Mary Anne. *Between Husbands and Wives: Communication in Marriage*. Newbury Park, CA: Sage, 1988. This book presents a scholarly treatment of power, conflict influence, emotional expression, self-disclosure, and nonverbal communication within the marriage relationship.

Knapp, Mark L. *Interpersonal Communication and Human Relationships*. Boston: Allyn and Bacon, 1984. Knapp was one of the scholars who formulated a theoretical explanation of relational stages. This is an excellent source for learning more about relational development.

9

CLIMATE

PREVIEW

The old saying "We always hurt the ones we love" means that when we argue with those who are close to us, the arguments often end in hurtful behavior because there seems to be no way to deal with communication that creates defensiveness. This chapter helps you understand why and how we get into defensive spirals. Beyond this, the effects of defensiveness in relationships are discussed, and suggestions for avoiding defensiveness are provided.

Relationships are enhanced when you create and maintain a supportive climate because it enables understanding and adjustment of viewpoints in a nonthreatening environment. This chapter presents the communication behaviors that help foster this climate. Suggestions are offered on how and when to be more supportive. You will find, too, that supportive behavior has many benefits for your relationships.

Relational growth occurs when we manage a relationship so that we keep a satisfying level of interest and meaningfulness. Growing relationships meet our needs. We can do a great deal to enhance the growth process if we know how. This chapter presents six specific relational concerns that we can influence in our relationships.

KEY TERMS

affection	certainty
compatibility	control
cooperation	defensive behaviors
description	emotional support
equality	evaluation
inference	intimacy
neutrality	problem orientation
provisionalism	relational growth
role agreement	rule agreement
satisfaction	self-disclosure
stagnation	strategy
spontaneity	support
supportive behavior	supportive communication

OBJECTIVES

1. Discuss the major reasons people defend themselves in interpersonal communication situations.

2. Specify and explain the two basic strategies people use to defend themselves.

3. Identify the characteristics of a defensive interpersonal communication climate.

4. Discuss the consequences of defensive communication behavior.

5. Identify the characteristics of supportive communication behavior.

6. Explain the benefits of supportive communication behavior.

7. Specify how you can remain supportive when you have a difference with a partner in a relationship.

8. Define "appropriate self-disclosure."

9. Explain and illustrate the concepts of roles and rules in interpersonal relationships, discussing their significance to relational growth.

10. Discuss the kinds of support that promote relational growth, illustrating each with an example.

11. Suggest ways to demonstrate affection and liking in various contexts.

12. Assess relational satisfaction using table 9.3.

13. Develop a plan for managing a relational difference.

14. Indicate what specific actions might be taken to guard against stagnation in a relationship.

DEFENSIVE COMMUNICATION

A group of college students decided to go out after class one Thursday night to relax after a particularly tiring week. Midterm exams were finally over, and this was an opportunity to have fun. After they had settled in and ordered their second round of drinks, Susan noticed that something seemed to be bothering Phyllis. She had chosen to ignore Phyllis's sullenness but finally decided that Phyllis was spoiling the good time they all had hoped to have. Susan confronted her. "Phyllis," she said, "you're being pretty hard to get along with. What's your problem?"

Phyllis was experiencing a problem, but she was doing her best to keep it to herself and did not think she was bothering anyone—she certainly was *not* being hard to get along with. Instead of responding directly to Susan, Phyllis picked up her drink and moved to another table. Apparently, she was more upset than anyone had imagined, because in a few minutes she came back long enough to say, "Susan, you think you know everything. Well, you aren't so much fun to be around either! I'm leaving and don't expect me to come back!" She then turned and left before Susan could speak.

Susan began to say something, and Tim ran to try to stop Phyllis. Phyllis would not come back, so he returned. Susan was really angry and continued to make negative statements about Phyllis. It was not long before the group left the restaurant.

What about Susan's communication had so angered Phyllis? After all, Susan seemed to sense that Phyllis was experiencing some kind of problem. Susan even appeared to want Phyllis to remain involved with the group in spite of the situation. The problem seems to lie in the language Susan used to talk to Phyllis. Her statement "You're being pretty hard to get along with" is not only a negative evaluation of Phyllis but also an implication that Susan thinks she has some right to evaluate Phyllis's behavior. Susan was also labeling her behavior as a "problem," which likewise assumes she has a right to do so. Susan's language pushed Phyllis to choose to become defensive.

Both Phyllis and Susan regretted their behavior after they had had time to reflect. They talked about the event and were able to be supportive and show that they cared. We frequently regret our defensive behavior.

It seems that just living life exposes us to conflict. We communicate in ways that trigger unexpected emotional responses from the other. Of course, sometimes the response is not unexpected. We could have predicted the response if we had paid close attention to the language used. Evaluative statements almost always will yield an urge to defend.

We can often predict a defensive response just by listening to the language we use.

This chapter will explore *defensive behavior*. We begin with a discussion of why we defend ourselves. Next, we present a detailed explanation of when and how we defend ourselves. We conclude with suggestions for responding differently to defensive communication behavior.

WHY WE DEFEND OURSELVES

Carl Rogers, a therapist who has studied how to create a supportive climate, and Fritz Roethlisberger have suggested that we have a natural tendency to evaluate and judge others. They believe that a "major barrier to mutual interpersonal communication is our very natural tendency to judge, to evaluate, to approve (or disapprove) the statement of the other person or the other group."[1] Rogers and others that share his concern provide suggestions for counteracting this natural tendency.

But why do we have this natural tendency? Perhaps we disapprove of someone's behavior that does not match our expectations, and thus we judge that person. Then, if the issue is important, we tell the other how we think he or she should think or behave. Sometimes the tables are turned, and someone else evaluates or judges us; when this happens, we often become defensive.

But why do we react in this way? Why was Phyllis so anxious to counter—or at least stop—Susan's judgment of her? The answer might be quite simple. Susan's judgment, or definition, of Phyllis was quite different from Phyllis's image of herself. This threatened her self-concept. If she had not perceived Susan's judgment as threatening, she might have ignored her or perhaps acknowledged the problem and asked Susan for help. But instead, she chose a dramatic way of saying, "I disagree with your evaluation."

This defense of self-concept specifically involves two areas. First, we defend our view of the outside world. We want our view of correct behavior and thinking to be confirmed. But even more importantly, our defense of our self-concept involves our defense of our worth as a person. We want to be respected, listened to, and understood. Phyllis felt misunderstood; her response was to defend herself by leaving the situation. But you may be surprised to know that Susan's behavior, judgment, is a category of defensive behavior, too. When she approached Phyllis, she was acting on her interpretation that Phyllis's sullen behavior was denying Susan's worth as a friend.

Worth as a person is at the heart of our defensiveness. We believe that we cannot always be right and are willing to tolerate being wrong some of the time. Yet, we find it intolerable to be denied our worth as a person *and* to be wrong, too. We cannot listen to talk that says that we do not count, that we are inferior, that we do not have the right to have an opinion. When another person evaluates us, we are likely to defend ourselves unless we make a conscious decision not to.

WHEN AND HOW WE DEFEND OURSELVES

There are two basic strategies we use to defend ourselves. We can *avoid* or we can *confront*. There are a number of circumstances in which we decide to ignore or avoid, but two seem especially important. One occurs when we decide the opinion of the other person does not count. In order to care about an evaluation, we must think the other person's view matters. We can decide that for ourselves, or we can decide it because other people, people we value, think the opinion does not count. If you do not care about the other's evaluation, you can ignore it.

A second reason to ignore another person's evaluation is because we do not want to hear it. Leaving allows us to avoid the evaluation altogether. Can you think of anyone you avoid because you believe that they will say things you do not want to hear?

People also engage in direct confrontation when they feel and believe that they are being attacked. These people—especially those who behave aggressively toward others—take the offensive to defend their self-concepts. They believe the best defense is to counter directly the other person's attack. This kind of confrontation can be carried out supportively if we are willing to utilize assertive and supportive communication behaviors. (*Supportive behavior* is talk that affirms the other person and the relationship.) But often people engage in aggressive communication behavior that generally creates further defensiveness.

DEFENSIVE BEHAVIOR

In a classic essay, Jack Gibb described the behaviors he observed while listening to groups engaged in defensive communication.[2] He noted that six such behaviors appear regularly: evaluation, superiority, certainty, control, neutrality, and strategy.[3]

Evaluation

Defensive communication involves *evaluation*. We voice a judgment about the other person. We might say, "You are stupid," if we are sufficiently angry. Or we make some assessment of the other person's behavior, such as "You're not doing your best." Sometimes we question the other person's viewpoint or motives: "I know what you are trying to do. You are trying to manipulate me." Evaluations of this kind are almost always seen as challenges to self-concept and produce an urge to defend ourselves.

Susan's remark, "you're being pretty hard to get along with," judges Phyllis. It suggests that there is something defective in her. The statement is not a challenge to one of Phyllis's ideas about the world but rather to her ideas about her self. It in effect is saying,

"You are not a fun person to be around." This negative definition affects the relationship between Susan and Phyllis.

Superiority

Superiority is behavior that implies that you are better than another person, that you are somehow wiser, and that you can make judgments that overrule the other person's sense of self. The question "How can you say that?" provides an example. The implication of this statement is "I can't imagine any right-thinking person saying what you said. Explain yourself." This suggests that we have some superior knowledge that qualifies us to question the other person's statement. This superiority is often enhanced by avoiding the intonation of a question and using the intonation of a statement.

Evaluation and superiority are closely linked. When a person is in the position to evaluate, that person is assumed to have some superior knowledge or insight. To judge another person, to offer suggestions as to how that person should behave, implies superiority. It implies that we have set ourselves above someone else. Thus, the superior attitude is often a direct attack on the other's self-concept. Susan implied superiority when she judged Phyllis.

Certainty

Certainty is represented by rigidity in view. It suggests confidence in our interpretation of the facts of a particular situation. It often establishes a win-lose situation—if we are right, the other person must be wrong and proven wrong. This attitude has great potential to harm a relationship. Once we become rigid in our position, we often believe we must put the other person down to "win." When this person resists our attempt, we escalate our effort and risk further damage to our relationship.

There is a clear relationship among evaluation, superiority, and certainty. Superiority and certainty are often necessary if our evaluation of another person is to have its intended impact. In other words, evaluation requires superiority, which in turn requires certainty. Consider how Susan spoke to Phyllis. There was no hesitation or sense of doubt in Susan's judgment. She did not say that Phyllis *might* be hard to get along with or that she *might* be experiencing a problem. She said, with confidence and certainty, that Phyllis was hard to get along with and that she had a problem. This was a direct affront to Phyllis's self-concept, one that she could not let go unchallenged.

The use of language that indicates certainty of judgment will, in all probability, cause negative reactions. Since views frequently differ, and since there seems to be no room for negotiation when certainty exists, the most likely response is confrontation and challenge.

Certainty has great potential to harm a relationship.

Control

Control means creating messages that either intimidate or suggest inadequacy in an attempt to get what we want from the other person. You may try to impose an attitude or viewpoint because you want someone else to believe as you do. Control may also come in the form of a threat in an attempt to keep the other person from doing something or prod them to do it. For example, you might say, "If you do not spend more time with me, I'll start seeing other people."

Attempts to control imply that the other person is somehow inadequate. This implies a judgment and superiority. We often imply, "I am right and you are wrong. Adopt this way of doing it. Think this about yourself. Do what I want."

Researchers found that communication of abusive couples is characterized by this opposition to the other's viewpoint.[4] This is not surprising because most people will feel hurt when the other person in the relationship exercises this kind of excessive control. The result may be an attempt to make a defense and perhaps to withdraw from he relationship.

Neutrality

A defensive climate is also created by *neutrality*. Neutrality suggests that we have little concern for the other person's viewpoint. When we attempt to control the other person, we often display neutrality. It is as if we are saying, "I know that you have a view, but I am right and I don't care if you have a different view. Agree with me." Not wanting to hear and understand the other person's view communicates that she does not count; that her view is not worth considering. This neutrality will surely result in an attempt at self-defense.

Neutrality also indicates that we do not care about the other person's feelings. Imagine a fight with someone who is crying and showing other signs of being deeply hurt. You are so angry that you say, "Cry if you like. This is the way it is going to be!" This verbal disregard of the other's feelings, usually accompanied by nonverbal displays of disregard, often causes the other person to lash out in an effort to hurt and show disregard.

Strategy

The final behavior that produces defensiveness is the application of a *strategy* designed to force another person, perhaps by trickery, into making the decision or thinking the way we want.

This strategy may be overt or covert. An overt strategy might be to employ some or all of the behaviors that cause defensiveness. For example, if you show that you are not interested in someone's opinion and indicate that you want that person to believe that your opinion is the only one that counts, you are deliberately planning to gain an advantage over her. If the other realizes you are using a strategy of manipulation, she may then resent you. She will object and do what she can to defend herself, most likely by attacking you in the same ways that you have attacked her. A covert strategy, on the other hand, might be to cause her to believe that you are interested in her viewpoint while subtly trying to cause her to accept your own. You may be successful, but resentment and hostility will result if you are found out!

Table 9.1 lists the characteristics of each of the six behaviors that create defensiveness. You can use it to analyze communication in your relationships. Careful analysis may uncover some surprises. You may find, as many have, that you are not as conscious of your behavior toward the other person as you might be. You may also discover that you want to change your communication behavior.

CONSEQUENCES OF DEFENSIVE BEHAVIOR

When we become involved in defensive communication, we begin to focus on ourselves. We plan messages to use in self-defense. We stop listening, so we are not likely to hear the other person's position. The other person might be making some important points and even trying to accommodate our position but all in vain. We find that being firm in our position often keeps us from losing, so we become even more rigid. Often we repeat the position as a response to whatever the other person says. We get absorbed in our own thoughts and become less sensitive to nonverbal cues. Our percep-

---

Table 9.1   Characteristics of Defensive Climates

Evaluation—To make a judgment about another person; to make an assessment of the other; to raise questions about the other's viewpoint or motives

Superiority—To communicate that you are superior; to suggest that the other person is inadequate in comparison

Certainty—To be rigid in your viewpoint; to try to correct the other; to assume a win-lose position

Control—To try to manipulate the other; to attempt to impose an attitude or viewpoint on another; to try to keep the other from doing something; to imply that another person is inadequate

Neutrality—To show little or no concern for the other or his problems and viewpoint; to treat the other as an object rather than a person

Strategy—To plan what you want and then trick the other into thinking he is making the decision; to cause the other to think that you have an interest in her when you do not

Source: Jack R. Gibb, "Defensive Communication," *Journal of Communication* (1961): 142–45. Adapted by permission.

tion becomes distorted. Finally, if the other person persists—and this is likely because the other person has also stopped listening and becomes rigid—we try to lash out and hurt that person. We are most likely to go from here into an escalatory conflict spiral. This is characterized by one behavior reinforcing the next.[5] It is difficult to understand this hurtful behavior, except to suppose it is related to winning. It is as if by hurting the other, we win despite what that person does. But have we reallly won?

Regret

Perhaps you can remember a time when you lashed out. But did you actually win much of anything? More likely, you regretted the event. Especially in close interpersonal situations, in which you really do have a stake in the outcome, the result is usually regret. We wish that we had had more control and that we had not hurt the other. Susan's willingness to talk with Phyllis about their difficulty may well have been motivated by regret.

Hostility

Defensive behavior also often leads to hostility because both the aggressor and the defender are manipulating. Their strategies are calculated to achieve their personal ends. This is not to say that people should not achieve their own goals. Rather, when manipulation is used to achieve personal ends at the expense of another, hostility often follows. The outcome of hostile behavior appears to be neutrality, the "I don't care" attitude. What often follows is "I want to hurt you."

Damage to the Relationship

Defensive behavior does serve the function of defending oneself, but seldom does it achieve any lasting or satisfying results. When people become rigid in their positions and stop listening, they have no way to resolve their differences. At least, they have no way that is likely to be satisfying to all involved. Certain strategies are often employed by a given individual, but the results are generally damaging. For example, you might lash out—hurt the other person so badly that she lets you have your way. This is winning only in the sense that you got your way. However, you lose in the sense that you may have damaged the relationship.

Another strategy is pulling rank. This involves imposing your viewpoint on the other person because you are in a position of power. Resentment is generated, and the relationship is probably damaged. In the workplace, this means that the damaged worker is likely to be less productive and may even sabotage the work effort. Even though the boss "won," she also lost.

REFLEXIVE BEHAVIOR

Is it necessary to engage in defensive behavior? We believe that it generally is not. You can select an alternative and then have more control of your own behavior. You can decide not to use defensive behaviors—and instead use supportive behavior—once you understand what they and the alternatives are. Knowing the general outcomes of defensive behavior may be helpful in persuading you to remain supportive. If you know that "winning" usually also means losing, you will be more likely to choose behaviors that have a greater win-win potential.

At a second level, many interpersonal transactions are *reflexive behaviors*. This means that what we do affects what others are likely to do. This principle operates when we decide to become defensive. But we can decide *not* to become defensive. In this case, the other person will find it more difficult to continue the attack. Thus, the other is encouraged to adopt more reasonable and perhaps supportive behavior.

Refusal to accept the definition of the situation as defensive can have a profound effect on the other person's ability to define it. It is difficult to fight with someone who will not fight! But in addition to not fighting, you also counter the wrong definition of a situation with your own definition. Remaining supportive (instead of defensive) is saying to the other person, "I want to talk about the situation. I want to talk in a way that won't damage our relationship. I want us both to be satisfied with the outcome. Let's cooperate in deciding."

Many interpersonal transactions are reflexive, especially when the parties involved have some commitment to the relationship. Commitment may spring from liking and affection, or it may spring from interdependency. Interdependency means that each person needs the other for some reason. For example, the boss needs you to get the work done, and you need the boss—or at least you need a job. Commitment makes a difference in how the other person is treated. If one person ignores the other's attempts at fairness, the commitment is damaged. If both parties behave badly, both have ignored the commitment. Then, to the degree that they understand the commitment, remaining supportive should have an influence on the outcome.

This was essentially what happened with Susan and Phyllis when their communication broke down. Both behaved defensively. This damaged their relationship. Because the group had a stake in the relationship (even though the other members did not participate in the exchange), other group members could legitimately demand that an attempt be made to restore the relationship.

SUPPORTIVE COMMUNICATION

The kind of behavior you use when you sense a difference with another person is related to your previous experience with that person. If you have developed ways of managing differences that utilize supportive behaviors, then your communication is likely to reflect a supportive attitude. If the opposite is true—you have managed differences utilizing defensive behavior—then your communication is likely to reflect a defensive attitude. Supportive communication, like defensive communication, reflects an attitude that the communicator has toward the other person in the relationship. And even if the methods you use are not particularly productive for you, you are likely to continue to use them unless you make a conscious decision to initiate change. You must decide to work toward a more supportive relationship. *Supportive communication* is talk that affirms the other person and the relationship; defensive communication disconfirms the other person and the relationship.

Carl Rogers captured the essence of the supportive attitude with his term *unconditional positive regard.* He explained the therapist's attitude and its effects on the other person:

> [A supportive attitude] . . . means that he prizes the client in a total, rather than a conditional way. I mean that he does not simply accept the client when he is behaving in certain ways and disapprove of him when he behaves in other ways. He experiences an outgoing, positive feeling, without reservations, without *evaluations.* The term we have come to use for this attitude is "unconditional positive regard," and we believe that, the more this attitude is experienced by the therapist and perceived by his client, the more likelihood there is that therapy will be successful and that change and development will take place.[6]

Rogers was referring to the therapeutic setting and the healing that takes place when the supportive attitude of a therapist is perceived by the client. This principle is also important in our day-to-day communication. A supportive communication climate allows for *change* and *development.* It enhances the relationship by enabling the participants to understand and adjust their viewpoints in a nonthreatening environment.

CHARACTERISTICS OF SUPPORTIVE CLIMATES

Consider this short dialogue that took place when Jean was trying to help her friend Ryan overcome a difference he had with a group to which they both belong. Jean tried to be supportive. She went to Ryan the next morning to talk. "Ryan," she said. "I wonder if we can talk about what was going on last night at Stan's? I can see that you are pretty upset with Phil, and perhaps the group, too. I wonder if you're willing to talk about what we did to cause you to feel so frustrated and angry. The group asked me to talk to you. We like you and want you to come back." "Well, Jean," Ryan answered, "Phil was being absolutely impossible. He's always on my case and I'm not going to take any more of it. If he'd change his attitude about people, he'd be decent. I'm through with him—and those other people, too!"

We can decide to work toward more supportive relationships.

What is this person doing? Your answer is an *inference*—a conclusion based on your interpretation of what you observe.

Jean was being generally supportive, and Ryan sensed this. Her supportive behavior set an atmosphere for potential understanding. Her communication defined how she saw their relationship, and Ryan was willing to accept that definition. We will use her language to illustrate some of what we have to say about supportive communication.

Jack Gibb identified six categories of supportive communication behavior: description, equality, provisionalism, problem orientation, empathy, and spontaneity.[7] We present each of these and illustrate how this communication might be carried out within a relationship. Then we discuss the benefits that supportive communication can have for a relationship. Finally, we present some ideas that can help you be supportive.

SUPPORTIVE COMMUNICATION BEHAVIOR

Description

Description is nonjudgmental communication that presents factual information about a person's perceptions of a situation. It may be about feelings, actions, or events. The communication does not imply or ask that the other person change his behavior. It also includes straightforward requests for factual information.

You can avoid the defensive communication called evaluation by using descriptive behavior instead. To do this, you must be able to recognize an *inference.* An inference is a conclusion based on your interpretation of what you observe. In many cases, an interpretation involves your subjective evaluation. It is close to what Gibb called evaluation: it is an opinion about what *you* observed. Thus, an inference is not a description; it's an evaluation.

There is really very little description in the conversation between Jean and Ryan, but neither is there any evaluation. Jean made only one inference: "I can see that you are pretty upset with Phil . . .." Her use of the word "are" made the inference sound like a judgment. She could have made it sound like an inference by saying "you seem to be."

Equality

Equality is the presentation of ideas in such a way that the other person sees us as like her in status. It has nothing to do with the actual status of the person or the definition of status within the relationship. It is a statement about how we are viewing the other person in relation to us for the immediate communication event. We display equality by not "pulling rank;" minimizing differences in ability, status, and power; treating the other person's views with the same respect that we give to our own views.

Notice also that Jean did not "pull rank." She was careful not to put herself in a superior position. She picked a time and place when she could talk to Ryan on his own ground. She went to him, even though she could have called him and asked him to come to her place to talk. She also did not offer him advice or give her interpretation of what had happened at Stan's. She tried to remain an equal by minimizing any differences in status and position. Remaining equal helps a person feel supported.

Provisionalism

Provisionalism is behavior that suggests tentativeness in presenting ideas. The word *seems* conveys tentativeness; the word *is* conveys certainty. Provisional language suggests that if more data were presented, you might be willing to change your attitudes and views. It allows for the possibility that the other person could have a view that is different from yours and that you would be willing to consider.

Jean also tempered her approach with provisionalism. She included several tentative statements in her dialogue. For example, she said, "I wonder *if* we can talk about what was going on last night at Stan's?" The use of "if" allows Ryan to choose not to talk. In the second part of the sentence, Jean avoids certainty by suggesting that she is open to interpretations other than her own.

Jean also said. "I can *see that you are* pretty upset . . . ." No provisionalism exists in this statement. Instead, she exhibited certainty, one of the communication behaviors most likely to yield defensiveness. She could not *see* that Ryan was upset. She could perhaps see his facial expressions, body posture, and tension and hear his tone of voice, phrasing, and pausing. But Jean could not *see* that Ryan was upset. She had to *guess* that her observations meant something, and she called that something "upset." Jean's guess was correct—Ryan *was* upset.

But what if it had been incorrect? Suppose your interpersonal communication instructor meets you outside the classroom. She knows that your mark on the midterm examination was low. She also believes that you will not like the mark because she has an image of you as an achievement-motivated individual who takes pride in a consistently high grade-point average. So she hands you your paper before class begins and says, "I know you'll be upset with the grade. Would you like to talk about it?" What does her guess do to your relationship? It puts you on the defensive.

You now have to process the low grade in her presence and, perhaps, in the presence of other students. You also have to do so on very short notice, and moreover, you have to deal with your emotional condition using language she has placed upon it—"upset." She *knows* that you *will be* upset, so, clearly, you must be upset. You are not allowed any other options, such as, for example, surprise, relief (if you didn't get the F you expected), or confusion. Or suppose the paper she handed you was not your paper. Does this mean that in all other interactions, she did not know who you were?

To defend yourself, you may do a number of things. You might, for example, play the passive role—that is, play it cool. Do not let anyone know what you are experiencing. Above all, do not involve yourself with the teacher, since that individual carries all the power in the teacher-student relationship.

You might also defend yourself by attacking her. You might use strong language. For instance, you might judge the quality of the test, complaining about the vagueness of the questions and the unfairness of including certain subjects. If she buys into your game, your low mark would be her fault, and you would have successfully defended yourself.

Problem Orientation

Gibb defines a *problem orientation* as an approach to talking about differences that conveys "a desire to collaborate in defining a mutual problem and seeking its solution."[8] We are saying by our words and actions that we have no solution, viewpoint, or behavior *that we plan to impose* on the other person. The problem orientation requires that both people present their ideas and goals by using provisional communication so that they can jointly evaluate the situation and come to a decision.

A problem orientation suggests to the other person that we are willing to share in the problem-solving process. The exchange between Jean and Ryan also exhibits this. Jean's question, "I wonder if *we* can talk about what was going on last night at Stan's?," suggests a problem orientation. She seems to be saying, "Let's work together so that we can understand this and agree on how you can rejoin the group." She makes no attempt to control Ryan by either interpreting what was going on or giving him a preconceived solution to the conflict. She makes it clear that she expects to engage in joint problem solving with Ryan.

Empathy

Gibb recommended a fifth supportive behavior, empathy. *Empathy* means to experience the world from another person's point of view. It requires the creation of the other person's perspective on the particular situation, event or thought. Of course, it is impossible to experience another person's perspective completely, but our attempt to do so will allow us to get a better sense of the how the world appear to that person.

Empathy involves three dimensions.[9] First, it involves perspective taking, that is, the suspension of judgment and opinions for the moment so that you can try to take on the other person's perspective. Second, it requires us to go beyond the thoughts and to try to take on the experience of the other's feelings, that is, to experience their joy, fear, pain, or whatever. Finally, there is a caring element to empathy. It requires that we generally care and are concerned about the other's well-being.

We can show empathy by listening carefully, perhaps using active listening, and telling the person that we understand how they feel and why. You might say, "Sue, you seemed really devastated when you did not get that job. I think that I might understand how you felt. I had a similar experience a couple of years ago." Genuine empathy can also be demonstrated by showing respect for the other person's value system and affirming that person's worth. Language such as "I think I can understand how you would see it that way" can achieve this.

Showing empathy is an important factor in promoting relational growth. Genuine empathy is very powerful because it represents an attempt to understand the other person's position and possibly even to identify with the problem. Empathy requires effort from the listener. Empathy is usually valued and viewed as supportive. For example, Jean could attempt to empathize with Ryan by saying, "I have had some frustration myself, so I can *understand* how you might have that kind of experience with the group." By establishing a caring atmosphere, she would likely reduce any sense of threat to his self-concept.

An empathic attitude is also communicated nonverbally. Your face and body can signal that you do care about the other person. False concern can produce mixed messages; you can say that you care with your words but that you do not care with your actions. When messages are mixed, the receiver usually believes the nonverbal behavior.

A display of empathy, if it is to be effective, must flow from a sensitivity to the other person. Gerald Miller and Mark Steinberg said that it must be a transactional process.[10] By this, they meant that we receive information from a person about his or her experience. Then, we must read these messages accurately and decide to respond empathically. Sometimes it is difficult to read these messages because they may take the form of subtle nonverbal cues. At other times, the verbal and nonverbal messages might contradict each other. We must thus carefully and skillfully analyze what the other person is telling us. Finally, we must make a decision about the effect of empathy. Miller and Steinberg suggest that we ask, "Would an empathic response be rewarding to this person?" It might be that the person is having a bad day and would rather not be reminded of the fact.

Spontaneity

Finally, Gibb identified *spontaneity* as a quality of supportive communication. Spontaneity is direct, honest, and straightforward behavior and communication. It suggests that we present our views openly while using other kinds of supportive behavior. When spontaneity does not involve description, equality, and provisionalism. the straightforwardness can be hurtful.

Sometimes circumstances are such that being open about our feelings would be destructive to the communication. If you are feeling very angry, you have thoughts that you would not have if you were in a different frame of mind. Perhaps you should wait to talk about the differences you are having. There are things in every relationship that might be better left unsaid. Spontaneous communication behavior must be tempered with good judgment if it is to promote relational growth.

Spontaneous behavior is not planned. What this means in practice is that we have not carefully selected the words we use to express our ideas. Sometimes you may want to carefully select the precise words you will use. But consider how such careful selection might be interpreted. Your nonverbal behavior might suggest that you have something to hide or that you are trying to manipulate. Spontaneous behavior is often the better choice.

Jean was straightforward when she spoke to Ryan about the problem. She stated exactly why she wanted to talk and what she wanted from the communication.

Table 9.2 summarizes and compares defensive and supportive behavior. The two types are presented in column form so that you can compare them.

Table 9.2	Defensive and Supportive Behavior
Defensive	*Supportive*
Evaluation	*Description*
To make a judgment about another person; to make an assessment of the other; to raise questions about the other's viewpoint or motives	To be nonjudgmental; to ask straightforward questions; to request factual information; to present descriptions that do not force the other person to change behavior or attitude
Superiority	*Equality*
To communicate that you are superior; to suggest that the other person is inadequate in comparison	To avoid pulling rank; to show the other respect; to minimize differences in ability, status, and power
Certainty	*Provisionalism*
To be rigid in your viewpoint; to try to correct the other; to take on a win-lose position	To be tentative with your behavior, attitudes, and views; to convey the attitude that more data might change your mind; to solve problems with the other, rather than to impose your own view; to share data and work jointly on a task in a give-and-take fashion
Control	*Problem Orientation*
To try to manipulate the other; to attempt to impose an attitude or viewpoint on another; to try to keep the other from doing something	To want to engage in mutual problem solving; to suggest by your words and actions that you have no solution, viewpoint, or behavior to impose on the other
Neutrality	*Empathy*
To show little or no concern for the other or his problems and viewpoint; to treat the other as an object, rather than a person	To identify with the other person's problems and feelings; to show respect for the other's value system; to affirm the other's worth as a person
Strategy	*Spontaneity*
To plan what you want and then trick the other into thinking he is making the decision; to cause the other to feel that you have an interest in her when you do not	To express straightforward behavior; to avoid deceiving; to have unhidden, uncomplicated viewpoints and motives; to be honest

Source: Jack R. Gibb, "Defensive Communication," *Journal of Communication* (1961): 142–45. Adapted by permission.

BENEFITS OF SUPPORTIVE COMMUNICATION

Supportiveness can have a positive effect on the communication providing two requirements are met. First, the behavior must be perceived as genuine. For example, if you are being so frank that it is out of character or beyond the bounds of normal behavior, the spontaneity may be seen as a manipulative strategy to gain the other's trust and is apt to produce defensiveness.

Second, the quality of the relationship may affect the success of an attempt to be supportive. Some caring, or at least some dependency, must exist if the attempt is to matter to the other person. If you do not care what a friend thinks about you, you can treat him in almost any way you want. You can, for example, try to hurt him without worrying about the effect.

Providing these two requirements are met, four important benefits are possible from supportive communication: encouragement, acceptance, dialogue and understanding, and relational growth.

Supportive Behavior Provides Encouragement

It is easy to be discouraged about our ability to handle our interpersonal relationships. Supportive behavior counters these sources of discouragement. Instead of discouraging, supportive behavior improves interpersonal relationships and affirms the other person in an encouraging way. It also provides a greater chance of achieving interpersonal goals because it encourages us to talk through our differences without feeling threatened.

Supportive Behavior Enhances the Possibility of Acceptance

The person who causes another to "give in" wins the argument but does not gain real acceptance of either the outcome *or* himself. But supportiveness can produce acceptance in both areas. When you convey acceptance of the other person and the other's ideas, you are likely to create a feeling of trust and confidence. Even if the final decision is not to the other's liking, such a feeling is beneficial to the relationship.

Supportive Behavior Encourages Dialogue and Understanding

Supportive behavior encourages us to listen. When we listen, we are more likely to understand the other. If we are both listening and trying to understand, genuine dialogue can take place. In contrast, defensive behavior often leads to ineffective listening and rigidity. Obviously, defensiveness does not encourage productive communication.

Supportive behavior offers a far greater chance of success and growth in our relationships because it encourages us to approach others as equals, to engage in joint problem solving, and to listen carefully in order to express empathy. The result is honest, straightforward communication.

Supportive Behavior
Encourages Relational Growth

Supportive communication promotes self-esteem, self-disclosure, and growth in our relationships. Supportive behavior allows us to feel more confident. Trust develops, which, in turn, promotes sharing. Sharing helps us to understand ourselves more fully, to be confident, to try new things, and to grow as people. If we engage in defensive communication, we risk potentially negative consequences for both ourselves and our relationships. The attack on another person's self-concept and the lashing out that often accompanies such defensive communication can lead to a disengagement process.[11] Obviously, there is no growth in the relationship when this occurs.

Supportive behavior encourages relational growth.

Growth and engagement result from sharing made possible by the trust we develop in each other. We are able to decrease risk because we believe that there is greater likelihood of support. Trust allows self-disclosure. The opportunity to get to know another person in a nonthreatening environment, even when there is disagreement, provides an opportunity to find what we have in common. This, in turn, can promote liking and attraction. Thus, supportive behavior is a key to a growth-promoting atmosphere in our interpersonal relationships.

REMAINING SUPPORTIVE

Supportive communication sounds simple, but it is very difficult. Because it is not as easy as it seems, we want to offer some pointers on remaining supportive.

You Can Disagree and Remain Supportive

You do not have to suppress your viewpoint and accept the other person's to be supportive. Supportiveness is not a matter of right and wrong. You can disagree and still work out an understanding without attacking the other person. For example, you might say, "I disagree with your position, but I do understand how you can believe as you do. Can we work out a cooperative position?" A statement like this says that, while you disagree, you know the other person has a legitimate viewpoint and that you are willing to cooperate in coming to a decision. This kind of relational affirmation will make it easier for you and the other person to talk about your disagreement.

Understanding the Need for Interdependency

Try to figure out if there is some sort of caring or mutual need in your relationship. Every relationship has some degree of interdependence. Understand the strength of this interdependence. If it is strong, there is a chance that a particular need will cause the person to be concerned about how she treats you. Interdependency helps check the other's tendency to treat you badly in the face of your supportive behavior. Sometimes it helps to affirm the other as a way of beginning a talk. One young person started a difficult conversation with her parents by saying, "I need to talk with you about a decision I've made. I first want to say that I care a great deal for you and your opinion. But as I am growing up, I need to make some decisions for myself." Then she talked to them about a young man she had agreed to marry.

Look for the Best Time to Talk

Sometimes people get caught in an emotional rage and are unable to respond to supportiveness. Under such circumstances, it is better to postpone the talk. The other is probably incapable of listening. Withdraw from such an unproductive moment without damaging the relationship, but make a commitment to talk later. Be sure to carry through with your stated intentions; approach the person at a more appropriate time.

Practice the Supportive Skills, Especially Empathy and Equality

Incorporating supportive communication skills into your routine behavior may be a slow task. Try being supportive at the very next opportunity. Practice the skills aloud. For example, how many ways can you think of to say or suggest:

1. "You seem to feel . . . ."
2. "We share this problem. Let's work at solving it cooperatively."
3. "I understand and can relate to your problems and feelings."
4. "You and I have equal status, power, and ability. We're both OK just the way we are."
5. "Your position is legitimate. You have a point of view. I am willing to discuss this issue with an open mind. I am not certain . . . ."

Remember that the habitual tendency to be critical is difficult to overcome. As you increase your skill with language and nonverbal communication, practice in more difficult relational settings. You will discover that you can be supportive, that it does make a difference, and that this gives you a new and welcome freedom.

Focus on empathy and equality. If you are empathic, you will listen more carefully. If you avoid "pulling rank," you will avoid the notion of superiority. These two attitudes generate a definition of the relationship that promotes the other supportive behaviors.

BUILDING A PRODUCTIVE CLIMATE

Relational growth occurs when partners maintain a satisfying level of interest in each other and their relationship. Although most of us have learned from experience some of the basic skills needed to keep relationships healthy and growing, we sometimes have difficulty doing so. The last section of this chapter is designed to help you sharpen existing skills and add some new ones. We will discuss six means of promoting relational growth: engaging in appropriate self-disclosure; achieving role and rule agreement; giving support; demonstrating affection and liking; managing relational problems constructively; and guarding against stagnation.

ENGAGING IN APPROPRIATE SELF-DISCLOSURE

Sidney Jourard said that we cannot possibly love another person unless that person fully discloses to us.[12] He meant that we must know a person in order to develop affection for that person. This knowledge is important for at least three reasons.

First, knowing provides a basis for discovering similarities or common areas of interest. This is very important to the development and growth of a relationship. Obviously, you feel more comfortable with those who are similar to yourself. And you also trust the person because that person's behavior seems predictable.

Second, the act of *self-disclosure* promotes self-disclosure. When a person shares with you and you see that disclosure as appropriate, you generally respond by disclosing yourself. Over time, this kind of talk maintains intimacy in a relationship. Greater intimacy can be achieved by greater self-disclosure. If you choose to deepen a relationship, you can reveal more of your experiences (breadth of disclosure) and more of the personal and private parts of those experiences (depth or intimacy of disclosure).

> The act of self-disclosure promotes self-disclosure

Finally, self-disclosure stimulates the relationship. A stagnant relationship may be characterized in part as one in which nothing is new. When disclosure drops off to the point that we stop learning about each other, the relationship does not—cannot—grow.

Appropriate self-disclosure means that we tune into the kind of self-disclosure the other person is willing to give. Appropriate self-disclosure means balanced self-disclosure. Each person in a relationship should disclose at approximately the same depth and breadth as the other. Some questions may help in discovering what level of self-disclosure is appropriate; How well do I know the other person, especially in terms of his more private life? To what extent has the other person revealed his feelings, values, and beliefs? How does my own self-disclosure compare to his? The breadth and depth of appropriate self-disclosure will also grow if we are in a relationship that we hope will move along the stages in engagement. (See Chapter 8.) Do you see progression through the stages? Do you see increased breadth and depth in disclosure over the life of the relationship?

ACHIEVING ROLE AND RULE AGREEMENT

Satisfaction in a relationship is contingent upon achieving *role* and *rule agreement.* Once these are negotiated, continued satisfaction depends upon successfully changing as a relationship changes. As it matures, ideas of what is appropriate must mature as well. When change is not recognized, renegotiation of the relational roles and rules is unlikely; thus, adjustment and growth are not occurring. Although negotiation involves many of the skills discussed in previous chapters, the techniques of conflict management are especially important, for when we express our dissatisfaction with some role or rule, the potential for conflict is introduced into the relationship.

GIVING SUPPORT

There are two kinds of *support* you can give a person in a relationship. First, the other person needs to be supported, affirmed, and valued. Carl Rogers called this "unconditional positive regard.[13] You can provide unconditional positive regard by telling the person directly that he or she is valued and needed. This creates a positive climate that promotes relational growth.

Second, a person needs support and confirmation when the pressures of daily living create a need for bolstering. Earlier you learned that people are motivated to engage others because of a need to share. You particularly need to share bad news so that you can be supported. It is psychologically much easier to handle a problem when you can share it with a friend. Active listening and empathy are the two main communication activities used to convey such support. It is also important to reassure the person: "It must have been hard to deal with your boss today. You did a good job." Support is essential for maintenance and growth in a relationship, as it contributes directly to the psychological health of our partner.

DEMONSTRATING AFFECTION

One of the three primary interpersonal needs in William Schutz's model is *affection*.[14] Each person in a relationship has some particular need for being liked. If the relationship is to grow and prosper, we should try to meet this mutual need. The first step in being able to give affection is to discover the nature of this need in the other. For example, some people want affection to be demonstrated more frequently and more directly than others.

In Eric Berne's theory of transactional analysis, a display of affection is called stroking.[15] When you stroke an infant, you physically touch the child. Adult stroking does not always involve such overt acts as touching. Of course, stroking may happen in intimate relationships, but it does not usually occur in others. Instead, Americans tend to engage in verbal stroking. You might make it a point to remember to tell the other person from time to time how much you appreciate her. Be sure also to recognize the other's positive achievements. Noticing how good the other person feels is a powerful way of stroking. You might say, "I see that you are feeling really good about the report you have been working on all week. And then George liked it too. That's really neat!"

Therapist Muriel James suggests that good friends give each other this kind of stroking.[16] She recommends that you agree to help each other when necessary by directly signaling the need. You might say to a good friend, "I really feel beat down today. Things have just not gone right for me." Your friend then might reassure you about his affection by saying. "Let's talk. I want you to know that I care."

This kind of reassurance is also very important to the relationship, since knowing that you can share your disappointments and still be liked will almost certainly enhance its growth. But keep in mind that the individual who repeatedly asks for support can become "needy." That is, this person may be seen as forever dependent, which the other may come to resent. Each pair must decide how much of this kind of sharing is healthy for their particular relationship.

MANAGING RELATIONAL PROBLEMS CONSTRUCTIVELY

People who are not successful in managing relational problems cannot expect their relationships to grow. In fact, problems that are not managed carefully can promote resentment and bitterness. A history of resentment and bitterness is a serious relational problem in itself. It can lead to movement through the stages of disengagement: differentiating, circumscribing, stagnating, avoiding, and, finally, terminating the relationship. Successful problem management, on the other hand, can provide a sense of accomplishment, growth, and optimism. It is important, therefore, to sharpen your relational diagnostic and problem management skills.

Assessing and Understanding Relational Problems

Problems are part of any relationship. We are sometimes frustrated because we do not know exactly why we are having a difficulty. Following are tools for diagnosing your relationship, and developing a constructive course of action for managing relational difficulties.

Sometimes an effort to improve a relationship can be cooperative because both parties recognize a need and want to participate. Clearly, this is the best situation for successful problem solving. But it is possible to work on a relationship even under less-than-optimum conditions. If possible, both people might fill out a diagnostic form (table 9.3). This will bring you closer to an understanding of each other's view of the relationship. Only then are you ready to develop a course of action.

Developing a Course of Action

Relational problem solving can be a difficult task because it usually involves conflict management. Each of the differences you uncover in a diagnosis of your relationship can raise the need for negotiation. (We are assuming that the process of understanding each other did not alter the differences you originally uncovered.) The following

Table 9.3   Diagnose Your Relationship

Step 1

Working separately, place an initial on the continuum line in response to each statement. Take as much time as you need to think about each item. Do not discuss your responses while you are working. When you finish, proceed to Step 2.

1. *Cooperation*

A. We identify, define, and solve our problems together. We respect each other's competence.

   Rarely ◄─────────────────────────────────► Often

B. We work together as a team without competing or putting each other down.

   Rarely ◄─────────────────────────────────► Often

C. We make decisions together. We make the most of what each of us has to contribute.

   Rarely ◄─────────────────────────────────► Often

D. We share our opinions, thoughts, and ideas without becoming argumentative or defensive.

   Rarely ◄─────────────────────────────────► Often

E. Overall, I am satisfied with our mutual respect and cooperation in thinking, deciding, and working together.

   Rarely ◄─────────────────────────────────► Often

2. *Compatibility*

A. We accept and work through our differences to find agreement on lifestyle and social and public images.

   Rarely ◄─────────────────────────────────► Often

B. We accept and work through our differences to find common values with regard to religion, morality, social concerns, and politics.

   Rarely ◄─────────────────────────────────► Often

C. We accept and work through our differences with regard to social life and choice of friends.

   Rarely ◄─────────────────────────────────► Often

D. We accept and work through our differences with regard to a basic approach to roles and rules.

   Rarely ◄─────────────────────────────────► Often

E. Overall, I am satisfied with the way we deal with our differences, maintain a shared lifestyle, and share values.

   Rarely ◄─────────────────────────────────► Often

3. *Intimacy*

A. We often play together. We put fun into what we do together.

Rarely ◄——————————————————————————————► Often

B. We express our emotions and feelings openly and freely. We say when we are scared, sad, hurting, angry, or happy.

Rarely ◄——————————————————————————————► Often

C. We tell each other what we like and dislike. We ask openly for what we want from each other.

Rarely ◄——————————————————————————————► Often

D. We "let go" with each other. We play, relax, and have fun with each other.

Rarely ◄——————————————————————————————► Often

E. Overall, I am satisfied with the level of openness and intimacy in our relationship.

Rarely ◄——————————————————————————————► Often

4. *Emotional Support*

A. We listen, understand, and empathize with each other's disappointments, hurts, or problems.

Rarely ◄——————————————————————————————► Often

B. We encourage and support each other when one of us is making basic life changes or trying new behavior.

Rarely ◄——————————————————————————————► Often

C. We take responsibility for nurturing one another when either of us is sick or hurting.

Rarely ◄——————————————————————————————► Often

D. We are emotionally supportive of each other when either of us feels anxious, dependent, or in need of care.

Rarely ◄——————————————————————————————► Often

E. Overall, I am satisfied with the nurturing and support we give and receive from each other.

Rarely ◄——————————————————————————————► Often

Step 2

A. Still working separately, review each item and analyze how *satisfied* you feel. You may have marked an item low on the continuum—and *like* it that way. Or you may have marked an item high, but feel uncomfortable about it. One person's intimacy is another's anxiety. In the margin next to each item, put one of the following: S = satisfactory, OK = acceptable but not exceptional, or D = somewhat disappointing.

B. Take turns telling each other how and why you marked each item on the continuum.

Source: Adapted from David L. Luecke, *The Relationship Manual* (Columbia, MD: The Relationship Institute, 1981). pp. 13–14. Used with permission.

suggestions may prove helpful in developing a course of action for managing your problems:

1. *Review what you have learned about conflict management.* The tools of conflict management are very important in an examination of relational problems.

2. *See if you can agree that change is important in the particular area.* This is important because unless you both agree that change is desirable, further discussion will only be frustrating. If you cannot agree at this time, you might agree to think more about it and to talk again later.

3. *List as many concrete proposals as you can for achieving the desired end.* Suppose you discover that you and the other person want to share opinions, thoughts, and ideas more often, without becoming argumentative. Some techniques you might try are: (1) set aside a specific time for sharing, (2) write down what you think and make a date to discuss what you have written, (3) agree to discuss whatever is on your mind before the end of the day, and (4) wait until the other person says, "I've finished presenting my side," before you talk. List your ideas and even write them on a piece of paper if that will help. The more ideas you can generate for achieving your desired goals, the better.

4. *See if there are any particular ideas that the other person does not understand.* Exchange lists. Before you start talking about your ideas, be sure that you understand each other. If one person does not understand an item on the list, she should mark it and return the list. Confer until all marks are eliminated.

5. *Look over the list and make a proposal.* This proposal might even include a statement of expectations about the other's behavior. For example, you might say, "I'd be willing to set aside a time to talk, if you'd be willing to allow at least thirty minutes for us to do so."

6. *Allow the other person to consider the proposal and respond.* It is helpful to limit the response to one of three types:

    a. acceptance

    b. a specific modification

    c. a specific counterproposal

7. *Continue modifying or making counterproposals until you can both agree.* Make sure that you fully understand any modification or counterproposal. A good way to do this is to engage in active listening. Usually, if partners are willing to stick with this kind of negotiation, they will be able to come to agreement.

The negotiation process will go much more smoothly if you are flexible and open to change. There is no magic formula that will *cause* you to be this way; you must resolve to be flexible. Begin your

Make a proposal about a desired change. Negotiation will go more smoothly if you are flexible.

conversation by talking about the need for give and take. You might also talk about and try to agree that there is a need for change. If you can reach some agreement, you have laid the groundwork for successful negotiation.

You can also encourage agreement by avoiding extreme positions. As soon as one of you takes a position that involves absolutes, such as "I want you to *guarantee* that you will *always* . . . ," the other person is likely to become defensive. When this happens, a counter-proposal that is just as absolute and rigid will likely result.

Finally, recognize that you can agree to talk at another time if tempers flare. This is not *always* a good idea, of course, because avoidance can develop into a habit and does not solve the problem. Use it only to allow tempers to cool and to give you both time to think about the issue privately.

GUARDING AGAINST STAGNATION

Stagnation occurs when a relationship ceases to be stimulating. The solution to this difficulty, therefore, is to find ways to increase stimulation. We could never offer a complete list of suggestions for increasing stimulation, but we can list five of the most important ones.

Set a Time for Sharing

You are often so busy that you do not spend enough time sharing and disclosing. Sometimes when you think you are sharing, you really are not. Joint activity often includes very little sharing at all. For example, going to a movie, watching a favorite television program, or taking classes together may not give you the opportunity to engage the other person interpersonally.

Sharing through disclosure is an important source of stimulation for relationships. Without it, a relationship will soon be in trouble. Conversations become predictable, and, if there is no news, listening becomes almost impossible. Such conditions are deadly to relational growth. We can avoid this by taking advantage of opportunities for sharing. Our recommendation is to find activities that allow for time alone with the other person: have lunch; walk; go to the beach; play a game that requires interaction. When you are involved in such activities, you should try to share yourself. However difficult this may seem, sharing is worth the effort, for it promotes reciprocal self-disclosure.

Agree to Do Something New Together

Another way to stimulate a relationship is to move in a new direction. Take stock of potential interests and set aside time to plan something new. This can prove to be a refreshing experience. The

Take advantage
of opportunities
for sharing.

activity and challenges that go along with new, joint experiences create numerous stories that can serve as a relational history and establish the relationship as meaningful and unique.

Express Caring Frequently

Often we forget to say what we are thinking. This is especially true in long-established relationships. We assume that the other person knows that we care. However, there is no substitute for saying, "I care!"

Understand That It Is OK to Disagree

You cannot always agree with the other person. Most of us understand this principle in the abstract, but find it difficult to apply to a specific relationship. A disagreement that we have been unable to resolve can create problems in our relationships. Resentment or guilt may build. Managing a disagreement does not directly prevent stagnation. It can, however, create a climate that helps us focus on the positive and grow. (You will learn to manage interpersonal conflict in Chapter 10.)

Give Your Relationship a Periodic Checkup

Use the form in table 9.3 to diagnose all your relationships—not just relationships that are in trouble. Such a check can suggest ways to stimulate already healthy relationships.

SUMMARY

This chapter focused on the behavior displayed when you are engaged in defensive communication. Rogers argued that people engage in defensive behavior because there is a natural tendency to evaluate others. He concluded that this is a major barrier to effective interpersonal communication. This tendency to evaluate is often met with defensiveness. Evaluation suggests some defect in the other person, who may feel a need to defend his self-concept—to say that his view counts and that he has a right to his perspective.

Sometimes you defend yourself by ignoring or avoiding the other person altogether. But if these choices are unavailable, you may attack.

Defensive behavior involves six categories of communication: evaluation, superiority, certainty, control, neutrality, and strategy. The consequences of defensive communication behavior are numerous. Perhaps the most damaging are

1. Defensive communication may signal rejection or disconfirmation. Rejection is an outright denial of the other person's definition of self. Disconfirmation suggests that the person or the person's opinion does not exist.

2. Defensive communication may lead a person to stop listening, become rigid in her position, and perhaps lash out at the attacker.

3. Defensive communication may lead to hostility. When others do not seem to care and do not seem to take you into account, you will likely become hostile.

The alternative to defensiveness is supportiveness. Supportive communication is characterized as descriptive, equal, provisional, problem oriented, empathic, and spontaneous. Supportiveness produces many important benefits for both the person and the person's relationships: it gives encouragement, enhances the possibility of acceptance, encourages dialogue and understanding, and promotes interpersonal growth.

There are four ways to improve supportive communication. Tell yourself that you can disagree and still remain supportive. Understand the need for interdependency. Look for the best time to talk. Practice the supportive skills that Gibb suggests. If you learn to communicate supportively, your relationships will be better, more satisfying, and more productive. These benefits seem worth the effort necessary to obtain them.

Relational growth occurs when people maintain a satisfying level of interest in each other and their relationship. Growth is encouraged by appropriate self-disclosure of about the same breadth and depth as your partner's disclosure. This self-disclosure provides a basis for discovering similarities, thereby promoting disclosure from the other person and stimulating the relationship. As the relationship grows, we risk slightly more.

We also need to achieve role and rule agreement by discovering what kinds of behavior and tasks are appropriate at various stages of our relationship, and we must provide the support necessary to nourish the relationship. This involves affirming the other as a valued person. It also means bolstering each other during times of disappointment or discouragement. A key part of offering support is demonstrating affection. It is crucial to give verbal and nonverbal signs of affection to promote relational growth.

When conflict arises we must manage our relational problems constructively. The chapter includes a scheme for assessing rational problems as well as plan for action.

Finally, we can guard against stagnation in our relationships by engaging in certain activities: set a time for sharing, agree to do something new together, frequently express caring, understand it is OK to disagree, and give the relationship a periodic checkup.

DISCUSSION QUESTIONS

1. In what social contexts are you likely to behave defensively? What behavior in particular do you use to express defensiveness? Given what you have learned in this chapter, how will you work to alleviate defensiveness?

2. Identify three people you know well. What causes them to behave defensively? Does your behavior produce this?

3. Use Gibb's six categories to analyze defensive situations in which you have been involved. Do you think his categories are valid? Are your behaviors consistent with what he says will produce defensiveness?

4. Using Gibb's six categories of supportive communication, analyze a situation in which you successfully managed a difference. Were your behaviors consistent with what Gibb said would produce a supportive climate? Give examples of your supportive behaviors.

5. How can you remain supportive when you have a difference in opinion with another person? How can you help the other person remain supportive?

6. How do we know what kind of self-disclosure is appropriate for a relationship? What are the possible outcomes of too much or too little self-disclosure?

7. Consider a male-female relationship in the integrating stage of development. What kinds of role and rule agreements might be a part of this relationship?

8. How is it possible to give support when you are having a disagreement?

9. What kinds of demonstration of affection and liking would be appropriate in each of these relational stages: initiating, experimenting, intensifying, integrating, and bonding?

10. What have you found to be the most important aspects of managing a relational difference constructively?

ENDNOTES

1. C. R. Rogers and F. J. Roethlisberger, "Barriers and Gateways to Communication," *Harvard Business Review* (July–August 1952): 28–34.

2. J. R. Gibb, "Defensive Communication," *The Journal of Communication* 11:3 (September 1961): 141–148.

3. Gibb's theory has received considerable support from textbook authors because it makes sense and is easily applied. Some empirical support for the theory also exists. See J. V. Civikly, R. W. Pace, and R. M. Krause, "Interviewer and Client Behaviors in Supportive and Defensive Interviews," *Communication Yearbook I*, B. D. Ruben, ed. (New Brunswick, NJ: Transition Books, 1977), 347–362; and W. F. Eadie, "Defensive Communication Revisited: A Critical Examination of Gibb's Theory," *The Southern Speech Communication Journal* 47 (Winter 1982): 163–177.

4. T. C. Sabourin and G. H. Stamp, "Communication and the Experience of Dialectical Tensions in Family Life: An Examination of Abusive and Nonabusive Families," *Communication Monographs* 62 (1995): 213–243.

5. J. L. Hocker and W. W. Wilmot, *Interpersonal Conflict*, 4th ed. (Dubuque, IA: Brown & Benchmark, 1995), p. 34.

6. C. R. Rogers, "The Therapeutic Relationship: Recent Theory and Research," in *The Human Dialogue: Perspectives on Communication*, F. W. Matson and A. Montagu, eds. (New York: The Free Press, 1967).

7. J. R. Gibb, "Defensive Communication," *The Journal of Communication* 11:3 (September 1961): 141–148.

8. Ibid., 143.

9. J. B. Stiff, J. P. Dillard, L. Somera, H. Kim, and C. Sleight, "Empathy, Communication, and Prosocial Behavior," *Communication Monographs* 55 (1995): 198–213.

10. G. R. Miller and M. Steinberg, *Between People: A New Analysis of Interpersonal Communication* (Chicago: Science Research Associates, 1975), 174–176.

11. I. Altman and D. A. Taylor, *Social Penetration: The Development of Interpersonal Relationships* (New York: Holt, Rinehart and Winston, 1973), 173–180.

12. S. M. Jourard, *The Transparent Self* (New York: Van Nostrand Reinhold, 1971), 5, 49–57.

13. C. R. Rogers, *On Becoming a Person* (Boston: Houghton Mifflin, 1961), 62, 283.

14. W. C. Schutz, *Firo: A Three-Dimensional Theory of Interpersonal Behavior* (New York: Holt, Rinehart and Winston, 1958).

15. One of the best treatments of Berne's idea of stroking is found in M. James and D. Jongeward, *Born to Win: Transactional Analysis with Gestalt Experiments* (Reading, MA: Addison-Wesley, 1971), 44–67.

16. M. James, as cited in a lecture given by members of the staff of the Center for Transactional Analysis at Ghost Ranch Conference Center, Abiquin, New Mexico, summer 1982.

READ MORE ABOUT
DEFENSIVENESS IN RELATIONSHIPS IN THESE SOURCES

Gibb, Jack R. "Defensive Communication." *The Journal of Communication* 11 (1961): 141–148. This is the classic essay that laid the groundwork for much of what we know about defensive and supportive communication behavior.

Rogers, Carl R. and Fritz J. Roethlisberger. "Barriers and Gateways to Communication." *The Harvard Business Review* (July–August 1952): 28–34. These authors explore why and how we create a climate that restricts our interpersonal effectiveness.

Wells, Theodora. *Keeping Your Cool Under Fire: Communicating Non-Defensively.* New York: McGraw-Hill, 1980. This excellent book expands on our treatment of defensiveness, relating the topic to organizational settings.

READ MORE ABOUT
SUPPORTIVENESS IN RELATIONSHIPS IN THESE SOURCES

Albrecht, Terence L., Brant R. Burelson, and Deana Goldsmith. "Supportive Communication." In *Handbook of Interpersonal Communication*, 2nd ed. Mark L. Knapp and Gerald R. Miller, eds. Newbury Park, CA: Sage, 1994. This chapter discusses the negative consequences of not having social support and the variety of ways people can provide it through their communication.

Garnet, Alan. *Conversationally Speaking: Tested Ways to Increase Your Personal and Social Effectiveness.* New York: McGraw-Hill, 1991. This practical guide to confirming relationships addresses these topics: starting and maintaining conversations, handling criticism constructively, and reducing anxiety in social situations.

Rogers, Carl R. "The Therapeutic Relationship: Recent Theory and Research." In *The Human Dialogue: Perspectives on Communication*, F. W. Matson and A. Montagu, eds. New York: The Free Press, 1967. In this essay, Carl Rogers captures the essence of the supportive attitude with the term *unconditional positive regard*. The relationship Rogers paints between climate and healing is fascinating.

READ MORE ABOUT
PROMOTING RELATIONAL GROWTH IN THESE SOURCES

Berg, J. H. and R. L. Archer. "The Disclosure Liking Relationship." *Human Communication Research* 10 (1983). These authors provide an interesting review of the research literature that examines the relationship between self-disclosure and interpersonal attraction.

Fitzpatrick, Mary Anne. *Between Husbands and Wives: Communication in Marriage.* Newbury Park. CA: Sage, 1988. This book presents a thorough examination of marital communication. Topics include power, conflict, influence, emotional expression, self-disclosure, and nonverbal communication.

Stewart, John. *Bridges Not Walls.* 5th ed. New York: McGraw-Hill, 1990. Stewart's excellent reader is well worth looking into. It covers a broad range of interpersonal issues from a variety of perspectives.

10

CONFLICT

All relationships involve needs and dependency. We have a great deal of power because of these factors. This is why power for us is primarily a relational issue. In this chapter, you will discover that the type of power available for use varies greatly from one situation to another. We can learn to use power more effectively when we understand the types that are available and the costs and benefits of the use of power.

U.S. society defines most conflicts as either winning or losing situations; there must thus be a winner and a loser. Conflict situations can, in fact, present creative opportunities for cooperation in overcoming differences. In this chapter, we propose a set of skills and a plan for learning to manage conflict more productively. Effective conflict management can enhance the growth and development of your relationships.

Perhaps the most frustrating experiences are relationships that just do not work. In fact, some people insulate themselves from this by expecting only a few relationships to grow, mature, and prosper. But in spite of this emotional preparation, they are surprised and even saddened when they discover that a valued relationship is failing.

In this chapter, we describe the stages through which a deteriorating relationship will pass unless something is done. We also make suggestions about what can be done to intervene at each stage.

317

KEY TERMS

avoiding	circumscribing
coercive power	compromise
confrontation/problem solving	control
deterioration	differentiating
displaying	dysfunctional conflict
emotional appeal	empathic understanding
expert power	expressed struggle
forcing	functional conflict
incompatible goals	information/persuasive power
interdependent parties	interpersonal conflict
legitimate power	lose-lose techniques
manipulation	nonnegotiation
perceived differences	personal rejection
power	referent power
reward power	scarce rewards
smoothing	stagnating
terminating	win-lose techniques
win-win technique	withdrawal

OBJECTIVES

1. Define the concept of power.
2. Tell how power is relational and how relational factors affect it.
3. Describe and illustrate the various power bases.
4. Describe power games, including strategies for managing them.
5. Define interpersonal conflict.
6. Explain when conflict may be dysfunctional.
7. Identify each interpersonal intervention technique, and classify it as to its win-lose potential.
8. Discuss how partners typically manage conflict in close relationships.
9. Develop a plan for managing interpersonal conflict that uses the confrontation and problem-solving technique.
10. Describe the major causes of relational deterioration.
11. Name and explain the stages of relational deterioration.
12. Specify behaviors that are helpful in managing the loss of a relationship.

POWER

It is difficult to imagine a relationship in which power does not play an important role.[1] There is a power dynamic in family, work, and social relationships. The idea that power is a part of life seems so obvious that we will not take the time to present our evidence. You must understand power if you are to manage your relationships effectively.

We begin this chapter by defining power and showing how it is relational. Then we examine the types that are available for use. Finally, we present some common power games with representative language that might be appropriate for managing them.

POWER DEFINED

Power has been defined as the ability or potential to influence others.[2] But what exactly is this "potential to influence"? Wally Jacobson suggests that it involves two factors—needs and dependency:

> If we want or need certain things, material or nonmaterial, that another person possesses, we are dependent upon that person in proportion to the strength of our desire for these things. Further, our dependence upon another is simultaneously related to whether we can get those same things from sources other than the person on whom we are originally dependent.[3]

Power, then, is perceived influence that one person has over another and is based on the other's dependency. To the extent that the other person is dependent upon us and perceives that dependency, we have power over him. Further, this person's dependency is reduced by the degree that he believes that these needs can be fulfilled elsewhere.

POWER IS RELATIONAL

One of the important facts about power is that it is relational. It is generally not an attribute of the power user. Instead, it belongs to the social relationship. Thus, power is only effective if someone allows us to use it. If the other person does not wish us to use power, she might choose to ignore us, to withdraw from the relationship, or to otherwise prevent us from exercising it.

Endorsement Factors

Willingness to allow an attempt to use power depends, in part, on the appropriateness of the source of power. One of the appropriateness factors is the relational definition. Every relationship is based upon some definition of how the partners stand in relation to each other. A number of terms might help you think about power in relationships. One set is "equal/equal" versus "superior/subordinate." Imagine how one of these definitions might affect your willingness to allow someone to use power. The use of *coercive power*—power based upon threat of punishment—provides an example. If a relationship has been defined as equal/equal (perhaps a friendship), one of the friends may reject the other's attempt to exercise coercion. On the other hand, in a superior/subordinate relationship (perhaps in the workplace), the subordinate may be willing to accept coercive power even though he does not particularly like it.

A second factor (one that may override the definitional factor) is *importance*. Two aspects of importance may have an effect. First, you may endorse an attempt to use power because the relationship is more important than the issue. Suppose, for example, that a friend wants to borrow ten dollars. You have a strong aversion to lending money to anyone, yet your friend says, "I can't understand why you won't lend me ten dollars. What are friends for? I guess we aren't as good friends as I thought!" Perhaps you sense that this issue is going to threaten your relationship and thus lend your friend the money.

The second aspect of importance is the value assigned to some issue. You may go along with power use because you realize the issue is more important to the power holder than the relationship. Suppose you have a significant dating relationship with a person who is not as serious about religion as you are. This person says to you, "Quit bugging me about going to church with you. When you do this, I don't think you love me. You know I don't want to go to church. If you don't stop, it is going to affect the way I feel about you." You reply, "My church is very important to me. You will go with me if you want to date me." If your strategy worked, it did because you figured correctly that the relationship was more important than the issue of going to church. In such a situation, both kinds of importance are operating to allow coercion in an equal/equal relationship. So the two factors that control the exercise of power are (1) how we define the relationship and (2) importance.

Commitment to the Relationship

Compliance with an attempt to use power is related to the commitment each person has to the relationship. We can imagine situations in which we are equally committed and thus equally dependent on each other. In these cases, neither person has more power.

Many relationships, however, are not evenly balanced. When one person is less committed to the relationship, she has more power because she may be willing to risk the relationship to get what she wants. The person who cares more may go along with a power play rather than risk the relationship.

The relationship itself is not always the issue. Instead, the rewards that are available in the relationship may be at stake. Imbalance in the need to be rewarded can be a source of power. For example, if I need your love and affection very much, I may do what you want in order to keep receiving them. You would have a great deal of power under these circumstances.

POWER BASES

One of the best descriptions of power is by John French and Bertran Raven and their associates,[4] who identified five bases or categories of power: referent, expert, legitimate, reward, and coercive. Raven and his colleagues later modified their bases of power to include a sixth: information/persuasive power.[5]

Referent Power

Referent power is available when someone identifies with you because that person likes you and values several of your attributes. The more this is true, the more that person will want to please you. Thus the referent power increases.

One of the clearest examples of referent power is the emulation a younger sibling attempts because of the attraction to an older sibling. A seven-year-old girl we know does all she can to emulate her

Referent power is based on liking.

eleven-year-old brother. She wears clothes like his, refusing to wear dresses. She asks for toys that are like his, rejecting dolls. She asks to enroll in karate because she admires his involvement. He has power because he serves as her referent. He can get her to do many things for him.

The use of referent power may or may not be conscious. For example, if you are attracted to someone, you may do things without being told. A teacher may hear from former students who, years after they have left the university, report on how influential the teacher was—much to the surprise of the teacher! In this case, the teacher exerted unconscious influence on the student. The same kind of influence occurs in other relationships. Parents, for example, often exert referent power that guides their children's behavior when they are not present.

Expert Power

Sometimes we are able to exert *expert power* over others because we have knowledge that they do not possess. A physician, for example, can influence you in matters of health but may not be able to help you remodel your house. You might follow an accountant's recommendations on tax matters but not on managing a relationship conflict. In fact, you may consider an attempt to influence outside an area of expertise to be a matter of poor judgment.[6]

We are sometimes influenced by the comments of a well-respected person because we think that the person's superior intelligence in one area may be representative of a more general expertise. Thus, we may think that an accountant or even a physician may know something about investing money or that clergy are able to advise on interpersonal relations.

We are also more apt to be influenced if the source of power seems to be unbiased. The fact that an expert does not have anything to gain by what she says may give her greater power.

Legitimate Power

Legitimate power usually comes with position; a belief that people in certain positions have a right to direct and influence the activities of others. Those who exercise leadership in our society—clergy, political officials, industrialists—may have influence because of their accomplishments and positions. A parent is also in this position in relation to young children. A supervisor is in this position in relation to employees. Legitimate power is a result of the role and has little to do with the person occupying the role. Legitimate power is not limited to formal role relationships. Our culture extends legitimate rights to exercise power to certain people. We can sometimes be influenced by a sports personality we admire or an older person, for example.

Legitimate power relates to a person's role and has little to do with personal traits.

Reward Power

Reward power, sometimes called reinforcement power, comes from control of something that is valued by the other person. This may be tangible (perhaps money or material goods) or intangible (love or faithfulness). Of course, the significance of the possession is an important factor in the amount of power we have to exercise. If the person values the fact that you do little favors, he might do a great deal to please you so that you continue to do them.

A relationship usually implies some kind of reward power. We maintain relationships because they are rewarding in some way. The more rewarding the relationship, the greater the reward power. Rewards may include affection, stimulation, meaningfulness, material goods, security, and confirmation of the other person. Their significance can vary according to the nature of the relationship. In a friendship, for example, you might emphasize affection; in a work situation, you might emphasize material rewards.

Coercive Power

Coercive power is generally associated with force: we threaten in some way. You might threaten to do something (perhaps dissolve the relationship) or to withhold something (perhaps affection). Teachers might reward with high grades and punish with low grades. Parents might reward by increasing allowance and punish by withholding allowance.

Coercive power is only effective when the person toward whom it is directed actually believes that it may be used. For example, parents who threaten but rarely follow through find that their threats do not seem to have much power. In a dating relationship, if someone threatens to withhold affection but only withdraws it temporarily and then "kisses and makes up," he may find his attempt to use coercive power ineffective.

The strength of coercive power depends upon how the other person views the punishment. If it seems mild, we may decide that we will do as we please to see if the other is really willing to carry through. Coercive power is strongest when the punishment seems severe and highly likely to be administered.

Information/Persuasive Power

Sometimes we have power because the other person believes that we are well-informed and think logically about issues and problems. The other person expects that we have significant information and are able to make well-reasoned, well-thought-out arguments. This kind of power is a combination of the speaker's abilities and the communication content that is produced. When you believe a friend who makes a well-reasoned argument that a particular movie is a better choice for an evening's entertainment, your friend has used *information/persuasive power.*

COSTS AND BENEFITS OF POWER USE

The use of power may be costly for the user.

Some attempts to use power are costly. Coercive power may be the most costly. It is most effective when the power agent does not have to carry out the threat. The primary method of convincing a person that we might carry out a threat is to have done so in the past. Punishment yields negative feelings that are difficult to overcome. Thus, coercion is costly because it decreases attractiveness. In addition, a power agent must be prepared to receive hostile and angry feelings from the other.

Coercive power affects the recipient's ability to perform and learn. A study by K. Sheley and Marvin Shaw showed that use of coercive power caused people working in a group to *decrease* their performance following their leader's plea for *greater* effort.[7] In a classroom setting, Virginia Richmond and her associates found that coercive power decreased both cognitive and affective learning.[8] These same findings seem also to apply to excessive use of legitimate power.

The use of coercive power can also backfire. Coercion can create a martyr of the recipient of an attempt to use power. In this case, the person may become angry and gain increased satisfaction by not complying. The noncompliance may then create anger in the power user that may reward the target of the coercion.[9]

There can also be an unexpected cost associated with the use of expert power. When information is shared, the other person is no longer dependent on the expert for the information. This is why in work contexts, some managers carefully guard certain knowledge. A manager may fix a machine rather than teach the employee how to repair it. The administrator of a medical clinic shared her information about the budget with a group of physicians. Once they knew how much money was available and who was getting it, they could exert power over her with respect to spending on their own projects. By giving up information, she had allowed each of them to gain expert power.

The main benefit in exercising power is that we can gain greater control over the various contexts in which we find ourselves. We can gain more power and control if we understand and exercise power to our advantage because we are seen as someone who is in control.

The use of power can offer other benefits to a relationship. When we use reward power to gain compliance, for example, the other person is more likely to be positive and happy. He is also more likely to comply. Reward power also seems to increase attractiveness. People like those who have rewarded them. Finally, reward power seems to increase the effectiveness of most other bases of power. Legitimacy is less likely to be questioned. Referent power increases because of liking, and others are more open to our persuasive attempts.

MANAGING POWER GAMES

Game playing often involves some attempt to exercise power. Five such games and strategies for managing them are discussed here.

Ignoring the Partner

One power play is a game that ignores the partner. One person pretends that the other is not there or in some way does not count.

This game can take one of several forms. One is to ignore the person completely—the "cold shoulder" treatment; to remain silent when addressed. Another form of this game is not taking "no" for an answer. Someone may also choose to ignore another's rights by breaking the rules of common courtesy (for example, by standing too close, using the person's personal property, or talking too loudly). When such behavior is confronted, the usual response is to plead ignorance to the rules of social behavior.

One way to combat game playing is to confront the person directly and assertively. Describe the behavior specifically and ask what it means. Then, tell the person that you do not appreciate the power game and that you mean what you say. Say, for example, "I notice that you have been picking up papers from my desk and reading them. Why are you doing that?" Pause here to hear an answer. Then say, "I don't want you to pick up papers that are on my desk and read them. I want you to stop doing that, and *I mean what I say.*" If the person is ignoring you, you might say, "I notice that you are being quiet when I am around. Is something going on?" If the person says nothing is happening, you might respond, "I'm really glad to hear that. I'd like to talk about . . . ." Here you believe the person and get on with your agenda. If the person says that there is a problem, you can engage in mutual problem solving.

Creating an Obligation

Another power game uses the principle of fair treatment. The game player deliberately does something to create an obligation. The essence of the game is embodied in the words, "You owe me one." We all engage in this kind of exchange, but it becomes a power game when it is deliberate.

This game sometimes occurs between grown children and their parents. The parents have sacrificed a great deal, as most parents do. In this case, however, the sacrifice was made with the expectation that some day the children would be able to repay the effort. For example, a parent may say to their grown child, "Why can't you be here for Christmas? You know how much this means to me. After all we've done for you, can't you take a little time to be with us?" Or consider this example: "How can you do so poorly in your classes? We are sacrificing and spending money that we need for other things just to get you to college. Show us you appreciate our effort by making good grades!"

This kind of game is played in dating relationships, too. Perhaps the man spends a great deal of money on a present, trying to make the woman feel obligated to grant him sexual favors she may be otherwise reluctant to give. This same game can be played the other way. Perhaps the woman gives sexual favors and, in return, demands a marriage promise. A less extreme example of this game might be to help a person do a term paper and then demand an evening out.

Again, the best way to stop this game is to confront it directly. You might say, "I'm surprised you are suggesting that you want something because you helped me with my term paper. I would enjoy taking you out for a good time, but I resent these conditions. I'd like you to stop doing things for me if you are going to ask for something in return. I want you to do things for me because you want to do them. And I want to do things for you because I want to do them—not because I feel obligated."

> A good way to stop power games is to call attention to them.

Name Calling

A third power game has its basis in name calling. The person playing this game exercises power by seizing the opportunity to define the circumstances by calling a name. For example, a man might say to his male friend who is dating a woman he does not like, "How can you date that *dog?*" The strongly negative language is used as a power play. The man is assuming the right to label this situation in a way that will influence his friend. Or consider how you might feel if a colleague said of your proposal: "How could you do that? That is a worthless, bankrupt plan!"

Counter this kind of power play by redefining the situation. Call attention to the overstatement of the issue and then present your view. You might say, "That's pretty strong language—'dog.' I'd say 'that nice, enjoyable sophomore' is more accurate. You might not like her, but I do." Or you might make a stronger statement: "I am amazed that you would see my plan that way. I resent such strong, negative language. If you want to talk about this, OK. But you don't have a right to treat me this way."

Expressing Utter Disbelief

Sometimes a person attempts to gain the upper hand and win compliance by expressing utter disbelief. Undoubtedly you have heard someone say, "I must not have heard you correctly. *What did you say?*" Or, perhaps, "You can't mean that!" or "You can't be serious!" Of course, the tone of these statements sends a pointed message: "That's an incredible statement. Defend it!" The person using this power game is attempting to question you with such force that you back off from your position.

We recommend you confront this behavior by saying something like, "It appears you didn't hear me. I said, Do you have a question you would like to ask me about this?" This kind of communication turns the tables—it requires the questioner to explain him or herself and relieves you of the burden of explaining. If you wish to make an issue of how the person confronted you, you might say, "You seem to suggest I must not be serious about what I said. I resent it when I'm serious and you suggest I'm not. I'd like to talk to you about this if we can take each other seriously."

Interrupting

Some people play a power game calculated to disrupt your thoughts. These persons may constantly interrupt you and try to "steal the floor." By the time you get a chance to talk again, you may have forgotten what you wanted to say. Another way to interrupt is to talk over what you are saying with "editorial" comments.

This behavior may be deliberate or an unconscious habit. Even if it is a habit, it may still be a power game. We recommend a direct approach in dealing with it. Perhaps you might come right out and say, "I notice that you have interrupted me three times in the last several minutes. That makes it difficult for me to come back and complete my thought. I may be interrupting you, too, but I promise not to interrupt if you'll also try hard to let me finish my idea before you talk. Is that OK with you?" Generally, calling attention to the situation and asking for cooperation will put an end to this game, at least for the time being.

CONFLICT

Because Phil believed that conflict is harmful, he tried to avoid conflict in the group as much as possible. Tim had been showing up late for group meetings, and Phil could tell that something was going to happen soon. Cheryl was saying in private that she had had "about all of the lateness" that she was willing to take. Phil dared to suggest that she needed to keep her feelings to herself for the good of the group. He said, "After all, Cheryl, you know that if you tell him off and make a big deal out of his being late, he might get mad and not come to the meetings at all. He might even cause trouble. Let's just plan to start late."

You can imagine how Cheryl reacted to this suggestion since she never holds back. She addressed Phil directly: "What do you mean? Start the meeting late? How can you suggest such a thing? I'm not going to let him mess up our project just because he can't get here on time. Next time you get an opportunity, ask him to start getting to the meetings on time."

Phil said no more. All he was trying to do was to make things run smoothly. Now he was going to have to talk to Tim. He expected that Tim would be upset and that he would be right in the middle. Now, he was even more anxious than he had been before he had tried to help. He could feel the anxiety in the pit of his stomach. When he left the meeting, he thought that maybe he would be sick.

Phil's experience is not unusual for those who believe that conflict ought to be avoided. Phil tried to smooth over the conflict in the hope that it would go away. Cheryl, on the other hand, realized that the conflict resulting from Tim's lateness and the group's need to have him there on time was necessary to discover some reasonable way for the group to proceed. When Phil tried to smooth over the conflict, Cheryl would not let him do so. Thus, conflict broke out over the attempted cover-up.

Phil did not talk to Tim. At the next meeting, Cheryl brought up the difficulty. She had considerable experience managing conflict and knew of several options for talking with Tim. She had found that confronting the problem directly and problem solving with the person involved worked best for her. She was thus able to manage this conflict without damaging her relationship with Tim or his relationship with the group. Phil was both amazed and relieved.

Here we will examine options for managing conflict. We begin by defining conflict and then move to a discussion of general intervention techniques and their likely outcomes. Next, we discuss how to use two general strategies for managing conflict. Finally, we present a plan for working through conflict.

INTERPERSONAL CONFLICT DEFINED

Joyce Hocker and William Wilmot have defined *interpersonal conflict* as an *expressed struggle* between *interdependent parties*.[10] This definition has several implications. In particular, the word *struggle* implies that the parties understand that they have incompatible goals, that the rewards are scarce, and that the other person (or persons) involved is keeping them from achieving their goals. The aim of each party is to prevail or to gain the rewards. Opponents in intense conflict may even attempt to damage, neutralize, or eliminate each other.

Expressed struggle

Interdependent parties

The important terms related to this definition are *perceived differences* and *incompatible goals*. There must be perceived differences between the individuals as well as striving for what we think are incompatible goals or *scarce rewards*. If there is no striving, there is no motivating force for the conflict. Note that sometimes the differences between people are real; other times they are merely imagined. Yet, in one sense it does not matter if a difference is imagined, for if the persons involved *believe* that there is a difference, real or imagined, they will act on what they think is true.

Incompatible goals

Scarce rewards

FUNCTIONAL AND DYSFUNCTIONAL CONFLICT

There can be both positive and negative outcomes from conflict. Morton Deutsch pointed out that destructive conflict exists when we believe we have lost as a result of the conflict and so are dissatisfied with the outcome.[11] But if we are satisfied, functional conflict has occurred. Although most conflict management does not result in either of these extremes, the goal is to make the outcome as functional as possible.

In *dysfunctional conflict,* we expand the conflict step-by-step, even though there are other options. In fact, we often lose sight of the initiating causes altogether. This expansion in conflict often includes an increase in the size and number of issues, the number of participants, negative attitudes, and our willingness to bear costs. Reliance upon direct or passive aggression, control, threats, force, and deception increases dramatically. There is also a movement toward uniformity in position. Pressure is applied on members of a side who might listen to the other point of view. This reliance on aggression, control, threats, force, and deception is destructive to relationships and therefore dysfunctional.

Direct aggression can have a significant negative impact on the target person. Recipients can feel humiliated, hopeless, embarrassed, inadequate, desperate and depressed. This impact can carry over to the person's job and personal relationships causing decreased effectiveness.[12] The negative effect of aggression can also carry over into the relationship of the individuals involved. An aggressive remark leads to an equally combative remark from the other, starting a destructive spiral that often expands well beyond the original issue. The end result is often relational damage. Of course, couples in these kind of relationships report significantly less relational satisfaction than do those who communicate about their differences in other ways.[13]

Functional conflict is managed so that some satisfaction is achieved and the relationship is not seriously damaged. It is usually controlled, whereas dysfunctional conflict is usually out of control. *Control* is the careful management of both the relationship and a decision about the basic difference you have with the other person. Conflict is functional if: (1) some personal and/or organizational goals are accomplished by some of the participants, and (2) the relationship is not permanently injured. Control is an important aim in selecting an appropriate intervention technique.

Effective communication during a conflict can benefit a relationship. The effect of this kind of communication is evident in years of research on marital conflict management. All marriages have conflict, but the happy marriages have partners who manage conflict very differently from those in unhappy marriages. A 9-year study concluded that unhappy couples argue in ways we have suggested are destructive.[14] These couples failed to listen carefully to each other, they had little or no empathy for each other, they used evaluative language, they ignored each other's nonverbal relational messages, and were more concerned with defending themselves than being problem-oriented.

In contrast, satisfied couples view the whole process differently. They see conflict as healthy and something that they need to face.[15] They may argue vigorously, but understand that they need to stay tuned into where the other person is and what that person is thinking. They use some form of active listening to do this. Finally, they are willing to admit their mistakes and not insist on their view.[16]

INTERVENTION TECHNIQUES

Research has produced a list of general methods used in managing conflict: forcing, withdrawal, smoothing, compromise, and confrontation/problem solving.[17] Briefly, they involve the following:

1. *Forcing*—using power to cause the other person to accept a position; each party tries to figure out how to get the upper hand and cause the other person to lose.

2. *Withdrawal*—retreating from the argument.

3. *Smoothing*—playing down the conflict (differences) and emphasizing the positive (common interests) or avoiding issues that might cause hard feelings.

4. *Compromise*—looking for a position in which each gives and gets a little, splitting the difference if possible. Both parties lose some and gain some.

5. *Confrontation/problem solving*—directing energies toward defeating the problem and not the other person; encouraging the open exchange of information. This is the best solution for all: the situation is defined, the parties try to reach a mutually beneficial solution, and the situation is defined as win-win.

Each of these strategies for managing conflict has a likely outcome. Filley has provided us a useful way to classify these techniques according to their outcomes.[18] Some are win-lose methods, in that one person seems to win and the other seems to lose. Others are lose-lose methods, and one is win-win. Let's see how the strategies are classified when we look at them based on the most likely outcome.

OUTCOMES OF INTERVENTION TECHNIQUES

Win-Lose Techniques

Two methods are classified as *win-lose techniques,* that is, one person will win, and the other person will lose.

Forcing is usually a win-lose strategy. It uses power (or perhaps majority rule in the case of a group) to cause the other person to accept a goal. The loser is forced to abandon her goal. Often the mechanism for keeping the other person in line is the "good loser ethic"—it is not nice to complain when the majority votes against you.

Most of us are willing to accept forcing to manage conflict in such a situation when a majority vote is the result of deliberation. We are even willing to accept the decision of our boss if it seems equitable. However, we generally do not feel comfortable with forcing in an interpersonal relationship in which we view the other person as an equal. Forcing strategies under these circumstances can damage the relationship.

Withdrawal may not seem as if it involves conflict at all since this method does not necessarily involve direct communication. But in most cases of withdrawal, there is some nonverbal communication, maybe some interpersonal communication, and certainly intrapersonal conflict on the part of the person who retreats. The winner wins because the loser, by withdrawing, gives permission to the other person to proceed.

Often the loser resents the winner because the loser believes she was forced into withdrawal. The force that brought about the retreat may have been a fear of the consequences of voicing a difference. Thus, to avoid an uncomfortable feeling or perhaps potentially significant damage to the relationship, one person withdraws and allows the other to have what she wants. In either case, damage may have been done to the relationship. The damage arises if resentment is caused in this process. Resentment causes dissatisfaction that might lead us to look for and emphasize the differences between the other person and ourselves. This emphasis can produce further dissatisfaction as we begin to think that we do not have as much in common with this person as we once had.

Lose-Lose Techniques

With *lose-lose techniques,* both people give up something. Two such methods are frequently applied to manage conflict in interpersonal relationships.

Smoothing falls into the lose-lose category because we usually settle nothing when we use it. Sometimes we can "bury the hatchet," but this is not often the case. More frequently, one or both parties continues to suffer intrapersonal conflict. Sometimes the intrapersonal conflict becomes so intense that we decide to bring up the difference again.

Buried, unresolved issues generally do not promote relational health. The resulting tension is often hard to ignore. Resentment can build when we believe that we cannot talk about certain things with another person. For those who feel this tension due to smoothing, a more productive strategy for managing conflict may be available.

Withdrawal often involves nonverbal communication.

Sometimes a person in a relationship will get greater satisfaction from a conflict-free relationship than from the resolution of a difference and the release of tension associated with managing it. Smoothing is a viable option for this person.

Compromise is viewed as a lose-lose method because both parties have to give up something. They may not manage the issue to either person's satisfaction. We do not often think of this method as a lose-lose strategy because each party voluntarily agrees to give up something. If each gives up a fair share, they may feel they have reached an equitable agreement. This is often satisfying.

Genuine compromise can promote growth in our interpersonal relationships. Most of us realize that we will have differences that cannot be resolved so that the goals of both people can be met. However, it is satisfying to know that the other cares enough about the relationship to be willing to compromise. See if a win-win strategy might work before deciding that compromise is necessary.

Win-Win Technique

The alternative to these win-lose and lose-lose conflict management strategies is the *win-win technique* of confrontation/problem solving.

Confrontation/problem solving is practiced when we bring a problem out in the open and try to use a joint problem-solving approach. This problem solving may take one of two forms. If the parties are not too far apart in their positions, they may merely need to focus on the goals and sort through the information each of them has about the problem. In such cases, it may be relatively easy to reach an agreement. If, however, they are far apart on an issue, they may need to go through a more careful, step-by-step decision-making process. The important consideration here is to focus on the goals that each partner hopes to achieve, to reach an agreement, and then to work toward fulfilling the goals.

Talking about a conflict as a problem to be solved is a win-win approach to conflict management.

This kind of problem solving can produce satisfaction as we work through and successfully manage differences. We gain a sense that we are capable. We gain confidence and trust in the other person if the problem solving is handled supportively. You will learn how to follow this kind of strategy in the last section of this unit.

USING FORCING STRATEGIES

Mary Anne Fitzpatrick and Jeff Winke[19] examined how people address conflict in an interpersonal setting. They used the Kipnis Interpersonal Conflict Scale to determine factor categories and then provided representative tactics for each conflict strategy. Their results are shown in table 10.1

Notice that the first four strategies are related to forcing. The tactics involved in *manipulation* are attempts to use a particular behavior to get the other person in a good mood. Although such behavior

Table 10.1   Interpersonal Conflict Strategies and Representative Tactics

Strategy	Representative tactics
Manipulation	Be especially sweet, charming, helpful, and pleasant before bringing up the subject of disagreement.
	Act so nice that the other person does not want to refuse when you ask for your own way.
	Make this person believe that he is doing you a favor by giving in.
Nonnegotiation	Refuse to discuss or even listen to the subject unless the other person gives in.
	Keep repeating your point of view until the other person gives in.
	Appeal until the other person changes their mind.
Emotional appeal	Appeal to this person's love and affection for you.
	Promise to be more loving in the future.
	Get angry and demand that the other give in.
Personal rejection	Withhold affection and act cold until the person gives in.
	Ignore the other person.
	Make the other person jealous by pretending to lose interest.
Empathic understanding	Discuss what would happen if you each accepted the other's point of view.
	Talk about why you do not agree.
	Hold mutual talks without argument.

Source: Mary Anne Fitzpatrick and Jeff Winke, "You Always Hurt the One You Love: Strategies and Tactics in Interpersonal Conflict," *Communication Quarterly* 27 (1979): 7.

is an attempt to build a climate that will permit less open conflict, it is manipulative because it puts on a false image to achieve a particular end.

This strategy may not be particularly harmful to our relationships for it does not involve treating the other person badly. Obviously, when the other is sweet and charming, acting nicely, and seems to be doing you a favor, you may not mind giving that person what he wants. We all sense that we nourish a relationship by being helpful. This strategy can promote relational growth when the giving is not one-sided and the issues are not too important. Resentment can set in when we relent on an important issue in order to give the other person what she wants. Perhaps the other person will think that she is "forced" to give in because of the "obligation" created when the person is not nice.

The second strategy, *nonnegotiation,* avoids open confrontation either by refusing to discuss the issue unless certain conditions are met or by repeating a viewpoint until the other gives up. This strategy assumes that the other person will become so frustrated by the stalemate that he will give up to relieve the tension. This approach denies the other person's view by avoiding or ignoring the individual altogether. The attitude that the other person has no right to be in disagreement is often part of the tactic, too.

A strategy of nonnegotiation can be especially damaging to a relationship because it is disconfirming. It says, in effect, that the view of the other person is not important. Insistence on having your way implies superiority, thus creating an imbalance in the relationship that may not be acceptable to the other person. If someone won't negotiate, you might give him what he wants because you have no alternative at the moment. Or you may decide that the issue is more important than the relationship—at least, the relationship at that moment. You may engage in very hurtful behavior that may damage the relationship. On the other hand, you may just feel resentment and not engage in any hurtful behavior. Here, too, the relationship may suffer. In both cases, the communication has not promoted growth.

The strategy of *emotional appeal* relies on the use and abuse of the other person's affection. You may promise love and affection in return for achieving an end. One kind of emotional appeal is *displaying.* Its tactics include crying, pouting, or even venting anger to cause the other person to agree. An appeal might be, "If you really love me, you will give up studying for the test and go out to dinner with me." This is an attempt to force a viewpoint by demanding that you do what the person wants as a sign of affection.

In their least harmful form, strategies of emotional appeal are frustrating. It is difficult to know what to do or say when someone is pouting. This kind of behavior might not be damaging if it does not happen often. In contrast, behavior that says "You would really give me what I want if you loved me" can be damaging. Giving in to the other's demands is a cheap definition of love. This strategy may get us what we want but is likely to cause deep resentment if used regularly. Strategies of emotional appeal clearly can retard interpersonal growth.

Personal rejection is yet another forcing strategy. Fitzpatrick and Winke define this strategy as an "attempt to make their partner feel stupid, absurd, and worthless."[20] The message is "You are not good enough for me to love, to give my attention to, or to be interested in, unless you give in to me." Thus, this strategy involves such tactics as attacking the other person's self-worth to achieve an end. Differences are not usually managed using this method. Instead, if we get what we want, we usually do so at the expense of a damaged relationship. The relationship will heal if we care for each other and if we do not employ this strategy too often. Frequent personal rejection can seriously damage a relationship.

USING A CONFRONTATION/PROBLEM-SOLVING STRATEGY

Empathic understanding is the fifth and final strategy presented by Fitzpatrick and Winke. This is a cooperative method similar to what Burke has called confrontation/problem solving. It is a win-win technique in that we attempt to understand each other and to accept the other person's point of view. Empathic understanding coincides with Carl Rogers's and Jack Gibb's ideas of supportive communication described earlier in this book. It requires that you express your thoughts, needs, and feelings directly and clearly, without judging the other person. Thus, an assertive style of communicating is usually appropriate to a confrontation/problem-solving strategy. Remember too that this is a cooperative effort to manage a difference—both parties must be willing to give a certain amount.

The goal of confrontation/problem solving is to manage the conflict without damaging the relationship. You promote relational growth when you are able to do so. When using this strategy, discuss what would happen if you accepted your partner's view. Discuss why you seem to be disagreeing. Remain supportive. Avoid arguments based on personal opinion. You can learn to manage conflict in this way by carefully studying and implementing the plan we will present shortly.

TYPICAL USE OF INTERPERSONAL CONFLICT STRATEGIES

The title of the essay by Fitzpatrick and Winke, "You Always Hurt the One You Love: Strategies and Tactics in Interpersonal Conflict," summarizes their major discovery about use of conflict strategies: people hurt those they love. They use strategies that inflict pain more frequently than they use empathic understanding.[21] The people in their study who were involved in the most committed relationships were more likely to use emotional appeal or personal rejection to win their way than people who were less committed. People in less committed relationships were likely to use conflict avoidance techniques. They would divert attention by using a strategy of manipulation or nonnegotiation.

The apparent inconsistency in always hurting the one you love is simple to understand. The bonds of a committed relationship are strong enough to withstand the risk of destroying it altogether. Less committed people are more concerned about their relationship. Think of a committed relationship you are experiencing. For example, do you or your parents use these tactics in relating to each other? How do you work out differences? Compare your style in these relationships to that in your dealings with friends. Is there a difference? We think, if you're honest, you'll find that Fitzpatrick and Winke were right.

In examining tactics used with same-sex best friends, Fitzpatrick and Winke found that typical patterns for males differ from typical patterns for females. Men were more likely to use nonnegotiation strategies. Women use personal rejection, empathic understanding, or emotional appeals. Fitzpatrick and Bochner found that males rate themselves as more detached and controlling in their same-sex friendships.[22] Women, on the other hand, usually have greater social skill. Although generalizations, these may explain the differences. Nonnegotiation techniques do offer a greater degree of control. In contrast, the techniques women seem to favor require the social skill of empathy.

One annoying problem remains. Why is the empathic understanding strategy not the most frequently used tactic for managing interpersonal conflict? Although not substantiated by research, it may be that forcing tactics are viewed as more likely to be successful, easier, and less time-consuming than empathic understanding or confrontation/problem solving. Forcing tactics that avoid direct conflict, or those used most often when the relationship is less committed, allow the participants to think about what they want. They also allow each person to hold fast to a viewpoint.

This kind of behavior occurs in dating relationships. Suppose, for example, that you are dating a person who is so set in his or her beliefs that the person finds it difficult to acknowledge any other point of view. Perhaps the person will not even discuss an issue that you do not see in the same way. We suspect that you would pick the time to discuss such an issue very carefully and that you would be helpful and pleasant before bringing up such an issue. It is as though you hope your behavior will keep your friend from rejecting you and from being emotional.

Amazingly, people seem to think such efforts will be more successful than if they actually tried to understand the other person's viewpoint. There is irony in the statement: "If you understood the other's view, you might be forced to give up your own view in favor of one that seems more reasonable!"

A strong desire to maintain a committed relationship appears to be the factor that makes forcing successful. It is difficult to withdraw from such a relationship since most people do not want to experience the pain of breaking up. So, they give in to the other person's view. In most instances, the only casualty appears to be a slightly damaged relationship and pain for one or the other. The damage is usually short-lived, but what accounts for the high rate of divorce? Is there a connection? If so, learning and practicing an alternative strategy—empathic understanding or confrontation/problem solving—can be very useful.

MANAGING INTERPERSONAL CONFLICT

Confrontation/problem solving is a conflict *management* technique. It is not a conflict *resolution* technique. Management implies working with a conflict situation in a way that allows for a variety of solutions. Not all efforts will resolve a problem. Sometimes, in fact, differences cannot be settled satisfactorily. Understanding and empathy may be all that a pair can hope for. The following plan might resolve the difficulty. It might also lead to understanding the other's position in a way that allows for empathy. Either of these is a desirable alternative to hostility.

A Plan for Managing Conflict

1. *Begin by understanding your typical conflict management strategy and its consequences.* If you assume that your usual conflict behavior is not useful to you and if you want to change that behavior, you need to know what you are trying to change. Although this prerequisite seems obvious, people do tend to engage in conflicts over and over again, sometimes using the same language and the same behavior.

   For instance, a father and his son often experience conflict over the use of the family car. The father wants his son to be able to use the car, but he also wants the son to put some gas in the tank. And, of course, dad wants him to bring the car safely home by a reasonable hour. The son wants to use the car but knows that he is often short on cash. Sometimes he forgets the time and returns home after the gas stations are closed. Thus, the conflict episode between the father and the son over the use of the car often repeats itself.

   > "Dad, can I use the car tonight?" The son sees the muscles in his father's face tighten.
   >
   > "Uh . . . well . . . uh . . . Son, I want you to be able to use the car, but I want you to bring it in at a reasonable time. And I want to find gas in the thing in the morning." The father sees his son's posture tense.
   >
   > "OK, Dad." The son heads for the doorway.
   >
   > "Remember," says the father, "Come in at a reasonable hour. And put some gas in it." This sounded like a "zinger" to his son.
   >
   > The son turns, asking a question that guarantees the same old conflict: "What time is 'reasonable'?"
   >
   > "We've been all through that over and over." Dad is getting hot. "I think you know what 'reasonable' is. Can't

you take some responsibility for yourself?" That does it. Father and son have the same fight again.

The key to managing such conflict behavior begins with knowing what you actually do. Otherwise, it is impossible to *change* your behavior or to develop ground rules that might help you and the other person avoid the conflict.

Suppose that you and your best friend find that you often engage in the strategy of personal rejection. You treat each other to the "cold shoulder." You ignore each other when you engage in conflict. You might say to your friend, "It seems as if we tend to ignore each other when we are having a disagreement. When I do this, I feel frustrated afterward. I don't like the frustration. And besides, it doesn't seem to do anything for the problem. What do you think?" If the other person agrees, you might offer, "I suggest that we try to sit down and understand each other, instead of ignoring each other. Would you be willing to do that?"

If you can agree to a basic rule like this, you are well on your way to changing your conflict style. You may need to go further and establish other agreements. If, for example, either or both of you engage in emotional appeals, you may have to agree to hold these back, also. Of course, rules are broken and sometimes hard to follow, and you may not be totally successful in sticking to your agreements. Nevertheless, agreements are an important first step to successful conflict management.

2. *Agree upon general, overriding goals.* Each party in a conflict has a goal for any particular disagreement. This goal probably centers around gaining the other person's agreement. If a goal is the motivating factor in your current conflict style, you are more likely to engage in one of the forcing behaviors we described. If you wish to avoid forcing, you can begin by stating your goals for the relationship: "We want to understand each other's positions and talk in ways that show that we value each other." You can also set goals to counter your previous, unwanted conflict strategy: "We will sit and hear each other out. We will avoid the ignoring behavior we engaged in before."

> Agreement about an overall goal is a first step in helping you manage conflict.

Don't despair if you and your friend are unable to keep your new goals always in sight. Sometimes the habits you have depended upon in conflict situations are very well learned. Even a much desired goal can get lost in the shuffle of words during a conflict. You have to replace such a pattern with a new and more desirable behavior. If you find that you have difficulty keeping your overall goals in mind during conflict episodes, write them down, carry them with you, and refer to them frequently.

This mechanical device was once recommended to a friend who often engaged in conflict with his wife over the same things. At first he thought the suggestion was silly. But repeating a conflict episode again and again, especially one that left both him and his wife unhappy and that they didn't want to repeat, was even sillier. He agreed to introduce the idea to his wife that weekend. Three years later, this friend said that he and his wife always write down their goals when they are in conflict, then share these goals with each other, making copies for each one to keep, and bring them out each time they find themselves falling into the trap of habit. They still have conflict, but, reports the friend, they do not play the same old tapes over and over. Both he and his wife agree that their relationship has matured and grown.

3. *Allow each person to describe his or her position on the issue.* Each person needs to be as clear and specific as possible. Stating positions is important because this can resolve misunderstandings.

Suppose your friend had committed himself to helping you study for a geography exam but did not show up for the session. If you were a bit concerned about the outcome of the exam and if you needed two pages of his notes, conflict might develop:

> *You*: I am afraid to talk to you about this problem because I can't trust you anymore.
>
> *Your friend*: I am surprised that you say that. I think we need to talk. Can we agree to hear each other's side of this?
>
> *You*: OK. You promised to bring your notes over last night and to help me study for geography. I am sure that I didn't pass the exam today. You broke your promise.
>
> *Your friend*: I am really sorry about the test. I *am* willing to help you study, but I thought that I said that I would help you *if you wanted me to do so.* You didn't say anything, so I assumed that you didn't want help. I'm sorry.

Each person might go on to state the circumstances surrounding the conversation and the expected commitment, details that could be useful for future arrangements of this type.

The sample dialogue illustrates our point. If you believe your friend, it is clear that each of you had a different understanding of the commitment. Now you work out a way of being clearer about commitments. Perhaps your friend says, "Will you agree to call me next time something like this happens? I intend to do what I say I will. So if I fail to do it, it is because something beyond my control has happened or I do not understand what I am supposed to do."

4. *Engage in active listening.* Active listening encourages understanding because the other person must listen carefully enough to be able to repeat your position to you. You can also correct any apparent misunderstanding because you will hear the other person's interpretation of what you have said. Often errors in sensing and understanding surface when you take the time to use this kind of feedback. Remember that active listening has some real advantages, so try to incorporate it as a step in conflict management. (You may want to review some of our suggestions for active listening in Chapter 7.)

5. *Suggest a range of ways of approaching or managing the difference you are experiencing.* You force yourself to think of various perspectives when you name several approaches to managing a conflict situation. Many people get stuck in a particular definition of a situation and are unable to achieve the necessary flexibility for productive discussion. Give yourself the freedom to adopt different positions by forcing yourself to consider alternatives to your favored plan.

Consider also that your initial positions might be far apart. Other alternatives might be closer to what the other person can accept. When both persons are thinking of alternatives, you may be able to come up with some position that both are willing to accept. Win-win outcomes are related to discovering alternatives that allow both persons to accept the position without feeling as if it were necessary to give in to the other's position.

6. *Ask what would happen if each approach you have suggested were taken.* Visualizing the consequence of an action is an important step in making a decision. Sometimes what we are suggesting seems like it will work only because we have not thought of the implications. For example, a couple may decide that spanking children is not a

Table 10.2	A Plan for Managing Conflict

1. Begin by understanding your typical conflict management strategy and its consequences.

2. Agree upon general, overriding goals.

3. Allow each person to describe his or her own position on the issue.

4. Engage in active listening.

5. Suggest a range of ways of approaching or managing the differences you are experiencing.

6. Ask what would happen if each approach you have suggested was taken.

7. Implement the final plan by specifically stating who will do what, when, and where.

8. Assess the results of the implemented plan.

good idea. In practice, however, they find that this kind of physical deterrent is necessary to keep their eighteen-month-old from running into the street. An attempt to visualize the result of their decision may have led them to another alternative.

7. *Implement the final plan by specifically stating who does what, when, and where.* Commitment involves action. It is an important step to decide what action will be taken by whom. Equally important are when and where. Some plans never are begun because there is no commitment as to when or where to start. Set a time. Set a place. Set a time to talk again with each other about how the plan is going.

8. *Assess the results of the implemented plan.* Our ability to manage conflict is enhanced when we learn from our experience with it. We recommend that you assess the success of your efforts and use whatever you have learned from the process to enhance your conflict management ability. Of course, it would be best, particularly if the conflict took place within an ongoing relationship, to work on the evaluation process with the other person involved. The basic questions you will want to answer are: How successful was our attempt to manage this conflict? What, if anything, did we learn that will help us manage our differences in the future?

Finally, in all conflict situations, you should keep your relationship in mind. One way to do this is to remember to include statements about the relationship. For example, you might say, "I am feeling a little frustrated right now, but I know that we will be able to work out our differences. We have been good friends for a long time and have been able to settle problems." Or you might say, "I'm glad that we are able to talk about this without getting angry with each other." Comments like this make a positive statement about both you and the other person. They also help to keep the relationship at a conscious level. This can help both of you keep your differences under control so that you can avoid hurtful remarks.

When Agreement Is Not Possible

This is not a world of fantasy in which all differences can be managed through communication. Sometimes disagreements cannot be resolved. For example, one of the ongoing problems for some college students is a parent who is providing financial support and thus feels justified in imposing controlling behavior that treats the student as a child. Sometimes this relational problem is impossible to solve. Further discussion of the issue might only lead to a more impossible situation.

In cases like this, the decision to withdraw from the conflict may be the best answer. Avoid withdrawal, however, that is intended to hurt the other person. Some people part saying, "I am not going to listen to reason. I will move out and never see you again." This attitude says, "The conflict cannot be managed. The issue is impossible. The problem will never be solved. I will make sure of that by completely breaking off contact." This is both an unnecessary and an unfortunate announcement. Try to keep the communication channels open for the future. Saying, instead, something like: "It is clear that we can't agree on this. I love you, and because I do, I'm not willing to fight with you now." Then, try to change the subject. Or if you must walk away, find something positive to say to the other. "I'll be back soon. I just have to get away from this for a moment."

RELATIONAL CONFLICT

There are many signs that relationships are coming apart. Our alarming divorce rate attests to the difficulty many people experience in maintaining healthy, growing relationships. In fact, by 1998, one of every two marriages ended in divorce.[23] If it is assumed that people do not enter marriage expecting failure, we must also assume that they attempt to manage their relationships in ways that will make them work. So why do half of U.S. marriages fail? There is surely no simple answer to such a complicated question. Part of the answer lies in the fact that people do not understand the relational deterioration process and how to counter it. This section will help you understand this process and later we tell how to combat it.

We begin this section by discussing the major reasons that relationships stop working. Then we move to a description of the deterioration process. Finally, we will present several suggestions for managing the loss of a relationship.

WHY RELATIONSHIPS DETERIORATE

An attempt to discover why relationships deteriorate is a very ambitious undertaking. There may be nearly as many reasons as there are relationships.[24] However, the causes may be grouped into three general categories: loss of attractiveness, unfulfilled needs, and inability to manage differences.

Loss of Attractiveness

Attraction is based on physical attributes, social behavior, and task enjoyment. As time passes in our relationships, we discover that the physical attributes that originally caused us to engage have diminished. Loss of hair, added weight, changes in muscle tone, and lines in the face may all contribute to a different and less attractive appearance. Even though we may not want to admit it, research suggests that we emphasize physical appearance. When appearance slips, we may be less attracted.

Attention to the social presentation of self often changes as our relationship ages. We take extra care about how we present ourselves when we are courting a new friend. We make sure that we look just right. We are careful to be polite and observe all the social niceties. These are essential to nourishing the relationship during the initiating and experimenting stages. We drop some of this behavior as the relationship becomes more stable, when it moves to the "long-term" category. In a male-female relationship, this may mean not bothering to call when we will be late. We may give other people fewer signs and symbols of affection. All of these are significant indicators that the relationship has changed. We may accept these changes, or they may serve as proof that we are falling apart and thereby decrease attraction.

We may lose our attraction to our partner because we spend less time enjoying tasks together. This may occur because we have become busier now that our situation has changed. In a long-term, committed relationship such as marriage, we may take on professions and perhaps have children to raise. These tasks take time—time that we used to spend with our partner. Our interests may also diverge as we grow older. Our partner may not enjoy some new activity that we find interesting. We may find someone who does, which might contribute to our dissatisfaction with the troubled relationship. This development of separate activities reduces the stimulation that we can give each other and creates a feeling that we are different and that we are not receiving the kind of enjoyment we once did.

Unfulfilled Needs

We all enter relationships with expectations that the other person will fulfill our needs. Three of the more important needs are affection, inclusion, and control. We expect the other person to show signs of affection. If we are engaged in a sexual relationship, we have certain physical expectations. Display of affection is likely to change as a relationship becomes more commonplace. We take a person for granted and may no longer fulfill each other's needs.

We take each other for granted.

We have certain expectations about how we will be included in other people's lives. You may be disappointed if someone cancels a lunch appointment. You may usually spend Friday nights with your friend but find that he or she is with someone else. You may notice that your friend has become more involved in his or her work. This takes time from your joint activities.

You may also find that the time you spend discussing and structuring your lives changes as your relationship goes on. Perhaps you had engaged in mutual planning and decision making.

As time passes, physical attraction may diminish.

However, as relationships move beyond the initial stages, we make assumptions and take things for granted. As a result, the other person may feel that he or she has lost some control. This can be a source of dissatisfaction.

The reverse side of this problem is too much control. You may enjoy being seen as a pair of friends or as a couple. Yet some of us do not want to feel like we are owned. Such a feeling interferes with your need for controlling your own life. Ownership restricts your personal freedom. It may place demands on you that make you uncomfortable. For example, in a dating relationship, you might be told that you cannot have any other opposite-sex friends. You might even think that your friend resents time that you spend with same-sex friends. This problem is often characterized by language peppered with *my*—"*my* man," "*my* woman," "*my* wife," "*my* husband." Inappropriate intimacy claims often produce stress because they make demands that we cannot fulfill. All of us need stimulation from other friends. We cannot always find enough time to be with our friends. Unwillingness to be controlled in this fashion can be a source of considerable discontent.

Sometimes we begin to feel as though we own and are owned by the other.

Either we or our friend may turn to a third person to meet needs if they are unfulfilled. Of course, the likelihood that this will happen depends on whether these needs are strong enough to cause sufficient dissatisfaction to push us into new relationships. (We are likely to leave an existing relationship if we develop a new one in which our needs are more fully met.)

Inability to Manage Differences

Failure to manage our differences successfully is the final source of relational deterioration. Of course, a broad range of factors may create differences. Relational problems, financial problems, child-rearing problems, concerns over management of behavior problems, such as alcohol use, or even trivial problems related to doing various chores are some common sources of difficulty.

Ability to manage differences is related to three factors. First, we must have some level of commitment to be willing to put out the effort to manage the difficulty. Do you care enough? Is the relationship important enough? Strong commitment will push you to find ways to resolve your differences.

Second, we must know how to manage conflict productively. Many people do not. These skills for managing conflict can be learned, but knowing them will not guarantee success.

Third, we must practice conflict management skills. Success is related to a history of effective management in the relationship. Success yields greater confidence. Greater confidence yields a greater willingness to try to manage differences. It seems clear that people should become as skillful at managing differences as they can.

Each of the causes listed above creates some level of dissatisfaction in relationships. Relationships may begin to come apart if we do not manage them skillfully. What follows are two cases, taken from interpersonal communications literature, that illustrate what happens when partners begin to experience some of these problems and the accompanying dissatisfaction.

Many relationships slip somewhat during the process of evolving. Sometimes this happens intentionally. Of course, deterioration may also occur while we are totally unaware of what is going on. At still other times, we know a relationship is coming apart but either do not know how to stop it or are powerless to do so.

This section can be very helpful for two reasons. First, when you know the stages in the *deterioration* process, you will often find that you can reduce the chances of this happening without your awareness. Second, understanding this process and some of the options for reversing it can help you discover what to do when you want to counteract deterioration. You may thus be able to give new life to the relationship. These stages in deterioration can be reversed at any time and growth begun anew.

Case I: Kathy and Joe

Kathy and Joe had gone together during the year she was a sophomore and he was a junior. Both of them agreed that Kathy was the one who wanted to break up. She felt they were too tied to one another and that Joe was too dependent and demanded her exclusive attention. Even in groups of friends, he would draw her aside. As early as the spring, Joe felt that Kathy was no longer as much in love as he, but it took him a long time to reconcile himself to the notion that their relationship was ending. They saw less and less of each other over the summer months, until finally she began to date someone else. The first time the two were together after the start of the next school year, Kathy was in a bad mood but wouldn't talk to Joe about it.

The following morning, Joe told Kathy, "I guess things are over with us." Later, when they were able to talk further, he found out that she was already dating someone else. Kathy's reaction to the breakup was mainly a feeling of release—both from Joe and from the guilt she experienced because she was secretly dating someone else. But Joe had deep regrets about the relationship.

The loss of a relationship can cause feelings of grief and guilt.

For some months afterward, he regretted that they did not give the relationship one more chance. He really thought they might have been able to make it work. He said that he had learned something from the relationship but hoped he had not become jaded by it. "If I fall in love again," he said, "it might be with the reservation that I'm going to keep awake this time. I don't know if you can keep an innocent attitude toward relationships and keep watch at the same time, but I hope so." Meanwhile, however, he had not begun to make any new social contacts and instead focused on working through the old relationship, and in learning to be comfortable in her presence since Kathy and he sometimes see each other at school.[25]

Case II: David and Ruth

David and Ruth had gone together off and on for several years. David was less involved in the relationship than Ruth, but it is clear that Ruth precipitated the final breakup. According to Ruth, David was spending more and more time with his own group of friends, and this bothered her. She recalled one night in particular when *The Last Picture Show* was being shown in one of the dorms and they went to see it.

"I was sitting next to him, but it was as if he wasn't really there. He was running around talking to all these people, and I was following him around. I felt like his kid sister. So, I knew I wasn't going to put up with that much longer." When she talked to him about this and other problems, he apologized but did not change. Shortly thereafter, Ruth wanted to see a movie in Cambridge and asked David if he would go with her. He replied, "No, there's something going on in the dorm." This was the last straw for Ruth, and she told him she would not go out with him anymore. David started to cry, as if the relationship had really meant something to him, but at that point, it was too late. At the time we talked to her, Ruth had not found another boyfriend, but she said she had no regrets about the relationship or about its ending.

"It's probably the most worthwhile thing that's ever happened to me in my twenty-one years, so I don't regret having the experience at all. But after being in the supportive role. I want a little support now. That's the main thing I look for." She added, "I don't think I ever felt romantic [about David]—I felt practical. I had the feeling that I'd better make the most of it because it won't last that long."[26]

THE STAGES OF RELATIONAL DETERIORATION

The process of coming apart, commonly referred to as relational *deterioration*, can be represented in stages, which have been given various names. Here, we present the work of Mark Knapp[27] to illustrate how this process works. We have summarized the five stages with representative dialogue in table 10.3.

Differentiating

In *differentiating*, the first stage of deterioration, we make clear the differences we see in each other. In the later stages of the coming together process, the partners ignore their differences and focus on commonalities. They are preoccupied with creating new language patterns that show unity. Differentiating, however, represents a shift in the relationship's focus from the couple to the individual. If you perceive yourself as separate from the other person and the relationship, you gain the distance necessary to differentiate effectively. If you have "glossed over" important differences, these differences may resurface and become the subjects of conflict during the differentiating stage.

Signs of differentiation are the opposite of what we witness in the coming together. The "we," "us," and "our" language returns to "I," "me," and "mine." The shared possessions and friendships return to their "owners" or become less important. Conversation turns from the shared values, activities, and interests to questions

Table 10.3	Stages of Relational Deterioration
Stage	*Representative dialogue*
Differentiating	"I just don't like big social gatherings."
	"Sometimes I don't understand you. This is one area where I'm certainly not like you at all."
Circumscribing	"Did you have a good time on your trip?"
	"What time will dinner be ready?"
Stagnating	"What's there to talk about?"
	"Right. I know what you're going to say, and you know what I'm going to say."
Avoiding	"I'm so busy, I just don't know when I'll be able to see you."
	"If I'm not around when you try, you'll understand."
Terminating	"I'm leaving you and don't bother trying to contact me."
	"Don't worry."

Source: M. L. Knapp, *Social Intercourse: From Greeting to Goodbye* (Boston: Allyn and Bacon, 1978), 13.

about why we no longer share those values, activities, and interests. Too often, *why* isn't even asked. Rather than talk about our relationships, we privately dwell upon our awareness of them.

Circumscribing

If you are involved in a deteriorating relationship, you may engage in *circumscribing*. That is, you may tend to avoid both topics and intimacy because either might lead to self-disclosure. You may avoid the expected response by substituting some less appropriate topic for talk about your relationship. You can actually count a decrease in the number of your interactions, in the number of subjects you discuss, in the depth (intimacy) of those subjects, and in the length of the communications.[28] This is just the opposite of what occurs in the engagement process.

Knapp found that we try to avoid risky topics when circumscribing. But as the relational deterioration progresses, this becomes increasingly difficult to do. He points out that "any new topic becomes dangerous because it is not clear whether the new topic may, in some way, be wired to a previous area of static.[29]

Another characteristic of circumscribing is the lack of reciprocal behavior. While this is true of self-disclosure of all kinds, it is especially true of relational disclosure. The statement "I know we are not agreeing, but I want you to know that I still like you" may be met by a neutral statement or perhaps even by silence. A statement about a concern may be similarly met. For example, we might say, "I feel bad about our disagreement last night. Let's talk about it." The other person might either reply, "I don't want to talk about it," or meet the suggestion with silence. Either way, the effect is to isolate, cut off, and disconfirm the other—something we would not do if the relationship were healthy.

Stagnating

Stagnating, the third stage of deterioration, is characterized by motionlessness and inactivity. Silence in the other's presence is indicative of this stage. Even though you may be physically together, you close off verbal communication. But nonverbal messages are not so easily extinguished. The other person still detects discomfort and negation.

Silence means that something is happening in the relationship. We carry on conversations in our heads, imagining how the other would respond. We make judgments about the other person. Many of these are negative judgments, which lead to further resentment and separation. We rarely confirm these thoughts with the other person because we want to avoid the potentially negative outcome. We say to ourselves, "I really can't bring any of this up because I know just what will happen, and I'll feel worse if I try."

Avoiding

The *avoiding* stage begins the process of ending the relationship. In this stage, you might hear "Quit calling me. I don't want to talk to you anymore" or "Can't you see that it is all over? I don't even want to see you anymore." Statements can be as blunt as these, but they can also be quite subtle. For example, "I don't really have time to see you today" is avoidance. You might also hear "I'm sorry, but I really can't stay long." Sometimes avoidance is evidenced in an evasion, as with "I'm busy tonight." The other person then replies, "How about tomorrow?" That invitation is avoided with "I told my boss I'd work late." The person persists, "When can I see you?" The avoiding answer is: "I'll call you when I'm free."

Terminating

It is not clear that *terminating* is a stage at all. It seems to be more an ending point or announcement. People physically separate. They may move to different parts of town or perhaps different cities. At this point, the relationship is usually dead, and both parties know it. They want to acknowledge this fact publicly. Generally, some parting statement about expectations regarding contact is made. This might be "I want to make it clear that you are not welcome in my house" or "We'll stay in touch by phone about the children. But don't come over to the house unless you call and I agree."

The relationship is over. When there has been a lengthy commitment, there is usually a grieving period. As with physical death, people experience loss when a relationship dies. We will frequently go through a period of intense negative feelings and blaming. Although painful, this seems to be a necessary part of the healing process for many people.

WARNING SIGNS OF RELATIONAL DETERIORATION

John Gottman, who studied couple relationships for over twenty years, identified four key warning signs that signaled a troubled relationship.[30] These are:

1. Criticism: Attacking the other's personality or character rather than specific behavior, usually with blame and personal comments.

2. Contempt: Intending to insult and psychologically abuse the other person; contempt may be verbal or nonverbal.

3. Defensiveness: Denying responsibility, giving excuses, whining, repeating themselves, saying "yes, but."

4. Stonewalling: Withdrawal, not responding to the other person; becoming minimally engaged in the relationship.

Of course, nearly all couples experience some of these behaviors in their relationship. Yet, in Gottman's study the single best predictor of divorce is stonewalling. If all four warning signs are consistently present, there is a 94 percent chance the couple will divorce.

GENDER AND TERMINATING RELATIONSHIPS

Men and women are different when it comes to the ending of a relationship. Women tend to be more in tune with the relationship, so they often see the trouble before the men do. They are also more likely to initiate the termination of the relationship than men. Perhaps that is because of their sensitivity to the relational health.[31]

When men decide they want out of a relationship they behave in ways that women find totally unacceptable. This situation allows both partners to think they were the ones who initiated the breakup and therefore to save face. Men often see the later part of the breakup as more difficult, but the women saw the period just prior to making the decision the most difficult.[32]

MANAGING THE LOSS OF A RELATIONSHIP

All of us have experienced the end of a relationship sometime in our lives. When the overwhelming feeling is relief, the loss of a relationship does not usually cause us much problem. However, we may experience considerable loss if it was a close, long-term relationship. We may not have done what we thought we should to manage the differences that finally brought the relationship to an end. The result may be a feeling of some guilt.

Here, we do not address the issue of reversing this process, as that was a key topic of Chapter 8. Instead, our focus is on managing the feelings and circumstances associated with the end of a relationship.

Understanding and Coping with the Loss

The ending of a relationship can bring with it feelings of loss, emptiness, and loneliness. Perhaps you sit alone thinking about the times you had together. Thoughts may turn to sadness and then to depression.

Depression is a serious psychological problem. Usually the depression associated with the loss of a relationship is temporary. If it becomes debilitating, get professional help. Consider talking with a counselor or clergy friend. One task in coping with this loss and the feelings that accompany it is to find ways to fill the void. Dis-

Many people get satisfaction from being able to help their friends.

cover productive things to do during the time that you may have spent with this person. Avoid just sitting around. Idle time feeds such a depression. Feelings are related to the specific situation. You can change the situation by doing something else; you can eliminate or reduce your feelings of loneliness and depression.

Utilizing Your Support System

When we are grieving a personal loss, we often fail to realize that many people would be pleased to help. Who would not be willing to talk with and help a friend under similar circumstances? Consider who might be helpful. Some people seem to spend a lot of time being negative. In fact, Eric Berne described their behavior as playing a game called "Ain't It Awful."[33] Such people like to complain about their circumstances. Complaining has only limited therapeutic effect. It has a greater likelihood of making the situation seem worse. Our advice is to avoid these people.

Instead, turn to someone who can be positive. Many people get great satisfaction from being able to help their friends. Go to someone like this and describe your circumstances, to the extent you feel comfortable. Avoid dwelling on the negative: extremely negative statements may feed your doubts about yourself and others, instead of speeding the healing process.

Avoiding Reminders of the Relationship

When you are trying to move away from a hurtful relationship, encountering reminders of it does not help you redirect your focus. We recommend that you remove mementos of your relationship from your living space. Some people throw them away or burn them; resist this urge. You may feel differently about the situation later and wish you had these mementos. Avoid places where you spent time together. While you are attempting to redirect your attention, it helps you to enjoy other places.

Engaging in Healthy Self-Talk

Sometimes when our relationships fail, we think that we are partially to blame. When this happens, it is very easy to feel guilty. We think that we should have behaved differently, perhaps been more tolerant. We may feel inadequate. Such feelings can lead to unhealthy self-talk. We carry on a conversation in our head that leads to the conclusion that we are somehow unable to manage relationships, that we are inadequate. Negative self-talk does nothing to help us begin anew. Instead it is discouraging.

You can help yourself by engaging in positive self-talk. Recognize that you still have a number of successful relationships and that you even managed the failed relationship quite well for some time. You are a skillful, likable person. Remind yourself of your successes.

Beyond this positive self-talk, you can take other actions to help bolster self-esteem. Take a few minutes to assess activities in which you have successfully engaged. Perhaps they have included helping others. For some, the act of helping others is rewarding and an excellent ego builder; it also tends to be noticed by others. This gives you a chance to interact with people under pleasant circumstances.

Finally, we often gain a positive experience by treating ourselves well. This might mean doing something you really enjoy or buying something you have wanted for a long time. Such activities can be rewarding. They help us focus on the positive.

Learning from the Experience

Try to learn from experience. Although this is a difficult assignment, it is worth the effort. This book, or ones like it, can help you in this process.[34] You can engage in introspection and gain some insights. You can use the knowledge gained from studying interpersonal communication and gain even greater insights. As time passes, what you have learned can fade from your memory. Using this book as a handbook to troubleshoot problems in your relationships can help you discover how you might do things differently.

You may decide to model the relationships you are entering differently. You may try not to have the same expectations of the other person as you did in past relationships. You may also discover specific ways of encouraging growth in your relationships. You can learn a great deal about nourishing and maintaining relationships by carefully reading and taking some of the advice presented in this book. This chapter addresses the issue of promoting relational growth.

SUMMARY

Power is the influence one person has over another. It is based upon dependency. Power is relational because of this dependency; this means that the other person in a relationship must endorse—that is, submit to—your attempts to exercise power. Willingness to endorse attempts to use power depends on how the relationship is defined and how important the issue is. Commitment to maintaining the relationship also has a significant impact on power. Generally, the person who cares the least has the most power because that person is more likely to exit the relationship if wishes are not granted.

Power has six bases or sources. It may come because we admire a person and are therefore trying to please—referent power. It may be a function of some superior knowledge—expert power. Sometimes, someone's office or position gives that person a recognized right to control the other person—legitimate power. Power can also come from being able to reward or punish—reward power or coercive power. Finally, power can be a result of having significant information and being able to use it to persuade—information/persuasive power.

The exercise of power has both costs and benefits. Generally the use of power connected with arousal of negative feelings leads to undesirable side effects. Coercion can lead to decreased effort, martyrdom, and increased antagonism and hostility. Costs can also be incurred when expert power is used. We make others experts in the particular area when we give information. Sometimes the given information is used as a basis of power by the receiver. The exercise of power also has its benefits. It provides greater control. In addition, reward power can produce a happier and more positive partner in our relationship. It also enhances the ability to use other kinds of power.

Finally, we described five kinds of power games. The first, ignoring the other person, involves pretending that the person does not exist, pretending not to hear what was said, or ignoring common courtesy and rights. Direct confrontation is the best way of countering this behavior. The second game, creating an obligation, is played when one person deliberately does something nice to obligate the other. Direct confrontation, along with saying you will not respond to this behavior, is the best response. Name calling is the third power game. To counter it, reject the other person's definition of the situation and suggest your own. A fourth game is expressing utter disbelief. It can be countered by standing your ground and asking the other person to explain. The final game, interrupting, can be countered by seeking cooperation in using polite behavior.

Interpersonal conflict takes place in both one-to-one and group settings. Sometimes this conflict is not useful, and sometimes it is functional. Functional conflict manages the situation without damaging the relationship. Nonproductive conflict often damages the relationship. People employ various strategies for intervention in such conflict.

Lose-lose and win-lose strategies are often not productive. Forcing strategies are win-lose methods that are frequently employed to manage conflict. The major forcing strategies are manipulation, non-negotiation, emotional appeal, and personal rejection. In close relationships, you most often use strategies that will hurt the other person and thereby allow you to gain your way. Withdrawal is another win-lose strategy, and smoothing and compromise are lose-lose strategies. Although some of these strategies may be appropriate in certain situations, they are generally not the best choice. An alternative strategy is confrontation/problem solving, a win-win strategy.

Relational deterioration is the weakening of the bonds that hold a relationship together. This may occur for a variety of reasons. Attraction for a partner may lessen because of changes in physical appearance, social presentation of self, or a decrease in the enjoyment experienced in doing tasks together. You may also find that your friend no longer fulfills your needs. There may be less affection and inclusion or problems may arise related to the amount of control you have in your relationship. Deterioration may also result from not being able to manage differences. You may have neither sufficient commitment to the other person and the relationship nor the necessary information and skills to make a serious attempt at managing problems.

Relational deterioration can be understood by knowing how the process progresses through its stages. First, we may focus primarily on *differentiating*, or noticing differences. Then we may engage in *circumscribing* behavior—we talk around certain uncomfortable topics. After this, we spend a great deal of time together in silence. This is described as *stagnating*. The silence becomes uncomfortable as we realize that the relationship is ending. We engage in *avoidance* during this stage. Successful avoidance moves us to the end, *terminating* the relationship.

We presented some suggestions for managing the loss associated with ending a relationship. Feelings of loss, emptiness, and loneliness may lead to depression. This can be alleviated by finding things to do, utilizing the support of your friends, and avoiding circumstances that remind you of the relationship. You can also try to engage in healthy self-talk by recognizing that you have been successful in other relationships and that you are a skillful and likable person. Helping others may increase your self-esteem, and you may also consider doing something positive for yourself. Finally, we recommended learning from your experience. After you have time to gain some objectivity, use your knowledge of interpersonal communication, with this or a similar book serving as a handbook, to discover how to improve future relationships.

DISCUSSION QUESTIONS

1. How does viewing power as relational affect your use of it?

2. We have suggested several endorsement factors that affect the willingness of a person to accept another's attempt to exercise power. Can you think of others?

3. What effect does the exercise of power from each of the six bases have on a relationship?

4. Consider the five power games discussed in this chapter. What strategies would you suggest for managing them? Have you experienced other power games? How could they be managed?

5. It has been noted that we frequently hurt the ones we love. Is this true in your experience? Why? How might you avoid this behavior?

6. Describe what you believe to be your most successful conflict management method. Would you describe this strategy as win-win, win-lose, or lose-lose? Why? Having studied this chapter, how satisfied are you with your method? What do you like about the method? What do you dislike?

7. Which of the intervention techniques suggested in this chapter would you be most comfortable using?

8. How does your method for managing conflict compare to those recommended in this chapter?

9. Why is so much time spent causing yourself and others pain when trying to manage conflict?

10. More than half the marriages in the United States end in divorce. Where do these relationships go wrong?

11. Suppose you were counseling young people who were engaged to marry. What advice would you give them with respect to avoiding relational deterioration?

12. This chapter has presented several suggestions for managing the loss associated with the ending of a relationship. Can you offer others?

ENDNOTES

1. An appreciation for the many relational contexts in which power is a concern can be gained from M. S. Hanna and G. L. Wilson, *Communication in Business and Professional Settings*, 4th ed. (New York: McGraw-Hill, 1998); and K. M. Galvin and B. J. Brommel, *Family Communication: Cohesion and Change*, 3d ed. (Glenview, IL: Scott, Foresman, 1990).

2. C. C. Manz and D. A. Gioia, "The Interrelations of Power and Control," *Human Relations* 36 (1983): 461.

3. W. D. Jacobson, *Power and Interpersonal Relations* (Belmont, CA: Wadsworth, 1979), 4.

4. J. R. P. French and B. H. Raven, "The Bases of Social Power," in *Studies in Social Power*, D. Cartwright, ed. (Ann Arbor, MI: Institute for Social Research, 1959), 150–167; B. H. Raven, C. Centers, and A. Rodrigues, "The Bases of Conjugal Power," in *Power in Families*, R. E. Cromwell and D. H. Olson, ed. (New York: Halsted Press, 1975), 217–234.

5. Raven. Centers, and Rodrigues, "Bases of Conjugal Power," 217–234.

6. French and Raven, "Bases of Social Power," 164.

7. K. Sheley and M. E. Shaw, "Social Power to Use or Not to Use," *Bulletin of the Psychonomic Society* 13 (1979): 257–260.

8. V. P. Richmond and J. C. McCrosky, "Power in the Classroom II: Power and Learning," *Communication Education* 33 (April 1984): 125–136; V. P. Richmond, L. M. Davis, K. Saylor, and J. C. McCrosky, "Power Strategies in Organizations: Communication Techniques and Messages," *Human Communication Research* 11 (Fall 1984): 85–108.

9. N. Miller, D. C. Butler, and J. A. McMartin, "The Ineffectiveness of Punishment Power in Group Interaction," *Sociometry* 32 (1969): 24–42.

10. J. L. Hocker and W. W. Wilmot, *Interpersonal Conflict*, 3d ed. (Dubuque, IA: Wm. C. Brown, 1991), 12.

11. M. Deutsch, "Conflicts: Productive and Destructive," in *Conflict Resolution Through Communication*, F. E. Jandt, ed. (New York: Harper and Row, 1973), 158.

12. D. A. Infante, A. S. Rancer, and F. F. Jordan, "Affirming and Non-affirming Style, Dyad Sex, and the Perception of Argumentation and Verbal Aggression in an Interpersonal Dispute," *Human Communication Research* 22 (1966): 315–334.

13. T. C. Sabourin, D. A. Infante, and J. E. Rudd, "Verbal Aggression in Marriages: A Comparison of Violent, Distressed but Nonviolent, and Nondistressed Couples," *Human Communication Research* 10 (1993): 245–267.

14. D. A. Infante, S. A. Meyers, and R. A. Buerkel, "Argument and Verbal Aggression in Constructive and Destructive Family and Organizational Disagreements," *Western Journal of Communication* 58 (1994): 73–84.

15. S. E. Crohan, "Marital Happiness and Spousal Consensus on Beliefs About Marital Conflict: A Longitudinal Investigation," *Journal of Science and Personal Relationships* 9 (1992): 89–102.

16. D. A. Canary, H. Weger, Jr., and L. Stafford, "Couples' Argument Sequences and Their Associations with Relational Characteristics," *Western Journal of Speech Communication* 55 (1991): 159–179.

17. R. Burke, "Methods of Resolving Superior-Subordinate Conflict: The Constructive Use of Subordinate Differences and Disagreements," in *Readings in Interpersonal and Organizational Communication,* 3d ed., R. C. Huseman, C. M. Logue, and D. L. Freshle, eds. (Boston: Holbrook Press, 1977), 234–255.

18. A. C. Filley, *Interpersonal Conflict Resolution* (Glenview, IL: Scott, Foresman, 1975).

19. M. A. Fitzpatrick and J. Winke, "You Always Hurt the One You Love: Strategies and Tactics in Interpersonal Conflict," *Communication Quarterly* 27:1 (1979): 3–11.

20. Ibid., 7.

21. Ibid.

22. M. A. Fitzpatrick and A. Bochner, "Insider and Outsider Perspectives on Self and Other: Male-Female Differences in the Perception of Interpersonal Behaviors," *Sex Roles* 7:5 (1981): 523–535.

23. Source: National Center for Health Statistics, Public Health Service, Washington, D.C.

24. See, for example, M. L. Knapp, *Interpersonal Communication and Human Relationships* (Boston: Allyn and Bacon, 1984), especially Part IV.

25. From *Divorce and Separation: Context, Causes, and Consequences,* G. Levine and O. C. Moles, Eds. Copyright © 1979 by the Society for the Psychological Study of Social Issues.

26. Ibid.

27. M. L. Knapp, *Social Intercourse: From Greeting to Goodbye* (Boston: Allyn and Bacon, 1978), 29–57.

28. Knapp, *Social Intercourse,* 24.

29. Ibid.

30. J. Gottman with N. Silver, *Why Marriages Succeed or Fail* (New York: Simon and Schuster, 1994).

31. S. W. Duck, *Understanding Relationships* (New York: Guilford, 1991).

32. G. O. Hagestad and M. A. Smyer, "Dissolving Long-Term Relationships: Patterns of Divorcing In Middle Age," in S. W. Duck, ed., *Personal Relationships 4: Dissolving Relationships* (New York: Academic Press, 1982).

33. Eric Berne, *Games People Play* (New York: Grove Press, 1964).

34. For an excellent additional resource, we suggest W. J. Lederer, *Creating a Good Relationship* (New York: Norton, 1984).

READ MORE ABOUT
INTERPERSONAL POWER IN THESE SOURCES

French, J. R. P. and B. H. Raven. "The Bases of Social Power." In *Studies in Social Power,* D. Cartwright, ed. Ann Arbor, MI: Institute for Social Research, 1959. 150–167; Raven, B. H., C. Centers, and A. Rodrigues. "The Bases of Conjugal Power." In *Power in Families,* R. E. Cromwell and D. H. Olson, eds. New York: Halstead Press, 1975, 217–237. These essays are primary sources on power and well worth reading.

Hocker, Joyce L. and William W. Wilmot. "Power in Interpersonal Conflict." In *Interpersonal Conflict,* 5th ed. New York: McGraw Hill, 1998. This chapter provides an easy-to-read extension of the ideas in this unit.

Korda, Michael. *Power! How to Get It: How to Use It.* New York: Ballantine, 1975. This excellent, popular, and well-written book provides an overview of power and issues surrounding its use.

READ MORE ABOUT
INTERPERSONAL CONFLICT IN THESE SOURCES

Canary, Daniel J., William R. Cupach, and Susan J. Messman. *Relationship Conflict.* Thousand Oaks, CA: Sage, 1995. This is a useful summary of the research on conflilct. It addresses a variety of relationships: friend–friend, child–parent, and romantic.

Jandt, Fred E. and Paul Gillette. *Win-Win Negotiating: Turning Conflict into Agreement.* New York: Wiley, 1985. This book presents a readable description of win-lose and win-win problem solving in a variety of contexts.

Kohn, Alfie. *No Contest: The Case Against Competition.* Boston: Houghton Mifflin, 1986. Kohn builds a case that competition is destructive, both for society and interpersonal relationships. He contrasts this with cooperation, which he believes makes people happier, more productive, and more secure.

Paul, Jordon, and Margaret Paul. *Do I Have to Give Up Me to Be Loved by You?* Minneapolis: CompCare, 1984. These marriage and family therapists seek to explain why couples fear and avoid conflicts. They show how couples can manage conflicts without giving up their own identities.

READ MORE ABOUT MANAGING RELATIONAL DETERIORATION IN THESE SOURCES

Bach, George R. and Peter Wyden. *The Intimate Enemy.* New York: Avon, 1968. This popular best-seller helps the reader understand destructive styles of managing differences in marriage. Bach and Wyden then describe the "fair fight" as a productive alternative.

Cahn, Dudley D. *Letting Go: A Practical Theory of Relationship Disengagement and Reengagement.* Albany, NY: State University of New York Press, 1987. This book looks at communication in various stages of relational development from a variety of relational perspectives: friends, married couples, supervisors and subordinates, and teachers and students.

11

ETHICS AND DIVERSITY

PREVIEW

Important growth-promoting aspects of our interpersonal relationships are that we be perceived as behaving ethically and respecting diversity. This chapter proposes six ethical standards against which we can measure communication behavior. White lies, equivocations, and evasions are examined in terms of these ethical standards. Ways we behave when we encounter a person who is different from us are explored, along with six guidelines to help a person communicate more effectively in these situations.

KEY TERMS

authenticity	culture
dialogue	diversity
empathy	equality
equivocation	ethics
face-saving lie	inappropriate humor
monologue	name calling
prejudging	stereotyping
white lie	

OBJECTIVES

1. Describe potential ethical dilemmas faced in maintaining our interpersonal relationships.
2. Cite and explain three general criteria for making ethical decisions in our relationships with others.
3. Describe ethical interpersonal behavior from a dialogic perspective.
4. Tell why complete honesty is not always possible in our interpersonal relationships.
5. Distinguish between lying and equivocal language.
6. Present and defend your position on the question, "Are white lies and equivocations an ethical alternative to absolute honesty?"
7. Describe the general nature of diversity in people.
8. Name and describe the four most common inappropriate approaches to communicating with diverse people.
9. Identify six guidelines for communicating sensitivity to diverse people. Apply these to your communication.

ETHICAL COMMUNICATION IN INTERPERSONAL RELATIONSHIPS

Concern about ethical behavior has risen dramatically in our country from the time of the Watergate scandal in the 1970s to the present day. *Time* magazine's May 1987 cover story seemed to capture the concern of average Americans when editors posed the question, "What Ever Happened to Ethics?" *Time* went on to report that legal and ethical charges were leveled against more than one hundred members of the Reagan Administration. (In fairness, it must be noted that all charges did not result in indictments.)

Further evidence of this rising skepticism about ethical practices appeared approximately two months earlier in *U.S. News & World Report* (February 23, 1987). A survey of the U.S. public conducted by *U.S. News* and Cable News Network found that more than half of the respondents believed people to be less honest than they were ten years earlier. Seven out of every ten of those surveyed were dissatisfied with the current state of honesty as they perceived it—the largest portion since Watergate.

Ethical behavior continues to be a concern in the United States. In one four-month period in 1989, for example, the *New York Times Index* included ninety-nine different subtopics under the general topic of ethics. During that same period, a total of 420 articles were referenced under these subtopics. We conclude that ethics is an important issue that pervades every facet of our lives. It requires our careful attention if we are to be responsible in our relationships. The purpose of this unit is to examine what it means to be ethical in our interpersonal relationships. Opportunities to make ethically responsible decisions abound in our daily lives. Consider just a few of the many possible situations that might confront you on any particular day. For example, on the job, what do you do with company time? Do you arrive at work on time if nobody is clocking you in? Do you use an hour or so during the work day to take care of some personal business without asking the boss? How about lunch time? Do you stay away from your work longer than you ought? Many people do not even realize that such questions are ethical questions.

Decisions we make about how to handle the truth in our relationships provide additional examples. Perhaps you have been involved in a work project to a limited degree. The boss does not fully understand your level of involvement. She compliments you for the key role you have played. Do you explain your role as a lesser one and correct the impression? Suppose, again, you hear a person say something about a friend that you know is not true. It is awkward for you to counter the remark. You have the choice: don't say anything or endure the awkwardness. Consider another example. Sue, a classmate, seems to be creating real disharmony in your class. If someone from outside the class asks you about the situation, will you answer honestly? What would you do if an honest answer would harm Sue's reputation around campus?

As a final example, suppose at work you might be able to pull some kind of a trick and gain an advantage over a fellow employee. Do you do so, even though you are uneasy about this kind of behavior? Or do you avoid the possibility of engaging in questionable behavior?

We could provide example after example of decisions we are each forced to make every day that involve ethical considerations. Remember the parlor game called "Scruples" that was very popular during 1989 and the early 1990s? The fun of the game was guessing, then discovering, how other people would handle ethical dilemmas. We think the foregoing examples are sufficient to show the impact and widespread nature of ethical issues we all face.

We begin our discussion of ethics by defining the term. Next, we present three general principles of ethics. This is followed by specific application of ethics to our interpersonal relationships. Finally, we look at the ethics of white lies, equivocation, and evasion.

ETHICS DEFINED

Ethics are a body of principles (or values) regarding good and bad, right and wrong conduct that guide a person in socially acceptable motives and actions within a particular context.[1]

GENERAL PRINCIPLES OF ETHICAL BEHAVIOR

Gary Kreps[2] presents three general criteria for making ethical decisions that are useful in a wide range of situations: (1) honesty, (2) avoiding harm, and (3) justice. Let's look at each of these principles.

1. *People should not intentionally deceive one another.* Very few of us would be willing to argue against an honesty principle. But absolute adherence to candor might very well be damaging. And so, while we would be unlikely to argue against such a principle, many of us cannot always live by it. We know more about most situations than mere facts. We know how we feel, what we want, and our images of other people and situations, for example. We might even believe that telling the mere facts would mean deceiving the other person. Do we tell just the facts? Or do we go beyond the facts and add our opinion, which we believe to represent the truth? Do we present our opinion as opinion, or do we present it as fact?

   This principle suggests more than honesty in what we say, though. We have a responsibility to check out our inferences *before* we discuss the issues involved with others. If we have not checked or cannot check out our judgments, then we have the responsibility to be clear that what we are saying is our opinion, rather than facts.

2. *People's communication should not purposely harm any other person.* This principle suggests that people have the responsibility to assess the harm that may befall others as a result of their communication. But what kind of assessment of harm are we talking about? Suppose a colleague is stealing from your organization. Perhaps she is regularly claiming expenses for reimbursement that she has not incurred. You are aware of the theft on a couple of occasions because you are working together on the same project and have seen her expense paperwork. Is it ethical for you to say nothing because what you say may harm the person? Most of us would think that we have a responsibility to tell the truth, particularly if asked. We might also think we have a responsibility to speak to the coworker. So, assessment of all aspects of this situation would dictate our action.

   On the other hand, we often have occasion to say things about others that do not need to be said. And sometimes we might make statements of which we are unsure. Certainly in such cases, the principle of purposeful harm applies. To speak out when we are unsure would be unethical because it would harm another person.

3. *People should be treated justly.* The interpretation of justice obviously varies from one situation to another. For example, in one organization, executives may be permitted to take their privately owned vehicles to the company motor pool for servicing. Another organization may not allow this. So, behavior that

might be seen as unjust in one organization may be considered just in another—a fringe benefit, a perk, of higher status. Justice or fairness may have a different meaning for different situations. So, to be ethical, we must make an informed judgment about what is just within a particular context.

The justice principle helps us apply Principle 2, the harm rule. Justice may dictate telling the truth even when telling may produce harm. For example, justice would dictate telling what you know about a person accused of cheating on an exam. Principle 2 says you should not purposely harm a person, but Principle 3 calls for justice.

These basic guidelines offered by Kreps provide a good foundation for developing ethical standards. We look now at ethics in interpersonal relationships to deepen our understanding.

INTERPERSONAL ETHICS

You are likely to communicate ethically if you think about interpersonal communication events as *dialogues.* Charles T. Brown and Paul Keller developed this idea in their book, *From Monologue to Dialogue.*[3] A *dialogue* is a communication event in which each participant understands himself or herself as both speaker and listener. Dialogue can be characterized in two ways: it is fundamentally empathic, and it is fundamentally authentic.

In contrast, a *monologue* is a communication event in which one or both participants focuses upon their own feelings, attitudes, and ideas, without particular regard for the other person. Thus, monologue is essentially a one-way communication event.

Empathy suggests an attempt to identify with the other's experiences, feelings, and problems and to affirm the other's self-worth. Thus, to communicate ethically in an interpersonal event is to respect the other's right to a position, to think of the other person as worthy, and to encourage the other's free choice.

Authenticity suggests an attempt to present oneself as direct, honest, and straightforward in communicating feelings and information. This is not to say that everything is communicated; it means that we communicate what is relevant and legitimate.

Applying the above components inherent in dialogue, we see that ethical behavior in an interpersonal communication event is both empathic and authentic. An ethical person assumes the responsibility to share in the communication process as both sender and receiver. An ethical person tries to understand the other's point of view and to empathize with the other as much as possible to encourage the other's ability to make free choices. An ethical person tries to present information accurately and candidly.

Three principles of interpersonal ethical communication emerge from this perspective:

1. *Ethical communication shows respect for the other person.*
2. *Ethical communication shows respect for the other person's ideas.*
3. *Ethical communication encourages (or at least does not inhibit) another person's ability to make free choices.*

Following these principles leads to three specific behaviors. First, *respect of a person and his or her ideas suggests that lying and distortion of facts and figures are not generally ethical behaviors.*

Second, *respect for the person's ideas also suggests that we behave in such a way that the other person feels free to disagree with us if his or her position is different from ours.* To accomplish this, we must often maintain an attitudinal perspective of *equality.* This means that we attempt to minimize differences between us and the other person in status, power, and intellectual ability, for example.

Third, *preserving the other's free choice requires refraining from extreme emotional appeals.* If we use tactics that create strong emotional reactions—perhaps a strong fear appeal, such as threatening dire consequences, or a strong emotional threat, such as withholding affection—we are not behaving ethically. Manipulative strategies of all kinds restrict the other person's choice and, within this perspective, fall into the area of questionable interpersonal ethical behavior.

WHITE LIES, EQUIVOCATION, AND THE ETHICS OF EVASION

Most of us realize that complete honesty and openness in our relationships can be quite damaging. There are no easy answers to finding acceptable alternatives, however. Given this, we think that you might find exploring the issue of white lies, equivocation, and the ethics of an evasion quite useful.

We can all think of situations where we make a decision to stretch the truth or avoid saying something in order to protect another person from the hurt that what we might say could cause. Suppose, for example, that you are attracted to your best friend's spouse or perhaps the person he or she is dating. Would you say so if your friend asked you directly? Most of us would try to avoid saying so because doing that might strain our relationship with our friend. Consider another example. A friend just paid a big price for a new outfit. She asks you what you think. You think it looks awful on her. Do you tell her? Most of us would find some tactful way to duck out of telling her exactly what we think.

We do not present these situations in order to build a case for lying to our friends and others around us but only to point out that total honesty can be very hurtful in particular circumstances. Most of us would like to avoid situations like these but find that an impossible task. So, we select between the two alternatives: white lies or equivocation.

White Lies

Lying is an intentional attempt to hide or misrepresent the facts of a situation by telling or leading someone to believe something that is not true. Lies are often told to protect ourselves from a damaging consequence we would experience if we were to tell the truth or to gain some unfair advantage over another person.

White lies are defined by those who use them as lies told without malicious intent and often with the intent of protecting the other person who might be hurt if he or she were told the truth.

It may be impossible to know how often white lies are told, but we do know that they are used often enough to have become a subject of study. One group of researchers, R. E. Turner and associates, asked 130 subjects to keep a record of the truthfulness of things they said in everyday communication.[4] One interesting finding is that only about a third of these people reported themselves as being totally honest. The other two-thirds encountered one or more circumstances where they chose to tell a lie.

This study also sought to help us understand how people account for lying. Five reoccurring reasons emerged for their lying.

1. *To save face.* We often think of lying under certain circumstances as merely exercising tact. We wish to prevent either our own or the other person's embarrassment. In fact, over half of the recorded lies of the 130 subjects of Turner's study were justified by this reasoning. This kind of behavior has been labeled "tact;" the dilemma is described by one researcher: "It would be unkind to be honest but dishonest to be kind."[5]

   Face-saving lies can be told to protect the teller, the receiver of the communication, or both. For example, if somebody comes up to you at a party and seems to know you, you may pretend that you recognize the person, even though you do not. You are protecting yourself from the embarrassment of not remembering and the other person from the embarrassment of being forgotten. Face-saving lies are also told to cover up mistakes we have made, perhaps blaming the problem on circumstances. You might say, "I've just not been able to find a time when all our committee members can meet," when the truth is that you have not gotten around to arranging a meeting time.

2. *To be seen as a polite member of society.* Some lies are told in order to be polite to others. You may not actually like to be around particular people; nevertheless, you are quite pleasant in your interactions with them. You might agree to lunch with a colleague when you do not really want to be with that person. Yet,

as you part company after lunch, you say how much you enjoyed having lunch with the person. At a dinner party, you might say that you liked the main dish the host served, even though you actually did not.

3. *To avoid tension or conflict.* Sometimes we will tell a lie to avoid anticipated unpleasant reactions from others if we were to tell the truth. Suppose a friend makes an unkind remark in criticism of you. You may make a joke of it, as if you do not mind, when you actually do. Or if you do react honestly and your friend notices, you might lie to avoid the confrontation. Perhaps you will pass off your irritation with "I didn't get much sleep last night. Sorry I'm so sensitive."

4. *To gain power.* We may see telling a lie as an opportunity to misrepresent the situation and gain more power. We might, for instance, exaggerate our expertise to gain an important assignment at work. Or we might tell a person we want to call us for a date, "Don't expect me to be waiting around for you to call," when we know that is exactly what we will be doing. We may also claim involvement or interest in something in order to gain confidential information.

5. *To increase or decrease engagement in relationships.* We may claim, for example, that we enjoy boating because we know the other person does. We may pretend that we want to help a person, perhaps by offering a ride, when we would rather not do so. We might compliment a friend on his or her new clothes, even though we think our friend looks ridiculous. We might also tell lies in order to reduce our contact and engagement with another person. When asked to attend a party Friday night, we might say we are busy when we are not. We break off a casual conversation in the hall by saying, "I really have to go," when we know that we are not in a hurry to be anywhere. A teenager might break off a steady dating engagement by saying, "I really do enjoy being with you, but I think I need to date lots of different people." The fact probably is that the teenager wants to disengage from the relationship but does not want to tell the truth.

These five categories of white lies help us gain a picture of the motivations for lying. The picture seems most often to be a harmless one, with little clarity as to who is gaining the most from this practice. Researchers have sought to shed some light on this issue.

One study reported that two out of every three lies have a "selfish reason" as their underlying motive.[6] Another piece of research conducted by Carl Camden and associates addressed this issue.[7] These researchers categorized lies by their basic purpose and the party the lie benefited. Table 11.1 displays their data. Notice that the majority of the lies (75.5 percent) were told for the benefit of the teller. Only 22 percent were told for the benefit of the other party, while 2.5 percent were for the benefit of a third party.

Table 11.1   Purpose of Lies Told and Party Benefited

	Benefit self	Benefit other	Benefit third party
Basic Needs	68	1	1
A. Acquire resources	29	0	0
B. Protect resources	39	1	1
Affiliation	128	1	6
A. Positive	65	0	0
1. Initiate interaction	8	0	0
2. Continue interaction	6	0	0
3. Avoid conflict	48	0	0
4. Obligatory acceptance	3	0	0
B. Negative	43	1	3
1. Avoid interaction	34	1	3
2. Leave-taking	9	0	0
C. Conversational control	20	0	3
1. Redirect conversation	3	0	0
2. Avoid self-disclosure	17	0	3
Self-Esteem	35	63	1
A. Competence	8	26	0
B. Taste	0	18	1
C. Social desirability	27	19	0
Other	13	5	0
A. Dissonance reduction	3	5	0
B. Practical joke	2	0	0
C. Exaggeration	8	0	0

Source: C. Camden, M. T. Motley, and A. Wilson, "White Lies in Interpersonal Communication: A Taxonomy and Preliminary Investigation of Social Motivations," *Western Journal of Speech Communication* 48 (1984): 315.

If the 75.5 percent makes you think that we are a nation of self-serving liars, we urge you to think of this in terms of other kinds of interpersonal communication. Most intentional communication has the goal of achieving the speaker's goal, rather than to directly serve the goals of the other person. So, it is not surprising that self-benefit is also a predominate goal of lying behavior. It turns out that if we look at behavior that denies something of the other person in favor of self, then only 111 lies (34.5 percent) fall into the selfish category.

Equivocation

Equivocation, avoiding a direct answer through use of ambiguous or unclear language, is an option that many of us take when faced with choosing between a lie and telling an unpleasant truth. We are all familiar with the situation where we are asked what we think of another's new outfit when our evaluation of it is less than positive. Rather than say what we think about it, we may say, "I think it really fits you." We have avoided telling a lie or unpleasant truth by answering a different question altogether. In this case, we have avoided embarrassment but have not given the other person the positive stroke he or she may have desired.

Dodging a question with an equivocal communication often turns out to be risky. If the other person is persistent, we may find ourselves back where we were to begin with. Thus, we may be forced to tell the truth or lie. On the other hand, equivocation has the advantage of avoiding the pain of being caught in a lie if our attempt to lie is discovered and pursued.

It turns out that most of us are likely to select equivocation over telling a lie when given the choice. Bavelas's research found that given the option of telling a face-saving lie, the "harmful" truth, or choosing equivocation, only 6 percent of the subjects chose the lie. Of the remaining subjects, 4 percent told the painful truth and 90 percent chose equivocation.[8]

The Ethics of Evasion

What can we conclude from our discussion of white lies and equivocation? Are these behaviors that research says so many of us use ethical? Our answer may seem to be an equivocation in itself because we cannot directly answer this question for you. If you apply the criteria we developed, white lies and equivocal behavior do meet most of the standards. Most of the time, these behaviors

1. do not purposely harm another person,
2. treat others justly,
3. show respect for the other person,
4. show respect for the other person's ideas, and
5. do not inhibit the other person's ability to make free choices.

The criterion these behaviors do not meet is the one that states: "People should not intentionally deceive one another." Perhaps a decision about whether a particular white lie or equivocation has created an ethical problem lies not in the truth but in whether the behavior is really in the interest of the receiver and whether this behavior is the only viable way to manage the situation.

DIVERSITY

According to the U. S. Census Bureau information from 1990, America's racial and ethnic distribution was about as indicated in table 11.2. The numbers do not total 100 percent because some people do not give their racial identity, while others give more than one response.

Table 11.2 U. S. American Racial and Ethnic Distribution	
American Indian	0.8%
Asian	2.9%
Black	12.1%
White	80.3%
Other and unknown	3.9%
Hispanic (may be any race)	9.0%

The year 2000 census will undoubtedly show a shift in these figures. The percentage of Whites will fall as the percentage of other groups—especially Black and Hispanic groups—increases.

Diversity Defined

Diversity refers to difference and variation.

We use the term *diversity* to refer to difference and variation. In this sense, racial diversity refers to different races. Ethnic diversity refers to different ethnic groups. Gender diversity refers to females and males. Age diversity refers to differences in age groups. To say the least about it, the human race is diverse.

The Difficult Side of Diversity

The problem with such diversity is that people, generally, are highly sensitive to their own uniqueness, and, unfortunately, too often ignorant about and insensitive to other people's uniqueness. This insensitivity often results in damage to others.

To illustrate, U.S. American people are not generally sensitive to the kinds of diverse families that exist in the United States. The mass media continue to assume—and foster—the extended family unit as an ideal, but with little regard for the harm this brings to people who do not fit that stereotype.

How many different kinds of families there are in our society! There are couples without children, for example. Why would it necessarily be the case that a childfree couple should be pitied? Many couples are voluntarily childless. In U.S. American society there are also one-provider families and two-provider families. There are previously married single parents and never-married single parents. There are custodial parents, divorced parents, and stepparents. There are cohabiting-couple parents. There are homosexual partners, many of whom are parents. There are married couples who live great distances apart, and whose marriages might be called "commuter marriages." There are families with three or more generations of one family linked to and sharing their lives with two or three generations of another family. Thus, we can find enormous diversity in family structures.

The differences in structure almost certainly imply different sex roles, different messages about marital devotion, about authority, about sexuality, and the like. How can anyone assume that their own particular situation, with the consequent default settings that situation implies, fits all? And yet, we often act as though everyone's family is just like ours.

When we interact with people who are more obviously different from ourselves—people who look and act differently, who do not share our basic cultural, racial and ethnic assumptions and beliefs—problems can arise. We may find it difficult to read the nonverbal cues, so we are uncertain about what others are thinking or feeling. We aren't sure what others expect of us, or we of them, and so we feel suspicious. We may be reluctant to speak to people who are different, or even feel afraid the other person will take offense to something we say or do inadvertently.

Differences Do Make a Difference

Indeed, some people are so different from us that we may find them hard to understand and difficult to like, or even accept. If we could only learn to tap into the enormous resource of skill, insight, and ability such differences represent we could generate a whole new world of creative ideas. But too often, instead, we choose to stand back and stare.

Some people are so different that we find it difficult to accept them.

Biology Makes a Difference

No one comes close to being exactly like anyone else, not even identical twins. Skin, body shape and type, hair texture, eye color set us apart. Gender sets us apart, too, in both physical features and in attitudes, beliefs, and values. Thus our identities as men and women, our self-concepts, and how we've learned to respond are part of our personal perceptual filters. To see the world as a woman is to see it from a feminine point of view. In a male-dominant society, the feminine point of view may very well cause a woman to allow herself to be dominated. She may not even be able to imagine an alternative. From the masculine point of view in a male-dominant society, men may not see anything wrong with dominating, or attempting to dominate the women in their acquaintance. More basically, they may not even be aware of their tendency to do so. Indeed, so much is this the case that, in U.S. American society, gender equity has become a very potent political issue.

Culture Makes a Difference

The term, culture, refers to the way people live their lives. Put another way, the term refers to the ways people learn to solve their problems. Culture tells us what makes sense. It binds like-minded people

Culture make a difference.

together. It provides guidelines for values, beliefs and behaviors. It produces a common language, then flows from that language to create tastes, habits, preferences and perspectives on the world. Culture tells us who "we" are (the ingroup) and who "they" are (the outgroup.)

This idea of ingroups and outgroups may be very helpful to you. The ingroup is whatever group you belong to. Anyone who is not in that group is part of the outgroup—a dichotomy that is true for everyone.

Consider what being part of the ingroup or outgroup does to your way of thinking about and relating to others! If you are a member of the majority group you may think of yourself as someone who treats other people's cultures with respect. You probably believe you treat everyone fairly and equally. And yet, people in the majority group are often accused of being insensitive and prejudiced. If you are a member of a minority group you may well have difficulty "reading" situations—especially tense situations. You may feel people don't take you seriously or that they "put you down." Since anger and hostility can flow from such feeling, you may also exhibit prejudiced behavior toward the majority.

COMMUNICATION AND DIVERSITY

From a communication perspective, a culture is a set of rules that apply when we talk with each other. Such rules fall into six overlapping categories: (1) etiquette, (2) values, (3) language, (4) traditions and customs, (5) food, dress, artistic tastes, and (6) belief system/world view. Thus the culture controls how we think about age, social class, religion, gender, even sexual orientation, and what is appropriate behavior. If the culture sanctions the behavior, then to the ingroup, the behavior is appropriate. If the culture censures the behavior, then to the ingroup the behavior is inappropriate. If you are not a member of the ingroup, however, there could be problems!

Culture controls how we think about age, social class, religion, gender, and sexual orientation

Remember—we are all members of one or more in groups.

Some Approaches are Inappropriate

The most common problems tend to fall into four categories of behavior: (1) prejudging, (2) stereotyping, (3) name calling, and (4) inappropriate humor. We choose to behave in these categories, and the behavior is informed, at least, by the culture of which we are members.

Prejudging

We prejudge others on the basis of similarity and differences. Usually, prejudgment is self-serving: We are good, they are bad. We are right, they are wrong. We are beautiful, they are ugly. We are God's chosen people, they are not. We are heroes, they are villains. We are innocent, they are aggressors. We are freedom fighters, they are terrorists.

The worst form of all prejudging is: We are people, they are things. Since they are things they have only functions. Since they are things they can be treated without regard to their humanity. Since they are things they can be bought or sold or given away or thrown away.

Stereotyping

To stereotype is to make an inflexible statement about all the members of a group. A stereotype is a generalization based on one's own limited experience with the members of a group. A stereotype is a short cut to understanding.

We need our stereotypes because they allow us to move into and work successfully with groups of strangers. They allow us to relate to people we do not know. For example, you have a stereotype of "professor" that lets you interact successfully with a professor you have not met before. The problem, however, is that a stereotype allows us to ignore individual uniqueness in a human being. The stereotype may keep us from seeing and understanding the person. That's why stereotypes can be so destructive—a stereotype tells us that the other person is not a unique individual.

To get an idea of the damage that can be done by stereotypes, consider these statements, each of which reflects a negative—and untrue—stereotype:

1. The auditors are always messing around where they're not wanted.
2. Hispanics want everything given to them.
3. Doctors are so arrogant! How can they dare make you wait for two hours?
4. Blacks are lazy—they never come to work on time.
5. Of course he's greedy. He's a lawyer, isn't he?
6. Women just aren't cut out for organizational leadership.
7. Asians never want you to succeed.
8. An Indian can't be trusted to stay sober.
9. Americans are all egotists.
10. You know he's gay—he's too sensitive to be normal.

Now, suppose someone should decide to act—to behave toward you—on the basis of one of these stereotypes. It seems a chilling thought to us, but it does happen.

Name Calling

Every noun is a name. Every name calls to mind something having particular features. A correct name calls to mind a correct image. An incorrect name creates an incorrect image. To illustrate, what image do you generate of a mixed breed dog when you hear the name "Cur," or "mutt," or "pound puppy," or "mongrel"?

Name calling is the use of a negative or diminishing word to categorize people. It happens often, and it is always damaging. Yet, many of us have become tolerant of such name calling. We "let it go" rather than confront it. But when we allow other people to put us or anyone else down we encourage their behavior. In the process we also damage ourselves.

Take care not to imply anything negative, such as pity or inability to function. Avoid insulting euphemisms. Do not demean any person or any group.

Inappropriate Humor

Humor can be used appropriately or inappropriately, too. What a wonderful thing to laugh with each other. We grow closer. We feel better. But humor has a cutting edge that can damage. To illustrate, the four categories of humor listed in table 11.3 can all be used to build up or tear down. How we use humor is always a matter of choice. How we respond to uses of humor is, also, always a matter

Table 11.3	Categories of Humor
Exaggeration	Overstatement related to persons, places, sizes, the way people feel or act, and personal experiences.
Surprise	Making use of unexpected or unusual feelings, events, or facts.
Absurdity	Using ideas and other humor materials that are illogical in thinking or in language.
Human problems	Situations in which a person appears foolish or is overcome by events. It includes situations where the speaker or the activity of the speaker appears laughable.
Playful ridicule	A sympathetic teasing and acceptance of human faults.

of choice. Why choose to tear down? Why not, instead, choose to build up?

COMMUNICATING WITH PEOPLE WHO ARE DIFFERENT

Consider, again, the five categories identified by the U.S. Census Bureau. This time think about how the lifestyles of these groups may well inform their behavior. Try to imagine yourself interacting with someone from each of the groups different from your own. What would be the implications for your conversation on almost any current topic?

American Indian	0.8%	Try to live in harmony with nature and the environment. Take a present-tense orientation, and are much more interested in group and collateral relationships than in individual relationships. They believe people are basically good. In general, they speak softly and slowly. They do not gaze directly at you when they are listening or speaking. They don't interject much, and they seldom do encouraging communication when they are listening. When someone else finishes speaking, they are likely to remain silent for quite a while before they respond because it would be rude to do otherwise.
Asian Americans Hispanics	2.9% 9.0%	Asian Americans and Hispanics tend to speak softly and avoid eye contact when listening and speaking to high-status people. They share similar rules about participating in conversation, and like American Indians, they do not interject often nor do they offer encouraging suggestions when they are listening. When another person finishes speaking they are likely to remain silent for a short while before responding. Their manner of expression is low-keyed and indirect.

continues

| Black | 12.1% | African Americans, in general, value living in harmony with nature and the environment. In general, too, African Americans tend to take a present-tense orientation. They are very comfortable with direct eye contact. Indeed while speaking they are likely to prolong eye contact with the listeners. Most African Americans are comfortable with interrupting, and they do so often. They are very quick to respond, and they tend to communicate in a highly emotional and affective style. Blacks tend to value being over doing. |
| White | 80.3% | In contrast to all the other groups, whites value mastery over nature and the environment. Moreover, whites tend to have a future orientation much more than past or present tense. Whites value individual achievement over group achievement, and they find their greatest satisfaction in doing rather than being. To Whites, people are both good and bad. Whites speak loud and fast, and often do this to control the listener. They make eye contact much more often when listening than when speaking. In addition, when they listen, Whites are given to head nods and other nonverbal markers. They are quick to respond, and they tend to favor an objective, task-oriented style. |

Source: The specifics in this table have been derived from Derald Wing Sue and David Sue, *Counseling the Culturally Different: Theory and Practice.* (New York: John Wiley & Sons, 1990.)

How you use language governs how well you work and play in the presence of diversity.

Using Language Appropriately

Ultimately, how you use language governs how well you work and play in the presence of diversity. To use the language more wisely and more effectively is to interact with diverse people more ethically, as well. We can avoid insensitive expressions, for example, only if we understand that they are insensitive. And we must learn to avoid insensitive expressions if we are going to communicate within the three ethical standards, (1) tell the truth, (2) do no harm, and (3) treat people justly. To illustrate, table 11.4 displays certain insensitive expressions and the alternatives we recommend. You can see how the expressions on the left violate these ethical standards.

Working in a Culturally Diverse Group

Different cultures have different ways of dealing with some of our most fundamental values. Working in a culturally diverse group implies, then, that the people in that group may not understand our value system, and we may not understand theirs.

Cultures differ, for example, in how they use time, in the appropriate roles of men and women, in style of dress, learning style, what constitutes appropriate bodily and social distance, appropriate levels of formality, and the like.

Table 11.4   Insensitive Expressions and Alternatives

Instead of saying:	*Try saying:*
1. The deaf person.	The person.
2. The woman doctor.	The doctor.
3. The black doctor.	The doctor.
4. The doctor, an Iranian guy.	The doctor.
5. The blind man.	The man.
6. The amputee.	The person.
7. The mentally retarded child.	The child.
8. Ellen is confined to a wheelchair.	Ellen uses a wheelchair.
9. Ellen is burdened with a disfiguring disease.	Ellen has acne.
10. Ellen is a victim of cancer.	Ellen has cancer.
11. Ellen, an exceptional child, . . .	Ellen.
12. Ellen is suffering from . . .	Ellen has . . .

Source: Michael S. Hanna and Gerald L. Wilson, *Communicating in Business and Professional Settings, Fourth Edition* (New York: McGraw-Hill, 1998) p. 83.

Now imagine yourself interacting with someone from a different culture. If you think of time as a series of evenly spaced ticks of a clock, 60 ticks to a minute, 60 minutes to an hour, and if you live your life by the clock, would that influence your thinking about someone who uses time differently? Let the other person in this illustration come from a culture that expands that five-minute period to thirty minutes. You agree the other person will pick you up promptly at 7:00 A.M. The other person arrives "just a few minutes late" at 7:45 A.M. What would you be likely to think of the other person? Would you judge the person inconsiderate?

Some societies believe women should be independent. Others believe women should be subservient to their men. Can you imagine any troubles that might arise in a work place where the two cultures meet? Can you imagine any troubles that might arise in a social setting from such different perspectives?

Some cultures think of a business dealing as a very formal affair. Others take a more casual, informal approach to business dealings. What if those two cultures were represented in your work place?

Some people find it offensive if you show the bottom of your foot. Some people never eat with the left hand, and would be offended if you do. Some people stand very close when doing business—others want much more space. Some people are comfortable touching others; other people do not want to be touched at all. Such differences can create very difficult working conditions.

What is a person who wishes to live gracefully to do in the face of such diversity?

Six general rules will help you communicate more effectively with people who are different from yourself.

1. *Learn everything you can about the other person's worldview.* Learn the rules of the other culture. Don't assume you're right and the other person is wrong. Delay or defer decisions and judgments until you know more about the other people. Do all you can to prevent a loss of face for the other person. In general, the farther east you go from the United States, the more face-sensitive the culture. In such a culture, be indirect and abstract. If you are of a face-sensitive culture, remain as flexible as you can. In any case, learn the rules and adapt yourself to them.

2. *Interpret for others.* Your understanding and insight may be just what the other person needs in order to make sense of a situation. If you need to, seek out such interpretations from others.

3. *Make allowances and remain flexible.* Tell yourself that other people are basically well intended. Try to get specific information about such questions as where, how, which, and when. Use language that is descriptive rather than judgmental.

4. *When appropriate, give and get feedback.* Keep the other person informed about what you think and how you feel. Keep yourself informed about what the other person thinks and feels. Try to

bring uncertainties and concerns up to the level of talk. But do be aware that some people are offended by directness while others have no trouble with it. Remain flexible and try to tune into the other person's level of comfort.

5. *Do not fall back on stereotypes.* Your observations of a particular culture will not apply to every member of the culture.

6. *Don't assume you know someone else's culture merely because you have read about it.* Broad personal experience is usually required before you can truly understand a culture different from your own.

What to Do When the Dominant Culture Is Different from Your Own

You may well find yourself a member of the outgroup working in a dominant culture that's different from your own. These six suggestions can make life simpler:

1. *Build self-esteem.* Build your own self-esteem and the other person's self-esteem.

2. *Try to identify the constructive contributions you can make because of the differences you bring to the dominant culture.*

3. *Adjust and adapt yourself as much as you can.* You do not have to give up your identity to adapt to another person's basic assumptions. When in Rome, do as the Romans do.

4. *Don't always cluster with your own kind.* Mix with members of the new culture. When you do refresh yourself by speaking your own language with friends from your own group, be sure to do this in situations that will not threaten your emerging relationships with members of the dominant culture.

5. *Work with others from both dominant and other nondominant groups to achieve common goals.* Identify those goals, agree on them, and try to make progress toward them and to help others make progress toward them.

6. *Avoid personal ethnocentrism or chauvinism.* Learn as much as you can, interpret for others, make allowances, and give and get feedback often.

SUMMARY

While a concern for ethics has always existed in the United States, that concern has been increasing dramatically since the time of the Watergate scandal in the 1970s. Competent interpersonal communicators should be aware of this concern and what constitutes ethical behavior.

Three principles of ethics serve as a guide for what constitutes ethical behavior in general. The ethical person should not intentionally deceive another. His or her communication should not purposely harm any other person. He or she should also treat others justly.

Interpersonal ethics are inherent in the concept of dialogue. Dialogue requires empathy and authenticity. Practicing ethical principles implies ethical behavior. Three principles derived from this perspective are: (1) ethical communication shows respect for the other person, (2) ethical communication shows respect for the other person's ideas, and (3) ethical communication encourages (or at least does not inhibit) another person's ability to make free choices.

We are all confronted by situations where we are tempted to stretch the truth, avoid saying something, or tell a white lie in order to protect ourselves and/or the other person. We employ these communication strategies: (1) to save face, (2) to be seen as a polite member of society, (3) to avoid tension or conflict, (4) to gain power, or (5) to increase or decrease engagement in relationships. How do these behaviors measure up against the principles developed in this chapter for ethical communication behavior? They may meet four of the criteria for ethical behavior. The one criterion unmet is that people should not intentionally deceive one another.

Diversity refers to difference and variations among people—race, ethnic, gender, and age. People are highly sensitive to their own uniqueness, but often ignorant about and insensitive to other people's uniqueness. This insensitivity can result in damage to others and serious impact on interpersonal relationships.

Some common communication approaches are problematic. These include prejudging, stereotyping, name calling, and inappropriate humor. Six guidelines are presented to use in improving communication with diverse people. They are:

1. Learn everything you can about the other person's world.
2. Interpret for others.
3. Make allowances and remain flexible.
4. Give and give back when appropriate.
5. Do not fall back on stereotypes.
6. Don't assume you know someone else's culture merely because you have read about it.

DISCUSSION QUESTIONS

1. Most of us have heard the expression "the ends justify the means." Are there situations where this might be true? What examples can you describe?

2. What is your view of ethical behavior in our time? Are people becoming more or less ethical? Are there particular arenas in our society where ethical standards are changing? Are there particular arenas in our society where ethical behavior is becoming more of a problem? Cite some of these arenas.

3. What ethical issues arise from your role as a student? Suggest statements that might make up a code of ethics for students.

4. How do you react when someone tells you a lie? Does the type of lie make a difference? Does the person telling the lie make a difference?

5. Are there times when lying is acceptable? If so, describe them.

6. Assume you are an employer and have the opportunity to hire a couple of new people. What do you see as some of the advantages of bring more diverse people into your workgroup?

7. Recall a time when you were a minority person in a group and heard inappropriate remarks that were related to your differences. What are some responses to this situation that you view as productive?

8. Your author provides you with some strategies for improving your communication with diverse people. What others can you add?

ENDNOTES

1. G. L. Wilson and D. K. Wright, "Ethics and Values in Organizational Communication." A paper presented to the Commission on Ethics of the Speech Communication Association (New Orleans, 1988).

2. G. L. Kreps, *Organizational Communication*, 2d ed. (New York: Longman, 1990), 250–251.

3. C. T. Brown and P. Keller, *From Monologue to Dialogue: An Exploration of Interpersonal Communication* (Englewood Cliffs, NJ: Prentice-Hall, 1979).

4. R. E. Turner, C. Edgely, and G. Olmstead, "Information Control in Conversation: Honesty Is Not Always the Best Policy," *Kansas Journal of Sociology* 11 (1975): 69–89.

5. J. Bavelas, "Situations that Lead to Disqualification," *Human Communication Research* 9 (1983): 132.

6. D. Hample, "Purposes and Effects of Lying," *Southern Speech Communication Journal* 46 (1980): 33–47.

7. C. Camden, M. T. Motley, and A. Wilson, "White Lies in Interpersonal Communication: A Taxonomy and Preliminary Investigation of Social Motivations," *Western Journal of Speech Communication* 48 (1984): 315.

8. Bavelas, 130–145.

Read More about
Interpersonal Ethics
and Diversity in These Sources

Bavelas, Janet B., Alex Black, Nicole Chovil, and Jenifer Mullet. *Equivocal Communication.* Newbury Park, CA: Sage, 1990. This book presents a scholarly treatment of deliberately vague communication and its relationship to telling the truth and lying.

Buller, David B. "Deception." In *Strategic Interpersonal Communication.* John A. Daly and John M. Wiemann, eds. Hillsdale, NJ: Erlbaum, 1994. This essay describes the role of deception in interpersonal relationships. It explores the verbal and nonverbal behaviors that are characteristic of deliberate and unintentional deception.

Jaska, James, and Michael S. Pritchard. *Communication Ethics: Methods of Analysis.* Belmont, CA Wadsworth, 1988. This interesting book raises ethical issues that provide food for thought for those who want to go beyond the ideas presented in this chapter.

Johannesen, Richard L. *Ethics in Human Communication.* 2d ed. Prospect Heights, IL: Waveland Press, 1983. This easy-to-read book provides a comprehensive treatment of ethical perspectives as they relate to communication.

Macrae, C. Neil, Charles Stangor, and Miles Hewstone, eds. *Stereotypes and Stereotyping.* New York: Gilford, 1996. This is a collection of scholarly works. It provides a comprehensive examination of the area, with chapters on the formation and development of stereotypes, how stereotyping operates in interaction, and how to minimize the harm of stereotyping.

EXPERIENCES

MILL AND MEET

Chapter 1: Interpersonal Process

This experience is designed to help you become acquainted with your classmates. List each of these descriptions on a single line of a sheet of paper. Then mill around the classroom and meet people who fit the descriptions. Ask the person to sign his or her name next to the description that fits.

1. Is an only child
2. Skipped breakfast today
3. Drives a van
4. Was born in the Northeast
5. Was born in the Southwest
6. Plays a musical instrument
7. Is a parent
8. Is left-handed
9. Is shorter than you
10. Has an unusual hobby
11. Is married
12. Has the same major as you
13. Writes poetry

14. Has been to Europe

15. Knows sign language

16. Is in love

17. Speaks more than one language

18. You have seen in another class

19. Is self-employed

20. Works evenings

OBSERVING AND FILTERING

Chapter 1: Interpersonal Process

This experience is designed to help you discover that you take in many different messages simultaneously and that you can find out a lot about another person without actually talking with that person. Begin by agreeing to work with a classmate you do not know for about ten minutes. Move your chairs so that you can see each other well. Do not talk with the other person during this activity.

Answer the following questions based on your observations of your partner. Do not compare notes or check their accuracy now.

1. Age?

2. Gender?

3. Ethnic identification?

4. Marital status?

5. Full- or part-time student?

6. Is the person employed?

7. If so, what does this person do?

8. Can you identify anything that happened to the person before coming into the classroom?

9. How is the person feeling now (eg., well, ill, tired, excited)?

10. What might happen to the person after leaving the classroom?

Compare notes with your partner. Check for accuracy, and share your thinking processes. What observations caused you to answer as you did?

Finally, discuss these questions as a class:

1. Were you able to draw inferences easily? Were you surprised by your accuracy or inaccuracy in doing so?

2. How do you account for your success rate in making inferences? What does this tell you about the communication process?

BELIEFS

Chapter 2: Self-Concept

This experience is designed to allow you to compare your beliefs about yourself with those of others. From the following list, select twenty characteristics that describe how you perceive yourself and how you believe others perceive you. How do these characteristics affect your interpersonal communication? Do you believe that others share this view of you? Test yourself. Ask a classmate or friend to look at your selections. How do these characteristics relate to your beliefs about yourself?

adaptable	competitive	diffident	friendly
ambitious	complicated	direct	garrulous
analytical	conforming	disagreeable	genuine
argumentative	conservative	disorderly	gregarious
arrogant	considerate	domineering	guarded
articulate	cooperative	driving	honest
autocratic	courageous	earthy	idealistic
belligerent	courteous	efficient	imaginative
calm	critical	egotistical	impulsive
candid	decisive	emotional	independent
careless	deferential	enthusiastic	indifferent
cautious	dependable	flighty	kind
cold	devious	frank	lazy
loyal	pessimistic	self-confident	systematic
manipulative	practical	self-conscious	tactful
materialistic	pretentious	self-starter	thorough
officious	probing	sensitive	thrifty
opportunistic	prompt	shrewd	truthful
optimistic	proud	shy	tyrannical
outgoing	rational	sincere	understanding
outspoken	relentless	skeptical	vain
overbearing	reliable	sneaky	warm
patient	reserved	stable	withdrawn
pensive	resourceful	stern	witty
persevering	rude	stubborn	
persuasive	ruthless	sympathetic	

VALUES

Chapter 2: Self-Concept

This experience gives you the opportunity to compare your values with those of another person. Return to the beliefs experience, and *rank* the characteristics you selected from most important to least important. Next place a check ($\sqrt{}$) by those that you perceive as positive characteristics. Compare your list with that of another person. How do they differ? Discuss both the differences and similarities with the other person to arrive at a better understanding of your own value system. Notice that some of your values are about you and what you want for yourself; others imply standards about the way things should be. You may also notice that some of your values are related to several beliefs. In fact, many values represent a synthesis of beliefs. Your values shape the images that you think are appropriate to present.

Thinking and talking about your values helps you to know more about who you are and who you want to be. A clearer idea about what is important to you enables you to express yourself more coherently and effectively.

COMMUNICATING ABOUT NEEDS

Chapter 2: Self-Concept

Working through this experience provides an opportunity to identify and communicate needs. In small groups, identify the needs that might motivate a communication with a friend in the following situations. (Recall that the needs presented in this chapter are physiological, safety, belonging, esteem, self-actualization, inclusion, affection, and control.)

1. You are short of cash to purchase books for the coming term.
2. You have two dates for Saturday night and must cancel one of your engagements.
3. You have just received a job promotion.
4. Your father and mother, who provide half of your school support, have just called to tell you that you will have to drop out of school because they are experiencing a temporary financial setback.
5. A close friend is moving to another city and you do not expect to see that person again.
6. You have won a week-long vacation.

After the needs have been identified, have one group member model communication to express the needs to a friend. Then have another member respond to the expressions. Answer these questions about each communication transaction:

1. Were the needs clearly stated? If not, how could they be clarified?
2. Was the response appropriate?
3. In what ways was the response satisfying or not satisfying to the person expressing the needs?
4. How could the response to the expression of needs be improved?

HOW DO PEOPLE AFFECT YOUR SELF-CONCEPT?

Chapter 2: Self-Concept

This experience is designed to allow you to understand how people with whom you come into contact affect your self-concept. The goal is for you to gain greater understanding of these situations and to discover ways to enhance the potential for you to feel valued, loved, and needed. The first part of this exercise asks you to consider your experience. The last part asks you to share the insights you gained with the class.

Step 1.   Identify a person with whom you have had recent contact and who you believe has had a positive effect on your self-concept. Write that person's name on a piece of paper. Identify incidents in which this person had a positive effect on your self-concept. In a paragraph, describe what that person did and/or said. Then analyze what you have written. Make a list of the kinds of things this person did or said to help you feel good about yourself.

Step 2.   Identify a person with whom you have had recent contact and who you believe has had a negative effect on your self-concept. Write that person's name on a piece of paper. Identify incidents in which this person had a negative effect on your self-concept. In a paragraph, describe what that person did and/or said. Now, analyze what you have written. Make a list of the kinds of things this person did or said to cause you to feel bad about yourself.

Step 3.   As a class, construct two lists on the chalkboard—one of things people do to positively affect self-concept, one of things people do to negatively affect self-concept.

Step 4.   Brainstorm about socially acceptable ways people can increase the potential for you to feel valued, loved, and needed.

ROLES AND RULES

Chapter 3: Perception

This exercise is designed to help you think about your roles and the communication rules that go with them. First list three roles that you very often assume. Working with a partner, share your lists. Then, for each of the following situations, choose one of your roles and either role play or just describe how you would approach the situation in that role:

1. Your new secretary seems upset. She feels frustrated and thinks that everyone expects her to do things the way your previous secretary did. How can you reassure her?

2. A friend borrowed one of your most prized books, which cannot be replaced. When it was returned, you found the cover was torn. What will you say to your friend?

3. A friend has asked you to help her husband find a new job as a decorator. You do not think very highly of his past work and do not especially want to put your reputation on the line by recommending him. What will you say to his wife?

4. Your new supervisor seems generally suspicious and is slow to come to trust people. You admire him and his work and would like to develop a positive working relationship. At your first evaluation, you have clearly done well, and your supervisor says so. What can you say to improve your relationship further?

Discuss how the communication rules that accompanied the roles helped to shape the interpersonal communication process in each situation. Then create your own situations, considering how communication rules and roles may either restrict or enhance interpersonal growth.

PERCEPTIONS OF RELATIONSHIPS: IDEAL RELATIONSHIPS

Chapter 3: Perception

This experience will allow you to explore your ideas of an ideal relationship with those of another person with whom you are involved. This experience is done out of class, and then the results are shared and discussed in one class session. The discussion often brings out hidden or easily overlooked criteria for establishing and maintaining relationships. This experience also works well as a term paper assignment. The basic idea for this experience was developed by Harville Hendrix, and a similar exercise appears in his book *Getting the Love You Want* (New York: Harper and Row, 1988).

1. Sit down with the person from one of your relationships that you wish to explore. Each person in the relationship should create a list of statements that describes his or her own personal idea about how an *ideal* relationship of the type shared by you and this person should work. For example, if you do this with your best friend, you might write "We have fun together" or "We know we can count on one another for someone to talk with."

2. You and your partner should then share your lists with one another, adding items from the partner's list to your own if there are statements there that you agree with but did not immediately think about.

3. Each partner should then privately rate each statement on his or her list from 1 to 4, with 1 meaning *very important,* 2 meaning *somewhat important,* 3 meaning *not very important,* and 4 meaning *not at all important.* Each partner should also circle the two most important statements in his or her list.

4. Now compare lists. Note where there are similarities and differences and mark those statements in some way. The areas of agreement between your two lists represent a "shared relationship vision." These are the things about which you agree and wish to have in or exclude from an ideal relationship of this type. Discuss these similarities with your partner. Also discuss the result of comparing your circled items. Did you agree on these?

5. Now each partner should go back to his or her list and underline each statement that represents something you feel you are both doing in your relationship.

6. Compare lists and discuss the similarities and differences between your perceived ideal relationship and your perceived real relationship. Did this discussion leave you with an agenda for improvement in the relationship? That is, were there things you both felt were important to your ideal relationship that you also felt are not happening in your relationship?

IMPROVING PERCEPTION

Chapter 3: Perception

This experience is designed to help you learn how to improve your perception. Sit comfortably where you will be undisturbed for about twenty minutes. Choose a spot slightly above your eye level and focus on it. As you focus, close your eyes, keeping your eyes raised slightly. Begin counting slowly backward from one hundred. As you count, you will find yourself becoming more and more relaxed.

When you arrive at one, check how your body feels, starting with your feet and working up to the top of your head, including your jaws and forehead. You might tense slightly, hold, and then relax each part as you progress. Inhale deeply as you tense each part, and exhale slowly and steadily as you relax it. Focus on each body part for as long as it takes for you to feel comfortable with it. You may find that your back, shoulders, and neck require greater attention. As you mentally climb your body, pay attention to what you are perceiving. Give some thought to each sense for every part of the body you relax.

You may get some images that seem unrelated to what you are doing, but this is O.K. It is important to accept whatever you think during the exercise and to go on. Do not try to change or avoid anything that comes to you. When you have finished this progressive relaxation, count down from twenty to one, recalling your environment as you go along. Remember the colors of the room, the arrangement of furniture, and what you expect to see when you open your eyes. When you reach one, you will open your eyes, feeling relaxed and refreshed, with an increased awareness of yourself because you have focused your perception.

After repeating this exercise several times, you may find that you can shorten, or even eliminate, the counting at the beginning and end of the exercise. If this is true, you can spend this time becoming increasingly aware of your bodily processes through focused perception.

Once you have developed a routine of performing this exercise, you will be able to attend to and concentrate on things outside yourself. For example, you might try this simple experience. Place a fresh orange in front of you. (It is important to start with a simple object that involves multiple senses.) After relaxing, and with your eyes still closed, concentrate on the orange. Imagine its smell, taste, texture, and appearance. Think about what sounds the orange will make when it is squeezed or when its skin is peeled or cut. Work to make your images as vivid as possible.

Next, with your eyes still closed, pick up the fruit and validate your sensory predictions. Concentrate on one sense at a time. Feel the surface of the orange for its texture, smell it, then open your eyes and examine it. Tear it open and focus on the sounds that come with that action. Taste the fruit and get a sense of its internal texture as well.

Try this same experience with different objects. Over time, the process of relaxing, predicting, and validating will strengthen your ability to perceive objects. Although your perception of people is more complex than your perception of objects, this exercise, with some modifications, can help you in perceiving others too. After you feel comfortable using this process with objects, apply your ability to create images to your experience of others.

As suggested before, relax and call to mind a familiar person. Exercise each of your senses as you concentrate on your image. The next time you see this person, verify your image, and you may be surprised at its accuracy. Having concentrated on this person, you may also find yourself paying more attention to your perception as you talk with and observe the individual.

When you feel comfortable creating images of people you know, try recreating and studying your communication events with them. By remembering and concentrating on your various perceptions and the contributions of your senses to your action in the encounters, you can better understand how and why the exchanges went as they did. Through this method, you can better understand how perception functions in your relationships.

This regimen for building your receptive skills can take some time, but it is well worth the investment. The benefits are increased personal health and interpersonal skill.

INFERENCES AND FACTS

Chapter 4: Language

This experience will help you understand the differences between inference and observation. Carefully read the following report and the observations based on it. Indicate whether you think the observations are true, false, or doubtful on the basis of the information presented in the report. Circle *T* if the observation is definitely true; circle *F* if the observation is definitely false. Judge each observation in order. Do not reread observations after you have marked them. Do not change any of your answers.

The Report

A well-liked college teacher had just finished making up a final exam and had turned off the lights in the office. Just then, a tall, dark, broad figure appeared and demanded the exam. The professor opened the drawer. Everything in the drawer was picked up and the individual ran down the corridor. The dean was notified immediately.

The Questions

Number on a separate sheet of paper from one to ten. Answer these questions true (T), false (F), or I don't know (?) on your paper. Please do not go back and reread the report. Please do not go back and change any answers on the questions.

 1. The thief was tall, dark, and broad.   T   F   ?

 2. The professor turned off the lights.   T   F   ?

 3. A tall figure demanded the examination.   T   F   ?

 4. The examination was picked up by someone.   T   F   ?

 5. The examination was picked up by the professor.   T   F   ?

 6. A tall, dark figure appeared after the professor had
     turned off the lights in the office.   T   F   ?

 7. The man who opened the drawer was the professor.   T   F   ?

 8. The professor ran down the corridor.   T   F   ?

 9. The drawer was never actually opened.   T   F   ?

10. In this report, references are made to three persons. T   F   ?

DESCRIBING RELATIONSHIPS

Chapter 4: Language

Words that people use to describe their relationships include the following:

friend	acquaintance
associate	person
companion	

Now write the answers to the following questions. Writing your responses will help you to think more thoroughly about the language you use to describe relationships.

1. Arrange the preceding list of words in order of increasing abstraction.

2. Examine each level of abstraction and list words or phrases that characterize relationships at that level. What behaviors are included at each level? How do the characteristics and behaviors differ from level to level?

3. In what ways do intensity, involvement, and expectations of the other person differ from level to level?

4. Evaluate each level as more or less impersonal versus more or less interpersonal.

5. How would communication between two people be described at each level of abstraction?

6. How would communication between people be affected if they used different levels of abstraction in defining their relationship?

7. What words could you add to this list? Where would each fit into the abstraction ladder? What effect do these levels have on relational growth?

8. Construct a similar ladder of the levels of abstraction in describing a romantic relationship. Compare your descriptions with others in class.

THE WORD IS NOT THE THING.
SOMETIMES IT ISN'T EVEN THE WORD!

Chapter 4: Language

This experience is designed to provide insights into language use. The following statements all mean the same thing as common proverbs you have heard many times. Can you supply the more familiar version?

1. All articles that coruscate with resplendence are not truly suriferous.

2. Sorting on the part of mendicants must be interdicted.

3. Male cadavers are incapable of rendering testimony.

4. Abstention from elevatory undertakings precludes a potential escalation of a lucrative nature.

5. Freedom from undesirable incrustations—that is to say, undefiled and unadulterated—is contiguous to rectitude.

6. Avoid becoming lachrymose concerning precipitately departed lactile fluid.

7. Eschew the implement of correction and vitiate the scion.

8. Surveillance should precede saltation.

9. The individual presenting the ultimate cachinnation possesses thereby the optimal cachinnation.

10. Eleemosynary deeds have their incipience intramurally.

11. Conflagration occurs in context with visible vapors having their provenance in ignited carbonaceous material.

12. Refrain, all individuals whose residences may be characterized as vitreous edifices, from catapulting petrous projectiles.

LANGUAGE AND RELATIONSHIPS

Chapter 4: Language

This experience allows you to explore how language use is affected by particular kinds of relationships. Write a letter to your family, describing your progress this term. Be as specific as you can, but limit your description to two pages or less. Then write another letter on the same subject, this time to your best friend. Finally, imagine that you have been asked to orient an incoming freshman. Write to this person about what and how you are doing this term. Compare letters with other interpersonal communication students, and consider these questions:

1. What similarities and differences did you find among letters addressed to the same role relationships? Did the assignment reveal any consistency in the pools of language used?

2. What did the letters reveal about the breadth of each relationship for which they were written? Did some letters have more information than others? Did the levels of abstraction differ?

3. What language indicated the intensity of the relationship between the correspondents? Did this language vary from letter to letter?

PRACTICING ASSERTIVE BEHAVIOR

Chapter 5: Feelings and Emotions

This experience provides practice in creating assertive responses to a variety of situations. You may either write scripts for these events or role play them in class. In either case, compare notes with your classmates to see if they have approaches to these problems that you may not have considered.

1. In a crowded movie theater, the person behind you is coughing so loudly that you cannot hear the film.

2. A professor is taking time from covering course material to express her views about university politics.

3. You see one of your neighbors taking materials from a construction site near your home.

4. Your television picture has been snowy for two weeks, and today it has gone out altogether. The bill from the cable company arrives. You do not think it is correct.

5. You think your spouse is taking you for granted by asking you to do more than your share of the housework.

6. At a lunch counter, the person after you in line ordered the same meal as you, a ham and cheese sandwich. When the cook calls out that the order is ready, this person goes quickly to the counter and takes your sandwich.

7. You want your best friend to stop smoking in your house.

8. You have learned that an acquaintance has said uncomplimentary things about you to another acquaintance.

9. Your neighbor visits frequently, uninvited, and installs himself in your kitchen to pass the time. You like him but wish he wouldn't always stay so long.

10. Your supervisor has criticized you in a way that you think is only partially true and fair.

IDENTIFYING ASSERTIVE, NONASSERTIVE, AND AGGRESSIVE LANGUAGE

Chapter 5: Feelings and Emotions

This experience provides practice in identifying assertive, nonassertive, and aggressive language. For each of the following situations, indicate what you might say in communicating assertively, nonassertively, or aggressively:

1. You are having a conversation with a friend who *never* makes eye contact when talking with you.

2. You have been offered a promotion at work, but the pay raise that comes with it is very small compared to the amount of increased work.

3. You were engaged last week, and today a person whom you find very attractive and would like to get to know as a friend asks you for a date.

4. While visiting the local health spa, a stranger asks to borrow your towel.

5. You are sober, but your best friend is intoxicated and wants to drive home.

6. You are sober, but your friend, who is also sober, thinks you have had too much to drink. You want to drive home, and she protests.

Compare your statements with those of some of your classmates. Are there any common feelings or ideas among the responses? Did any issues about the relationship (such as trust or understanding) influence your decisions about appropriate assertive language?

STATING GOALS CLEARLY

Chapter 5: Feelings and Emotions

This experience will give you practice in goal setting in terms of the amount of behavior wanted, quality criteria, and time limits. Clear statements about what you want require three kinds of information. This exercise will help you to identify your goals in terms of those three kinds of information.

1. State the goal in terms of *behavior that could be observed.*

Words that point to behavior that cannot be observed	*Words that point to behavior that can be observed*
believe	define
recognize	distinguish
feel	acquire
think	repeat
interpret	identify
interpolate	describe
conclude	translate
know	rephrase
determine	arrange
imagine	draw
enjoy	demonstrate
judge	choose
evaluate	classify
conceptualize	write
experience	tell
plan	propose

2. Tell the other person the *amount* of the behavior you want and any *quality criteria* you have in mind. Tell the other person how you will judge that he or she has given you what you want.

3. Tell the other person the *time limits* you have in mind. By what time and date must the other person give you what you want for you to be satisfied?

LEARNING TO TALK ABOUT WANTS

Chapter 5: Feelings and Emotions

This experience provides practice in talking about wants. Working with a partner, list at least six things that you each want from your relationships and from the people in your relationships. Discuss how you would describe these wants to someone in a relationship. Remember to include statements about the *observable behavior*, the *quantity* or *quality* criteria, and any *time frame* that might be involved. Finally, practice asking for the wants on your list, taking turns and helping each other to feel comfortable with the requests.

CREATING FEELING STATEMENTS

Chapter 5: Feelings and Emotions

The goal of this experience is to give you practice in expressing feelings. Form small groups and then select a situation from the left column and a person to whom you will deliver the message from the right column. Role play the communication with another member of your group. Then role play the same situation with a different receiver. Analyze how the expressions of feelings differ. Allow each group member to role play at least one situation with two different receivers.

Situations	*Receivers*
1. You have an appointment and the person did not show up.	1. A professor
2. The person next to you in class made sarcastic remarks about your test grade.	2. Your mother, father, or spouse
3. You have just been paid a compliment that you know you do not deserve. You are embarrassed, and the person who paid the compliment notices your embarrassment.	3. An acquaintance of several months
4. A friend came up to you this morning and sensed that you were feeling depressed. The friend smiled, invited you to sit down, and then listened to your problems.	4. A good friend

LEARNING MORE FEELING WORDS

Chapter 5: Feelings and Emotions

This experience will help you use a broader range of language. Begin by working alone to list at least five expressions of feelings for each of the following situations. Use any list of words you wish, including those provided in chapter 5. Keep in mind that there are both verbal and nonverbal message systems.

1. You discover that someone has stolen your textbooks from your car.
2. You realize that you have spent too much time in one activity and are now late for an important appointment.
3. Someone important to you has behaved in a way that you do not approve of and in a context that you care about deeply.
4. Someone important to you has rejected your invitation to spend an evening together, using language you find offensive.

5. Someone you trusted has repeated a secret that you told in confidence.

6. Someone you love has just been recognized for an excellent accomplishment.

7. You have just been paid a very strong compliment by someone important to you.

Compare your responses with that of someone seated close to you. Expand your own list if you wish. Practice using the words on your list by role playing the situations with your partner. Remember that you are trying to expand your feeling vocabulary.

Finally, discuss these questions as a class:

1. Did you find this experience easy or difficult? Explain your answer.

2. How could you more easily learn more feeling words?

PERSONAL APPEARANCE AND COMMUNICATION

Chapter 6: Nonverbal Communication

This experience demonstrates the impact of appearance on communication.

Step 1
(five to ten minutes; work alone)

On a separate sheet of paper, rank the following items in terms of their importance to you for women, then for men.

Women	Men
jewelry	breath/teeth
figure	facial hair
lipstick	cologne
breath/teeth	shoes
shoes	hair
pants/skirt	pants
perfume	physique
fingernails	fingernails
blouse	shirt
legs	shower
makeup	jewelry

Step 2
(twenty to thirty minutes; work in groups of five or six)

Arrive at a group consensus on ranking for the items on the list for women and men. Record each group's rankings on the chalkboard.

Step 3
(ten minutes; work as a class)

Discuss these questions:

1. Why do some items seem more important than others?
2. What effect does physical appearance have on interpersonal communication?
3. Having seen the lists and heard the discussion, would you change your rankings on your personal list? If so, why?

THE MESSAGES OF PERSONAL SPACE

Chapter 6: Nonverbal Communication

This experience will help you understand your use of personal space. You will need to understand the following definitions. *Freeze* means to stop all movement, including gestures, eye motion, and the like. *Melt* means to continue natural movements until "freeze" is called.

First, select a partner—someone from the class whom you do not know well. Stand facing each other, about ten feet apart. Move slowly toward or away from each other, until you find a comfortable distance for each of the following:

1. Public distance—one that requires you to recognize the other person (between ten and eighteen feet)
2. Social consultive distance—one that allows you to talk with each other comfortably but not to touch (between four and ten feet)
3. Personal distance—one that allows you to tell secrets to each other and to touch (between two and four feet)

When you come to a comfortable distance, call "freeze." If your partner calls "freeze" before you do, stop all movement instantly.

Discuss these questions with your partner:

1. Did your experiences of each appropriate distance differ? Why or why not?
2. Was it difficult to "freeze" when asked to do so? Why or why not?

Now, face your partner again. Move slowly toward each other until one of you becomes so uncomfortable that you call "freeze." Stop all movement, study the distance between you, and then move to a comfortable distance and discuss these questions:

1. How close were you to each other?
2. Do any gender-related variables control how close you can get to each other?

Conclude this experience with a class discussion. Try to discover if women and men experience personal space differently. Are there any rules that control how closely two men can stand? A man and a woman? Two women? If so, how do you account for them? How do you suppose you learned them?

EMPATHIC LISTENING

Chapter 5: Feelings and Emotions

Chapter 7: Listening

This experience is designed to allow you to practice empathic listening and discuss the verbal and nonverbal cues that are associated with this kind of listening. Divide the class into groups of three or four. Together, read the first statement in the following list, and spend two or three minutes thinking about a response. When all group members are ready, discuss the idea. *Each person should paraphrase the ideas of the previous speaker before making a new comment.* Repeat this process with the other statements.

1. People should limit the size of their family to two children.
2. Dependent college students whose parents make less than twenty thousand dollars per year should be granted a government scholarship of not less than five thousand dollars.
3. College courses not in a student's major area of study should be taken on a pass fail basis.
4. For a tuition rebate of five hundred dollars, a student should be required to contribute one hundred hours of service to the university or college during an academic year.

After discussing each topic, answer these questions:

1. What nonverbal cues were displayed by the person doing the empathic listening?
2. What verbal cues were displayed by the person doing the empathic listening?
3. How did you feel about the other participants during the discussion? Did you feel any different in this group than in others? Why or why not?
4. When is empathic listening best used?

ROLE PLAYING ACTIVE LISTENING

Chapter 7: Listening

This experience gives you the opportunity to practice active listening through role playing. In small groups, act out each of the following situations for a few minutes. Designate one member to be the initiator and another to be the active listener. After role playing each situation, discuss as a group the effectiveness of the active listening. Rotate roles so that each member has an opportunity to listen actively.

1. You are single and would very much like to find someone to date seriously. You are telling your closest friend that you have met a very nice person who seems to be exactly whom you have been looking for.

2. Your boss has just told you that the due date for a project you spent most of the night completing has been extended. You gave up tickets for a very special concert to finish this work, and your boss forgot to tell you that you had the extra time. You meet a close friend and coworker as you are walking down the hall.

3. You have just learned that the person who is both your academic advisor and friend has been fired. You go home and find your roommate (or spouse).

4. A good friend who has been engaged to marry for a year tells you that the engagement is off.

5. You have borrowed a car and accidentally backed into the concrete base of a light pole. You know the owner of the car will be very angry. A friend walks up as you are examining the damaged car.

6. You were counting on all A's this term. You receive a C on the last speech in your public speaking class, which you suspect will drop your grade for the course to B-. You decide to share your feelings with a friend.

7. You are depressed about living with your parents. You would like to move out but are not sure they will like the idea. You decide to talk with your mother about this issue.

8. A friend has had her car in the shop for over a week. You are tired of providing taxi service for her. She approaches you to ask for a ride to town.

9. Your marriage is not going well. You are not fighting, but all the excitement seems to have disappeared. You decide to discuss this with your spouse.

10. You are pretty tired of school. You have been in classes for almost two straight years with no summer vacation. You are facing an enormous paper that is especially depressing you. A close friend has noticed that you seem down.

After finishing your role playing, discuss these questions with your group and the class:

1. How successful was your active listening?
2. Why is active listening sometimes difficult?
3. What can be done to make active listening easier?
4. What would happen if you engaged in active listening every time someone tried to communicate to you?
5. Under what circumstances would you want to use active listening? Contrast these with the circumstances in which you would *not* want to practice active listening.
6. How did you feel when you were the active listener? Focus on the intensity of the feeling.
7. How did you feel toward the listener who paraphrased what you said?

Personal Time Line

Chapter 8: Relationships

This experience provides an opportunity for you to review your personal history and to share as much of it as you wish. This is a good experience for helping your group members get acquainted.

Everyone has a history, beginning with birth and leading up to the present moment. Your images of yourself and your world evolved out of interactions with important other people in your history and out of the lessons you have learned from the connections you have made among all the experiences you have had. Sometimes it is useful to review that history. That is the purpose of this exercise.

Step 1.   Draw a time line similar to the one that follows.
Step 2.   Try to include as many truly significant events as you can remember. If you can't remember everything, don't worry.

Among other things, you might want to include

- important people you have met
- influential books you have read
- important anniversaries and events—for example, graduation, first car, first job, first date.

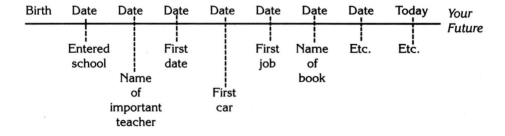

Step 3. In a group of three or four, share as much or as little of your time line as you wish. Discuss these questions:

1. What was significant about what you included?

2. How did what you included on your time line influence your emerging concept of yourself and your world?

3. Can you notice any interesting patterns among the items you have listed?

4. Are there any notable similarities or differences between your own time line and the time lines of the other group members?

SELF-DISCLOSURE MODELS

Chapter 8: Relationships

The purpose of this experience is to give you an opportunity to discuss how the quadrants in the Johari Window affect communication and relationships. Examine the Johari Windows below. Consider these questions, first alone and then with a group:

1. For each window pair, describe the communication that would occur.

2. Are there any kinds of relationships for which the window seems especially appropriate? If so, why?

3. Do you think this figure depicts a growing relationship?

4. What would you do to increase the openness in this relationship?

How is communication affected by these Johari Windows?

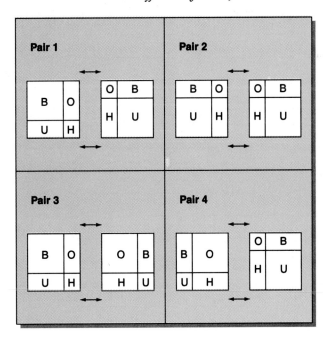

LANGUAGE OF SELF-DISCLOSURE

Chapter 8: Relationships

Following is a series of semantic differential scale items for you to use in a self-discovery experience. Take a moment to produce two copies of this scale. On one copy, place a check on the continuum to represent the degree of the attribute you think you possess.

After you have marked all items, use a different color of ink to mark the items to indicate how you believe others see you. Finally, give the unmarked copy of these scales to someone who knows you fairly well and ask that person to indicate how he or she sees you.

	7	6	5	4	3	2	1	
relaxed	___	___	___	___	___	___	___	tense
confidential	___	___	___	___	___	___	___	divulging
confident	___	___	___	___	___	___	___	ill-at-ease
enthusiastic	___	___	___	___	___	___	___	apathetic
trustworthy	___	___	___	___	___	___	___	untrustworthy
safe	___	___	___	___	___	___	___	dangerous
considerate	___	___	___	___	___	___	___	inconsiderate
friendly	___	___	___	___	___	___	___	hostile
involved	___	___	___	___	___	___	___	detached
straightforward	___	___	___	___	___	___	___	tricky
respectful	___	___	___	___	___	___	___	disrespectful
reliable	___	___	___	___	___	___	___	unreliable
secure	___	___	___	___	___	___	___	insecure
sincere	___	___	___	___	___	___	___	insincere
stimulating	___	___	___	___	___	___	___	boring
sensitive	___	___	___	___	___	___	___	insensitive
not deceitful	___	___	___	___	___	___	___	deceitful
pleasant	___	___	___	___	___	___	___	unpleasant
kind	___	___	___	___	___	___	___	cruel
honest	___	___	___	___	___	___	___	dishonest
skilled	___	___	___	___	___	___	___	unskilled
informed	___	___	___	___	___	___	___	uninformed
experienced	___	___	___	___	___	___	___	inexperienced
bold	___	___	___	___	___	___	___	timid

When you have collected data from all three ratings, transcribe the numbers associated with the spaces checked on the grid on below. When you have entered all the numbers, consider what they mean in terms of your self-concept.

Remember that self-concept is not necessarily static. If there are areas in which you would like to see change, you can. Remember, however, that *the rating from the other person is the perception of one (and only one) other person.* It is subject to selectivity and subjectivity.

Self Analysis Grid

Attribute Scale	Self-Rating	My Perception of Other's Rating	Other's Rating
Relaxed–tense			
Confidential–divulging			
Confident–ill-at-ease			
Enthusiastic–apathetic			
Trustworthy–untrustworthy			
Safe–dangerous			
Considerate–inconsiderate			
Friendly–hostile			
Involved–detached			
Straightforward–tricky			
Respectful–disrespectful			
Reliable–unreliable			
Secure–insecure			
Sincere–insincere			
Stimulating–boring			
Sensitive–insensitive			
Not deceitful–deceitful			
Pleasant–unpleasant			
Kind–cruel			
Honest–dishonest			
Skilled–unskilled			
Informed–uninformed			
Experienced–inexperienced			
Bold–timid			

INVESTIGATION OF MALE/FEMALE RELATIONAL DIFFERENCES

Chapter 8: Relationships

This experience will allow you to explore interpersonal concerns that make relational development between males and females difficult. You can prepare for this assignment by listing those things that members of the opposite sex do, say, or think that impede meaningful interpersonal relationships.

Form two groups, one of men and one of women. If possible, they should work in separate rooms. Each group is to list ten things that members of the opposite sex do, say, or think that act as barriers to relational development. Rank the items on each list, and then write them on the chalkboard.

The instructor will lead a discussion based on the following procedure:

1. The group will be asked to clarify each item, giving examples when requested.

2. The group about whom a statement is made will be asked if they believe it is true.

3. Class members should discuss what difference knowing this information might make in their effort to promote relational growth.[1]

MANAGING DIFFICULT FAMILY COMMUNICATION SITUATIONS

Chapter 8: Relationships

This experience is designed to help you identify difficult family communications and discover effective techniques for managing them. Begin in small groups by brainstorming for answers to the question, What are difficult family communications? List as many of these situations as you can. Next, narrow the list to five on which to concentrate your effort. Develop a specific scenario for each situation. Then identify members of the group to play the roles in your first situation. Work through the situation as if you were in it, using communication techniques you have learned in this course. Then analyze the communication by answering the following questions. Go on to role play and discuss each of the remaining situations, rotating the players.

1. What specific communication techniques were used to try to achieve successful management of these situations? How successful were you with them?

2. Are some techniques more important to success than others? If so, list them. Why are some more successful than others?

3. How successful were these efforts when compared with your experience with situations like these in your own life? If they were better, how do you account for this? What factors acted in previous situations to make them less successful? How can these be avoided? If your answer was "worse," account for this.

4. What have you learned from this experience that you hope to take to your communication with family members?

EXAMINING RELATIONAL DEVELOPMENT

Chapter 8: Relationships

The purpose of this experience is to provide practice in analyzing a dialogue to discover various aspects of the relational development process. Read the following dialogue that took place between Jill and Stephen, who are engaged to marry:

Steve: Jill, tell me what annoys you about me.

Jill: I get really upset when you sit in the living room and watch TV while I'm fixing dinner.

Steve: There wasn't any other place for me to sit. I wanted to watch the news, anyway. You know I like to watch the news.

Jill (interrupting): There was, too, a place to sit. And besides, I'm more important than watching news.

Steve: I didn't mean that you weren't more important than the news. I meant that I ought to get to watch the news for fifteen minutes.

Jill: I'm glad you are so considerate. You're nearly perfect—I guess.

Steve: Shut up! You're making fun of me.

Jill: You deserve it. Do you get mad when I make fun of you?

Steve: Yes.

Jill: I've changed my mind. You aren't even close to perfect.

Steve: Now it is my turn to tell you what annoys me! It annoys me when we are on a date and you make eyes at other guys.

Jill: It does?

Steve: Yes. It does.

Jill: You poor boy, you sure do have your problems.

Steve: There you go again. You can't carry on a serious conversation without teasing me. I hate it! I'm sorry you asked me over for dinner.

Examine this dialogue with these questions:

1. Speculate on why Steve and Jill might have initiated their relationship.
2. What stage of the relational development process do you think Steve and Jill are in? Why did you come to this conclusion?
3. Identify the self-disclosure in this communication. What effect did it have on relational development?
4. Identify the statements that positively or negatively affect the relationship. What effect did positiveness, or the lack of it, have on the relationship?
5. Did either person try to deal with potential conflict seriously? If not, speculate about how their attitudes affected the outcome of the relationship.
6. Assume that Steve and Jill would like their relationship to grow. Make a list of suggestions that would help them achieve this goal.

PRACTICING SUPPORTIVE COMMUNICATION

Chapter 9: Climate

This experience provides the opportunity to practice supportive behavior through role playing.

Step 1.   Work with a small group. This step takes about fifteen minutes. Read each of the cases and decide on a course of action for managing the problem in each. What skills should be used? How might the situation be handled best? Make notes.

Step 2.   The members of the group agree to role play the cases, taking turns practicing the skills agreed to and serving as observer-coaches for the role players.

Siblings

Brother Robert and sister Ellen have been competing for parental affection since childhood. Now they are adults at home for the holidays. Robert decides to poke his nose into Ellen's private life. He doesn't like that she is—he suspects—spending many nights in the apartment of her boyfriend, Charles.

Parent-Adult Child

Mother has spent a lifetime controlling her daughter. Now, at sixty, she still involves herself, uninvited, in the rearing of her daughter's two children. Michael, the nineteen-year-old grandson, is a model kid—all *A*s in school, productive on the job, fully involved in social and extracurricular activities at school, and so on. Judy, the seventeen-year-old high-school senior, is rebelling. This late-maturing child is beginning to experiment with drugs, sex, and alcohol and is flaunting the fact that she cuts school, is rude to her teachers, and so forth. The grandmother decides to do something by putting a guilt trip on the mother.

Boss-Employee

Jill, twenty-four-year-old graduate with a major in English, has been working as an executive assistant to the forty-four-year-old married president of a small construction firm in the city. She is confident of herself socially but uncertain that she is good enough to have a career and uncertain, in any case, what that career should be. "English majors wait tables," she says often. Now the boss has started hitting on her with this line of analysis: "You can have your promotion and your career right here in this business. All you have to do is be friendly." He emphasizes the word *friendly* with a body scan and a leer.

Lovers

Lisa and Bert have been seeing each other regularly. Indeed, they lived together for two years—their senior year in college and the first year after they graduated. Then Bert got a promotion and moved to a neighboring city about four hours away. Each weekend, one of them traveled to the other's town. The commute has begun to wear on them both, and now Lisa has met a very attractive guy in her own town, and the guy has been showing evidence of being very interested. He is a successful sales representative for a large manufacturing firm and must travel a lot. Bert has gone to Lisa's place for the weekend, and he has determined to find out why Lisa has been distancing herself from him.

ASSESSING SUPPORTIVENESS AND DEFENSIVENESS

Chapter 9: Climate

This experience provides practice in assessing supportiveness and defensiveness in a dialogue. In small groups or as a class, analyze this dialogue for examples of defensive and supportive communication. Identify Gibb's category or categories that a statement illustrates and tell why the statement might produce defensive or supportive behavior in the other person. Then, if it is defensive, create an alternative statement that might be seen as supportive. If small groups are conducting the analysis, they should share their work with the class when they have completed the analysis.

This conversation takes place between Phil and John, who have been roommates for two years. They will both be seniors next year and are trying to decide whether to live together for their final year. Phil has some reservations about living together, but John thinks it is an excellent idea.

> *Phil:* I really want to talk about our plans for sharing an apartment next year. But I know you won't want to talk about it.

> *John:* I thought we made that decision last week. I don't have anything to say to you about this. There is nothing wrong with living together next year. You always want to talk.

> *Phil:* I just want to find out how you think some things will go next year. We've had a few differences and I want to talk.

> *John:* Things will go just fine. I don't see any reason to talk about this. Besides, when you decide we are going to "have a talk," we always end up having a fight. Why can't we just drop this whole "talk" idea and keep things as they are? You're trying to bump me out so Linda can move in. That's it.

> *Phil:* That's not true. I did talk with Linda about living together, but that was in December. I can't believe that you are bringing that up now!

> *John:* Well, you didn't tell me anything about it then. I had to find out from a friend of mine. Then I confronted you with it and you lied.

> *Phil:* I'm telling the truth now. Can't you let the past be the past? I am sorry that I did that. I've told you that six times. I am telling you the truth.

> *John:* I've noticed you hanging around Linda—I saw you talking in the corner of the snack bar yesterday. You didn't even notice me until I walked right up and grabbed a chair. You were talking to her about next year.

> *Phil:* Linda is not trying to get me to let her move in here.

> *John:* Then you are trying to convince her to move in.

> *Phil:* I tell you there is nothing to this! This is one of the problems I wanted to bring up. You are *always* jealous of my friends. You think that being a roommate means that

you have a right to impose decisions about my social life. I am sick of this!

John: Wow!

Phil: I am going to ask Linda to move in, and I expect you to get out.

John: Wait, Phil. We've roomed together for two years. We're good friends—or at least I thought we were. How can you just throw me out?

Phil: I don't know what you want me to say. I'm sick of this. I want you out. If you want to still be friends, we can try. I won't live with you—you can't change.

John: That does it! Forget that we ever roomed together. Every time you want to have one of these "talks" we have a fight. I'm leaving. I'll be back *when you're not here* to pick up my things. Linda can move in next week!

ANALYZING DEFENSIVE COMMUNICATION WITHIN A RELATIONSHIP

Chapter 9: Climate

This experience gives you an opportunity to analyze your defensive behavior within a relational context. This out-of-class assignment asks you to secure the permission of a friend to be interviewed about your own defensive behavior. Allow enough time to discuss the topic adequately. (This interview may require nearly an hour to complete the assignment.)

Understand that, in asking about your defensive behavior, you are asking for evaluation. This is one of the six characteristics of defensive-producing communication. Be prepared to control your urge to become defensive. Avoid arguing with the person and use active listening skills.

Begin the interview by explaining Jack Gibb's characteristics of defensive and supportive behavior. Next, ask your friend which of the characteristics you use most often. Probe for specific examples of the behavior. Take notes on what is said.

ROLE PLAYING DEFENSIVE AND SUPPORTIVE COMMUNICATION

Chapter 9: Climate

Form small groups, and have two members role play each of the following situations, first using defensive behavior and then using supportive behavior. Remember that supportive behavior affirms the other person but does not necessarily mean that you agree with that person's position. The other group members will act as observers. They should take notes so that they will be able to point out specific examples of defensive and supportive behavior.

After each role play, the observers should discuss with the actors how closely they kept to Gibb's categories. Continue to role play until all members have had an opportunity to practice both defensive and supportive behavior.

1. You have been bothered for three weeks by a member of the opposite sex who would like a date. You have no interest in the person. The person has caught up with you after class and is walking with you across campus, pressing you for a date.

2. You are living with someone who keeps an untidy apartment. You usually keep your belongings in their place. You have talked with this person several times. Your roommate's attitude is that he has a right to his own life-style and that you should move out if you don't like what is going on. Your parents are visiting in two days and you want the apartment cleaned. You do not have time to clean up your roommate's mess because you must study for a final exam.

3. You and your roommate share the cost of food and the cooking. When your roommate is cooking, she frequently invites a friend or two and cooks for four instead of two. This happens about three times each week. You believe it is not fair to split the cost of groceries if this practice is to continue. Your roommate says that it is just part of living and being sociable and that you are free to invite your friends when you cook. You might wish to do this once a week, but the paying arrangement still would not be fair.

4. You are selected as the leader of a group that is working on a class project. One member has missed a few meetings and is often late with his part of the work. The project is due next Monday. You have talked to this person before and he commented. "You got it, didn't you? You're lucky I had time to do it at all." You are concerned that his work will not be ready for the Monday deadline. You talk to him about the situation in hopes of getting a firm commitment.

MANAGING POWER IN CLOSE RELATIONSHIPS

Chapter 10: Conflict

This experience helps you understand how power is used in close interpersonal relationships. It also asks you to evaluate the effect of the use of various kinds of power in these relationships.

Work through this experience in small groups. Consider how power is used in close interpersonal relationships. Make three columns on a single sheet of paper. Label each column with one of these kinds of relationships: siblings, parent/child, and lovers. List the six kinds of power discussed in chapter 10: referent, reward, coercive, legitimate, expert, and information/persuasive. For each situation, identify a specific instance from your experience that illustrates each kind of power use in that kind of relationship. Make a record of these. Then conduct an analysis of power use in each relationship. Following are some questions to guide your analysis:

1. What kind(s) of power are most effective? Why?

2. What kind(s) of power are least effective? Why?

3. What do you mean when you consider the notion of effectiveness?

4. If effective use of power changes from relationship to relationship, how do you account for this?

5. Do any sources of power seem underdeveloped in these relationships? If so, how do you account for this? Do you think that this creates a problem? If so, why?

6. Do you often find coercive power used as a source of leverage in close interpersonal relationships? If so, what problems does this create for the relationship? What can you do to manage the problem of overuse of coercion in close relationships?

Win As Much As You Can

Chapter 10: Conflict

The name of this game is "Win As Much As You Can."[2]

1. Divide the class into groups of eight students or more. Further divide these groups into pairs, and seat them as follows:

X X

X X   X X

X X

Each pair is given a payoff schedule and scorecard and asked to study them for two or three minutes. The partners are asked to share their understanding of the game with each other—but not with their group.

Instructions: For ten successive rounds, you and your partner will choose either an *X* or a *Y*. Each round's payoff depends on the pattern of choices made in your cluster:

Payoff Schedule

4 *X*s: Lose $1 each
3 *X*s: Win $1 each 1 *Y*: Lose $3
2 *X*s: Win $2 each 2 *Y*s: Lose $2 each
1 *X*: Win $3 3 *Y*s: Lose $1 each
4 *Y*s: Win $1 each

You are to confer with your partner in each round and make a joint decision. In rounds 5, 8, and 10, you and your partner may first confer with the other pairs in your group before making your joint decision.

Scorecard

Round	Your Choice (circle)	Group's Pattern of Choices	Your Payoff	Your Balance
1	X Y	__X __Y		
2	X Y	__X __Y		
3	X Y	__X __Y		
4	X Y	__X __Y		
5 (bonus)	X Y	__X __Y	(x3)	
6	X Y	__X __Y		
7	X Y	__X __Y		
8 (bonus)	X Y	__X __Y	(x5)	
9	X Y	__X __Y		
10 (bonus)	X Y	__X __Y	(x10)	

2. The title of this activity is "Win As Much As You Can." Keep this goal in mind throughout the experience. There are three key rules:

   a. You are not to confer with other members of your group unless you are given specific permission to do so. Don't talk with them. Don't send nonverbal messages back and forth.

   b. Each pair must agree upon a single choice of X or Y for each round.

   c. You are to ensure that the other members of your group do not know your pair's choice until you are told to reveal it.

   There are ten rounds to the exercise. During each round, you and your partner will have one minute to mark your choice of X or Y on the scorecard. You will then have one minute to mark your choice for round one. (After one minute, a facilitator should make sure that each pair has marked the scorecard.)

   Share your decision with the other pairs in your group. (Here, a facilitator can assist the groups by pointing to each pair and asking, in turn, "Have you marked your scorecard? What have you marked?") Then enter the score on the scorecard according to the payoff schedule. A facilitator will ask if there are any questions about the scoring. (Note that the purpose of the activity is stated in the title of the game, Win As Much As You Can.)

3. A facilitator should guide the game as follows:

   a. "You have one minute to mark your decision for round 2 . . . 3 . . . 4."

   b. "Has any pair not finished?"

   c. "Share and score."

4. Round 5 is a bonus round. The scorecard shows that all amounts won or lost on this round will be multiplied by three. Before you mark your choice for this round, you may wish to discuss this experience with the other pairs in your group (three minutes for this).

5. After three minutes, please return to your pair positions. You have one minute to mark the scorecard for round 5. Remember, the rules are in effect.

   Has any partnership not finished?

   Share and score.

   Rounds 6 and 7 are conducted like rounds 1 through 4. Round 8 is a bonus round and is conducted like round 5. Round 9 is a standard round and is conducted like rounds 1 through 4.

6. At round 10, remember that this round is a bonus round. It will increase the number of positive or negative points by ten. Thus, by itself, round 10 can change the balance in this game. Because

that is so, you may wish to talk with the other pairs in your group. (After three minutes, proceed as in step 5.)

7. Each pair tallies its total points, and then each group tallies its total points from the combined pair scores.

Discuss the ideas of competition and cooperation in a conflict situation:

1. What are the usual outcomes of conflict situations? Is this the usual situation?

2. Why don't people cooperate? Under what circumstances might you have achieved cooperation in this experience?

3. Most people define this exercise as a win-lose experience. Is it necessary to define conflict situations as win-lose? Are most interpersonal situations really win-lose situations when conflict occurs?

4. How would you describe your feelings during this game? Do you think your feelings about the participants would affect your future relations with them if this were a real-world experience?

5. What implications might this experience have for your future conflict situations?

ROLE PLAYING CONFLICT MANAGEMENT

Chapter 10: Conflict

Practice role playing effective conflict management in each of the following situations. The actors should attempt to reach a decision about the problem. After each case, answer the questions at the end of this experience before moving on to the next case.

1. Mary has been with her company for approximately five years and has a responsible position. She is intelligent, efficient, and capable. She is an excellent employee except for one problem that mars her record. Now and then, she antagonizes her fellow workers by her defensiveness-producing behavior. For instance, one day she delivered material to a coworker by just tossing it on the desk as she hurried by.

She has also left the impression that a person should have known better when he or she handed her work that contained an error. For example, the other day a coworker asked her a perfectly reasonable question, but she walked by as if she had not heard.

You and several of your fellow workers can no longer tolerate this situation and have decided to talk with Mary about it. She is usually a reasonable person—except, of course, when she has these occasional problems. She might become defensive.

2. James Irwin is a new professor. He has just given his midterm examination, which includes sixty objective questions and six short-answer essay questions for a fifty-minute exam period. At the end of the fifty minutes, he called time and collected all the papers. Only two students had finished the exam. The course for which the exam was being given is a prerequisite for all upper-level courses in the department. Irwin has indicated that any incomplete questions will be counted as incorrectly answered. At the urging of the department chairperson, you and four other students decide to go to him to discuss the problem. He has seemed reasonable on other matters related to the course, but you do not know how he will react to this inquiry.

3. Paul Holbrook has been the business manager for Midwest Chemical Company for fifteen years. During this time, he has developed a number of habits that are annoying to his subordinates. About two years ago, he started eating lunch alone in his office with his door closed. In fact, he keeps his door closed most of the time.

   When members of the department have a question, they often get a brief and unsatisfactory answer. For example, Kay asked for the morning off to go to the dentist. Paul answered, "Two hours," without even looking up from his work. George put a note in Paul's mailbox, asking how to submit a report. Two days later, he received a one-word reply, "Typewritten." Upon hearing George's story, Stan, another employee, told George how lucky he was. Several months ago, Stan asked Paul a question as he passed through the office. Paul acted as if Stan hadn't said a word.

   Four of you in the office have decided that you must speak to Paul. If the climate does not change, you have all agreed to ask to be transferred to another department.

4. Karl Lewis is a thirty-year-old recent graduate of Northeastern University. He worked for several years and then decided to return to school for a degree in organizational communication and management. Karl has been hired by Southern Steel Corporation, a medium-sized producer, to direct its training and management development program.

   The director of personnel, Margaret Goodyear, had been directing the training program along with her other duties. She hired Karl but had some reservations. She had wanted someone with at least five years of experience directing a training department, but, for some reason, none of the other applicants seemed qualified.

   Karl's academic record and recommendations are outstanding. In fact, Margaret has no reason to believe that he cannot do well in the job. Nevertheless, she has assigned Karl only routine, predominantly clerical duties. He has been given no real authority over the department he was hired to direct. Karl has scheduled a meeting with Margaret to attempt to resolve this problem.

Discuss each case by answering these questions:

1. What conflict management strategy was followed?
2. How effective was this strategy for managing this conflict?
3. If the strategy was effective, how do you account for this?
4. If the strategy was ineffective, how do you explain this? What might be a better strategy? Why?

MAKING SOME CHANGES

Chapter 10: Conflict

This experience helps you identify habits that contribute to unwanted conflicts. It is possible to change habitual behavior, but you have to replace a habit—you can't just break it. This means you must practice and practice until the new behavior feels as natural as the old. Of course, you must first think about the habitual behavior you want to change.

Do you find yourself using habitual behavior in conflict situations that you want to change? For many, such habits center around child rearing, money, time, and sex.

Work through this series of requests for information on a separate piece of paper. You can move through the items for each habit you want to analyze.

1. Name a habit you would like to change and are willing to work on changing; then describe your behavior.
2. Describe, as specifically and positively as possible, the behavior you would like to substitute for the unwanted conflict habit.
3. What is the *worst* possible result from the habit you want to break?
4. How does the trouble caused by your habit usually start? That is, what behavior can you use to "trigger" your replacement?
5. What can you ask the other person to do to help you remember that you want to replace an unwanted conflict habit with the preferred choice?

SETTING A CONFLICT MANAGEMENT GOAL

Chapter 10: Conflict

This experience is designed to help you focus on goal setting as part of managing conflicts. Begin your work by identifying a relationship you have that is not going as smoothly as you might like. Find one in which you are experiencing some conflict. The key question you are answering in this experience is, What do you want from this relationship that you are not getting?

On a sheet of paper, write as many things as you can that you want from this relationship. Write each item on a separate line and allow a couple of inches between each item to write additional analysis. Next, under each item, describe what you would like the other person to do in relation to these things you want. Finally, write a complete goal statement for each item. This should state the following:

a. What behavior you want

b. What amount of behavior (if you know it)

c. How you will measure the amount

d. What criteria you hold

e. How you will measure these criteria

f. A time frame—date and time—by which you wish the goal to be accomplished

EXAMINING A CONFLICTUAL RELATIONSHIP

Chapter 10: Conflict

This experience will help you think through how you might improve a relationship. This is a private, introspective experience. By now, you should have no difficulty completing these steps on a separate paper.

Step 1.   Write down the name of someone with whom you have an ongoing relationship that you would like to make better.

Step 2.   Indicate what you want to change. Write down the goal, using whatever words best describe your intent.

Step 3.   Write down the behaviors the other person can perform that will cause you to agree that your goal has been achieved.

Step 4.   Write a complete statement for each performance. Describe the nature, quality, and amount that you will consider acceptable.

Step 5.   Have you ever asked for these behaviors? Can you ask for these behaviors? Will you ask for these behaviors? How will you ask for these behaviors? (Remember: talk about yourself, and stay in the present tense.)

WHAT MAKES A HEALTHY INTERPERSONAL RELATIONSHIP?

Chapter 9: Climate

Chapter 10: Conflict

This experience will help you understand the features of a healthy relationship by comparing your ideas with those of your classmates.

Step 1
(twenty minutes)

Working as a group, discuss how to maintain a healthy relationship. After twenty minutes, list the group's ideas on the chalkboard, collectively ranked according to their relative importance.

Step 2
(approximately ten minutes)

Still working as a group, discuss these questions:

1. Does the group share any ideas about healthy relationships? If so, what does this tell you?
2. Are there any notable differences in the listed ideas? If so, how do you explain them?
3. Based on the lists of other groups, would your group want to change its list? If so, how?
4. If you have made any changes in your list, rank the top five, write them on the board, and erase everything else.

Step 3
(approximately thirty minutes)

Select one member of your group to work at the chalkboard. Select another member to direct a conversation with the class. Identify at least one (or two, if this is easily done) implication for behavior for each item on the board.

ETHICAL ISSUES

Chapter 11: Ethics and Diversity

There are a number of ways to think about ethical issues. This experience is designed to allow you to share your ideas with others. Read and analyze each of these situations in small groups. Then share your judgment about what you think you should do and then what you actually would do. Tell also how you account for this difference. Tell what ethical principles are relevant to the decision-making process for each situation.

Dawn

Michael is a fifteen-year-old neighbor whom Dawn has known since he moved into her neighborhood, when he was three and she was eight. He sees her outside and comes over to talk. Michael asks her to promise not to tell his parents that he intends to run away from home. Dawn agrees. Michael goes on to tell her of his plans to take one of the family cars with him. Dawn tries to persuade Michael to talk to his parents and not run away. He refuses and stomps off. Assume you are Dawn.

Lashonta

Lashonta has been dating Charles for almost a year. He is the first man who is really exciting to her. Lashonta enjoys many of the same things as Charles, especially the long talks they have about many important issues. One important issue to both of them is attitudes about sex. Charles believes that it is important to save sex for marriage. He has asked Lashonta a couple of times what she thinks about this issue, but she sidesteps his question. Lashonta had sex with a friend once when she was sixteen. Charles senses that Lashonta is avoiding this issue. He decides to ask her directly about her sexual experience. Assume you are Lashonta.

Marisa

Marisa has a friend, Jerry, who has a fatal illness. Marisa has talked to Jerry's father and found out that Jerry has only weeks to live. Jerry senses that he is growing weak and wonders if he is dying. He asks Marisa if she thinks he is dying. Assume you are Marisa.

Rita

Rita, a close friend of Phillip, saw him pick up another student's textbook, tuck it in with his books, and walk off. She is shocked and concerned about what seems to be such a blatant act of stealing. Phillip walks down the hall to another room, where he sits, awaiting his next class. Assume you are Rita.

Mary Ruth

Mary Ruth, a friend of Linda, sees Linda sitting in a back booth of the Pizza House Restaurant with Ryan. It seems obvious to Mary Ruth that this is much more than a casual encounter. Again and again. Linda is involved with Ryan in "romantic" behavior. The problem is that Linda is engaged to Bill and Mary Ruth senses an obligation to let Bill know that this is going on. Assume you are Mary Ruth.

MANAGING CROSS-CULTURAL COMMUNICATION SITUATIONS

Chapter 11: Cross-Cultural Communication

This experience gives an opportunity to practice responses to a variety of cross-cultural communication situations. You can also compare and contrast your responses with others.

Following are some situations in which people are confronted by some differences brought about through contact with various microcultures. In small groups, discuss each situation. Then formulate a response that you think has the best chance of managing the situation. Record enough of your responses as necessary so that you will be able to share them with the class.

1. A person you know talks about people of other races in a derogatory tone. Although you like this person otherwise, you find these stereotypic references to people offensive. You decide to talk to this person. What do you say?

2. A good friend often engages in sexist language that reflects negatively on these men or women. This behavior bothers you very much and you decide you can no longer tolerate it. You value the friendship enough to talk to this person about the situation. What do you say?

3. Cynthia and Noel are of different races and have recently married. Prior to their marriage, Noel felt somewhat like an outsider when he was at gatherings of Cynthia's family. The situation has not changed; rather, Noel's fears seem to have been confirmed in that he and Cynthia are rarely invited to her parents' home. Cynthia, on the other hand, is frequently included in outings with her mother. Cynthia and Noel have talked about this situation and, over time, she has come to agree with him that there is a problem. They decide to talk to her parents. What should the couple say?

4. Charlotte, a lesbian, has a committed relationship and has enrolled in an interpersonal communication course to learn how to nurture this relationship. She is disappointed in the fact that relationships discussed in the course are assumed to be exclusively heterosexual. She decides to discuss her disappointment with the course instructor. What should she say?

5. You have formed a friendship with a person who sits next to you in class. You have two classes together, one immediately following the next and in the same classroom. Three weeks into the term, this person experiences a religious conversion and is obviously very much enamored with this conversion. This person is so "sold" on this conversion that it is the focus of all the talk

before, between, and after class. The person persists in an effort to get you to go to church. You don't want to put this person down but decide you must talk about this situation because it is having a serious negative effect on your relationship. What do you say?

DIALOGUES FOR ANALYSIS

Two Female Roommates

Roommate 1 (slamming the door): I thought I told you to clean this house. I went to work, I came back, and it's still a mess.

Roommate 2: Look—I just got home myself. I'm tired. I've had a long day and I don't have time to clean this whole apartment.

Roommate 1: Well, when I asked you to do it yesterday you sure seemed to have a lot of time. You were lying there watching TV.

Roommate 2: Look, I work full-time at two jobs. I go to school, you know, why should I . . .

Roommate 1: I have sympathy for you. I work too, and I go to school full-time. And, I have company coming in less than fifteen minutes, and this house is still a mess.

Roommate 2: Why should I have to clean this whole apartment?

Roommate 1: 'Cause you never clean! That's why! I'm sick of cleaning up after you.

Roommate 2: I *never* clean up? Now—I take out the trash, I stack the dishes every now and then. I do a little bit around here.

Roommate 1: Oh, maybe once a week—if I'm lucky to get even that much help.

Roommate 2: Now—who had that party this weekend?

Roommate 1: I had the party, but I believe more of your friends showed up at the end than mine. And they sure were wasted and making a mess.

Roommate 2: Well, look, you said it was an "open" party.

Roommate 1: Yeh—I said it was "open," but I didn't say you had to trash the place either.

Roommate 2: We didn't trash the place; there are just a few beer cans lying around. I can clean it up.

Roommate 1: You call this a few! Look around you! I can't even walk! And it smells bad. Look at those ashtrays. This place is gross!

Roommate 2: We can clean it together before your company comes tonight, I think. Let me finish watching . . .

Roommate 1: That's not the point.

Roommate 2: my TV show here.

Roommate 1: This is how it always happens. This is just how it *always* happens, and I'm sick of always cleaning up the mess.

Roommate 2: I think we need to sit down and make some arrangements.

Roommate 1: This is just why it is a mess; you're sitting there watching TV.

Roommate 2: You're being too bossy. You know, I just can't do everything around here.

Roommate 1: Well, I wouldn't have to be if I didn't have to keep asking you this over and over. After a while, I get sick of asking you.

Two Male Coworkers

First Version
Doug: Jim, dump that over there.

Ken: Doug, Doug—I got this call from a customer. He was irate. He received this entire shipment of a product and only some of it is right. He's just gone crazy! I wrote this order a week ago, and it means lots and lots of money to this company. And somehow it got screwed up. The only place I can see where that could have happened is down in shipping. You had all the parts, or you were supposed to have.

Doug: Ken . . . Ken . . .

Ken: Yeh? Yeh?

Doug: People from your department come down here all of the time and complain about us. You can tell by that chart on the wall that we've had 572 man hours of perfect employment. Bill Phillips put that chart right there to inspire us. It sounds like you're just blowing off steam.

Ken: Well, maybe I am. I've got to get some answers for this customer. He's sitting there with a product he didn't order.

Second Version
Ken: Doug, I got this call, and this customer told me that he had ordered three hundred of the 2400's and two hundred of the 2404's. The three hundred came in and the two hundred are only partial,

and some of them are broken and some of them are bent, to the point that he can't use them. We've got to come up with some solution.

Doug: Is this your customer, Ken?

Ken: This is my customer. The one that I've been working on for years and years, and he finally placed his first order with us.

Doug: Well, you know how organized we are in the shipping department. It's a rare day when something is broken. But, let's face it, you know truckers are pretty violent. Maybe that's the cause of the problem. Have they filed a report with the trucking company yet?

Ken: We shipped those in our trucks!

Doug: We did?

Ken: Yeh—our truck. We delivered it on *our* truck.

Doug: Our truck? Who is that driver on that job? I'm going to have to talk to that guy! But I've inspected almost every package that goes out of here. 'Cause you know, that's my job. And I don't see what you could be talking about. I think your customer, you know, has some . . . well, I don't want to talk about your customer. But he has some problems. I think he's screwed up the material himself. We have had some customers do that when we've known for a fact that the material was put on their docks in perfect order.

Ken: Well, maybe we better go back and check our receipts and the signatures . . .

Doug: We'll check them at our end.

Ken: . . . and see that he's checked them and that they were in good shape.

Doug: But this is our third complaint this week from people in your department. I'm getting sick and tired of people coming down here and trying to tell me how to do my job.

Working Mother and College-Age Daughter

Mother (talking to herself): It's two o'clock in the morning; she said she was going to be here at twelve. Where in the world is she? Why didn't she even call? This is ridiculous! She is never going out again! Never, ever, ever—or she's moving out. I can't stand this!

[door closes]

Daughter: Oh, Mother—what are you doing up at this hour?

Mother: I could ask you the same question. Do you know what time it is, young lady?

Daughter: Yes, ma'am, I do!

Mother: Well, do you want to relay it to me?

Daughter: It's 2:15 A.M., but we were having such a good time. I thought for sure you'd be asleep. It wasn't hurting anybody.

Mother: What time did you tell me you'd be home?

Daughter: I don't remember.

Mother: What time did you tell me you'd be home?

Daughter: 1:30 A.M. Gee—I'm only forty-five minutes . . .

Mother: Wrong!

Daughter: Oh, Mom, go back to bed. You need your sleep.

Mother: I've never *been* to bed! I haven't been to bed yet. I was up reading, and then it happened to have been twelve o'clock and I expected you in. And then you didn't come, and you didn't come, and you didn't come, and now I'm worried.

Daughter: Well, I'm home now. I'm tired. Good night.

Mother: No, ma'am! You come right back here. You're not going to bed. Have you ever heard of a telephone? I mean, just call and tell me you're not dead.

Daughter: Mom, you would have screamed holy murder . . .

Mother: I would not!

Daughter: . . . if I had awakened you at 1:15 A.M.

Mother: I would not.

Daughter: I was having such a good time.

Mother: I would not have screamed.

Daughter: Do you remember what it was like to have fun?

Mother: Oh, now, don't start that with me! Do not! I am the mother; you are the child.

Daughter: Mother, I could be a mother too. Why don't we just be roommates? Do you always have to be the heavy and me the kid?

Mother: As long as I'm the mother, I'm going to be responsible for you. It doesn't matter if you're eighty years old, and God help me, if I'm still living, I will still worry about you.

Daughter: Well, you *should* worry about me; I worry about you.

Mother: Well, what if I'd stayed out all night and you were sitting home? Would you have cared? What if I came moseying on in about

3:30 in the morning? And you said, "Mom, where have you been?" and I said, "Out." Would you deserve—or would you feel like you deserved—some kind of explanation?

Daughter: Curiosity would have killed me! Where would you have been until . . . ha, ha!

Mother: Well, that's not the point! That's not the point!

Daughter: What is the point, mother?

Mother: The point is . . .

Daughter: You're going to be tired, you're going to look like hell at work tomorrow—my class is at eleven tomorrow.

Mother: All right, Ms. Asterbuilt. That's what you do—you stay home and watch "The Young and the Restless" until it's time to go to school. You go to school; I work my butt off all day. I'm here by myself; the house is my responsibility. You don't even lift a finger to do anything around here.

Daughter: But that's your job.

Mother: Oh—no, ma'am! I have a full-time job elsewhere. You can help.

Daughter: Right now, I'm going to school and that's my job.

Mother: Going to school from eleven to two—*big deal!*

Daughter: I can never eat here; why should I wash the dishes?

Mother: Fine—all right—if we're going to be roommates—you pay half the rent—[pause] how does that grab you?

Daughter: Can we have deferred payments?

Mother: No, ma'am! Now—half the bills; half the electricity; half the water. Hey! That's what roommates do! Half the telephone bill . . .

Daughter: So you want me to quit school.

Mother: God knows you love the telephone and calling your boyfriend in Alaska or wherever he lives.

Daughter: I call collect.

Mother: Well, it's a good thing. [pause] And back to the subject at hand. Where have you been from 6 P.M. to two o'clock in the morning?

Daughter: Do you want it minute by minute? I thought you were tired. You're fussing 'cause I'm keeping you up all night.

Mother: You're not too old for me to slap you around a little bit. Tell me where you've been.

Daughter: All right. At 6:15 P.M. I went to Nancy's apartment.

Mother: Don't be smart—

Daughter: I was at Nancy's apartment until about 7:15 P.M., because we were waiting for Joann to come over, because we had to go to the cleaners. And then we had to—oh, let's see—umm—we went out for pizza. Nancy didn't want pizza 'cause she's on a diet, so we had to go get salad. Then we went to see what guys were hanging out at the 7-Eleven. And then we went to Adam's for a while.

Mother: That's a good place. See, I want to know—I wonder how much money I've spent at Adam's and the Acapulco Club, when I've never even been in the place.

Daughter: Precious little, Mother. I don't drink like a wino.

Mother: You better not—you better not.

Daughter: We just socialize.

Mother: And I mean to tell you, if I ever catch you coming in driving drunk—if you ever come home after you've had too much to drink—Honey—that will be the end of your automobile. *The end!*

Daughter: By whose standards—"too much to drink"?

Mother: By mine.

Daughter: You set pretty high standards for me, Mother.

Mother: Well, if you're going to live here, that's the way it's going to be. I am worried about you. As long as you're my child—which will be forever—I will be worried about you.

Daughter: But what about your two martinis at lunch with the girls? Don't you drive home after that? What's the liquor content of that?

Mother: Let's get back to the point here.

Daughter: What I'm trying to say here, Mother, is that you should trust me. And I've never given you any reason not to trust me. I do everything by the book. I don't do drugs. I don't sleep around—my God, I even go to church with you!

Mother: And that is why I expect you to do what you say you are going to do. Because you are a good child. You have always been good; you have never given me any problems. You're right, until just this minute.

A Brother and Sister

Steven: I don't want you going out with Owen.

Jamie: Why not, Steven?

Steven: Because he is an SAE, and he's only got one thing on his mind, and I don't want him messing around with my sister.

Jamie: You're a Kappa Sigma. They think the same thing that SAEs do.

Steven: That's different. Kappa Sig is the biggest fraternity on campus. Everybody in Kappa Sig is O.K.

Jamie: He didn't go to South Alabama; he went to Auburn. That makes a difference.

Steven: No, it doesn't.

Jamie: Why not?

Steven: You're not going out with him.

Jamie: Give me one good reason.

Steven: Cause he is no good. He's no good.

Jamie: That's not a good reason.

Steven: He's got nothing on his mind, and he's going nowhere.

Jamie: Nothing on his mind? *I'm* on his mind. I'm something.

Steven: No. That's beside the point.

Jamie: Steven, you're digging your own hole. *You're* not going out with Owen!

Steven: I'm not digging my own hole. You're not going out with Owen!

Jamie: And you're not big enough to stop me. What about that girl you went out with and I told you she was nothing but a slut. You went out with her anyway.

Steven: That's different. It's a double standard.

Jamie: Why?

Steven: 'Cause girls have to save themselves for marriage.

Jamie: So you just go ahead and take it from her so she can't save anything. Right?

Steven: I didn't take it from her, and that's none of your business. You are just not going out with Owen.

Jamie: Well, do you fear for your little sister?

Steven: Yes. You're not going out with Owen, because Owen . . .

Jamie: Well, have a talk with him.

Steven: You can't control Owen. And I can't be there on the date.

Jamie: Well, then, you talk to Owen and tell him to control himself.

Steven: It's not my place to . . .

Jamie: Well, then . . .

Steven: . . . talk to him.

Jamie: You can't stop me from going out with him. That should be Dad's job.

Steven: I'll tell Mom.

Jamie: Mother can't do anything. She went out with Daddy. [laughter]

Steven: I'll tell you what. I'll find you somebody to go out with.

Jamie: A Kappa Sig?

Steven: Kappa Sig is the best.

Jamie: No way! No, no, no! I've heard about them.

Steven: There's nothing wrong with them.

Jamie: I've heard about their games.

Steven: He's a freshman and in Kappa Sig. He's a nice guy.

Jamie: I had a class last quarter with a girl who used to date one. She had nothing but terrible things to say about him.

Steven: About a Kappa Sig?

Jamie: Yes!

Steven: I can't believe it.

Jamie: And his first name was Steve. I didn't think it was you.

Steven: You have a biased opinion here.

Jamie: You have a biased opinion against Owen as an SAE. And he went to Auburn. You don't know anything about that fraternity.

Steven: I know a guy you can go out with. His name is Gary. He's got glasses. He's a nice guy. He's a freshman.

Jamie: Glasses?

Steven: Well, they're neat looking. He's a nice Christian guy.

Jamie: Does he look like a bookworm?

Steven: No. He's a nice Christian guy.

Jamie: Don't be judging Owen. He may be also.

Steven: He's an SAE. None of those SAEs do that.

Jamie: In Auburn. He goes to South now.

Steven: An SAE is an SAE wherever they are.

Jamie: Are you going to be home Friday night?

Steven: No, I'm going out.

Jamie: See, you can't stop me then.

Steven: I can stop Owen.

Jamie: You wouldn't hurt him.

Steven: No. I'll cut his tires or something.

Jamie: You wouldn't do that 'cause then he'll take his dad's car.

Steven: I'll tie you up and put you in a closet.

Jamie: No, you're not big enough to tie me up and put me in a closet. Besides, I'm the one who took the rope-tying class. I could tie *you* up and put you in the closet. Where should we go on our date? Somewhere lighted?

Steven: You should go out with Gary.

Jamie: I've never met this Gary. And I hate blind dates. I hate them!

Steven: I'll set it up—he's not blind.

Jamie: You said he wore glasses.

Steven: It's just a vision impairment.

Jamie: Will he bring "Rover" with us?

Steven: Probably.

Jamie: A seeing-eye dog.

Steven: Gary is the ideal person for you to go out with.

Jamie: I'm not going out on another blind date.

Steven: You're not going out with Owen.

Jamie: The girl I tried setting you up with would have been nice. But you wouldn't go out with her.

Steven: That's different.

Jamie: No, it's not!

Steven: I can pick and choose whom I want to go out with. You are my little sister. You'll go out with whom I tell you to.

Jamie: How old are you now? One year older. Yeh. That makes you a real expert on dating.

Steven: It does. I've been around and seen more.

Jamie: When you were dating, I was double dating. And I wasn't double dating with your friends.

Steven: But you weren't going out with an SAE.

Jamie: Would you leave that aside?

Steven: I can't.

Jamie: That's not the point.

Steven: He's an SAE.

Jamie: He lives in Springhill.

Steven: He's too old. He's twenty-seven years old

ENDNOTES

1. The basic idea for this experience may have originated with Josepin DeVito of Queens College, although we have seen it in several places.

2. This experience has been widely disseminated. We have noticed variations of it in several sources. One version of it was formulated by William Gellerman. See W. Pfeiffer and J. E. Jones, eds., *A Handbook of Structured Experiences for Human Relations Training*, vol. 2 (LaJolla, CA: University Associates, 1974).

GLOSSARY

abdicrat One of three personality types identified by William Schutz and defined by the interpersonal need to control. Abdicrats have little need to control, preferring to give power and responsibility to the other person in a relationship.

absolute present Principle that we can only live in the present and that our relationships are therefore always in the present.

abstraction Process of moving, in language, farther from a referent; of perceiving and making sense of language; of translating experience into language. A general concept that partially represents some whole.

accommodation Process of adjusting the frame of reference to integrate new information and experiences.

acculturation The modification of a person's culture through contact with another culture.

active listening Technique that includes the skills of concentrating, frequent internal summarizing, interrupting, and paraphrasing what another has said.

adaptable-social One of three personality types identified by William Schutz and defined by the need for inclusion. Adaptable-social people balance needs for inclusion and privacy.

adaptor Movement or gesture displayed to alleviate psychological tension.

adjustment   The fourth stage of culture shock, in which the person adapts to a culture enough to feel comfortable.

affect display   Movement or gesture that reflects a feeling or the intensity of feelings.

affection   Fondness for or devotion to someone or something; liking. One of three interpersonal needs identified by William Schutz. In this context, affection is the desire to be liked by others and to develop loving relationships. Schutz identified three personality types related to the interpersonal need for affection: (1) overpersonal, (2) personal, and (3) underpersonal.

affirmation value   Benefit that a person derives from a relationship because of the other person's confirmation of that person and his or her beliefs.

agenda for talking about relationships   A list of all components of a relationship presented in an order convenient to follow in an interpersonal encounter. Included are observations, inferences, feelings, wants and expectations, intentions, openness, images, and checkout.

aggressive   Interactive style that is self-enhancing, belittling, controlling, and hurtful or damaging to others and to relationships.

allness   Making judgments and treating people based on limited experience but acting as if this limited experience has allowed us to know all there is to know about them.

ambiguity   Quality of a message that permits more than one interpretation.

analyst   Mnemonic device to assist in remembering a behavior that punishes talk about negative feelings. ("You feel that way because . . ..")

artifacts   Things people collect about themselves.

assertive   Interactive style that is self-enhancing, expressive, and self-supportive yet also protective of the choices of others. Not aggressive and not shy.

assimilation   Process of changing what is perceived to fit a frame of reference.

attending   In listening, the selective act of attention.

attention   Process of responding to stimuli.

attitude   "Mental and neural state of readiness organized through experience, exerting a directive or dynamic influence upon behavior, the individual's response to all objects and situations to which it is related" (Gordon Allport). Predisposition to respond.

attraction   See "interpersonal attraction."

attribution   Assigning motivations to another person's behaviors.

authenticity   An attempt to present oneself as direct, honest, and straightforward in communicating feelings and information.

autocrat   One of three personality types identified by William Schutz and defined by the interpersonal need to control. Autocrats feel a need to dominate, to rise to the top of a hierarchy.

avoiding   Stage in relational deterioration characterized by overt efforts to break off contact and end the relationship.

balance   State of emotional calm that results when perceptions seem consistent with expectations or our image of reality; a quality of a system that accounts for its ability to change so that its various elements suit its goals and environment.

belief   Statement about what is developed from information outside the realm of personal experience. Three categories of beliefs are primitive, surface, and derived.

bonding   One of five stages in a relationship in which the partners make a special, voluntary, ongoing commitment, usually, but not always, in a public ritual.

certainty   Defensive behavior characterized by a rigid viewpoint and both verbal and nonverbal suggestions that the speaker is correct and the receiver is incorrect. Closed-mindedness that creates defensiveness; behavioral opposite of provisionalism.

channel   The means of transmission; the vehicle through which messages are sent.

checkout   Colloquial term used to help remember the importance of getting and giving feedback when talking about relationships.

circumscribing   Stage in relational deterioration characterized by avoidance of topics and situations that might lead to self-disclosure.

classification level of abstraction   Communicating about the people in our relationships in terms of particular groups they belong to.

closure   Process of adding information to perceptions of otherwise incomplete events.

code   Set of symbols and signals used to convey messages. See "language."

coercive power   Power that derives from ability to remove another's actual choices or the perception that choices are available. Power that derives from force or the threat of force.

cohesiveness   Sense, feeling, or property of wholeness, unity, or togetherness.

communication   Process of transmitting and interpreting messages.

communication competence   Communication that achieves what one person wants from the other while maintaining the relationship in a way acceptable to both.

compatibility   Ability to coexist in harmony.

complementary relationship   Relationship, or view of a relationship, in which one person is superior and the other is subordinate, as in a parent-child relationship.

compromise   Conflict management strategy in which parties each give and get a little, splitting the difference if possible.

conditioning   Process of teaching or controlling behavior by making rewards and punishments contingent upon specific behavior.

conflict, interpersonal   Form of competition. Situation in which one person's behaviors are designed to interfere with or harm another.

confrontation/problem solving   Conflict management strategy in which energies are directed toward defeating a problem and not the other person. Parties look for a mutually beneficial solution.

connotative meaning   Personal meaning of a word. Affective associations that an individual brings to a word. Connotation imbues language with value (right/wrong, good/bad), potency (hard/soft, hot/cold), and action (fast/slow).

consistency   Perceptual process that causes us to perceive what we expect to perceive and to be uncomfortable when our perceptions and expectations don't match. In attribution theory, the expectation that an individual will exhibit the same behaviors in similar situations. We generally respond to consistency by attributing the behavioral cause to the individual and to inconsistency by attributing the behavioral cause to circumstances outside the individual.

content dimension   Part of a communication event having to do with topics, objects, and events outside the relationship.

context   Physical, social, psychological, and temporal environment in which a communication event occurs.

control   (n.) Defensive behavior characterized by manipulation in an attempt to impose an attitude or viewpoint on another. One of three interpersonal needs identified by William Schutz. The degree of desire to exercise power and authority. Schutz identified three personality types related to the need to control: (1) abdicrat, (2) democrat, and (3) autocrat. Behavioral opposite of problem orientation. (v.) To exercise restraint, dominance, or direction over; to command.

cooperation   Process of working or acting together for a common purpose.

critical listening   Part of the listening process in which four questions are asked to discover closed-mindedness or bias: (1) position, (2) agreement, (3) feeling strength, and (4) importance.

cue   Message that is not symbolic.

culture   Assumptions and rules of a group that render patterns of thought and behavior appropriate or inappropriate; the sum total of ways of living built up by a group of human beings and transmitted from one generation to another.

culture shock   The psychological reaction of distress brought on by being exposed to a culture very different from one's own.

crisis   The second stage of culture shock, in which the person actually feels distress because of the differences in the other culture.

decoder   Mechanism or agent that translates. In interpersonal events, each individual translates the messages sent by the other.

defensiveness   A position or attitude designed to protect against attack. In interpersonal communication, manifested in such behaviors as evaluation, superiority, certainty, control, neutrality, and strategy. Behavioral opposite of supportiveness.

democrat   One of three personality types identified by William Schutz and defined by the interpersonal need to control. Democrats are balanced and capable of taking charge or allowing others to be in control when appropriate.

denotation The dictionary definition of a word. Meaning of a word, as agreed to by a speech community.

derived beliefs Beliefs resulting from other beliefs.

description Supportive behavior characterized by factual information, absence of judgmental language, and straightforward questions.

dialogue A communication event in which each participant understands himself or herself as both speaker and listener and that is characterized by fundamentally empathic and authentic communication.

differentiating Stage in relational deterioration characterized by focus on the individual and perception of self as separate from the other person and the relationship.

disconfirmation Process of ignoring or denying another's self-disclosure.

dissonance Emotional discomfort resulting from conflict between related elements in the attitude-value-belief structure. In extreme form, dissonance and guilt are synonymous.

distortion In the perception process, changing the content to fit the frame of reference.

dyadic communication Two-person communication.

ego states In Transactional Analysis, patterns of behavior reflecting the self-concept. There are three ego states: the parent is the source of rules that govern behavior, the adult is rational and conceptual, and the child is emotional.

ego support value The benefits a person derives from a relationship because of the support of the other person.

emblem Deliberate movement that can be directly translated into words; discrete, categorical behavior that is generally known and accepted.

emotions Physical state within particular contexts.

empathic listening Part of the listening process; observing and identifying with another's feelings, wants and expectations, intentions, openness, and images and bringing them to the level of talk when they seem important.

empathy Supportive behavior characterized by identification with experiences, feelings, and problems of others and affirmation of another's self-worth.

encoder The component of the communication process that translates information from one form to another; in speech, that which translates ideas into spoken words. A telephone mouthpiece serves as an encoder when it translates spoken words into electronic impulses.

enculturation The process of transmitting culture from one generation to the next.

environmental interchange The exchange of information and resources between a system and its environment.

ethics   A body of principles (or values) regarding good and bad behavior.

equality   Supportive behavior characterized by respect for another and efforts to minimize differences in ability, status, power, and intellectual ability. Behavioral opposite of superiority.

equifinality   The quality of offering a system many means to achieve its final goals.

equivocation   A response that avoids a direct answer through ambiguous or unclear language.

ethnocentricism   The tendency to view people of other cultures through one's own cultural perspective, especially when it results in the conclusion that one's own culture is superior.

evaluation   Defensive behavior characterized by judgments, assessments, and questions about another's viewpoint or motive. Behavioral opposite of description.

evasion   A response that avoids addressing the issue at hand.

expectation   Anticipation of an occurrence; prediction; assumption that an event is likely to occur. Anticipated response from another.

experimenting   One of five stages in interpersonal relationships in which an individual explores another and searches for common areas of interest.

expert power   Power that derives from knowledge.

face-saving lie   Making a statement that is untrue in order to avoid embarrassment.

fact-inference confusion   Process of making an observation, drawing an inference about the observation, and acting on the guess as though it were a fact.

family   A network of people who live together over a long period of time and who are bound to each other by ties of marriage, blood, or commitment, legal or otherwise.

feedback   Messages sent from a receiver to a source to correct or control error. Can take the form of talk, verbalized cues, and nonverbal cues.

feelings   Physical body events experienced in the present tense. Body's response to physical stimulation.

freedom to be   The right to exercise reasonable control over one's life.

field of experience   Sum of an individual's experiences, plus all connections drawn among them, that allows a person to talk about and interact with the world. Some theorists believe that people cannot interact unless their fields of experience overlap.

forcing   Conflict management strategy that uses power to cause another to accept a position.

frame of reference   Interlocking facts, ideas, beliefs, values, and attitudes that give form to perceptions.

game   In game theory, a simulation with rules that govern the behavioral choices of players. Game may be played as win-win, win-lose, or lose-lose. In Transactional Analysis, a game is a dishonest, ulterior transaction in which the participant hides true feelings while manipulating another into providing a payoff.

gestures Body movements that express an idea or emotion.

hierarchy A set of systems, people, or objects related to each other by status, importance, or size. Hierarchy is usually pictured as stacked to illustrate the relationships among the elements.

honeymoon The first stage of culture shock, in which a person is unaware of differences in the other culture and is enchanted with it.

identity aspiration Desire to be recognized as a particular kind of person.

illustrator Deliberate movement used to reinforce and enrich verbal messages.

image Mental representation, idea, or form. Description or conception of something.

inclusion One of the interpersonal needs identified by William Schutz that includes an individual's desire to be accepted, to feel wanted, and to be a part of groups. He identified three personality types: undersocial, oversocial, and adaptable-social.

indiscrimination Failure to recognize the uniqueness of a person; interacting in terms of some class or category stereotype.

inference Guess, conclusion, or judgment derived from observations.

inferential level of abstraction Communication using language that suggests broad, often judgmental categories.

information In information theory, available data. The more available data, the more information and the less the uncertainty. More commonly used to mean anything that reduces uncertainty.

information overload Condition in which the complexity or amount of available information is too great to manage effectively.

information/persuasive power Influence over another person that comes from a person's control of information and/or ability to make believable arguments.

initiating One of five stages in interpersonal relationships in which an individual observes another and decides whether to invite interaction.

integrating One of five stages in interpersonal relationships in which partners move closer, talk more, and think of each other as a unit, using the terms *we* and *our* in reference to their relationship.

intensifying One of five stages in interpersonal relationships in which intimacy and trust increase as partners commit more fully to each other.

intention Will or determination to act or achieve some end.

intentional orientation Approaching people, objects, and events as if the words we use to talk about them are actually the people, objects, or events.

interchangeability Characteristic of language that makes it possible for individuals to function as both sources and receivers.

interdependence The quality of being interrelated and constrained by each other's actions.

interpersonal attraction   Willingness to communicate and develop a relationship with another.

interpersonal communication   Transactional process of exchanging messages and negotiating meaning to convey information and to establish and maintain relationships.

interview   Interpersonal communication context in which questions are asked and answered to achieve some goal.

intimacy   Characterization of a close, familiar, and usually affectionate relationship that results from self-disclosure and mutual acceptance.

irreversibility   Feature of communication process that makes it impossible to take back what has been said. Once a communication event has occurred, it cannot be "uncommunicated."

Johari Window   Illustration designed by psychologists Joseph Luft and Harrington Ingham to explain the relationships between self-concept and self-presentation. Includes four sections: (1) open self—things about the self that are known both to self and others; (2) blind self—things known to others but not to self; (3) hidden self—things known to self but not to others; and (4) unknown self—an area inferred to exist but not known to self or others.

judge   Mnemonic device used to describe the tendency in our society to punish clear expressions of negative feelings. ("You have no right to feel that way.")

language   Body of words and symbols, governed by rules, commonly used to communicate.

legitimate power   Power that derives from position.

leveling   Distorting a message by omitting details from what is perceived.

lie   An intentional attempt to hide or misrepresent the facts by telling or leading someone to believe something that is not true.

liking   To regard with favor. To have kindly, friendly feeling for someone or something. Related to "affection."

linguistics   Study of language that focuses on the rules of word usage and the relationships between words, meanings, and behavior. Sometimes subdivided into semantics (study of meanings), syntax (study of rules), and pragmatics (study of language-behavior relationships).

listening   Active process of receiving verbal and nonverbal messages.

map-territory confusion   Substitution of language for experience. Treating a symbol as an object that can be manipulated. Sometimes called "reification."

material me   Part of self-concept that focuses on body, home, and physical objects.

message   Any sign, symbol, or combination thereof that functions as stimulus material for a receiver.

metacommunication   Communication about communication.

model Physical representation of something. A metaphor that allows examination of some object or process in a particular way but also limits what can be observed in that way.

monologue A communication event in which one or both participants focus on their own feelings without regard for the other person.

naming Assignment of labels to objects, phenomena, events, and especially people.

naming level of abstraction Communication using language that acknowledges the uniqueness of the other person, often signaled by using the person's name.

negative reinforcement Removal of an aversive stimulus to strengthen behavior. Removal is contingent on the behavior.

neutrality Defensive behavior characterized by treating another as an object having only one or a limited set of functions or without showing concern for that individual's problems or viewpoint. Behavioral opposite of "empathy."

noise Any interference or distortion in message exchange. Noise exists in the communication process to the extent that message fidelity is damaged. Three broad categories: (1) physical, or channel, noise (2) semantic, or psychological, noise, and (3) systemic, or system-centered, noise.

nonassertive Interactive style characterized by self-denial, which allows or encourages others to choose and receive what they want, even at the expense of self. Sometimes called "shy."

nonverbal communication Communication other than words.

nonverbal level of abstraction Communication based upon our direct experience of the other person, involving our thoughts and perceptions in the immediate present.

observations In interpersonal communication, the results of noticing or perceiving the behavior of others. Process of taking in information about another person. One component of the relationship dimension of communication.

openness Willingness to receive and consider ideas from another. Sometimes called "latitude of acceptance."

operant conditioning Process of strengthening or weakening behavior by making rewards and punishments contingent upon the change desired.

optimist Mnemonic device used to describe the tendency to negate expressions of negative feelings. ("Everything will be all right.")

overpersonal One of three personality types identified by William Schutz and defined by the need for affection. Overpersonal people take special pains to avoid being disliked. They may spend great amounts of time talking about their feelings or inquiring about the feelings of others.

oversocial One of three personality types identified by William Schutz and defined by the need for inclusion. Oversocial people continually seek to join and feel a part of many groups.

paraverbal cues Variations in rate, pitch, force, and formation of suprasegmental elements of language that constitute how a word is spoken.

passive listening Attending to what is being said without actively providing feedback. Does not interrupt the speaker but may provide subtle, nonverbal feedback.

perception Process of becoming aware of sensory stimuli and selecting from available information.

perceptual accentuation Feature of perception process that distorts perceptions in the direction of wants. For example, we tend to see people we like as smarter and more beautiful than those we do not like.

personal One of three personality types identified by William Schutz and defined in terms of the interpersonal need for affection. Personal people can balance situations to be liked when affection is desirable or maintain distance when it is not desirable.

personalizing Using language that places responsibility for judgments and opinions upon oneself.

person perception Process of perceiving another, characterized by mutuality, clarity, and number of expectations. Derives from summary evaluation and includes and is influenced by feelings about self and others.

persuasion Process of influencing attitudes and behaviors.

persuasive power Power that derives from ability to argue logically and persuasively.

polarization Use of language in pairs of opposites without allowing any middle ground.

positive reinforcement Process of strengthening behavior by making reward contingent upon that behavior.

posture Carriage or position of the body as a whole.

power Ability or potential to influence others. J. R. P. French and B. H. Raven identified six bases of power—referent, expert, legitimate, reward, coercive, and information/persuasion—each of which is defined in this glossary.

problem orientation Supportive behavior characterized by a desire to collaborate with another in defining and solving a problem. Behavioral opposite of control.

process Ongoing activity. Continuous change in pursuit of a goal.

productivity Feature of language that makes it possible to create original sentences that will be understood and to talk about new ideas.

projection Process of attributing one's own feelings, attitudes, values, and beliefs to others.

provisionalism Supportive behavior characterized by willingness to be tentative, to share information, to suggest that additional information might change one's mind, and to work jointly with another. Behavioral opposite of certainty.

proximity Nearness in space that makes it possible for two people to develop a relationship. Part of interpersonal attraction.

punctuation Arbitrary assignment of beginnings and endings in the continuous process of communication, thus identifying separate sequences. One means of interpreting events.

receiver Person or thing that takes in messages.

recovery The third stage of culture shock, in which a person understands a culture well enough to feel relaxed most of the time.

referent Object, phenomenon, person, or event to which a symbol refers. Part of the triangle of meaning developed by C. K. Ogden and I. A. Richards.

referent power Power that derives from liking.

reflexiveness Ability of language to refer to itself.

regulator Body movement that fosters interaction. Gesture system that controls turn taking in the flow of communication.

reification See "map-territory confusion."

reinforcement Strengthening of another's behavior or self-concept.

relational definition Perception each person carries in language about a relationship at a particular moment.

relational deterioration Disintegration of a relationship resulting from loss of attractiveness, unfulfilled needs, or inability to manage differences.

relational growth Result of maintaining a satisfying, interesting, and meaningful relationship.

relational rules Societal assumptions and interpersonal agreements arrived at through self-disclosure that allows the prediction of behavior.

relationship dimension Part of a communication event, usually nonverbal, that allows interpretations about the nature of the relationship.

remembering Process of recalling by an effort of memory. Fourth component of the listening process.

response Any behavior that results from stimulation.

reward power Power that derives from ability to mediate another's rewards through possession of something valued.

rigidity in naming Process of fixing or hardening a label to some person, object, phenomenon, or event.

rip-off artist Mnemonic device used to describe a person who shifts the attention away from a person expressing negative feelings and to him or herself. ("This happened to me.")

risk Exposure to a hazard, danger, or loss.

role Behavior evidenced by an individual and sanctioned by others. Expectations of someone's dual behavior. Pattern of behavior. Routine associated with an individual in a particular context.

rule Pattern of behavior expected from certain role situation or context. Boundary for behavior in a relationship.

script In Transactional Analysis, the life plan an individual feels compelled to act out. Characterized by four basic themes, or life positions: (1) I'm OK, you're OK; (2) I'm OK, you're not OK; (3) I'm not OK, you're OK; (4) I'm not OK, you're not OK.

selective attention Process of choosing between stimuli.

selective exposure Process of choosing to expose oneself to certain stimuli while disregarding or avoiding others.

self-awareness Degree to which our self-concept matches the person others see us as.

self-concept Sum of perceptions, ideas, and images about oneself.

self-disclosure Revealing one's thinking, feelings, beliefs, and the like to another.

self-esteem Value of oneself. Self-love. Self-respect.

self-expression Word choice that reflects the feelings and status of the speaker. Sometimes strong language that was not intended literally.

self-fulfilling prophecy Process of making a prediction come true.

self-regulation A system's ability to sense the environment, monitor goal attainment, and adjust itself to the environment so that it can achieve its goals.

sensing Receiving stimuli through the five senses.

Shannon and Weaver model Model of the communication process.

shared beliefs Beliefs derived through experience and acknowledged by others.

sharpening In perception, process of focusing on details that reinforce the frame of reference while discarding the rest.

shy See "nonassertive."

sign Token. Indication. Something that stands for or announces the presence of something else when a natural relationship exists.

significant other Person who influences the formation of the self-concept. Person to whom one looks for information about appropriate behavior.

silence Absence of sound. Background upon which all spoken language is structured. Thomas Bruneau identified three forms: (1) psycholinguistic (part of the temporal sequence of speech), (2) interactive (pause or interruption used for decision making), and (3) sociocultural (culturally sanctioned or mandated silences).

similarity Perception that someone is like ourselves. Part of interpersonal attraction.

smoothing Conflict management strategy of minimizing differences and emphasizing positive, common interests or of avoiding issues that might cause conflict.

social comparison Comparison of oneself to others.

social me Part of self-concept that focuses upon how others perceive and experience oneself.

source Location of an idea. Originator of a message.

spiritual me Part of self-concept that focuses upon awareness of oneself as a thinking and feeling person.

spontaneity Supportive behavior characterized by the candid, straightforward, and uncomplicated presentation of the self.

stagnation Stage in relational deterioration characterized by inactivity, verbal silence, discomfort, and negation of one's partner.

static evaluation language Language that reflects fixed judgments and evaluations of people.

stereotype Application of a fixed set of beliefs about a group or subgroup that ignore the uniqueness of the individual member.

stimulation value A benefit derived from a relationship because the other person brings up interesting ideas.

strategy Defensive behavior characterized by attempts to trick another into thinking that (1) he is making a decision that in fact has already been made or (2) his best interests are being considered when they are not.

subcultural language Language specific to a particular subculture.

superiority Defensive behavior characterized by suggestions that another is inadequate or inferior and thus unable to entertain feedback or share in problem solving.

supportive behavior Communication behavior that affirms the other person and the relationship. It is characterized by description, problem orientation, spontaneity, empathy, equality, and provisionalism, each of which is defined in this glossary.

surface beliefs Flexible beliefs. Least central of all elements in the belief structure, for example, those dealing with matters of taste.

support relationship A relationship in which a person encourages another person to talk freely about all aspects of self.

symbol Something that stands for something else when no natural relationship exists. In language, words, phrases, and sentences that stand for thoughts.

system A set of objects or entities that interrelate with one another to form a whole.

symmetrical relationship Relationship, or view of a relationship, in which partners are essentially similar in status, responsibility, and the like.

terminating Result of relational deterioration. End of a relationship. Severance of contact, sometimes codified, as in a divorce decree.

territoriality Tendency for individuals to claim, "own," and use space as an extension of their own personal space. Lyman and Scott described four categories: (1) public (area that individuals may enter freely), (2) interactional (area marked by participants as theirs while they are interacting), (3) home (private space occupied by legal sanction), and (4) body (space immediately surrounding one's physical person).

thought Result of mental activity. Perception and interpretation of a referent, including feelings, past experiences, and related perceptions. Mental image of a referent.

time Cultural system of temporal or sequential relationships between and among events that has message potential. Some cultures are monochronic because they use time arbitrarily. Others are polychronic because they emphasize people and interactions, rather than an arbitrary understanding of time.

touching behavior, friendship/warmth Casual and spontaneous touching that signals mutual acceptance and positive regard (but excluding love or sexual touching), as in congratulatory back patting.

touching behavior, functional/professional Touching to deliver professional service, as between a physician and patient.

touching behavior, love/intimacy Touching that signals a special, or bonded, relationship, or that assumes or confirms intimate access to be appropriate, as in hand holding or lap sitting.

touching behavior, sexual arousal Touching that is pleasant because of the sexual meaning it conveys or the sexual stimulation it produces, as in petting and sexual intercourse.

touching behavior, social/polite Ritual touching to acknowledge someone's personhood or essential humanity and/or acknowledge or neutralize status differences, as in handshaking or kissing a cardinal's ring.

transactional Mutual negotiation of meaning. Mutual influence.

Transactional Analysis System developed by Eric Berne for analyzing relationship behavior as it occurs.

triangle of meaning Figure developed by C. K. Ogden and I. A. Richards that depicts the relationship among words, referents, and thoughts.

trust Feeling of comfort that derives from ability to predict another's behavior. A belief that the other can be relied on.

turn taking Passing initiative for talk back and forth between participants in conversation; signaled by various nonverbal cues.

two-valued orientation The tendency to experience a phenomenon or event in polarized terms without allowing any middle ground. See "polarization."

underpersonal One of three personality types identified by William Schutz and defined in terms of the interpersonal need for affection. Underpersonal people have little need for affection and avoid giving it to others.

undersocial One of three personality types identified by William Schutz and defined in terms of the need for inclusion. Undersocial people have little need for inclusion, isolating themselves from group involvement.

understanding Third component of the listening process. Interpretation and evaluation of what is sensed.

utility value The benefit a person gets from a relationship because of talents or things the other person brings to the relationship.

values What a person considers important; wants, goals, and guidelines. Characterized by statements of what should be.

vocalics Variations in rate, pitch, force, and formation of suprasegmental elements of language that constitute how a word is spoken.

wants Wishes, needs, and desires for a relationship.

white lie Saying something that is not true without malicious intent. The intent is often to protect oneself or the other person.

withdrawal Conflict management strategy of retreating from conflict.

wholeness The quality that makes the whole of a system greater than the sum of its parts.

INDEX

abstraction, 102, 107-114, 116, 125, 135-137, 394-396, 435, 437, 441, 443

accommodation, 62, 70, 73, 94-95, 435

acquaintanceship, 243, 247, 251, 265, 272, 274

active listening, 122, 192, 208, 219-220, 230-234, 296, 304, 308, 330, 341, 403-404, 413, 435

affection needs*****

affirmation value, 436

allness, 436

angle of interaction, 174-175, 196, 198, 200

assertiveness, 158, 169-171, 246

assimilation, 62, 70, 73, 94-95, 436

attitude, 38-40, 42, 55-57, 73, 85, 88, 90, 136, 243, 264, 272, 277, 286-288, 290-292, 297-298, 315, 335, 343, 347, 414, 436, 438

attraction, 22, 61-62, 74, 78-79, 81, 83, 91, 94, 216, 240-244, 248, 257-258, 260, 262, 264, 273, 275, 277-278, 301, 315, 321, 343-345, 355, 436, 442, 444, 446

attribution, 62, 78-79, 81, 83, 91, 94-97, 212, 436, 438

authenticity, 361, 365, 382, 436

avoiding, 281, 286, 305, 309, 311, 318, 330, 335, 348, 350, 353, 355-356, 364, 370, 423, 437, 446

blind self, 240, 252, 442

bonding, 26, 186, 213, 240, 259-261, 269, 271-276, 313, 437

certainty, 282, 285-286, 288, 294-295, 298, 311, 437-438, 444

channels, 4, 17-18, 21, 258, 343

Cipher in the Snow, 46

circumscribing, 305, 318, 348-349, 355, 437

closure, 62, 69-70, 94, 437

clothing, 9-10, 133, 174-175, 179, 187-191, 198, 208-209, 214, 266

cognitive control, 142, 147

combining, 102, 108

coming together process,
240, 260-261, 348
commitment, 114-115, 239,
260, 263-265, 267,
269-272, 274, 279,
291, 302, 320, 340,
342, 346, 350, 354-
355, 414, 437, 440
communication, 3-4, 6-10,
12-26, 29-32, 34-36,
38-40, 42-46, 48-50,
52, 54-59, 61-68, 70,
72, 74-78, 80-82, 84-
86, 88, 90-92, 94-97,
101-108, 110-112, 114-
120, 122, 124-126,
128, 130, 132, 134-
144, 146, 148, 150,
152, 154, 156-166,
168-171, 173-218,
220, 222, 224-230,
232, 234-235, 239-
242, 244, 246-248,
250-252, 254-258,
260-262, 264-266,
268-270, 272, 274-
279, 281-288, 290-
302, 304, 306, 308,
310-315, 318, 320,
322, 324, 326-328,
330-332, 334-336,
338, 340, 342-344,
346, 348-350, 352-
354, 356-358, 360-
362, 364-370, 372,
374-378, 380, 382-
384, 386-390, 392-
394, 396, 398-402,
404-406, 408-414,
416, 418-420, 422,
424, 426, 428, 430,
432, 434, 436-448
complementarity, 102, 121,
123, 137
compromise, 270, 318,
330-331, 333, 355,
437

conflict, 12, 37, 125, 145,
182, 192, 207, 268-
269, 279, 283, 289,
296, 303-305, 308,
310, 312-313, 315,
317-319, 321-323,
325, 327-343, 345-
349, 351, 353, 355-
359, 368-369, 382,
410, 414-415, 418,
420-422, 437-440,
446, 448
confirmation, 134, 270,
304, 323, 436
connotation, 103, 117, 119-
120, 438
context, 4, 17-18, 21, 23,
32, 50, 57, 82, 109-
110, 115, 120, 142,
145-149, 180, 184,
186-187, 191, 197,
205, 210-211, 215-
216, 234-235, 250,
255, 279, 358, 363,
365, 395, 399, 413,
436, 438, 442, 445
control, 17, 24, 29-31, 45,
47, 50-53, 56-57, 86,
89, 91, 102, 115, 120,
123, 129, 135, 141-
142, 146-147, 152,
158-159, 161-163,
165, 168, 176, 181-
184, 192-194, 199,
209, 211, 241, 244-
245, 253, 270, 272,
282, 285, 287-288,
290, 296, 298, 311,
318, 320, 323, 325,
329-330, 337, 340,
342, 344-345, 354-
355, 357, 369, 378,
383, 388, 402, 413,
432, 435-436, 438-
441, 444
critical listening, 219, 228,
438

culture, 13, 75, 102-103,
107, 118, 139, 173-
175, 177, 180, 182,
184-185, 190, 196,
200, 202, 204, 209,
211, 215, 217, 235,
241, 249, 277, 322,
361, 373-375, 380-
382, 435-436, 438-
441, 445

decoder, 4, 17-18, 21, 438
defensiveness, 54-55, 88,
192, 207, 225, 281,
284-285, 287-288,
295, 299-300, 311-
312, 314, 350, 411,
437-438
denotation, 439
description, 92, 155, 282,
293-294, 297-298,
343, 359, 385, 396,
439-441, 447
differentiating, 305, 318,
348, 355, 439
disconfirmation, 133-134,
311, 439
diversity, 76, 361-363, 365,
367, 369, 371-373,
375, 377-384, 422
dominant behavior, 40,
56-57

emotions, 76, 104, 138,
141-149, 151, 153,
155-157, 159, 161,
163, 165, 167-171,
177, 180, 182-184,
192, 194, 208, 307,
396-399, 402, 439
empathic listening, 228-
229, 235, 402, 439
empathy, 21, 97, 119, 167,
184, 219-220, 225,
228-229, 234, 246,
293, 296-298, 300,
302, 304, 313, 330,

337-338, 361, 365, 382, 439, 443, 447

encoder, 4, 16-18, 21, 439

engagement, 26, 239-242, 244, 246-248, 272, 301, 303, 349, 368, 382, 403

environmental inter-change, 439

equality, 125, 268, 282, 293-294, 297-298, 302, 361, 366, 440, 447

equifinality, 440

esteem needs, 50

ethics, 40, 59, 361-363, 365-367, 369-371, 373, 375, 377, 379, 381-384, 422, 440

evaluation, 77, 102, 129-131, 222, 228-229, 282-286, 288, 294, 298, 311, 342, 370, 390, 413, 438, 440, 444, 446, 448

evaluative listening, 219, 228

fact-inference confusion, 440

family communication, 84-85, 96, 357, 408

feedback, 4, 17-18, 21, 23, 37, 44, 164, 166, 192, 207-209, 224, 226-227, 246, 256, 341, 380-381, 437, 440, 444, 447

feelings, 8, 10, 15, 21, 53, 70, 74, 77, 87, 89, 97, 104-106, 113-115, 122, 134-135, 141-151, 153-157, 159, 161, 163-165, 167-171, 173, 178, 182, 184, 187, 192, 207-208, 226-227, 229-232, 234, 247, 252, 254,

272, 287, 293, 296-298, 302-303, 307, 324, 328, 330, 336, 347, 350-355, 365, 377, 396-399, 402-403, 418, 436, 439-447

focusing, 35, 67, 73-74, 102, 108-109, 446

forcing behavior*****

frame of reference, 4, 30, 33, 56-57, 61-64, 68, 70, 73-75, 78-79, 82-83, 85, 88, 90, 93-95, 97, 104-107, 117, 123, 127, 130, 136, 207, 228, 241, 435-436, 439-440, 446

friendship, 49, 84, 87-88, 120, 124, 131, 174, 186, 235, 243, 260, 265, 274-275, 277, 279, 320, 323, 424, 447

hidden self, 240, 252, 274, 442

identity aspirations, 30, 40, 43, 56-57

ignoring, 102, 108, 123, 126, 311, 325-326, 335, 339, 354, 439

images, 10, 29, 31-32, 35, 45, 56, 65, 69, 75, 94-96, 107, 121, 125, 143, 184, 187, 191, 209, 234, 262, 306, 364, 388, 392-393, 404, 436, 439, 446

inferences, 69, 77, 92-94, 96, 127, 158, 179, 181, 191-193, 207-209, 219, 226, 241, 364, 386, 393, 436

information/persuasive power, 318, 321, 324, 354, 441

initiating, 118, 240-241, 245, 260-262, 264, 273, 313, 329, 344, 441

integrating, 240, 260-261, 266-268, 273, 313, 441

intentions, 22, 51, 70, 108, 114, 120, 136, 143, 173, 187, 195, 207, 210, 224, 302, 436, 439

interdependence, 301, 441

interpretation, 6-7, 62, 67-69, 83, 105, 118, 130, 192, 194, 208, 222, 225, 284, 286, 293-294, 341, 364, 436, 447-448

Johari Window, 240, 252-255, 273-274, 276, 278, 405, 442

kinesics, 174, 176, 210-211

language, 9-10, 16-17, 24, 51, 56, 75-76, 83, 85, 101-107, 109-129, 131, 133-143, 145, 147, 149, 151, 155, 158-159, 161-165, 167-169, 175-177, 193-194, 207-210, 212-213, 215, 217, 225, 265, 267-268, 283, 286, 293-296, 302, 319, 327, 330, 338, 345, 348, 362, 370, 374-375, 377-381, 386, 393-397, 399, 406, 424, 435, 437-448

lies, 18, 22, 92, 149, 161, 249, 343, 361-363, 366-370, 383

listening, 117, 122, 125, 158, 164, 192, 195,

208, 219-235, 283, 285, 288-290, 296, 299, 302, 304, 308-309, 311, 330, 341, 377-378, 402-404, 413, 435-436, 438-439, 442, 444-445, 448

Maslow's hierarchy of needs, 30, 48-49
message, 7, 9-10, 16-21, 23, 45, 69, 83, 115-116, 118-119, 122, 134, 156, 166-167, 173, 175-176, 178, 181, 191-196, 208-209, 217, 219, 222, 224-226, 228, 230-234, 252, 256, 258-259, 262, 327, 335, 399, 436, 438, 442-443, 446-447
multivalued orientation, 102, 135

naming, 102-103, 110-111, 121, 123, 129-130, 135, 137, 443, 445
narratives, 76
needs, 7, 13, 21, 29-30, 35, 45, 47-50, 53, 55-57, 59, 117, 129, 135, 158-159, 163, 184, 240-242, 244-246, 251, 272, 278, 281, 291, 304, 317, 319, 336, 340, 343-345, 355, 369, 380, 388-389, 435-436, 438, 441, 445, 448
neutrality, 53-54, 225, 282, 285, 287-288, 290, 298, 311, 438, 443
noise, 4, 17-18, 21, 23, 46, 66, 146, 443

openness, 30, 55-56, 73, 162, 240, 253, 259, 276, 307, 366, 405, 436, 439, 443
open self, 240, 252-253, 442
orientations, 205-206
overdisclosing, 253, 255, 274

perception, 17, 43, 55, 61-65, 67-79, 81, 83-87, 89, 91-97, 104-105, 110, 112, 123, 128-129, 196, 211, 213-214, 275, 357-358, 390-393, 407, 437, 439, 444-447
personal distance, 174, 200, 401
physiological needs, 48, 50
polarization, 102-103, 133, 136, 444, 448
power, 6, 51, 107, 133, 139, 169, 177, 193, 197, 201, 207, 210-211, 214-215, 229, 257, 279, 290, 294-295, 298, 302, 315, 317-327, 330-331, 354, 356-357, 359, 366, 368, 382, 414-415, 435, 437-438, 440-442, 444-445

self-disclosure, 4, 13, 20-23, 26, 29, 47, 53, 102, 104, 121, 239-240, 248, 251, 254-260, 264-267, 273-274, 276-279, 282, 300-303, 309, 312, 315, 349, 369, 405-406, 410, 437, 439, 442, 445-446

self-esteem, 49, 259, 300, 353, 355, 369, 381, 446
self-fulfilling prophecy, 102-103, 126-129, 137, 446
self-regulation, 446
sensitivity, 4, 14, 18, 21, 25, 82, 138, 297, 351, 362
silence, 173-175, 193-194, 207-209, 215, 218, 349, 355, 446
similarity, 240, 243, 248, 264, 272, 275, 277, 375, 446
social comparison, 30, 40-42, 56-57, 446
social needs, 49-50
source, 4, 12, 16-18, 21, 26, 33, 105, 167, 186, 198, 202, 235, 239, 242, 248, 253, 261, 277, 279, 288, 298, 307, 309, 319, 321-322, 334, 345-346, 348, 358, 369, 378-379, 415, 439-440, 446
space, 16, 69, 73, 135, 146, 173-175, 192-193, 196-203, 207-208, 215-218, 254, 353, 380, 401-402, 444, 447
spontaneity, 282, 293, 297-299, 446-447
stagnating, 305, 318, 348-349, 355
stereotyping, 62, 83, 102-103, 126-128, 361, 375, 382, 384
stimuli, 18-19, 21, 65-66, 68, 92, 222, 234, 436, 444-446
strategy, 282, 285, 287-290, 298-299, 311, 320, 331-339, 341, 355-

356, 420, 437-438, 440, 446-448

superiority, 285-288, 298, 302, 311, 335, 438, 440, 447

symbol, 7, 9, 102, 105-107, 131-133, 138-139, 185, 442, 445, 447

symmetry, 102, 123, 137

synthesis, 25, 30, 34, 388

terminating, 305, 318, 348, 350-351, 355, 447

territoriality, 174-175, 196-198, 210, 215, 447

thought, 39, 42, 46, 52, 54, 78, 102, 105-107, 112, 116, 124, 138, 140, 143, 145-146, 148-150, 161, 163, 167, 176, 194, 222, 229, 233, 241, 246, 249, 256, 296, 320, 327-328, 340-341, 347, 351, 376, 384, 392, 412-413, 425, 428-429, 438, 447

time, 6, 8-10, 14, 17, 23, 35, 40, 42, 44-45, 47, 51-53, 55, 66-67, 69, 73, 75-77, 79, 81-82, 85, 93, 110, 113-115, 118, 122, 125, 128-130, 133, 145-146, 150, 156-157, 159-160, 163-165, 168, 173-175, 181, 185, 189, 192-193, 198-199, 204-210, 212, 217-218, 224, 227-228, 232-233, 243, 246, 249-250, 252, 255, 259, 263, 265-266, 269-270, 272, 283-284, 287, 290, 294, 302-304, 306, 308-309, 311-312, 319, 326-328, 337-338,

340-348, 350, 352-353, 355-356, 362-363, 367, 370, 376-377, 379-381, 383, 392-393, 396-399, 403-405, 413-414, 419-421, 424-429, 440, 443, 445, 447

touching, 95, 134, 173-175, 180, 184-188, 213-214, 217, 266, 273, 304, 380, 447-448

transaction, 7-8, 389, 441

transactional analysis, 62, 85-86, 304, 314, 439-440, 445, 448

Triangle of Meaning, 102, 105-106, 135, 445, 448

trust, 4, 19-22, 26, 45, 55, 96, 151, 185, 192, 240, 255, 257, 260, 264-267, 299-301, 303, 333, 340, 390, 397, 430, 441, 448

unconditional positive regard, 292, 304, 315

underdisclosing, 240, 255

unknown self, 240, 252, 442

values, 30-33, 36-39, 41-42, 44-45, 56-57, 59, 63, 70, 91, 93, 122-123, 135, 139, 143, 145, 190, 244, 262, 264, 303, 306, 321, 323, 348-349, 363, 373-375, 379, 383, 388, 440, 444, 448

vocalics, 173, 194-196, 208, 218, 448

vocalizations, 193-195, 208

vocal quality, 175, 194-195, 208

wants and expectations, 142-143, 145, 156, 168, 170, 187, 195, 226, 436, 439

wholeness, 437, 448

withdrawal, 318, 330-332, 343, 350, 355, 448